FROM RAGTIME TO SWINGTIME

Isidore Witmark

The Story of

THE HOUSE OF WITMARK

FROM RAGTIME TO SWINGTIME

By ISIDORE WITMARK
and ISAAC GOLDBERG

LEE FURMAN, INC. • PUBLISHERS • NEW YORK

Printed in the United States of America

LOVINGLY DEDICATED TO THE

MEMORY OF MY DEAR WIFE

"ENGEL"

DEVOTED PARTNER FOR OVER

TWENTY-FOUR YEARS

—•—

For you, dear, my heart is yearning,
Little Woman of the West,
Just for you my soul is burning,
Little Woman of the West,
Yearning,
Burning,
Westward turning,
To the one whom I love best.

It is with profound sorrow that I record here the passing, on July 14, 1938, of Dr. Isaac Goldberg, my collaborator in this work from its beginning. His death was sudden and I feel his loss keenly.

I was able to secure the services of Mr. Frank Owen, author of "The Wind That Tramps The World" and "A Husband For Kutani," and with his assistance it has been possible to bring this work to completion.

ISIDORE WITMARK

"THANKS A LOT"

Without the invaluable help of the following friends this book would not have been possible, and their co-operation is hereby acknowledged gratefully.

Credit for the illustrations goes to Albert Davis, S. W. Todd, ASCAP, and the New York Historical Society.

For data and research placed at my disposal I record my appreciation of the assistance of Arthur Boucher, Victor Blau, Joseph McLaughlin, George Glenz, Herman Heydt, Jerry Vogel, Stanley Quinn, R. C. McPherson, Richard Tarantous, Thomas Grant Springer, John T. Washburn, Julius Rothschild, Knight MacGregor, Frederic Miller, George B. Wellbaum (of the New York Telephone Company), Trumbull White, Margaret Searle, and Grace Morse.

I am indebted for final proofreading and indexing to Joseph Greenbaum.

ISIDORE WITMARK.

CONTENTS

CONTENTS

CONTENTS

CONTENTS

CONTENTS

CONTENTS

ILLUSTRATIONS

ILLUSTRATIONS

ILLUSTRATIONS

FROM RAGTIME TO
SWINGTIME

CHAPTER I

THE PROPHECY

"I SHALL never work for another man as long as I live!" From the indignant lips of a fourteen-year-old boy, this declaration seemed like an idle boast. Yet it was oddly prophetic, for it marked the start of the famous House of Witmark.

That House, which the late Sam S. Shubert called "The Tiffany of the Music World," was built upon the slender asset of a toy, coupled with the confidence and determination of three boys, the eldest of whom was only fourteen.

It was the New York of 1883, the city of gas lamps and horse cars, of bustles and ballads. Chester A. Arthur had succeeded to the Presidency of the United States. Franklin Delano Roosevelt at the age of one year was cutting his first teeth. Brooklyn was a separate city. And ragtime was yet to be born. *Sweet Adeline* had not been written. The deathless music of Victor Herbert was still to be published. And in a modest home in West 40th Street were three eager youngsters who had an important part to play in spreading the songs that three generations of Americans have treasured.

Isidore, the eldest son, at work, helping the family meet expenses. Jay and Julius, eleven and thirteen, were still in school; Frank, seven, and Ed, five, had not yet seriously considered entering on a business career.

FROM RAGTIME TO SWINGTIME

There was about Jay an air of playful vigor. He was bubbling over with exuberance, too full of spirits to be good by rule. At school he had won the arithmetic prize, for which the usual reward was a medal. A medal, however, carried with it the implication that its winner also had been a model scholar in behavior. Much as Miss Christine Roy, the teacher, liked her pupil, she could not conscientiously allow him to wear such a medal. So she gave him his choice of a secondary award: a tool chest, a velocipede, a baseball outfit, or a toy printing-press.

It was a weighty problem. Jay decided that, although he had strong inclinations toward the tool chest, he would think it over and consult his family. His brother Isidore, just fired from his job, was miserable. His dismissal was inevitable because a relative of the owner had arrived from Germany and must be given a place in the business. Nevertheless, Isidore had worked hard and long hours, and the injustice of it hurt.

At noon, back from his job for the last time, Isidore walked up to the mother whom the boys all idolized and declared, "Queen, I shall never work for another man as long as I live!"

Mother Witmark smiled with patient sympathy. "Very well, my son," she answered. "What are you going to do?"

Isidore did not know. At that moment Jay walked in with his announcement of the prize. He was still in a quandary over what he should take. Then and there the Witmark boys went into their first important conference.

"Take the printing-press," Isidore suggested. Already his mind was outlining a campaign for orders. What matter that they knew nothing about type, paper, or ink? They had assets far better—enthusiasm and a driving force that was their heritage.

When the press had been finally chosen and delivered, with its diminutive bed and its three tiny drawers of type-cases, the boys were speechless with awe. Daddy Witmark, smiling proudly, shared their rapture. On the base was engraved the

22

trade mark, "Challenge." Here was a challenge, indeed, a challenge that M. Witmark and Sons promptly accepted.

New Year's day would be coming along. Printers did an enormous business in greeting cards. In those days, New Year's *was* a New Year's. The city put on its holiday attire and everyone was the soul of congeniality. There was nothing machine-made or synthetic about the jollity. The city was much smaller then, and people closer to one another. New Year's Eve was not spent in hotels and restaurants. The place of celebrations was the home. Christmas ushered in a week of glowing social warmth that reached its climax with the ringing out of the old year and the ringing in of the new. Almost everyone had his own New Year's cards printed. People called upon one another, sometimes even hiring carriages for the occasion, and in this ceremony the card was an important feature.

It was the New Year's card that put the Witmark brothers in business. They would print cards at ten cents and upwards per dozen. The printery was established in the bedroom of one of the boys. It was a modest room at best, and, with a printing shop added to its normal furnishings, it was somewhat crowded.

One of the space-saving devices was a folding table hinged on to the door that led to the hall. One evening Daddy Witmark dashed impulsively upstairs to see how business was progressing, but alas! he forgot the folding table. The next moment press, type, cards, bronze ink were sprawling in printer's pi on the floor, and a very confused Daddy stood on the threshold, surveying the wreckage. Yes, business was progressing—all over the room.

During that winter season of 1883 the boys made about thirty dollars, and their earnings might have been greater if they had had facilities to meet the demand. A local tailor, for example, submitted his business card for an estimate on a thousand. The estimate department returned a figure of $9, with the statement that it would require four days for printing. The amazed tailor showed them that for the same order he had been paying $1.75.

23

To the boys it was a blow, revealing how ill-equipped they were to handle work demanding speed and economy.

The boys went into a huddle. Something drastic must be done to meet the disaster of competition that faced them. It seemed almost hopeless, and yet they found a solution, a solution amazingly simple—expansion. They would expand until they were on a par with other firms. Their present equipment was far too rudimentary; they must move to a regular printing office with a large supply of types, the latest accessories, and, above all, a power press.

Fortunately, at that time Daddy Witmark was taking over the agency for a new patent music-binder, and it was quite easy for the boys to convince him that he would need a quantity of "literature" to promote the binder.

"Buy us a power press," they said, "and we'll do all your printing."

Dad, as usual, consented and before long a gas-driven press was humming away in the Witmark household. It was working from early morning until late at night. Sometimes it threatened to continue running until dawn. But Dad put a stop to that by going to the cellar at 3 A.M. and turning off the gas. It was a point of honor with the boys never to accept an order that they did not mean to have ready on time for delivery.

Meanwhile, Daddy Witmark was waiting day after day for his "literature." But nothing happened. The boys were so busy with outside printing that they had no time for his. At last he wearied of waiting, and, despite the fact that he had bought the gas-driven press for his work, he was obliged to go to another printer. The irony of it!

CHAPTER II

DADDY AND QUEEN

1. Prussia to America

MARCUS WITMARK was born in a small town in Prussia, the third of four brothers. His father, a prominent contractor, died during the cholera epidemic of 1849, and the business might have collapsed if his mother had not stifled her grief and taken up her husband's work for the sake of her little ones. There is little doubt that she was a remarkable woman, for in an age when women in business were practically unheard of she assumed her husband's obligations and directed the completion of the public buildings that had been under construction at the time of his death.

The revolution of 1848 had widened horizons. Completely captivated by accounts of opportunities in the United States, Simon and David Witmark joined the mass immigration of Germans to America. Soon they were writing home vivid accounts of their experiences. Young Marcus began to dream of the day when he, too, could join his brothers in the new land. Some day his ticket would arrive for one of the auxiliary steam sailing vessels that took weeks to make a crossing. That ticket would be a passport to a new existence. One day unbelievably it came. It was arranged that Marcus was to embark upon the hazards of new fortunes with two friends who had sung with him in the church choir.

There were tearful farewells. On the outskirts of the town where they lived was a last symbolic bridge to cross on the way to the railway station. On that bridge stood a young fraulein, Henrietta Peyser. Her hair was like honey and she wore it in two long braids. Saying good-bye to her was almost as difficult as his farewell to his mother. And he wondered if he would ever see her again.

The voyage to America would have been uneventful but for a tragic accident. Sailors at work repairing a sail dropped a pulley-block upon the deck, and in falling it struck one of Marcus' pals and killed him instantly. The tragedy brought the two remaining boys closer together than ever. Thereafter they remained friends to the end.

Marcus was not afraid of the water. At home, out of sheer exuberance of spirits, he had often dived for pfennigs, just as black sea-urchins do in tropical ports. From the neighboring orchard across the edge of the lake near where they lived, he would steal an apronful of green apples and swim back munching his loot. He seemed proof against punishment. Once, returning from a bakery with some loaves of bread, he had seen a head bobbing in the water helplessly. Fully clothed, he had jumped into the water just in time to rescue the drowning boy who had come up for the third time. It proved to be his own brother Elias, or Alec, as he later became known in the United States.

The New York of 1853 was a quiet, leisurely city. It was only twenty-eight years since the first gas lamps had been placed upon the streets, and many thought them a waste of public funds. Oil lamps were illumination enough for persons foolhardy enough to be prowling around at night. Timid souls still prayed that the scourge of yellow fever would not return. That year the Astor Place Opera House, built in 1848 and never a success, finally gave up the ghost and was purchased by Donetti and

26

turned into a menagerie. But its loss was somewhat compensated for by the opening of the World's Fair for the Exhibition of the Industry of All Nations at the Crystal Palace on July 14, 1853, perhaps the most important event in the administration of Mayor Jacob A. Westervelt. In the same year the printing and publishing establishment of Messrs. Harper and Brothers in Franklin Square was destroyed by fire and six hundred employees were temporarily thrown out of work. All in all, it was an exciting year for the city, a year in which the Administration was repeatedly attacked for passing an act authorizing the purchase of Central Park, a gloomy, uncultivated wilderness, far removed from the reach of anybody.

Marcus Witmark had heard that America was a cold country. Therefore he had come provided with a huge fur coat. Although the ship steamed into New York harbor on July 4, 1853, he was so assured of the rigorous climate and so proud of his coat that he encased himself in it, prepared to astonish the natives with his regalia. Marcus was an inquisitive soul; no sooner had he been taken to his temporary home than he set forth to see the city. At the City Hall a large crowd had gathered to hear the speeches and watch the fireworks. Marcus enjoyed oratory and display and to City Hall he went, still wearing his heavy fur coat which incidentally was growing heavier by the minute. Being in the crowd was suffocating, and, weighed under by his garment, he grew faint. There was no room to fall, so down to the ground he slipped out of his coat, which was held up by the pressure of the crowd. In a short time he was revived, and his notion of the American climate revised.

His brothers had settled in the South, one in Fort Gaines, Georgia, the other in Eufaula, Alabama. Already they had mapped out for him his start as a peddler through the Southern states. Much credit must be given to peddlers for the opening up to commerce of the United States from coast to coast. With their little rickety wagons or their pack-horses the peddlers formed a little band, intrepid, fearless, venturing to the outmost reaches of settlers. Many of the earliest peddlers came from New England and it was largely due to their efforts that Massachusetts and Connecticut became the manufacturing centers of the country; peddlers at first and, a few generations later, merchants and bankers as the tide of progress swept on. Daniel Frohman in his autobiography has told of his father, who was a peddler. If the history of peddlery were written it would be indeed the saga of America.

Before long Marcus was on his way to Fort Gaines, Georgia, while his companion of the voyage, Ralph Davis, headed for Joplin, Missouri. Marcus had inherited the initiative of both his father and mother. He was awake and up before dawn. A quick breakfast, then out on his peddler's route while others were still sleeping. His progress was rapid. From the peddler's pack he graduated to the hand-cart; from the hand-cart to a horse and wagon. He hired an assistant. He opened a store, and soon he had two branches. He built a modest home, and acquired slaves. A favorite sister from the North had brought disgrace upon herself by marrying a man of whom her family disapproved. Marcus sent for her and made her husband an associate in his business. When war was declared in 1861 and the brother-in-law was invited to join a troop then organizing, Marcus called him aside and persuaded him to let him go in his place.

He equipped his own company, trained it, and received his commission as Lieutenant from Governor Brown of Georgia, whose son eventually occupied the same office. For a short time Lieutenant Witmark was placed in charge of the city of Macon. Later he commanded a battery at Richmond. He saw plenty of active service, and rose to a Captaincy on the battlefield. On the third day of fighting at Gettysburg, at Sugar Loaf Mountain, he was wounded. He never surrendered his sword, however, managing to pass it on to one of his regiment as the soldiers strode by him in retreat.

DADDY AND QUEEN

Captain Witmark had dash and gallantry. During the Richmond days he had come to know, as one of a number of social contacts, a beautiful young heiress and leader of society; it looked as if the fraulein with the honey-colored braids in Prussia had been forgotten, and that the Southern belle was to be the choice of his heart. There was a dinner at her home, and a proposal on Captain Witmark's lips. The proposal was never spoken. Why? The reason is more important than the failure itself. Witmark had noticed at the dinner that the father and mother were not on speaking terms. Family solidarity may be regarded as a hereditary trait of the Witmarks; distaste for domestic dissension blighted the wartime romance.

The wounded captain, captured at the battle of Gettysburg, was transferred to a hospital on David's Island, opposite New Rochelle, New York. Here he received attention from Mrs. James Gordon Bennett, Sr., wife of the proprietor of the *New York Herald*, and from other social leaders who were in sympathy with the cause of the South.

He was discharged from the hospital a few months later and together with 3,600 other Southern officers was transferred to Johnson's Island, across from Sandusky, Ohio. Here began a period of mental torture. At Andersonville and in Libby Prison Northern officers were being executed; at Johnson's Island, reprisals were taking place, shot for shot. Every day officers were called out, never to return. At last came the dreaded call for Captain Witmark, and he murmured a good-bye to the world.

He had escaped death on the battlefield, only to meet it now in the cold, unromantic calculation of reprisal. He was young, and the world was oh, so fair! The war could not last much longer. His death, in any case, would be as purposeless as it seemed ironic. But who was this before him? Where was the firing squad? In the anxiety of his position, Captain Witmark had forgotten that, in anticipation of a possible exchange of prisoners, he had ordered a suit to be made by a local tailor before

Christmas. In honor of the same holiday, he had been fattening a cat for dinner. (Food was distressingly scarce. He had paid an Indian five dollars for a brace of rabbits.) And the cat, incidentally, had been stolen.

This was no summons to a firing squad. It was his tailor. It was a reprieve from the execution to which he had thought himself condemned. It was virtually resurrection! In his joy, Captain Witmark seized the amazed tailor in a hearty embrace and kissed him.

Reprisals gave way in time to exchange of prisoners. Captain Witmark was on the list of officers marked for early return when the shot that killed Lincoln reverberated across the horror-stricken North. At once all exchanges were cancelled; Captain Witmark remained at Johnson's Island.

By the time the War had come to an end, he was mourned as one killed in battle. So great was the rejoicing when he returned that for a week he was feted by everyone. He was offered an appointment as probate judge, but declined. He had gone to war leaving behind a flourishing business. He had returned to find himself all but ruined, until he made the happy discovery that friends had nailed up in an isolated barn some $60,000 worth of his cotton.

There was a magnetism about the man that inspired confidence and affection. His slaves had been freed by the war, yet when he closed out his Southern interests and made up his mind to go North to live they refused to be left behind, and followed him. In New York, however, they found they were unwelcome —New York resented the influx of plantation hands—and he was obliged to send them back to the South.

In after years, talking to his sons about his slaves, Dad used to say, "Boys, some of the slaves may not have slept on a bed of roses; but on the whole they came in for much consideration. When we were sick we tried to cure ourselves with home remedies, but when our slaves were sick we generally sent for a specialist."

It was not only his personality that his children inherited, but also his sense of domestic harmony. As a child he had sung in the church choir and possessed an excellent soprano voice. He was musical by nature. He could accompany himself on the flutina, or, as it is called today, the piano-accordion. Once in the early sixties a teacher of the guitar, making his rounds of the Southern states, spent a week or so among the society belles and swells of each town. Marcus Witmark was the only one who had not taken these lessons; when the teacher left, he was also the only one who was competent to play the guitar.

Perhaps the one thing that determined him more than any other to go North was the visit to the devastating ruin wrought by Sherman on his famous march to the sea. He could not endure the sight of the havoc. He had loved the South as a second home. Now all its charm was gone.

2. Happy Ending

In New York new adventures awaited him. A group of boyhood friends, who in the meantime had come from his home town in Prussia, asked him to a party where the chief guest was to be a young woman who had arrived recently from the old country and was visiting her married sister, the wife of Dr. David Bendan, a professor at New York University in Washington Square. It was Henrietta Peyser, the little fraulein with the long, golden locks—the last face he had gazed upon before he had crossed the bridge to go to America. Ah, her father and mother were on speaking terms! Now he knew why he had not proposed to the belle of Richmond.

They were married on October 4th, 1866.

There followed a series of business ventures, now with his brothers and again with the brother-in-law whose place he had taken in the Civil War and in whose hands he had left his affairs, the brother-in-law who systematically robbed him. After a number of disappointments he found himself in the children's lace cap trade, in partnership with a certain A. M. Morris. Witmark built up a list of customers below the Mason and Dixon line. Down South, cotton was king. With cotton, business rose; with cotton, it fell and failed. It was with the eventual decline of cotton that Witmark and Morris sank into bankruptcy.

On the day that he failed, he came home with a dollar bill and a cat, all that he had salvaged out of the ruins. He was not defeated, however, even though his friends took him to task for having been so honest, so impractical as to settle up and pay his debts, leaving himself unprovided for. He had a ready answer: "I have five good reasons for doing this—my sons. When they grow up, I don't want them to bear a name they'll be ashamed of. We have our home. I'll make a living for them!"

And now Marcus decided, because of his reduced capital, that he would have to go into a business in which his host of friends would be of help to him. He hit upon the idea of a family trade in wines and liquors. It was an immediate success, and Marcus was on top of the world again.

He made his sons his companions. He dressed them alike. Saturday afternoons were devoted almost ritually to the Grand Opera House at Twenty-third Street and Eighth Avenue, then the most attractive theater in the country. Unfortunately for Dad's comfort, however, each show did not end with the curtain, but continued at home for hours afterward with his boys staging their own versions of the pieces. And in these childhood revels Jay was always the villain.

Getting the children to bed was a problem. In the summer, Dad would walk them around the corner to the bakery and buy cookies. Upon their return they would all go to the dining room in the basement. Thereupon, like a modern Pied Piper, he would strike up a stirring operatic tune on his piano-accordion and

Daddy Witmark

"Queen"

Photo from oil painting by Brown Bros., N. Y.

Marcus Witmark when he received his commission as Lieutenant from Governor Brown of Georgia.

march them in file behind him three or four times around the room, luring them then up the stairs to bed. In his hearing they would say their prayers and good nights.

That was Daddy Witmark's way; everything with a flourish, like the sweep of a signature. He liked the visible evidences of success. When little Julie first showed signs of developing into a singer, it was not the possible money returns that interested Marcus Witmark. Although the child was in demand by clubs and other associations, his father never set a price on Julie's services. He stipulated simply that after Julie had sung his solos the organization was to present a gold or silver medal to the boy. Showmanship! There were times when a club could not afford the price of such a medal. When this happened Daddy Witmark footed the bill, for a medal and public presentation there must be!

Some time later, when little Frank, too, gave every evidence of turning into a prodigy of music and memory, Marcus was very proud. At once he set about securing publicity for the boy. In 1881 the pseudo-science of phrenology was popular. Almost as many people went to have their bumps read as to have their palms read. Among the leading phrenologists were Fowler and Wells, who had a store at Eighth Street and Broadway and published *The Phrenological Journal*. In the May, 1881, issue an entire article was devoted to the five-year-old wonder, Frank Witmark. Daddy looked very innocent but undoubtedly he had had much to do with it.

"Frank's talent," according to the article, "consists fundamentally in the possession of a remarkable memory, which is, however, specially related to music, he being able to name any piece of music when the score is shown him; and he can turn the leaves of music correctly for one who is playing it. He can give the names at once of upward of three hundred compositions when shown them. . . . He is not yet six years old, has never attended school, and does not know the alphabet. . . . He seems to have inherited his musical gift, as his mother possesses mu-

33

sical ability and he has two brothers but a few years older than himself who can perform well on the piano; but in its peculiar expression he is a phenomenon of which we know no parallel; and if he does not become an eminent composer and musical celebrity . . . we shall be greatly surprised."

The prediction was fulfilled, for Frank played an important rôle in the development of M. Witmark & Sons, both as an executive and as a composer of waltzes. He was at his height as a waltz composer during the middle nineties when, although not a second Johann Strauss, he was called The American Waltz King.

All this publicity for a mere tot would have gratified any ordinary father. But it was hardly enough for Daddy Witmark. One day there appeared in the show window of Fowler and Wells a life-size oil painting of Frank Witmark. It was an effective advertisement, for Broadway in the early eighties was like Fifth Avenue today. Fowler and Wells had not paid for that painting.

CHAPTER III

ISIDORE AND HIS BRETHREN

1. Jobs—and a Declaration of Independence

THE failure of the lace cap business had made a deep impression upon the eldest son of the Witmarks. Though but nine, he was mature and strong. He had never found much time for play. Now there would be less, for he became part of the delivery system of his father's venture into wines and liquors. His route covered all of Greater Manhattan, for his father had many friends. There were customers at 125th Street, off Fifth Avenue. Before leaving for them, Isidore would kiss his mother as if he were going on an ocean trip, and then embark—upon an Eighth Avenue horse-car. It required the better part of a morning for him to get there. The going and returning, indeed, consumed a day. The clang of the cowbells still haunts his ears, together with the cloppety-clop of the horses, burning up time. . . .

As likely as not, he would be told at three in the afternoon to carry an order to farthest Brooklyn or Williamsburg, and in those days a visit to Brooklyn was almost a transcontinental journey.

Part of Isidore's duties consisted in gathering up, en route, as many "empties" as he could carry. The loads, and they were often heavy, did not trouble him. There were childish contre-

35

temps, however. Once, on his way back from a trip to Brooklyn, he developed a sudden hunger, to which the answer seemed to come from the cheerily suggestive whistle of a peanut-stand. In Isidore's hands was a large basket filled with empty bottles that had contained Rhenish wine. In his pocket was a nickel, the fare home, and in his stomach, hunger. Out came a penny for a handful of peanuts; and then, too late, the realization that four cents could not take a fellow back to New York. With the heavy basket on his arm he walked all the way from Brooklyn by way of the bridge to Fortieth Street and Ninth Avenue, Manhattan. He reached home at midnight, half dead, where his parents, little more alive, were waiting anxiously.

Isidore had his own ample share of the Witmark gift for music. In these days, however, he was more interested in art. His spare time was devoted to drawing in colored crayons, but it is doubtful whether his father appreciated the murals that his ambitious son strewed about the office walls so profusely. Isidore fell in with an artist, Jacob Stern, who impressed him as much by his ten-gallon hat and huge beard as by any of the more subtle qualities of the master. He showed the man some of his efforts.

"There is something to them," said Stern, patronizingly. "Come around to my studio at nine Monday morning, and we'll see what we can do."

This was almost consecration; until Monday morning Isidore champed at the bit. Eight o'clock found him waiting at the office. So did ten o'clock. Mr. Stern never appeared. At eleven, the frustrated Rembrandt realized that he had been betrayed.

Had Isidore been successful with Stern, he would have left school, but as things turned out he decided to continue with his studies. Lessons, nevertheless, were not enough to consume his overflowing energies. He must be busy with something. Thus began a series of enterprises that served the purpose of a training-school for the youngster. A glance at the family album suggested his first business. No home, in those days, was complete without

36

its tome of thick, cardboard pages, bound in leather or in plush, with a gold or silver plate adorning the front cover and with clasp in front, the binding done in the rainbow hues. No sooner was school over than he made a beeline to home for his heavy sample case.

There was a Mr. Joseph Nathan who was a great friend of the Witmark children. He could be counted upon to start them off with flying colors on any venture that their boyish hearts embarked upon. So off went Isidore to Mr. Nathan, with his family album, payable at a dollar down and twenty-five cents per week. Mr. Nathan bought the album—for cash! It was a good omen, and forth went young Witmark to conquer the world. It was not long before the salesman learned that late afternoon, just before suppertime, was the best period. Husbands had not come home from work and sales-resistance was low; not low enough, however. A few discouraging experiences convinced Isidore that there were too few Nathans in New York.

One day while he was covering Forty-third Street between Sixth and Seventh Avenues, he had an exciting experience. This was a residential district, and he stormed the front door of every house. Some doors were slammed in his face; at others he received a firm though polite "No." His joy can be imagined when, after he had asked one woman, "Lady, can I interest you in a beautiful plush family album at a very low price?" she answered, "Come in and follow me."

He did so, and landed downstairs in the kitchen where he discovered that she was the cook. Resigned to the situation, he immediately opened his sample case and showed his wares, in which she displayed interest. Finally, he got her to select the shade of plush she preferred, and brought out a form which he filled out for her to sign. All had gone well until the moment he handed her the pencil.

"What's this?" she asked.

37

"This is for you to sign so that the album may be delivered to you."

She hesitated. Meanwhile the chambermaid came in. They began to giggle and exchanged words that made no sense to him. He waited patiently, doing everything he could to induce her to sign, to no apparent avail. After balking for almost an hour, she exclaimed, "Sign it yourself!"

At that he lost patience entirely. "I don't believe you can write!" he cried.

Immediately he became unpopular. It seemed as if everything in the kitchen began flying in his direction, and above the din he could hear her shouting, "Get out of here!"

He escaped through the basement door, barely missing a new barrage.

As the door slammed on his heels, he pondered whether or not he should smash a pane of glass as a balm to his ego. Fortunately his better judgment after a tough battle prevailed. The house next door was a very high-class boardinghouse, the proprietors of which turned out to be friends of his parents. They had heard of his prowess as a pianist. The lady of the house recognized him.

"I hear you play the piano well," she said. "Won't you play for us?"

Glimpsing a possible sale, he agreed, whereupon she summoned a number of her boarders and Isidore had an audience. They evidently expected to hear Bach, Beethoven and Brahms; but alas! he could not soar quite that high. Moreover, his mind was so intent on the prospective sales that he did not play well. So, even though he had a goodly assemblage at the start, by the time he had finished it had dwindled down to the proprietress, who remained to thank him for the entertainment. And now he tried to sell her an album.

"Oh, I've just bought one," she said. "I'm so sorry. Why don't you try next door?"

ISIDORE AND HIS BRETHREN

That shut the albums tight. Little man, what now?

The drinking water of New York was not, at that time, considered pure; the water works were being reconstructed, and the populace had become water-conscious. So had Isidore Witmark. He became the agent for a filter, consisting of glass containers of various sizes, filled with charcoal and supposedly purifying chemicals. His first customer, of course, was Mr. Nathan, who purchased the most expensive size and paid for it, in cash. Most of the sales were of the cheaper type, and business was good enough to be considered as a stop-gap. When, however, an opening occurred in the wholesale hat concern of Hilborn Brothers, on Houston Street and Broadway, Isidore seized the chance; from there he rose to a job at Eighth Avenue and Fortieth Street in the basement hat store of a Mr. Niner.

Whether the faithful Mr. Nathan visited Niner's for the pleasure of buying hats from young Witmark is not on the record. It was at this stage, however, that Mr. Nathan turned the tables. He had become interested, as a partner, in the manufacture of novelty bags for women, the novelty consisting of inch strips of colored metal that crossed each other, giving the bag the appearance of a checkerboard. He sent for Isidore; if that boy could sell things *to* him, he reasoned, he could sell them *for* him.

"Here's something," he said to Isidore, "on which you can make real money." For a time, indeed, the boy did very well with the article. But it was the first merchandise handled by him that he could not sell to Nathan!

There were interludes, such as the experience of the Witmark boys with subscriptions to home magazines, of which a large number were published in Maine. An advertisement offered, as an inducement for taking subscriptions to these periodicals, a complete agent's outfit of sample premiums for seventy-five cents. The samples proved to be a really attractive set of reproductions. Each set contained a dozen replicas of famous works of art, worthy of framing.

39

FROM RAGTIME TO SWINGTIME

The youngsters quickly discovered that taking subscriptions for magazines, even in the early '80's, was a crowded field. Whether the agents were working their way through college is not told; but certainly there were too many of them swarming the neighborhoods. Isidore, who had so nearly become an artist, could not take his eye off those chromos. Here, he felt, was the real business. If they could not sell the magazines, why not the premiums? Christmas was coming. The brothers arranged for a little stand on Eighth Avenue and Fortieth Street, decorated it with the chromos from the sample cases, and set a price of twenty-five cents on each reproduction.

In a week they were sold out, at a profit of some thirteen dollars. Later, it struck them that the sale of the chromos had not been quite ethical; the pictures were premiums, not merchandise. The conscience of the boys bothered them, until they salved it with the thought of the Yuletide joy that the chromos were bringing to their purchasers.

Niner's was not congenial to Isidore. Not long after his acceptance of the basement job he found the opportunity to apprentice himself for six months to the owner of a piano factory. He had learned to play the piano well enough to entertain possible customers for his album, and even, in his boyish manner, to teach ambitious friends.

The piano factory occupied a ramshackle building on what was then known as the Dump, at Thirty-fifth Street between Eleventh and Twelfth Avenues, which looked like a long railroad car. The proprietor's name was Fullam, and his firm was called the United States Pianoforte Company. Fullam was an eccentric; together with his wife and a cat he lived on the premises. He made a regulation piano that sold for $295, but he had invented a square piano for the less affluent music lovers—an instrument about 54 inches long and 30 inches wide that would fit in almost anywhere. The idea—the saving of space in small apartments—was the forerunner of the baby grand. The legs of this proletarian

40

instrument were flat, stencilled boards cut jigsaw fashion; its frame, however, was of iron, as in a regulation piano; the keyboard was miniature and, though quite practical, got out of order frequently. It was Isidore's duty to set up these pianos, which were rented at 25 cents per week, and to keep them in tune. Rentals flourished and the boy was kept busy.

The six months of apprenticeship expired, and in token of the firm's satisfaction, Isidore received a complete tuning kit and one of the infant pianos. He took the piano home by hailing the first wagon that came along,—it happened to be a fish cart. The piano was straddled on the wagon, over the ice, and brought to his home, but not unloaded there, for, in the meantime, he had rented it to a neighbor, and delivered it directly. It did not remain there long, alas! for with its tinny tone and lapses from proper pitch, it soon became a nuisance. Finally he took it back, and converted it to the uses of a sideboard. In time it was relegated to the cellar. One night after the family had gone to bed there was a terrible racket below stairs. Someone, examining the piano, had left the keyboard exposed, and the cats had a party on it that kept most of the neighborhood awake. Not long after that, Isidore sold it back to the widow of Mr. Fullam who had passed away in the meantime.

From Fullam's, young Witmark went to a real factory, the Weser Brothers, who were makers of a piano then popular and still being manufactured. Here he became proficient at tuning, accepting outside jobs, and on one of his rounds he met the ubiquitous Mr. Nathan.

"What now?" asked his patron.

"Oh," replied Witmark, proudly, "I'm a piano tuner."

"So? Fine! You must come up and tune my piano."

No sooner said than tuned. Mrs. Nathan, every bit as affable as her husband, went off on a visit, leaving the boy alone so that he would be free of disturbance. He found a large, old-fashioned square instrument, in need of key regulation and repair to the

41

action. The action was likewise old-fashioned and clumsy; for a twelve-year old, tall and sturdy though Isidore was, it was a task to remove it and place it upon the parlor table. He eased it to the edge of the case, but accidentally tilted it. The hammers caught on the rim and, breaking off, fell to the floor like so many soldiers in battle. The boy was stunned. He shoved the action back into the case and picked up the broken hammers. And he left a note: "I'm sending you a tuner on Monday." Farewell to tuning!

Two nights a week were free, which to Isidore meant freedom to do more work. He taught the piano. Among his pupils was the daughter of one of the attachés of the Metropolitan Opera House; the other was a maltster named Pauli. Pauli had enormous fingers, so wide that they struck two keys at the same time. It was impossible to teach him. His wife, who was ambitious for him, desperately asked the teacher what could be done. The only advice he could give was to have a special piano built. That sent Pauli back to his malt.

The last man for whom Isidore Witmark was to work was a milliner, Brown, who kept a shop at Eighth Avenue and Forty-fourth Street. It was from this establishment, one historic noon-day, that Isidore Witmark unknowingly walked from the millinery business into the smudgy fascination of types, paper stock, and printer's ink.

2. The Original Hell's Kitchen

The Witmark home was on the rim of Hell's Kitchen. The Kitchen itself originally was the name of a single building situated on a rock in Thirty-ninth Street, near Eleventh Avenue, a sanctuary for gangsters and thieves hiding from the law. Later the name was given to the whole district from Ninth Avenue to Eleventh, and from Fourteenth Street to Fiftieth. This was after the Gopher Gang took over and ruled the district with terrorism. While not the largest gang in the city, it was one of the most

42

feared because everyone of its five hundred members was notoriously vicious. They usually hung out in basements and cellars, plotting their forays; hence their name. They might in time have taken over the entire city had it not been for their incurable habit of quarreling among themselves. A leader seldom lasted over three months. Among the more notorious leaders were Newburg Gallagher, Marty Brennan, and Stumpy Malarkey. The Gophers frequented a saloon kept by Mallet Murphy who used to subdue annoying customers with a mallet, usually an effective silencer. The Gophers had a vexing habit of stealing overcoats from policemen that made them very unpopular at headquarters. Thereafter the police traveled four or five together and many a Gopher skull was smacked with a night-stick. The belle of Hell's Kitchen was Ida the Goose, until she proved untrue to her men and went over to the Five Points on the East Side.

While Hell's Kitchen was a dangerous place, the streets immediately adjacent to it contained the residences of some of the finest families in New York. Most of the houses had brownstone fronts and were three or four stories high. They had high stoops and a basement, representing a style of living that kitchenette apartments of today have done so much to banish. There were six high-stooped houses on the south side of Fortieth Street just west of Ninth Avenue, set in a row beginning with the Witmark house, Number 402.

Although the Witmarks lived on the rim of Hell's Kitchen, they would hardly have known there was such a place had it not been for the gangs that might have picked any street for their chance battles. The favorite day of the year for such a pitched battle was Election Day, when various gangs competed to set the biggest bonfire. Everything that was loose in the shape of wood, no matter how large, was appropriated, including cellar tops, doors, wagons, signs, counters, and even entire staircases. The old time elections were vastly different from those of the present. In front of the stores where the votes were cast were a series of high election boxes made of wood and covered with linen or paper posters. Those boxes looked like Punch-and-Judy theaters. There were men standing beside them and others inside of them with large bags full of election tickets, which they supplied to the voters, who in turn took them into the store. They voted by casting the tickets into large glass globes resembling fish bowls. The polls were controlled by the leaders of the districts and they were the scene of many fights during the day.

But the biggest rivalry and by far the biggest fights took place at the end of the day when the rival mobs came around to appropriate these Punch-and-Judy boxes. Some gangs came early to avoid too tough a battle. It made no difference whether or not the men in charge of the boxes were still inside. Over went the boxes, and a mob of young ruffians was ready to drag them down to their headquarters for the night's conflagration. From a safe distance, the Witmark children were excited spectators of the bonfire battles which they watched as they munched peanuts and enjoyed with all the awe and enthusiasm of youth.

Another neighborhood event was the old Thanksgiving parade. The boys and girls would dress up as ragamuffins, much as they do today at Halloween; the clubs would compete with one another for the distinction of parading the most novel array of costumes. There was always a fine band, behind which the first line of club members appeared in leather aprons and Busby hats, armed with axes or rifles. They carried a list of places to be visited for the appropriation of prizes to be shot for at the feast and celebration that followed the parade.

The foragers would proceed to a store or a private home, and, while the drummers stood beating a tattoo, two of the Busby men would stand in the doorway, axes or rifles crossed, while a third man entered the house for their trophy. The prize almost always turned out to be an old-fashioned silver-plated caster, a revolving stand for bottled condiments. It was awarded to the best shot, and the target of the marksmen, especially painted and decorated, was invariably riddled at the end of the day.

3. Going on the Stage

Through Dave Grant, who had gone to Public School 28 where he had been a chum of the Witmarks, Julie had been introduced into the profession of minstrelsy. Going on the musical stage in those days, before musical comedy and light opera had arrived to alter the complexion of things, literally as well as figuratively, meant joining a minstrel troupe, parading on the morning before the show opened, blacking up, participating in the "olio"—the variety acts between the first part and the afterpiece—and barnstorming.

Dave Grant had just joined the minstrel troupe of Billy Birch, a permanent organization that held forth regularly in San Francisco Hall on Broadway between Twenty-eighth and Twenty-ninth Streets. They needed another madrigal boy. Would Isidore care to join? For Isidore, too, in the grammar school days had possessed a good voice, as had all the Witmark boys except Jay. And a job as madrigal boy—we would say chorus man today—was the entering wedge into a fascinating career.

Isidore hesitated. The offer was tempting, but he felt that it would be wrong for him to leave Dad in the lurch. Julie, however, working in a millinery store, was eligible. As Isidore had spent his spare moments in tuning and teaching the piano, so Julie had begun haunting theatrical rehearsals, instinctively seeking an outlet for a remarkable voice. Here was just the opening for Julie, and he joined Billy Birch's San Francisco Minstrels on August 27, 1883. There were four madrigal boys: Julie, Dave Grant, Jakie Miller, and a fourth boy whose name was Shreiber. Jakie Miller became the protégé of Bob Slavin, the black-face monologist, took his name, and as Johnny Slavin soon was one of the most popular singing and dancing comedians on the stage.

45

The experience was valuable for Julie, and it proved priceless for the firm that he and his brothers were shortly to found.

In 1884, for a brief engagement Julie went from the minstrel troupe again as a madrigal boy to Lawrence Barrett and his spectacular production of "Francesca da Rimini," with Marie Wainwright, Louis James, and Otis Skinner at the Grand Opera House.

He was still to be graduated from the chorus and to sing his first solo on the professional stage. This occurred in the same year during a summer engagement with Leavitt's Gigantean Minstrels at Tony Pastor's Theater.

It was a gala occasion for the Witmark family. Tony Pastor's and Koster and Bial's spelled consecration for the contemporary performer. Mother Witmark and Isidore were nervous as they sat through that first performance. The Queen was fond of telling in after years how Isidore, intensely excited, had pinched her throughout the singing of Julie's number, *Baby's Lullaby*. Julie's salary was ten dollars per week, but it being Leavitt's practice to be careless in such matters, he never received it.

4. The Eden Musée

Later in 1884 he was engaged for eight Saturday matinee concerts at the Eden Musée. So great was his success with Harrison Millard's song, *When the Flowing Tide Comes In*, and *Always Take Mother's Advice*, by Jennie Lindsay, that he remained at the Musée for eight months.

The Eden Musée was one of the show places of the city. Its fame throughout the nation was widespread, second only to that of the Statue of Liberty. When it opened its doors on March 29, 1884, it was the latest idea in amusement from Paris, and many compared it favorably with Madame Tussaud's in London. The wax figures exhibited at the Musée were among the finest specimens to be found anywhere, and they were made on the premises. Some of the groups won renown. Among the best liked at the

46

EDEN MUSEE CONCERTS.

Original Hungarian Prince Lichtenstein's Celebrated Gypsy Band. - - - - - - Mr. Paul Olah, Leader.

SPECIAL PROGRAMME
— FOR THE —
GRAND CHILDREN'S MATINEE
Saturday Afternoon, February 21, at 2 P. M

Miss LINDA DA COSTA,   The Little American Nightingale

Master JULIUS WITMARK,   The Boy Soprano

1885

PRINCE LICHTENSTEIN'S CELEBRATED GYPSY BAN1

Will Perform the Following Selections:

PART I.

1. MARCH—"Boccaccio,"..Suppe
2. WALTZ—"Beggar Student,".................................Millocker
3. SONG—"A Mother's Watch by the Sea,"..................Howard
   MASTER JULIUS WITMARK.
4. OVERTURE—"Hunyady,".....................................Erke.
5. SONG—"Embarrassment,".....................................Abt
   Miss LINDA DA COSTA.
6. SONG— "Karl's Lullaby,"...................................Gardner
   MASTER JULIUS WITMARK.
7. WALTZ—"Gasparone,"..Millocker

SPECIAL PROGRAMME
— FOR THE —
GRAND CHILDREN'S MATINEE,
Saturday Afternoon, February 21, at 2 P. M.

Miss LINDA DA COSTA, The Little American Nightingale

Master JULIUS WITMARK,   The Boy Soprano.

1885

PRINCE LICHTENSTEIN'S CELEBRATED GYPSY BAND

Will Perform the Following Selections:

PART II.

8. MARCH—"Les Volontaires,".................................Metra
9. SONG—Ballad "Si tu Savais,".............................Balfe
   Miss LINDA DA COSTA.
10. WALTZ—"Nanon,"...Suppe
11. SONG—"Always Take Mother's Advice,"...............J. Lindsay
    MASTER JULIUS WITMARK.
12. HUNGARIAN AND AMERICAN MELODIES,
    (Violin Solo, Mr. PAUL OLAH.)
13. SONG—"Coming' Thro' the Rye,".......................
    Miss LINDA DA COSTA.
14. POLKA—"Express,"...Fahrbach

A rare program of one of the famous landmarks of old New York in 1885. Julie was engaged to sing there for eight concerts and was such a success he remained eight months.

47

opening were the tableaux, "The Baptism of the Great-Grandson of the Emperor of Germany," "The Rulers of the World," and "The Abolition of Slavery in the United States." The Chamber of Horrors in the basement was one of the main attractions.

The building consisted of a magnificent hall and a gallery in which concerts were given. Some of the attractions that appeared in the Musée may be worthy of recounting: The first Hungarian Band ever to play in America; the Viennese Lady Fencers who, according to the Museum Scrap Book, created more of a stir than the Florodora Sextette; and one of the first troupes of Russian Dancers. In 1898 it produced and exhibited a cinematograph version of "The Passion Play" which ran for nine months. The film, taken on the roof of the old Grand Central Palace, was two thousand feet in length in days when five hundred foot films were the average. Among other Musée features were flower shows, it having been the scene of New York's first orchid exhibition in 1887. Incidentally the only day it was ever closed was the occasion of the funeral of William McKinley. Its largest single day's admissions were during the Dewey Celebration when 1200 passed its turnstiles. It was one of the few institutions in town that never altered its policies.

When the Eden Musée was opened, Twenty-third Street and Sixth Avenue was a busy thoroughfare, the center of New York's shopping district, but when the department stores commenced moving uptown or into oblivion its glory commenced to wane until at last in December, 1915, it closed its doors and its assets were sold under the auctioneer's hammer. Napoleon, Caesar, and Teddy Roosevelt went in one lot for $240, while Robert Emmet was bought by an Irishman for $2.

5. Domestic Blueprints

In an appreciative measure, the Witmark home had been transmuted into a theater. The home was the proof-sheet of every

402 West 40th Street, first home of the House of Witmark, about
1886, showing Frank, Julie, Jay and Eddie — all four born in that
house. Printing was then the major business. Note the title pages in
show window — most of them set up in type by Isidore.

Eddie and Frank

Favorite poses in their
vaudeville specialty which
was a big success.

ISIDORE AND HIS BRETHREN

activity in which the children engaged. Isidore was not yet sixteen; Julie was fourteen; Jay thirteen; and Frances, the only girl in the family, just under eleven. Having grown up with the boys, she was something of a tomboy and in the toy-press days she had proved valuable as a sort of runner between the boys' stand at the corner of Eighth Avenue and Fortieth Street and their home where the actual printing was done. She would wait until a few orders had accumulated at the stand and then hurry the copy and instructions to her brothers at the print shop, remain until the matter had been run off, and rush back with it to the stand. Frank, the first of the kids to receive printed publicity, was a veteran of nine, and Eddie, later to be known as Adolph S., was seven.

It was Jay whose skill in arithmetic and shortcomings in deportment had been responsible for the emergence of the boys into the printing business. It was Julie's voice that, together with Isidore's resourcefulness, was shortly to launch them into the publication of music. Isidore was to write the songs and Julie was to sing them. Isidore also made all the special medley arrangements that were such a big hit with Frank and Ed, and with the public, too. He devoted much time to these medleys; as a result, the boys' act stood well apart from the routine accepted formerly. The idea of the young arranger was not merely to assemble a tuneful potpourri of popular material, but to integrate it into what virtually became a miniature play. People were soon looking forward to new Witmark medleys as an event.

From the yellow, crumbling pages of Julie's scrapbook, it is possible to reconstruct, not only the sensational advance of "The Wonderful Boy Soprano" in the world of the theater, but the frequent performances of the Witmark household.

By 1885 the Witmarks had been in the printing business for two years, so that the programs for all these occasions were the work of "Witmark Brothers, Printers, 402 W. 40th St."

The evening of January 28, 1885, was a gala occasion at the
49

Witmarks'. The program for the "Entertainment and Birthday Party Tendered to Mr. M. Witmark" on that Wednesday was one of the most interesting documents of this salient year in the life of the young firm. It was printed, naturally, by Witmark Brothers. The Director of Entertainment again, naturally, was Isidore Witmark. In honor of the paternal anniversary the program was printed in blue ink. The entertainment had been arranged entirely by the six little Witmarks.

Daddy and Queen had cause indeed to be proud of their children. Wherever there was a prominent entertainment, the Witmark children were likely to be found on the program, which, often as not, was printed as well as provided by the same children. Julius was a drawing card and frequently had the position of honor. The youngest, Eddie, was already being billed before Court Abingdon, No. 6935, of the Ancient Order of Foresters, or the Christian Worker's "Helping Hand," as "The Youngest Character Artist on the Stage." He had a sketch, "The Poor Little Newsboy," which was in popular demand. Isidore played all the piano accompaniments. And as if these numerous appearances were not enough, in the banner year of 1885 the children organized an amateur musical and dramatic society with the modest name of "The Select."

The aim was to run, at the end of the season, a triumphant performance under the stage-direction of Isidore. What they thought of one another was evident not only from the name that they chose for their organization but from their courage in hiring for this public performance what was then one of the finest halls to be had in New York, "The Lyric," later known as Bryant Hall, which stood until a few years ago on Sixth Avenue between Forty-first and Forty-second Streets. Here for years hundreds of successful shows rehearsed within its walls, and of course also many failures.

In the middle Eighties it was customary to serve a supper after the amateur performance, whereupon dancing continued into morning. The lease of the hall carried with it the obligation on the part of the lessee to guarantee a certain number of suppers. Daddy Witmark, never far from the scene of activities, took over the guarantee of fifty plates. Tickets were going fast, so that no special risk was involved. On the night of the entertainment the house was packed. All the friends of the participants had turned out loyally to see what they could do, and it was generally voted that it was a bully show. Julie, incidentally, won another medal.

According to custom, no sooner had the curtain come down on the entertainment than the orchestra struck up the supper march. The glorious tones of a good old operatic procession smote the air accordingly. But where was the answering tramp of many feet? One march was played after another. Yet nary a marcher.

What was the explanation of the Grand March that failed to march? For one thing, virtually four-fifths of the audience was composed of the parents and relatives of the performers. They were elder folk who seldom went to such entertainments and did not stay for the dance. The other fifth were very young and had more appetite than money with which to purchase supper tickets. For that matter, the children of 1885 were not spenders.

From the kitchen came aromas that would have stirred an Egyptian mummy to appetite. Isidore looked at his father. His father looked at him. Daddy Witmark was a good sport.

"It looks as if I'm going to be stuck," he said. "Very well. It's worth it after that first-rate show you gave. Invite the crowd to supper on me."

The announcement was made. The band blared into another processional. This time they *all* marched.

6. Cruelty to Children

The middle of February, 1885, was a time of recurrent excitement in the Witmark household. Julius Peyser Witmark, the next

51

to the eldest, had been virtually taken off the stage of the Eden Musée, where he was appearing in the operetta, "The Mountain Queen," and summoned with his father before Mayor Grace to show cause why he should continue to appear upon the stage. Julius, though but fifteen, had already been singing in public for two years and it is somewhat astonishing that with all the publicity surrounding him he had never before this come to the attention of President Elbridge T. Gerry of the Society for the Prevention of Cruelty to Children.

Marcus Witmark was not the only indignant parent to attend the meeting in the Mayor's office. There was the mother of Linda Da Costa, a ten-year-old prima donna who, as the Queen of the piece, had been singing to Master Witmark's King. Resentment against Gerry ran high. Why, demanded Alderman Tony Hartman, this eternal interference of the high-minded President Gerry in the affairs of children well-cared-for, when there were so many manifestly abused and ill-clad, neglected waifs in the city who were far more properly the objects of his solicitude?

Julius had better luck than his little Queen Linda, for the Mayor granted him the right to sing at matinees. So joyful he was at his victory, and already so much the veteran trouper, that he left with a promise to send Mayor Grace a batch of complimentary tickets for the show.

The effect of the encounter with Gerry was to increase business for both children. Linda, though denied permission to act and sing on the professional stage, continued to appear in local concerts where Julius sang with her. Sweet are the uses of publicity, even though one's name, by a none too accurate press, is spelled Wittmark, Whitmark or Witmark.

7. Minstrels

The greatest date in the great year of 1885 was August 5, on which day Julius made his debut with a famous minstrel troupe,

Thatcher, Primrose and West, in Buffalo. The contract had the glory of an accolade. It had been signed as the result of a try-out arranged one night in the previous season in Williamsburg, Brooklyn, where Julie made his really first appearance with the Thatcher, Primrose and West troupe. On that evening it was stipulated that if Julie were engaged he would appear only in white face. He was a big success in his black-face try-out, yet never thereafter in his minstrel career did he face an audience from behind burnt cork! He was the only white-face in the famous minstrel First Part offered by his new employers. The concession to the boy was, in its way, and for the institution of minstrelsy, revolutionary.

At fifteen, Julie was well on his way to becoming a star—a singer over the national circuit, in company with singers and actors whose names were household words in the world of minstrelsy. When the time came to see Julie off, Isidore was to accompany him as far as Buffalo and there was great excitement in the Witmark household.

It was almost midnight, on August 4, 1885, their mother's birthday, when they pulled into Buffalo. The children had no notion where the troupe was staying, so, when the bus for the Tifft House hove into sight, they took it; one reason was that the rain was coming down in buckets. The Tifft House was the *de luxe* hotel of the city; it is not surprising that the drenched youngsters were informed, with smiling courtesy, that the minstrel troupe was not registered there. They picked up their luggage, took a bus to another hotel, and, within a couple of hours had made a tour of Buffalo's hostelries, returning unsuccessful in their quest to the railroad station from which they had set out. There, at the station, was the Continental Hotel; had they tried it first, they would have saved many bus fares. It was now two o'clock in the morning.

It was at the Continental that the brothers met Chauncey Olcott; they were to know him much better in the glorious days

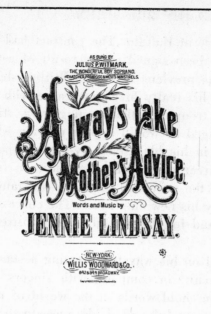

Original title-page of *Always Take Mother's Advice* (1885). This was Julie's first big song hit and the number that transformed the Witmarks from printers to music publishers.

First Witmark songs published by Willis Woodward & Co., before the boys were in the publishing business on their own.

ahead. Here they met, also, Barney Fagan, one of the foremost minstrels of the time, known too as an outstanding producer, and to be much better known within eleven years for his song, *My Gal's A High Born Lady*. The managers paid all hotel and railroad bills, and saved money by doubling up its personnel. Julie was about to be assigned to a permanent rooming partner. "Put *me* with the boy," Fagan urged; and thus was initiated a friendship that lasted long after the minstrel days.

The company took Julie to their hearts. He was, after all, a child. He sang that night and was a big success. Next morning the Buffalo *Courier* described him as "a handsome lad with a singularly sweet and musical voice. His enunciation is especially distinct and he sings with unmistakable refinement and intelligence."

The song he sang, entitled *A Mother's A Mother After All*, was composed by brother Isidore. It was his first published composition, and bore the imprint of Willis Woodward & Company. To the listener of today, the mother in popular song is identified largely with Al Jolson and his synthetic Mammy. Our sophisticated youngsters know the differences that distinguish a mammy from a mother, and a mother from a mama, hot or cold. Mothers, the original crooners and singers of the race, have always been a staple of song. Long before Al Jolson yearned on bended knee, with outstretched arms, for his coal-black (say, rather, lampblack) mammy, Julie had been singing of the perennial mother to audiences that could not hear enough about her. He had already made tremendously popular the Jennie Lindsay song, *Always Take Mother's Advice*, also published by Woodward, and was to increase its vogue all over the country, wherever he traveled with the minstrel troupe.

Woodward did not know it at the time, nor did Julie, or Isidore, but the Witmarks had already been started upon their career as publishers of music, and by nothing other than the failure of Woodward to live up to a promise.

FROM RAGTIME TO SWINGTIME

On August 6, the Thatcher, Primrose and West minstrels left for Bradford, Pa. Isidore's duty as a guide and chaperon had been accomplished. Julie now had, as it were, five parents to watch over him: Mr. and Mrs. Thatcher, Mr. and Mrs. Primrose, and Mr. West. They all promised to take care of him. When the train pulled out for Bradford, Isidore felt lonely. Buffalo seemed deserted, and it required an effort to pull himself together. Nevertheless, as long as he was in Buffalo he might as well see the sights, so to Niagara Falls he went, and, amid the crude bridges, the rough fences and rustic walks, he enjoyed a haunting sense of solitude.

As for Julie, whom the Thatchers, Primroses and West were going to watch over tenderly, he remained unspoiled. Indeed he was the only one of the minstrels to maintain his poise and his common sense. At the end of three weeks he had become the confidential banker of the entire company. The rôles had been reversed. He was the "father," not the child.

It was on this tour that he had an experience the memory of which never left him. With the company there traveled the English troupe of acrobats, the Nelson family, in theatrical lingo a "sensation" wherever they played. The youngest of the family, Charley, was the top-mounter and was about Julie's age. He took it into his head, childlike, to annoy Julie as much as possible, until finally Barney Fagan insisted that the young ones should have it out in the ring. Barney, a splendid specimen of a man and a fine boxer, trained Julie for the event, and one day a ring was roped off on the stage of the town in which they were playing, and the boys went at it in earnest. It was only natural that Charley Nelson should be the favorite, because he was an acrobat and in fine condition. But through Fagan's expert training, Julie proved to be a sort of dark-horse and held his own magnificently with his opponent. Charley did not bother him any more.

Not long afterwards, the Nelson family, who practised every day of the week, were going through their regular routine and

The song written to "measure" for Julie and sung by him all over the country with
Thatcher, Primrose and West's Minstrels and with the great Billy Emerson in San
Francisco, 1899.

had finished everything but their six-high feat, with little Charley on top. The stunt was that, at a given signal, the six-high line was to lean forward and suddenly break and all of them roll over and land on their feet. It was a tremendous finish to a remarkable act.

On this day they were rehearsing carelessly, and by the time they reached the big stunt they were nervous. It was never discovered why, but when the signal was given for the break it was as quickly recalled, and the five remained in position while poor little Charley fell. He never performed again; the fall paralyzed him from his hips down. He was brought to the New York Hospital, New York, and Julie was his constant visitor until he passed on.

A more pleasant reminiscence of Julie's was the last performance given by Chauncey Olcott with the minstrel troupe of Thatcher, Primrose and West. Olcott had been engaged by the Lillian Russell Opera Company to sing the leading tenor rôle in Edward Solomon's "Pepita." This was his farewell to blackface. All the old minstrel shoes that had been accumulated over years of trouping were gathered together and thrown after Chauncey, as tokens of good luck for his new venture.

And a lucky venture it proved, for this was the beginning of Olcott's greater fame. He went to England where, for two years, he sang in light opera. On the death of the beloved Irish singing comedian, William J. Scanlan (many will remember his *Sweet Molly O*, and *Peek-a-Boo*), Olcott returned to America to succeed him under the same management, that of Augustus Pitou, and he became the foremost Irish romantic singer of his time.

Meanwhile, Julie was seeing America. Besides singing solos, he took part in travesties. One of the most popular of these was "The Black Mikado." Gilbert and Sullivan's white "Mikado" was only a few months old, yet the parodists had seized upon it with a burlesque glee that had been rampant since the days of "H.M.S. Pinafore" but six historic years before. Julie sang now as Yum Yum, again as Pitti Sing. A fellow had to be versatile on the road.

Robert H. Davis, the veteran columnist, was a boy editor in the days when Julie was trekking across the country with his companions in minstrelsy. He recalled, years later, his first sight of the boy soprano, in far-off Nevada.

"I see Carson, Nevada," he wrote, "with a flashing, black-haired, vibrant Julius P. Witmark, the boy tenor, stepping down the main street in a mauve overcoat with the Thatcher, Primrose and West invaders. I still hear your voice reaching the very rafters of the opera house and penetrating the dome of heaven. They were glorious days to remember."

CHAPTER IV

THE BEGINNING OF TIN PAN ALLEY

1. The Late Eighties

*J*ULIUS WITMARK was a natural-born "plugger." For him to sing a song was to start the song on the road to possible fortune. In 1885 there were no phonographs, no gramophones, no radios, to duplicate simultaneously the singing of a piece. For that matter, long after the invention and the commercialization of the phonograph, the singer would remain the great vehicle of publicity for composer and publishing firm. Julie had been promised by Woodward an interest in the song, *Always Take Mother's Advice.* At the end of the season, however, he found it as hard to collect this promise from the publisher as he had found it to collect his ten-dollar weekly salary from "Mike" Leavitt. For his share in making a song the song of a nation he was patted on the back and presented with a twenty-dollar gold piece as a bonus. Perhaps these entrepreneurs thought themselves above keeping faith with a child. If so, they reckoned without their host.

Isidore once again arose in his youthful wrath against the injustice of the publisher. If he could not hold a job to which he was entitled, he could start a firm of his own. If a song-publisher tried to take advantage of Julie's personal magnetism as vocalist and living advertisement for sheet music, he and his brothers

60

could retaliate by going into the publishing of music on their own. To vary a familiar fighting rhythm, they had the press, they had the singers, and they had the composers, too.

At that time very few music houses specialized in the publication of popular songs. First among them was Willis Woodward and Co., who published also *Woodward's Monthly Magazine* and were situated in the Star Theatre Building, Thirteenth Street and Broadway. Woodward had issued many of the current successes: *White Wings*, by Banks Winter; *The Song That Reached My Heart*, by Julian Jordan (the title, suggested by Henry J. Sayers, author of *Ta Ra Ra Boom-de-Ay* and manager of the Thatcher, Primrose and West Minstrels, brought that gentleman a royalty of two cents on every copy sold); *If The Waters Could Speak As They Flow*, by Charles Graham, later to write *The Picture That Is Turned Toward the Wall* and *Two Little Girls In Blue*; *Always Take Mother's Advice*, by Jennie Lindsay.

Another was the original firm of T. B. Harms and Co., consisting of Thomas and Alex Harms, the founders, two fine men— too good for their own benefit—who published most of the musical productions of the day, including the DeWolf Hopper vehicles, "Wang," "Dr. Syntax," "Panjandrum," and "Castles in the Air." Among their many hits were Scanlan's *Peek-a-Boo* and *Molly O!*, and Gus Williams' *Pretty Little Dark Blue Eyes*, from the play with music, "Captain Mishler."

Another was Harding on the Bowery, established in 1860; he was really the pioneer house of this type, publishing Tony Pastor's hits, including *I Have Only Been Down to the Club*, and the famous *Marriage Bells*, by "Matt" O'Reardon. These houses were practically wholesale publishers, but did a little retail business on the side.

Among the wholesale-retail houses was William A. Pond & Co., publishers of the Harrigan and Hart songs, by David Braham, and the authorized versions of the Gilbert and Sullivan operas.

61

FROM RAGTIME TO SWINGTIME

Another house, Spear & Denhoff, located in the New York hotel block at Broadway and Waverly Place, had published some big ballad successes, including Skelly's *Old Rustic Bridge By The Mill, When The Flowing Tide Comes In, Babbling Brook,* and *Baby Mine.*

Out in Cincinnati, the John Church Company was active in popular publications. They had all of the J. K. Emmett songs: Emmett's *Lullaby,* Emmett's *Cuckoo Song* and others that Emmett sang in his "Fritz" series of plays. They also published songs for the great minstrel, Billy Emerson, and for Gus Williams. They became the publishers of the operas and marches of Sousa, and of the early operas and choral works of Julian Edwards. John Church was indeed a live house, and it had grown to primary importance before it was taken over by Theodore Presser Co., of Philadelphia, one of the largest musical publishing houses in America today. By coincidence, Church had published the first set of teaching pieces written for the piano, around 1883, by the then unknown Theodore Presser.

Presser became one of the outstanding figures in American music publishing and, incidentally, one of the best friends of the Witmarks. He studied music here and abroad. At the Royal Conservatory, Leipzig, he numbered among his teachers the renowned Jadassohn and Reinecke. He taught at college; it was while at Ohio Wesleyan University that he conceived the plan to organize the Music Teachers' National Association. This was a pioneer organization that led, in time, to the clubs, federations, and conferences now constituting a national network of musical educators. In 1883 he founded *The Etude* as an organ for the Association. The organ preceded the music publishing business that it still distinguishes.

It was a visit to Italy, and to the Verdi Rest Home For Musicians in Milan, that planted the idea in his mind for an American Home for Aged Music Teachers. The idea met with a lukewarm reception. In 1907, however, Presser founded and endowed the institution now known as *The Presser Home for Retired Music Teachers*. Nine years later he established the *Presser Foundation*, which he had preferred to call "A Foundation for the Advancement of Music." It is a worthy monument to the man whose altruism it symbolizes, well described in its pamphlet as "the institutional continuation of the founder's life." Theodore Presser died at Philadelphia on October 28, 1925. On July 3 of that year he had celebrated his seventy-seventh birthday.

The most energetic of all the "popular" firms of the earlier days were doubtless Woodward and Harms. They anticipated, in a modest way, the future of the popular music publishing business by their primitive method of introducing and "plugging" songs that showed any signs of life. In fact, they and Harding had the call on all the public singers and minstrels as introducers of their respective numbers. These concerns boasted no more than one piano each; they had no regular pianist or demonstrator on salary. They adhered to no particular promotion programs and, with the exception of one or two small advertisements in the *New York Clipper*, the *Variety* of that day, they did no advertising.

After the advent of Witmark, the first firm to imitate them was Spaulding & Gray, composed of two energetic young men. Spaulding had been a music clerk with Charles Ditson & Company; also a writer and composer, afterwards head of the Educational Department of M. Witmark & Sons. Gray was a variety performer and song writer. The two outstanding successes published by them at this time were *Down Went McGinty*, by Joe Flynn, and *Two Little Girls In Blue*, by Charles Graham,—big money hits. The house of S. T. Gordon, general publishers, also had a great popular success, *Silver Threads Among The Gold*, by H. P. Danks, which it took over with the catalogue of the Troy house of C. W. Harris. This song has the reputation of being the most successful "revived number" ever published, having proved more popular and a greater seller in its second life (copyright renewed in

63

1907) than in its first; the original copyright is dated 1873. It was revived in 1902 by that famous minstrel singer, Richard J. José, who was with Primrose and West's Minstrels at the time.

This, then, was the field into which the Witmark children had determined to break. The new publishing firm was greeted by its chief competitor, Willis Woodward, with a blaspheming prophecy, "I'll give those blankety-blank-blank Witmarks just six months in this business."

A half-century later the Witmark firm was still flourishing. Woodward's had long been a reminiscence of old-time publishers.

The Witmarks, ancestrally, had been noted for a powerful drive that took now the form of strict self-discipline and again even a moralistic turn. In the boys, this heritage was evident from the moment that they started their own firm. It was nicknamed "The Hatchery," by the competitors who were predicting its early failure, because it was composed of fledglings. Years later, a notice in one of the music trade papers, commenting upon the dynamic methods of Isidore, wrote "Isidore Witmark won't let any employee of his do more than he does, but he works twenty-six hours a day." The early habits had remained.

During his minstrel tour Julie had made many friendships with responsible dealers in the West and the Middle West. He not only sang songs; he sold them in generous orders to the commercial houses. His delightful personality gave him access, though a mere boy, to the heads of the most important companies. Big men, such as Mr. Healy of Lyon & Healy, Chicago, and Mr. Sherman, of Sherman, Clay & Co., San Francisco, the prominent music firm of the far West, entertained him; their buyers and clerks were quick to follow suit.

There was yet another aspect to this and similar tours which eventually was to stand the Witmark company in good stead. Julie, as a public performer acquainted with the taste of the people in all sections of the country, developed into that most valuable of men in what came to be known in Tin Pan Alley—

Eddie in his popular singing specialty.

Frank M. Witmark

The Eden Musee

a hit-picker. He had an almost uncanny aptitude for spotting future song successes at first hearing. Brother Isidore, in the musico-dramatic end of the business, was to develop a similar gift. He was a song-and-show doctor long before that term had become current on Broadway, and had a hand in several stage productions on which his name did not appear.

If the year 1885 was the big year for song and dance in the Witmark ménage, 1886 was doubly big for the inauguration of the music-publishing firm and for a stream of juvenile successes from the pen of Isidore.

Yet, through overenthusiasm and its very excess of alertness, the firm came near being wrecked at the start.

2. President Cleveland Marries

One day, Jay Witmark happened to read in the newspapers that President Grover Cleveland was about to marry. It was a mere rumor, lacking any trace of confirmation. Here, suggested somebody in the group, was a good spot for a specially composed wedding march. That was all Isidore needed to hear. He stopped his press, laid aside his ink-smeared apron, and disappeared.

A moment later the professional noises in the old printing shop were intermingled with the rhythmic strains that came thumping down from upstairs, and before the day was many hours older, Isidore had added to his *opus* numbers a *President Cleveland's Wedding March*. In the heat of this eagerness to win a scoop over the publishing business of New York city, the boys rushed through a large, lithographed *édition de luxe* of the composition.

And then came the news that the rumors of the President's wedding had been a hoax. One may well imagine that this announcement fell upon the ears of the boys like the crack of doom. It seemed as if the President, with malice aforethought, had let them down. The croakers among their competitors began to sing again the song of defeat that they had sung from the first.

Daddy Witmark read the papers also. And one bright morning, before his early-rising sons had been able to consult the dailies, he walked in with the gladsome tidings that there had been no hoax after all—that Grover Cleveland was to marry the beautiful Frances Folsom—and that wedding marches were in order now.

The Witmark printing-shop-musical-publishing-firm began to hum with presidential-marital activity. "Foot kicking" as a motor power had been replaced by gas; Witmark Quick Print could now print more quickly. The other publishers, who, like cautious business men, had been holding off until they could see which way the cat was going to jump, were caught off their guard. The Witmark brothers had the wedding-march market all to themselves. It was an important coup, and placed the boys firmly upon the music-publishing map of the country.

"The tempo," said the *New York World* of May 30, 1886, "is not quite lively enough for the old Jacksonian Democrats who have called at the White House for offices and have been compelled to retreat, but nevertheless it is to be hoped that the music will become popular." Popular? The reporter should have asked the other publishers who had had a *march* stolen on them by a trio of kids!

No sooner had the children opened up their music firm than they had a Catalogue. "Charles E. Dobson's compositions for banjo and piano . . . Send for catalogue," reads the advertisement. And what is this already at the birth of the venture?

Wanted:
> Boys or young men for orchestra, who double in brass preferred; also boy quartet and singers: salaries paid. Call or address Witmark G. B. Minstrels, 402 W. 40th St., New York.

They knew where they were going, these Witmarks. Having founded a music firm to get revenge upon Woodward, out of friendly rivalry and sheer exuberance of spirits they contemplated a troupe to put Thatcher, Primrose and West out of business!

What were the "G.B." minstrels? The *Great Boy* troupe! And what had been the prime motive behind the organization of the Great Boys? Gilbert and Sullivan.

From the first, with the unabating popularity of "H.M.S. Pinafore," the operas of the satiric Gilbert and his collaborator had been seized upon by juvenile companies, white and black, inside of the church and out. Julie, Frank, and Ed were singing on the stage and in concert halls. Through Barney Fagan, Julie had learned something about the practical details of staging ambitious minstrel acts; he could hardly have had a better teacher. Jay already seemed a born treasurer; Isidore was an organizer, and could be depended upon to provide special material.

Through the advertisement in the *World* they organized a club of clever boys, set weekly dues at five cents, hired the Adelphi Hall on Fifty-second Street near Broadway—paid for out of the dues—and rehearsed every Sunday afternoon.

It was no idle children's affair. More than one of these Great Boy Minstrels was graduated into professional eminence. Young Lang, for instance, was soon known as a member of the popular team, Dixon and Lang. Frank McKinney, a bricklayer's apprentice, had a beautiful tenor voice, and it won him a place in one of the best-known quartettes of the day. There was a kid named Filehne, a cornet soloist, who also went professional.

The advertisement called for youngsters who could "double in brass," and certainly they doubled with a vengeance, whether the word "brass" refers to instruments or to "nerve." The orchestra thus formed was a fluctuating affair. Sometimes they had three pieces, and sometimes seven. Ike Stone played the violin. It has been said in these pages that Jay was the only non-musical child of Daddy and "Queen" Witmark. We did Jay wrong. In this orchestra he played the bass drum. Isidore played the piano.

The Great Boy Minstrels, alas, rehearsed for six months, and gave only one performance; hardly that, to tell the truth, for they were but one of the acts on a variety program. The show was given for one of the Posts of the G. A. R., who had given the Witmark boys all their printing. Included in this patronage was a small sixteen-page program that Isidore set himself and stayed up until three in the morning "making ready." At three he was relieved by Jay, who hopped out of bed and started running the press into the next day.

They rehearsed the show until midnight, when the performers were hustled out of the shop so that the Witmarks could get busy on that printing.

The one performance, nevertheless, was a success, particularly an intricate Fagan routine entitled *Colored Knights of Labor.* Julie directed the number, and Isidore wrote the words and music.

✓ Tin Pan Alley is the Newspaper Row of music. It is a species of song-and-dance journalism, intimately bound up with the current trend of events. The story of *Grover Cleveland's Wedding March* is a symbol of the whole industry. By a good half, that industry is a melodious opportunism, just as today the moving-picture industry is a celluloid opportunism, annexing to itself, and exploiting, the news-values of the day.

The Witmarks were among the first, before Tin Pan Alley was founded, to sense the importance of turning to profit the major happenings of the time. Popular songs, particularly ballads, have always sung of popular interests and of historic and contemporary events, whether great victories, great conflagrations, murders, acts of God, or other such memorabilia. What Tin Pan Alley did for the songs was to quicken the time-interval between events and report. Its music, generally, is the doggerel of song, as its rhymes are the doggerel of verse.

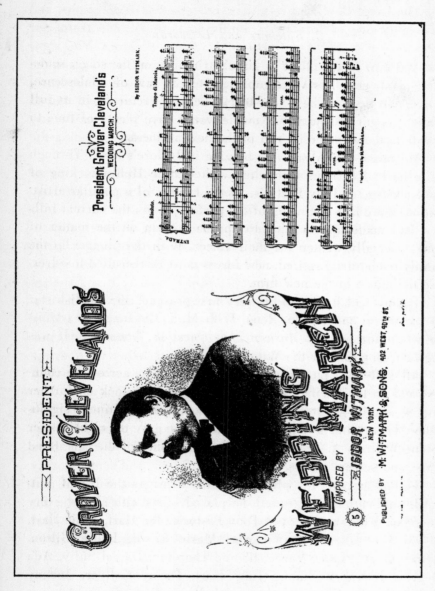

A Wedding March with a musical history. Witmarks' "40th Street" first big hit, that opened the door to the music business for them.

3. Butchers and Blizzards

And now in the midst of Julie's triumphs on the stage, something happened. His voice, obedient to the law of adolescence, broke, and it would be a year or two before it returned in its full adult strength and quality. Now he would have plenty of time to devote to the commercial end of the new business.

Meantime new ideas were buzzing in Isidore's head. Through Julie he had become acquainted with George Hoffman, king of the backstage at Tony Pastor's. As the brother of a popular artist, Isidore there had met many of the performers on the current bills and had made up his mind to approach them on the matter of songs specially written for their voices. With the plugger in the family temporarily retired, new forces must be recruited to advertise the music of the new firm.

Isidore had luck with his very first prospect, the English star of the music halls, Mlle. René. With M. J. Cavanagh as lyricist he wrote for her *I'll Answer That Question Tomorrow*. It was the first song to bear the Witmark imprint.

Mlle. René popularized the song in her tour across the country, and on the Pacific Coast the title of the tune took on for her and a certain gentleman a very personal and pertinent significance. There came a tomorrow on which she gave the right answer to one William A. Brady. René was the mother of the celebrated stage and screen actress, Alice Brady.

Isidore became the plugger for the firm. As the list of Witmark publications lengthened, he placed songs with almost every top-notcher who appeared at Tony Pastor's: Joe Hart, Katie Hart, Bessie Bonehill, Vesta Victoria, Marie Lloyd, Lottie Gilson, Arthur West, Eunice Vance, Bonnie Thornton, Daniel Sully, Ada Deaves, Jennie Williams, Tony Hart, Danny Collyer, Johnny Wild, Florrie West, Monroe and Rice, Tom Seabrooke——Vanished singers, vanished songs!

THE BEGINNING OF TIN PAN ALLEY

During the summer days Tony Pastor's was used as a tryout house for unpretentious comedies, many with music, one of which, at this time, had scored a hit. It was Daniel Sully's "Corner Grocery," and the success of the piece encouraged Sully to try again. Isidore, learning of Sully's new piece, looked it over and suggested that he turn it into a comedy with music. Why not? Here were a few numbers that Isidore had written, waiting for such an opportunity. Sully heard the numbers; one of them, *Mike Nolan, His Mule And His Cart*, so pleased him that he altered his plot to center around it and even named his piece "Daddy Nolan," making his part that of a junk man, to conform with the song. Not this alone; Sully, delighted with the success of the song—he spoke rather than sang it, for his singing left much to be desired —ordered 45,000 copies, which were given away as souvenirs. Here was a double stroke of luck for a new music firm! Such a distribution would seem large even today; in 1886 it was a glorious advertisement that sent the Witmarks up with the spring of a jack-in-the-box.

The same year they published as independent songs, *The Village Choir, The Ship's The Home For Me, Breathe Those Tender Words Again*, and *King of the Swells*, all written by Isidore.

Next year, he wrote two more songs *Sweet Autumn Flowers* and *Too Whoo, You Know*, the words of the latter by M. J. Cavanagh; it was Isidore's first big hit.

Cavanaugh had written the lyrics for *As I Sat Upon My Dear Old Mother's Knee*, to music by Joseph Skelly, and both the words and music of *Bring Back My Fisher Boy*. Cavanagh was prolific and versatile and was responsible for one of the big popular successes then—*Mr. and Mrs. Malone*. Between 1887 and 1890 he wrote a number of lyrics for Isidore, to the songs *'Tis The Sweetest Song of All, Since Reilly Took An Oath He'd Take My Life, Jack Won't Forget You*, and *He Was A Pal Of Mine*. The pal song is, in the composer's opinion, one of his best compositions. He had written it for Julie, who was highly successful with

Two "Currier and Ives" of the music business. *Mike Nolan*, fifty years old; *Only A Butcher*, over forty years.

it. Considering the descriptive type to which the song belonged, Cavanagh's lyric was first-rate. At benefits to which they all contributed, the torch singers of the day—Lottie Gilson, Bonnie Thornton, Emma Carus, and Imogene Comer—fought for the privilege of singing *He Was A Pal Of Mine.*

In 1888, the theatrical Rialto was on Fourteenth Street between Broadway and Fourth Avenue. Indeed, it was almost concentrated in front of the celebrated Morton House and the Union Square Theater. A number of important considerations had convinced the Witmarks that they were too far from the center of operations. Time was to reverse the direction of their move, and discover them squarely back in the Fortieth Street district whence, at this moment, from their home and office at 402 West Fortieth Street,—they had made up their minds to move to 32 East Fourteenth Street.

It was another great day when the firm moved into its first independent office. Separation of office from home was a visible token of new self-determination.

The dealings discussed in that office were not always of the sort that portended epical advancement for the cause of native music. For example, there was the visit, in February, 1888, from Jacob Mayers, who edited a trade paper, *The Butcher's Advocate.* Mayers, on the committee arranging for the annual ball and reception of "The Butchers and Drovers," to be held at Lexington Opera House, Fifty-eighth Street and Third Avenue, was eager to have Isidore write a waltz especially for the occasion. He had written *President Grover Cleveland's Wedding March,* and it followed that a writer good enough for Cleveland was good enough for Mayers and his esthetic companions.

Jake Mayers was a positive fellow. Had the firm been less in need of money, their senior member would have proved equally stubborn. Isidore suggested calling the composition, *Protective Waltzes.* Mayers insisted that the name be *Only a Butcher,* which

73

hit the poor composer like a cleaver across the throat. They argued until they were hoarse. Mayers promised a marvelous rendition of the piece by an augmented orchestra under the direction of Louis Eppinger, which inducement was as if he were to dangle the promise of a Whiteman or a Vallee today. He also offered twenty dollars in cash.

Isidore, afraid to let the order slip through his fingers, finally agreed to Mayers' title on condition that if he wrote another waltz for the next ball it should be entitled *Only A Slaughter-House*. Mayers' wit was not so keen as his butchers' knives; he missed the boy's sarcasm and consented at once . . . *Only A Butcher* turned out to be a successful effort in its *genre,* but it ended Witmark's connection as staff-composer for the "Butchers and Drovers." There was no re-order for waltzes, for there was no ball the next year.

Nothing, it seemed, could stop the boys now; not even the famous blizzard of 1888, which saw the winter out on March 12th with a white celebration that no one who attended it ever forgot. The day became a focal point on the calendar, for reckoning backward or forward, like the "big wind" in Ireland. What was a mere blizzard, however, to make these executives lose a day at the new office? Suppose Chauncey Olcott were to come up and find the place closed? Not to go was almost to halt the business of the entire city.

That morning Isidore and Julie trudged over to Broadway, waited a tiny eternity for a University Place car to come along. At University Place and Fourteenth Street, their destination, the driver refused to stop the car; there was nothing for the boys to do but jump, and they landed almost to their necks in a drift. Before they had managed to extricate one another they had sunk even lower. Reaching No. 32 was a blinding progress through drifts, for the snow, already hill-high in spots, sent back a dazzling whiteness. The wags had got to work with the self-scathing humor

THE BEGINNING OF TIN PAN ALLEY

known to soldiers in the trenches; merchants, on top of what looked like their white dugouts, had stuck up signs; "Keep off the Grass"; "Who said Snow?"; "For Sale, A Fine Stock of Linen Dusters"; "This Way to the North Pole."

The boys remained at their office until late in the afternoon without a soul coming in and without a bite to eat. It was too stormy to go out, and as dreary as solitary confinement. Finally they decided to go home. They tied burlap bags around their legs, bundled up well, and started for the street. When they reached University Place they learned that no cars were running. Matters had become much worse since morning. More signs had appeared everywhere. And more drifts, with men attempting rather unsuccessfully to make paths. It was like going through canyons. They searched about to see if they couldn't pick up a vehicle to take them home. With difficulty they held their footing at the corner of Fourteenth Street and University Place. Out of the distance, through a flurry of thick snow, they saw a four-wheeler cab approaching. The driver was almost hidden from view, so covered was he with snow.

Isidore cried to Julie, "That looks like our salvation!" and shouted, "Hey!" to the cabby who was driving laboriously against the wind. He did not stop, but turned toward them in his seat. "Hey!" Isidore repeated, "What will you charge to take us to Fortieth Street and Ninth Avenue?"

"Go to hell," replied the driver, and drove on.

It was getting late and knowing their folks would be worrying, Isidore suggested they hoof it the best they could. It was slow work plodding through those drifts; running was out of the question. By the time they got to Thirty-third Street and Broadway, they were exhausted. Then appeared one of those coffee shops à la Dennett, which stood on the site where Saks' Thirty-fourth Street store now stands. Making a beeline for it, they were soon enjoying steaming cups of hot coffee, while they thawed out. With a new lease on life, they started on the last lap of their journey,

75

and the surroundings looked every bit like the picture, "The Retreat from Moscow." With extraordinary luck they might have managed to reach their parents by telephone. But such extraordinary luck was not theirs. In 1888 there were only a few hundred subscribers on the books of the Bell Telephone Company. The first commercial telephone exchange had opened only ten years before—not in New York but in New Haven, Connecticut, where it had eight lines and twenty-one stations. In 1888, New York itself had in the entire city but four pay telephone booths, situated in The Imperial, at Thirty-second Street and Broadway; The Gilsey House, at Twenty-ninth Street and Broadway; the old Astor House, at Broadway and Vesey Street; and the Hoffman House, on Broadway between Twenty-fourth and Twenty-fifth Streets. Four booths! One moderate-sized cigar store today has more than that. . . . They were as far from a booth at their end as their parents were.

When finally they reached home and the arms of anxious parents, their noses and ears were frostbitten and fingers and toes little better.

In 1935, forty-seven years after, Isidore joined "The Blizzard Men," a New York organization composed solely of the veterans of the big snow.

4. Organ Music

The tenure of the office at 32 East Fourteenth Street was short-lived. The building was owned by a publisher of magazines and patterns for women, William Jennings Demorest, with a pair of Christian names that pointed to a greater William Jennings— Bryan—in the decade to come. William Jennings Demorest, too, ran for the Presidency of the United States—on the Prohibition ticket. Nor did his prohibitory ideas limit themselves to wine. He must have included women and song, for despite their year's lease, the Witmark boys were found by the landlord to be a public nuisance, what with the racket that was always going on: new songs being bawled forth by ambitious songsters and songstresses. Out went the new firm, almost as fast as it had moved in.

It was in the Demorest building that the boys had their first and only trouble with union labor. The pianist, a member of the musicians' union, and a singer were in session—one of those sessions that had given the owner of the building his excuse for breaking the lease. They were in the midst of the number when the twelve o'clock whistle blew. Noon! The pianist stopped in the middle of a bar, as if the whistle had blown his hands off the keys. "There's the whistle. I'm off to lunch!" he announced, and left the singer high and dry . . .

The Witmarks found a place at 841 Broadway, and signalized their removal by the purchase of a Beatty organ. The organ, provided with all the necessary stops, was excellent value at $27.50. Beatty organs were manufactured by the thousands in Washington, New Jersey, where Daniel Beatty was Mayor at the time.

An organ in a publishing firm devoted to popular music—a firm just ousted from its previous quarters because of its raucousness—might have appeared incongruous. For something genteel still hovered about the humble instrument with its sacred associations. Harrigan, of the famous trio, Harrigan, Hart and Braham, would not be singing his song of *Maggie Murphy's Home* until the end of 1890, when "Reilly And The 400" was staged at the theater bearing his name. To a delightful tune Maggie looked upon the organ as a cachet of gentility:

> On Sunday night, 'tis my delight
> And pleasure, don't you see,
> Meeting all the girls and all the boys
> That work down town with me.
> There's an organ in the parlor
> To give the house a tone,
> And you're welcome every evening
> At Maggie Murphy's home.

5. *"Austerlitz"*

A proud day in Isidore's life was when he was called in to provide songs for the thematic accompaniments to Daniel E. Bandmann's production, "Austerlitz." The dress rehearsal took place January 20, 1889. Bandmann, a noted German actor, had mastered English and played in it exclusively thereafter. He played comedy or tragedy roles with equal facility, trouping the continent from Canada to Texas, from Oregon to New York. He was a discoverer of many stars, notably Julia Arthur. He was, moreover, a masterful director.

"Austerlitz," previously known as "Dead or Alive," was the work of the melodramatic expert, Tom Taylor, author of the immortal "Ticket of Leave Man" and of the Edwin Booth vehicle, "The Fool's Revenge." The latter play, derived from Victor Hugo, is the dramatic brother to Verdi's "Rigoletto." In the cast of "Austerlitz" were Fred Sidney, W. S. Hart (the Bill Hart of the yet unborn "movies"), Ann Sutherland and Richard F. Carroll, the comedian and dancer who was then her husband; a special feature was the clever little French actress and prima donna, Louise Beaudet. To Isidore the rehearsal looked like hopeless chaos, in which the vastness of the production engulfed the human beings taking part. At least a week would be required to get it ready, and the following night was set for the opening! It was five in the morning when Isidore and some of the players left the theater in a rainstorm, with no cab in sight. The actors were soaked waiting for transportation and Mlle. Beaudet went into a fit of sobbing hysterics.

Yet the storm abated, and on the following night the play went off without a hitch, as though it had been running for a year. Stage folk do not have to be told that the phenomenon is not so unusual as it appeared to the youthful composer. As gratifying to him as this proof of Bandmann's skill in direction was the success of his two musical numbers, *The Lullaby* and the duet, a vivandière song; the duet was sung by Mlle. Beaudet and Richard Carroll.

Meanwhile Julie had returned to the stage. His voice had shifted to baritone. In 1888 he played again with Thatcher, Primrose and West. In 1889 he joined Billy Emerson's Minstrels in San Francisco. The following year he played "legit" as Frank Howard in H. Grattan Donnelly's comedy, "A Pair of Jacks," starring R. G. Knowles and William Russell.

During the week of November 18, 1889, Frank and Eddie played with Lew Dockstader's Minstrels, in their novelty act, "The Three C's.":

> Character Duet—*The Ragged Urchins*
> Classical Duet—*I Would That My Love*—Mendelssohn
> Comic Medley—*Chestnuts*

Jay was the financial and commercial factor of the combination. Perhaps it was all to the good, too, that he was not musical and that he had much of the youthful stoic in his nature. Jay was the first "audience" that Isidore and Julius ever had. He was their Mr. Public, or, in less dignified parlance, their "try-out dog." He thus became the hard-headed member of the partnership. To him his elder brothers would come with the first manuscripts that found their way to the office of the new business. His patient and seemingly impervious ears they would assail with these promises of hits.

Jay was a good sleeper while asleep, and, when he wanted to be, while supposedly awake. The most enthusiastic efforts of Julie and Isidore worked upon him like a hypnotic. He would sit down, let them try one or two manuscripts on him, and be lulled off into sweet slumber. Finally, the older boys hit upon the plan of removing the chair that so easily became a bed. Thenceforward Jay was compelled to stand up. There was plenty—too much, indeed—for him to hear. Manuscripts were arriving from all over the country, sometimes reaching a total of a thousand in a month. The brothers would read to the standing Jay, satisfied that they now had him in a position where he could not help listening. When they had finished, they would look up for a sign of approval or disapproval and there stood Jay—fast asleep!

That settled it. It was decided to accept manuscripts on the principle of hit or miss, trial and error. Jay could take charge of the commercial end, which required a hard heart and a deaf ear, neither of which he really possessed.

Isidore, rarin' to write hits, was now to taste the pride of playwriting. The direct inspiration was the clever comedian, James Reilly, who was in the tradition of the famous J. K. ("Fritz") Emmett, and portrayed a juvenile immigrant. J. K. Emmett in the German dialect, William J. Scanlan and Chauncey Olcott in the Irish, and Gus Heege in the Scandinavian Ole Olson and Yon Yonson characters, were the favorite type of popular entertainer in the Eighties, Nineties, and early Nineteen-hundreds. The versatile Reilly could tell a good story; he had a pleasant singing voice; he could yodel, dance, act, and was good looking. Featured in Murray and Murphy's "O'Dowd's Neighbors" at the Union Square Theater, he was an outstanding success.

It was here that Isidore met him and the result was "The Broom Maker of Carlsbad," a comedy drama written by Isidore Witmark and F. B. Hawkins, with the songs by Isidore Witmark, produced at Tony Pastor's Theater, the week of August 18, 1890, with Frank and Ed Witmark as "Special Attraction." It was played for a couple of seasons and indirectly was responsible for the "e" in Isidore's first name.

The company had finished rehearsing, the scenery was completed, the route was booked, and the proofs of the lithographing and printing were sent in for O.K. Jim Reilly came into the office hail-fellow-well-met. "Ah, the printing! Fine!" he exclaimed, and proceeded to examine the sheets—when suddenly his whole de-

MINSTREL KINGS 1870-1900's

Press Eldredge   Happy Cal Wagner   Gorman Bros.   Billy Rice

R. J. Jose   Frank Howard   Eddie Leonard   Banks Winter

Frank Dumont   Al G. Field   Charlie Reed   Honey Boy Evans

Photos Albert Davis

J. L. Carncross   Jim McIntyre   Tom Heath   J. H. Haverly

MINSTREL KINGS 1870-1900's

Billy Emerson   Geo. Thatcher   George Primrose   William West

Billy Birch   The Only Leon   Charley Backus   Barney Fagen

Luke Schoolcraft   Hughey Dougherty   Willis P. Sweatnam   George Wilson

Photos Albert Davis

Frank McNish   Carroll Johnson   Bob Slavin   Lew Dockstader

meanor changed. He threw the proofs on the desk. "The show is not going out."

The men in the office were flabbergasted. Then, thinking it was a joke, they burst into laughter.

"I mean it," said Jim. "I was never more in earnest in my life."

"What's wrong, Jim?"

"Count the letters in Isidor's name on those lithographs."

Up to this time the name had been spelled "Isidor." They counted the letters. There were thirteen.

"I'm not superstitious," explained Reilly, "but that's an omen of ill luck and I'm not taking any chances."

Isidor did some quick thinking. Taking out his pencil he added an "e" to his first name. "How's that, Jim?"

"That'll do it!" He was the same old Jim, and the author was the new Isidore.

At 841 Broadway the boys came to a decision between music-publishing and theatrical production as a career; not, however, before they had taken a flyer in burlesque. The burlesque company had already been organized, the backer—in the way of theatrical "angels"—had taken wing, and the Witmark boys had the opportunity of taking his place.

Their ambition was in the direction of the type of entertainment now historically associated with Weber and Fields. Adah Richmond had grown friendly with the new firm; she sang its songs. A fellow named Streibig, who had risen to stage production from the old circuses, had organized and offered for a few weeks the Adah Richmond Burlesque and Specialty Company in "Chow Chow," a former Richmond success. But Adah and he had quarreled, and Streibig had bowed out, leaving the entire production in the air. Here was an opportunity for aspiring producers, and the Witmarks availed themselves of it.

The company was reorganized, and played the variety houses

in New York as well as the Eighth Street Theater. Incidentally, on the program were "Masters Frank and Ed Witmark, The Singing Prodigies." After this appearance, "Chow Chow" went on the road with Jay as treasurer. It was not a happy tour; the burlesque was an old-fashioned affair, and it was all they could do to last long enough for a return to Gotham.

6. A Gallery of Old-Timers

Among the actors in the company was Charlie "Nix" Grapewin, who was one of the actors in the screen version of Eugene O'Neill's "Ah, Wilderness!" Later he played the rôle of Wang Lung's father in "The Good Earth" for which he has been acclaimed by the critics. Grapewin, in the old-time burlesque, took the rôle of His Royal Nibs, Emperor of China. In the variety on the same bill he appeared three times: with "The Three Clovers" in their "Artistic Acrobatic Act entitled, 'Excitement In Chinatown'"; in "Spanish Rings" (with Silbon and King) and in "The Silbon Trio," which introduced a "Triple Trapeze Act and wonderful backward and forward swings and hand-to-hand catches, leaps, etc." A man worked for his salary in those days!

Grapewin had a curious habit of ordering, in every town that the Witmark company played, a sewing machine sent up to his room on approval. As an old circus man, he was accomplished with the needle and self-help. During his stay he would use the machine for repairs to his clown costumes or for the sewing of new ones. Then, when the company was ready to move on, he would call up the machine dealer, inform him that it was not quite what he wanted, and add, "Better send for it today, as I'm leaving town in the morning."

It was during the try-out for the chorus of the ill-fated burlesque show that the Witmarks almost alienated the affections of one of the most popular singers of the day.

An advertisement had been inserted in the press for chorus

THE BEGINNING OF TIN PAN ALLEY

girls, a quicker method than trying to reach them through the few agencies then established. The girls had come straggling in all day, and by twilight the quota had been selected. It may easily be guessed that after a gruelling day such as this even the softest masculine eye might have become dull, and that another girl and voice and shape were just another shape and voice and girl.

When yet another lass appeared in the doorway it was time to call a halt. Besides, she appeared not to know whether this was really the place she wanted; it was getting dark, too, and she was a slip of a thing, and not particularly good looking. "No more chorus girls!" yelled an assistant. "Company's full!"

The lass was nonplussed. Then, recovering, "I'm Miss Gilson," she said. "I have come to hear some new songs that you wrote me about."

Gilson! A magic name! At the sound of the voice Isidore was overwhelmed with embarrassment. He hastened to apologize. She was gracious, and the incident was passed over with a healing laugh.

Lottie Gilson was hardly a beauty off stage. While she made up wonderfully for performance, she looked more like a little German hausfrau in her street clothes. She became one of the best boosters that the Witmarks ever had.

Strangely enough, there was one Witmark plugger whom the Witmarks themselves found it necessary to discourage, close to them as he was. Dad, who was interested in everything his boys undertook, had suddenly found himself with what he thought was a new occupation. He acquired a big, heavy cane and, as a Witmark claque of one, would go to all the theaters where the songs of the firm were being sung, pounding the cane on the floor after each rendition.

One day, Isidore happened into the theater where Dad was giving one of his unique cane solos. "Dad," he inquired "what are you doing?"

"I'm boosting our songs."

83

Not wanting to discourage him, yet realizing that he would soon become a nuisance in the various showhouses, Isidore argued that the firm would never know how it stood with a song if Dad Witmark were the soloist at the plugging. "We don't want to deceive ourselves, Dad. If the song is there, the audience will respond; and if it isn't the quicker we know it the better."

Much disappointed, yet seeing the force of his son's argument, Dad agreed and his new occupation was renounced. Maybe he pounded all the harder when his sons Frank and Ed were engaged by Koster & Bial's, for the week of January 25, 1891; and harder still when the engagement expanded into a year of Sundays, during which his sons were featured. They made many appearances at Tony Pastor's; they were in William A. Brady's production, "The Inspector," by William Rannie Wilson, which starred the late Frazer Coulter, popular in his day, and opened at the new Park Theater, at Thirty-fifth Street and Broadway, on November 13, 1890; they were billed as leading attraction with Sheridan and Flynn's variety combination at Gilmore's Auditorium, Philadelphia.

"Limpy" Gilmore! He was the toughest manager in the variety game. He would take his seat on the stage, Monday mornings during rehearsals, and hand down his decisions without mercy. If an act was not to his taste, no matter what combination sponsored it, he would fire the members on the spot.

When Frank and Ed first appeared for rehearsal, "Limpy" craned his neck and growled, "Who are those kids,—the Witmark boys?" Told that they were, he said, "They're all right! I saw them at Tony Pastor's."

The Sheridan and Flynn combination centered about the vaudeville pair whose names it bore. Joe Flynn had been catapulted into success by his song, *Down Went McGinty*.

Koster & Bial's was situated at Twenty-third Street near Sixth Avenue, uptown side, and it vied with Tony Pastor's in the importation of foreign artists. It brought over among others Carmencita, the Spanish dancer; Fougère, the popular French chanteuse; Eugene Sandow, the king of strong men; Marie Vanoni and her sensational song, *Georgie;* Marie Lloyd, Amann, Dufour and Hartley, Paulus, Violette, Nada Reyval, and a host of others. It also featured condensed operettas and travesties on the various operatic successes. The operas burlesqued were "Madame Angot," "Billee Taylor," "Fra Diavolo," "Orpheus," "La Belle Hélène," "Blue Beard," "Robin Hood," and many others. The casts appearing in these travesties were household names in those days but today are forgotten by all but old-timers—Jennie Joyce, Josie Gregory, Agnes Evans, Ruth Davenport, Madge Lessing, Christine Blessing, Kate Howe, Georgie Denning.

These travesties were written and produced by Fred Solomon, who played the leading comic rôles, assisted by Sol, his brother, who played the second comedy parts. All the other parts, whether male or female, were played by the women mentioned. Fred Solomon was at Koster & Bial's for years; later he became one of the leading comedians in company with such men as Francis Wilson, Jefferson de Angelis, James T. Powers, and De Wolf Hopper at Rudolph Aronson's New York Casino in its palmy days.

Besides being a favorite New York comic, he was an author, composer, orchestrator, and stage and musical director. In the latter capacity he had charge of all the musical shows produced by Klaw & Erlanger. He came from the Solomon family of which his brother Edward, one of the husbands of Lillian Russell, was the star. Edward was the composer of the famous operetta, "Billee Taylor," as well as of "Claude Duval," "Vicar of Bray," "Paul and Virginia," "Polly," "Lord Bateman," "Pepita," and Marie Tempest's great success, "The Red Hussar." Fred, too, was a composer. He wrote the opera "King Kaliko," produced at the Broadway Theater, New York, in 1892, and many popular songs.

FROM RAGTIME TO SWINGTIME

His *Life's Story*, of which the following is the refrain, was the hit of its year:

> Just a little sunshine, just a little rain,
> Just a little happiness, just a little pain,
> Just a little poverty, just a little gold,
> Then the strange eventful tale of life is told.

Koster & Bial's was noted for two things—one, a stage curtain that was not a curtain at all, but a folding fan automatically rising from below the stage and unfolding (using the fan instead of a curtain was to save the expense of a theater license); the other, Koster & Bial's Cork Room, which could be entered either through the front of the house or through an entrance on Twenty-fourth Street west of Sixth Avenue. This Cork Room was the rendezvous of all who worshiped fashion and gaiety. It was the big night club of New York, and nothing but champagne was served in it. Its name was derived from the thousands of corks nailed into designs on its celling and walls and the curtain of signed corks dividing the Cork Room from the stage. Most of the corks had been signed by the patrons. The cast and chorus, when not on the stage, would spend their time there, and they were effective champagne "salesmen."

Koster & Bial's had a separate department on the corner of Twenty-fourth Street and Sixth Avenue, where they ran a bar and supplied families with domestic and imported beers, wines, and liquors. Before becoming a music hall, Koster & Bial's had been a concert auditorium, where families would spend the evening, eating, drinking, and listening to a high-grade popular orchestra under the direction of Rudolph Bial, and such concert artists as Dengremont, the Brazilian boy violinist, and Jules Levy, the cornetist.

When Koster & Bial's closed their establishment on Twenty-third Street they removed all the autographed corks, about 30,000, from the famous Cork Room. A great number of these they encased in coffin-shaped boxes and presented as souvenirs to the old patrons of the celebrated resort. It was a symbolic, if macabre, touch; the miniature coffins signalized the passing of a memorable landmark, the Cork Room.

The firm then became associated with Oscar Hammerstein in his first Manhattan Opera House in Thirty-fourth Street between Broadway and Seventh Avenue. This occupied part of the site belonging to R. H. Macy & Company, and ran through to Thirty-fifth Street. The opera house was renamed Koster & Bial's, opening with *éclat* on August 28, 1893. There was an excellent billing of stars, domestic and foreign; among the latter was Albert Chevalier, the immensely popular singer of coster songs, who made his American début in this theater. The house was eventually torn down to make room for Macy's.

Fred Solomon, chief comic of the old Koster & Bial's, later joined the House of Witmark in the special organization known as the Witmark Music Library, inaugurated in the late Nineties. Ernest Bial, son of Rudolph, eventually went with the Witmarks as a composer and arranger.

Among the songs that started the new firm on its long road was an interminable production by the team of Lawlor and Thornton known as *The Irish Jubilee*. The team had won wide popularity in vaudeville with their act, "The Upper Ten And The Lower Five"; and gradually were introducing numbers of their own.

The Irish Jubilee was a song on new lines; consisting entirely of what, to Tin Pan Alley, are verses, it lacked a refrain. It should be understood that a "verse," in the jargon of Tin Pan Alley, is what it is in no other land or clime. It means that part of a song which is not refrain or chorus; it does not signify a line, nor a stanza, if the stanza happens to be the refrain; it is the stanza or stanzas that lead up to the chorus. "Verse and chorus" would sound redundant outside of the Alley. Today, a set of verses without refrain would be regarded on Broadway as a freak or a conscious throwback. Indeed, the tendency for years has been to condense and all but eliminate the verses, and get to the chorus as quickly as possible. Radio singers and even radio bands frequently omit the verses and the music to the verses. We have no time for such lengthy narratives as *The Irish Jubilee,* which was long-winded even at the end of the Eighties, before the arrival of sentimental tabloid-novels that were to pass for popular ballads in the coming decade.

The Irish Jubilee ran on in this strain for some five minutes of un-refrained verses. It became very popular, and bred many imitations.

A couple of verses will suggest the doggerel quality of the patter:

Oh, a short time ago, boys, an Irishman named Doherty,
Was elected to the senate by a very large majority,
He felt so elated that he went to Dennis Cassidy,
Who owned a bar-room of a very large capacity,
He said to Cassidy, go over to the brewer,
For a thousand kegs of lager beer and give it to the poor,
Then go over to the butcher shop and order up a ton of meat,
Be sure and see the boys and girls have all they want to drink and eat,

Send out invitations in twenty different languages,
And don't forget to tell them to bring their own sandwiches;
They've made me their senator, and so to show them gratitude
They'll have the finest supper ever given in this latitude.
Tell them the music will be furnished by O'Rafferty,
Assisted on the bagpipes by Felix McCafferty,
Whatever the expenses are remember I'll put up the tin,
And anyone who doesn't come be sure and do not let them in.

It achieved a fairly large sale. It was also nearly the cause of a permanent estrangement between Thornton and his juvenile publishers.

Thornton, who was to become one of the best known among the early denizens of Tin Pan Alley, as much for his *joie de vivre* as for his songs and his devoted wife, Bonnie, had a friend in Montreal. This friend, a Mr. Kelly, was a fanatical devotee who ran a little stationery shop. He bought a few copies of *The Irish Jubilee* and placed them on sale—the only music that he ever handled. In the course of their tour, Lawlor and Thornton arrived in Montreal, where they were greeted by Kelly with the announcement that he had been selling *The Irish Jubilee* in the thousands.

It may easily be imagined that, when the Witmark boys rendered Thornton their semi-annual statement, according to which complete sales did not amount to as much as Kelly had told him he alone had sold, Thornton considered the boys anything but honest. They immediately got in touch with Kelly, only to learn that he had cited those figures to make Thornton feel good, and also to make himself out the big man who could sell a song if he went after the sales. Even today some clerk in a little music store on the road will try to ingratiate himself with a traveling singer-composer, giving him exaggerated figures of the sale of his song.

Both Lawlor and Thornton achieved record song hits. Poor Charlie Lawlor went blind and died a few years ago. He was the composer of *The Sidewalks of New York*. Thornton, who passed away in 1938, wrote a succession of song hits, among them *My Sweetheart's The Man In the Moon* and *When You Were Sweet Sixteen*. The latter took the country by storm. And thereby hangs a tale.

The Witmarks had bought the song from Thornton outright. They had laid it away for a while, awaiting the moment most propitious for its publication. When that moment came, they tried it out before publishing it, and were satisfied that they had a candidate for success. Their judgment was ratified by the big demand for the song. Naturally, they were delighted with the way things were going; they lined up the professional singers for a heavy campaign. In the midst of these exciting preliminaries they were served with legal papers by the firm of Joseph W.

Stern & Co., who represented themselves as the rightful owners of the composition. Unless the Witmarks stopped publishing the song, or made proper settlement, they would be sued. The rival publishing house demanded a statement of sales and the surrender of all profits to date.

The Witmarks did not know what to make of it. In their safe was a bona fide bill of sale, signed by the composer. The mystery was soon solved. Thornton, while in his cups, had sold the same song to two firms; the other firm, having been the first to purchase it, was the rightful owner.

A few months before, the same firms had been engaged in a similar mix-up, with the Witmarks on the winning side. The title in question was *The Girl Of My Boyhood Days*. The Stern Company was a younger firm than the Witmarks and the Witmarks, whose policy from the beginning had been to help rather than to hinder, got the author of the piece to agree to a transfer of the title. *The Girl Of My Boyhood Days* was presented to the Stern Company, and the Witmarks were content with a variation: *The Games Of My Boyhood Days*. This was not so good as the original; moreover, it required the rewriting of the lyric. Their competitors expressed deep gratitude, and promised never to forget the kindness; they looked forward to an opportunity to reciprocate. Here, surely, in the imbroglio over Thornton's song, *When You Were Sweet Sixteen*, was that longed-for opportunity.

Instead of notifying the Witmarks at once of their prior claims upon the later song, Stern's let the firm exploit the song, build up its sales and make it popular, and then pounced upon it. This strategy proved to be a boomerang. They had, by their delay, tacitly agreed to the publication of the song by the Witmarks; they could not take the title away, but they did compel the Witmarks to pay a good price in settlement. It was rather an original manner in which to carry out the promised reciprocity.

There is a story concerning James Thornton to the effect that he had been missing from the Rialto for some time and his cronies had begun to wonder what had become of him. To the joy of his followers, one day, he reappeared. Questions warmed his ears.

"Where have you been, Jim? We've missed you. You haven't been playing—we haven't seen you booked anywhere."

"No," he replied. "You see, I've been in another business for the last few months."

"What were you doing?"

"I was out with a temperance lecturer."

"*You*, with a temperance lecturer! What could you be doing with a temperance lecturer?"

"I was the horrible example," Jim retorted proudly.

"Well, what happened?"

"We closed up."

"Why?"

"Business was so bad we didn't take in enough to keep the horrible example in condition."

Many anecdotes are told about Thornton, who looked and dressed far more like a minister than like a minstrel. It is said in connection with his extensive vocabulary that on one occasion he was seen walking up Broadway studying the dictionary and tearing out page after page as he memorized it.

Speaking of Irish jubilees, there was Maggie Cline, the "Irish Queen" of the Nineties, who was a jubilee in herself. She was a generous soul and had never been known to refuse to appear at a benefit performance. She was booked for one every Sunday night, which made it a full week after all the other days at the regular performances. She sang many a song into success, but her name remains identified with one song: *Throw Him Down, McCloskey*.

It was her meeting in 1890 with John W. Kelly, "the rolling mill man," that brought her the song by which she is remembered. "I asked him," she has related, in typical Cline fashion, "if he had any loose songs about him, and he said he had one which no one wanted on the opera stage and I could have it, but not for a cent less than two dollars. I took the song and paid cash, and for twenty-three years I've used it in my business." The song was *Throw Him Down, McCloskey*—"musical, red-blooded, rough-house, scored for the piano and a strong voice."

Her rendition of it was not merely that of a song; it was practically a show in itself. At the words "Throw him down, McCloskey!" everybody backstage seized the first object at hand—a chair, a broom, an iron rod, or something heavier—and threw it on the floor with all his might. The result was bedlam. Those who could not find a heavy weight or a piece of furniture contented themselves with steam whistles, thunder sheets, or other "props" equally musical—and loud. The other actors on the benefit bill, together with the stage hands and vistors in the wings, could hardly wait for the moment of the charivari—the "grand slam," the "anvil chorus." It was a rivalry in pandemoniac din. Out front, the enchanted listeners demanded encore after encore, until Maggie and her troupe were exhausted.

A year before Maggie acquired the Kelly song, Joe Flynn had written *Down Went McGinty*, which was another Cline favorite in the Gay Nineties, second only to the McCloskey riot. The way she swung her hips as she strode across the stage, requiring as much room as a pugilistic match! The hitching of her belt, the swing of her arm, the summons to the Irish in the gallery to join in the chorus!

Maggie Cline died on June 11, 1934, at the age of seventy-seven. *Throw Him Down, McCloskey* is as ineradicably associated with her as "Rip Van Winkle" with Joseph Jefferson.

The four years at 841 Broadway were distinguished for a number of Witmark hits. The catalogue soon included Charles Graham's *The Picture That Is Turned Toward The Wall*; Andrew Mack's *The Wedding of The Lily And The Rose*; and John T. Kelly's *I Long To See The Girl I Left Behind*.

THE BEGINNING OF TIN PAN ALLEY

Kelly was an outstanding Irish comedian, featured in many of his own comedies, and one of the original stars at Weber and Fields' celebrated Music Hall. He remained with them until they closed. His song was popular for a full year and a half; in those days there were no radios to lift a song into nation-wide fame in one or two broadcasts—and then, by the same process, kill it early with high-pressure repetition. *I Long To See The Girl I Left Behind* was the predecessor, as a gang or barbershop number, of *Sweet Adeline*. Had *Sweet Adeline* not been written, probably Kelly's song would have continued to be used as the favorite "get together" quartette. It had the same qualities as its more famous follower, and is still in the repertory of some foursome harmonizers. Perhaps the refrain may recall it to more than a few readers:

> A little brown cot,
> A shady green spot,
> No happier place I find.
> My heart's fairly gone,
> I love only one,
> She's the girl I left behind.

When *Sweet Adeline* came along it, too, found a haven with the Witmarks. The song has a history all its own, which belongs to the early 1900's.

CHAPTER V

EXPANSION

1. Moving Ahead

HE Witmarks were accumulating a respectable catalogue. "Respectable" is the correct word, for it is the Witmarks' pride even today that they never published a vulgar song. Their business was run "one hundred per cent clean," and became known for that standard. In their later career, this quality even played a humorous part in the structure of their expanding professional rooms. A time was to come when it would be said of the Witmarks that they were the first to put popular song publishing into the big business class, even as Klaw & Erlanger had raised the show business from the status of barnstorming.

They were moving ahead. How long ago had it been since Isidore, in the first days of the home office, had had to meet the requirements of their correspondence with Jeffersonian inventiveness? They could not afford a stenographer, yet there were so many letters to answer. Necessity suggested the way out. He found that, while writing an answer himself, he could dictate a letter to his brother Jay, and another to their friend, Morrie Golland. The mail was cleaned up on the day that it arrived.

They had moved far, too, since the days when they could not

recognize a drunk on meeting one. This, in the pre-Tin-Pan-Alley era, was a phenomenon in itself, for song-writing half the time was merely a method of getting enough change with which to relieve the monotony of sobriety.

Thus, when Joseph P. Skelly (the ex-plumber with a fine flair for melody), George Cooper (recently eulogized, at his death, as one of our best verse writers), and Charlie Pratt (an ace among concert accompanists and arrangers in his time), first visited the Witmark home, how were the boys to know that the men were three sheets in the wind? The Fortieth Street Print Shop reeked of printer's ink, not booze. And the kids were flattered out of their senses at a visit from the three musketeers who were turning out so many hits of the day—*My Pretty Red Rose, The Old Rustic Bridge By The Mill, As I Sat Upon My Dear Old Mother's Knee.*

To be sure, the three fellows looked bleary-eyed and they had a queer walk. But human peculiarities are many. The trio had some numbers with them, and to think they had sought out the Witmarks! They all went upstairs to the piano and Pratt played the tunes. There were none that the Witmarks liked. But Julie, then at the beginning of his stage career, was looking for a song. Could they suggest one? They looked at Julie, took his measure, as it were, and returned in a couple of days with a ditty entitled *Is Mother Thinking Of Her Boy?* For this effort they demanded no less than fifteen dollars, then a high price for a song. They got their price, however, and plenty of advertising, for Julie featured it on his tour with Thatcher, Primrose and West. But not until someone called on them a week or so later, and heard of the visit paid by the three musketeers, did the truth dawn upon the Witmark boys.

"So Skelly and Pratt and Cooper were up to see you? Were they sober?"

So *that* was it!

95

FROM RAGTIME TO SWINGTIME

2. Charles Graham

The coming of Charles Graham to the Witmarks was another of the lucky breaks that fell to the lot of the boys. Isidore had been trying to land a hit, and had produced a few personal successes with *Jack Won't Forget You* and *He Was A Pal of Mine*. From the titles, they sound as if they might have been inspired by the type of song that Paul Dresser, brother of Theodore Dreiser, was putting out. The boys had taken over, from the Variety Publishing Company, *Bring Back My Fisher Boy*, and *As I Sat Upon My Dear Old Mother's Knee*.

Then one day, out of the blue, the gods of song-hits picked Charles Graham. He was a prolific Englishman whose output was too copious for any single firm of that day. Already he was well known for his, *If The Waters Could Speak As They Flow*, which was the one outstanding Graham number published by Woodward. The Witmark catalog had a dozen Graham pieces—he wrote both the words and the music—but none of them so far had rung the bell.

Many readers will recall the melodrama, "Blue Jeans," by Joseph Arthur, and how they thrilled to the scene in which the hero, strapped to the long carrier of a sawmill, with the villain at the lever, was saved in the nick of time. They will remember, too, the strict moralism of the old-time plays and songs, which visited upon errant girlhood the cruel vengeance of outraged tribal standards. It was at a performance of "Blue Jeans," then at the height of its popularity, that Charlie Graham was impressed by the ritual of turning the strayed daughter's picture to the wall. He was so deeply stirred that, changing the scene of the tale, he wrote the old-time tear-drainer, *The Picture That Is Turned Toward The Wall*.

Graham's songs, in the mode of their day were condensed novels set to music. The titles as often were an epitome of the

96

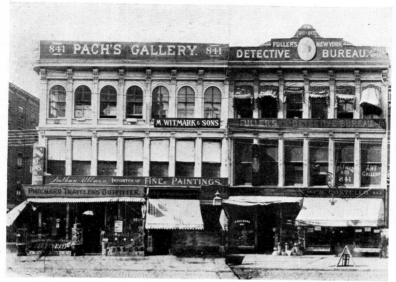

Photo N. Y. Historical Society

Corner of 13th Street and Broadway, across from the Star Theatre.
It was here that Witmarks had their first tremendous song hit —
The Picture that is Turned Toward the Wall.

Photo S. W. Todd

The Adams Express two-wheel money wagon that brought Julie's
salary to "402" every Thursday, sure as the clock, during his season
with Thatcher, Primrose and West's Minstrels.

Photo Albert Davis

Bob Fitzsimmons

Photo Albert Davis

James J. Corbett

song. The new piece was brought to the Witmarks, and these are the lines that the prospective publishers read:

Far beyond the glamour of the city and its strife
   There's a quiet little homestead by the sea,
Where a tender, loving lassie used to live a happy life
   Contented in her home as she could be.
Not a shadow ever seemed to cloud the sunshine of her youth,
   And they thought no sorrow could her life befall.
But she left them all one evening and their sad hearts knew the truth,
   When her father turned her picture toward the wall.

REFRAIN

There's a name that's never spoken,
A mother's heart is broken,
   There is just another missing from the old home, that is all.
There is still a memory living,
There's a father unforgiving,
   And a picture that is turned toward the wall.

The manuscript was received without enthusiasm, but Graham needed fifteen dollars far more than the Witmarks needed the song. So they paid him the fifteen and stored the song away among the unsung hits. There it might have reposed for the rest of time had it not been for a visit from Andrew Mack, the Irish actor and counter-tenor. They ransacked the catalog for a number that he might feature, but to no avail. There was nothing left but to run through the unpublished manuscripts, among them *The Picture That Is Turned Toward The Wall*, which had been turned toward the wall even by the publishers. Mack seized upon it. It had in it, he exclaimed, something of the sad spirit that sounds from the Irish "come-all-ye's." Then and there the *Picture* did a right-about-face. Night after night it was turned toward the tear-dimmed eyes of fond audiences. That girl had left home to some purpose, so far as the Witmarks were concerned.

Julie added it to his repertory. The title became a catch-phrase. It was the target for sly parodies, which crowned its popularity. After years of searching for a hit, the Witmarks had been hit by one.

Graham was as much surprised as his sponsors, nor did he seem to bewail his having sold the song outright. This part of it, by the way, was amply made up for by the Witmarks. Like all such free-lancers, Graham had his own pet songs which he could not forgive the public for ignoring. Soon he was to know another success, inspired by nothing more poetic than a glance through the window while he was shaving. He happened to catch sight of two little girls, dressed alike in blue, carrying their books to school. *Two Little Girls in Blue* he murmured to himself, without special intention. The phrase struck him as a song title, and he abandoned the razor for the pencil, but no pencil was to be found. For a moment he was in despair, not trusting to a shifty memory. Then he grabbed a piece of soap, sketched the title and a few key words on the mirror, and another mother-song was born. Unfortunately, though, the wandering minstrel wandered with it into the firm of Spaulding and Gray.

The Picture That Is Turned Toward The Wall was more than a financial success for the Witmarks. It brought them a coveted prestige. Formerly they had sold sheet music by the hundred copies; now they knew sales in the thousands. The presses all but smoked in their hot haste to fill orders, which came in by mail, by wire, by personal call. Jobbers who had scorned to deal with "children" were camping on their doorstep for copies. Dealers who had refused them displays now buried other songs beneath the *Picture*. Singers whom they had been obliged to chase now chased them. The pianos in the professional department were overworked and cried in their tinny voices for reinforcements. New instruments were added.

The Forward March of Tin Pan Alley had begun!

The success of the new firm suggested to Frank Tousey, publisher of "dime novels," "nickel libraries," detective tales, and a weekly periodical, that perhaps extra money was to be made in popular music. His entrance into the new field naturally brought qualms to the souls of his competitors. He might have made a go of it had he set about it in the right way. He chose the wrong way, however, and picked the Witmarks as target. Banking on the wide publicity attained by Graham's *The Picture That Is Turned Toward The Wall,* Tousey brought out a song titled *The Picture With Its Face Turned Toward The Wall.* Copyright law was not so well defined in the late Eighties as it is today. Nevertheless, the Witmarks sued and they won on the plea of colorable imitation. Tousey did not last long in his musical venture.

The victory increased the self-confidence of the boys, and won for them a new respect among their competitors.

3. Copyright—Abroad

Copyright! One broad aspect of the vexed question had been settled, for the moment, by the "International Copyright Law" of 1891, which admitted aliens to the protection of their works against piracy in the United States, and secured for Americans a like protection abroad. The international situation had been in a mess for years. Late in the seventies it had been dramatized in the eyes of the American public by the visit to these shores of D'Oyly Carte, and, hard upon his heels, of Gilbert and Sullivan, who had come to watch over their interests in "The Pirates of Penzance," which followed close upon the phenomenal success of "H.M.S. Pinafore."

Songs from England and the Continent were much easier to reprint than comic operas. As a result, the lyricists and composers of a long list of hits received nothing from our publishers. *Annie Rooney, That Is Love, Mary and John, Comrades, Drink Up, Boys, It's For Money, My Old Dutch,* and most of the big Albert Chevalier successes, *Some Day, Love's Old Sweet Song, Good Bye* and all the ballads of Tosti,—all had been free for the asking in the United States.

After 1891 domestic publishers could no longer help themselves to foreign productions. If they wished to handle music from England, they would have to come to terms with the English publishers, acting as their representatives in the United States. And *vice versa*.

By 1892 the Witmarks had come to regard themselves with pardonable pride as the leader among the new firms. They felt something of the expansive spirit that was beginning to throb in the pulse of the nation. They looked across the ocean, Londonward, toward the leading music publishers of England.

It was a question which of the boys should take the trip across the ocean.

First, however, there was a musical comedy to see onto the stage and through the press: "The Isle of Champagne," music by William W. Furst, book and lyrics by Charles Byrne, starring Thomas Q. Seabrooke. It was the first complete musical comedy score to be published by the Witmarks. Furst was another of the prolific composers of the day. He will be recalled as the conductor at the Empire Theater under Charles Frohman's management when Maude Adams ruled. It was he who wrote the *Babbie Waltzes* for her production of "The Little Minister," and a number of Empire successes. He wrote music also for William Gillette in "Sherlock Holmes." Furst was phenomenal as an arranger. Julius Caesar is said to have been able to write a different letter with each hand. Furst had a special knack of writing music with both hands; but it was the same music! With his right hand he inscribed the notes; with his left he set down the bars. It was a trick that gave him a speed enabling him to turn out manuscripts almost twice as quickly as the ordinary musical scribe.

It was decided that Julie should go to Buffalo and watch the première of "The Isle of Champagne." As Isidore was the eldest of the firm he was selected to make the voyage to London. He booked his passage on the North German Lloyd S.S. *Spree* and was in the British capital twelve days later, the first of the popular

NEW YORK CLIPPER
THE OLDEST AMERICAN SPORTING AND THEATRICAL JOURNAL

Copyrighted, 1891, by The Frank Queen Publishing Company (Limited).

Founded by
FRANK QUEEN, 1853.

NEW YORK, SATURDAY, OCTOBER 10, 1891.

[VOLUME XXXIX.—No. 31

Price 10 Cents.

AS TO WOMAN.

WRITTEN FOR THE NEW YORK CLIPPER.

What highest prize has woman won
In science or in art?
What unrelated work by woman done
Stands city, field or mart?
She has no Raphael—Painting saith,
No Newton—Learning cries.
Show us her statesships, her Macbeth,
Her thought-won victories.

Wait, boastful men, though worthy all
Thy deeds which these art true,
Things worthier still and holier far,
Our sisters yet will do.
For this the worth of woman shows
On every pompled place,
That still as man is wisdom grows
He honors her the more.

Oh! not for wealth, or fame, or power,
She man's true consort strives,
But silent as the growing flower,
To make of earth a heaven.
For in the "Garden of the Sun,"
Woman, brighteat rose, shall bloom,
For woman's God is undropped—
Her advent yet to come.

MARK KENYON

THE SPECTRAL TYPEWRITER.

A THEATRICAL GHOST STORY.

WRITTEN FOR THE NEW YORK CLIPPER
BY J. LLEW WILLIAMS

JULIUS P. WITMARK
COMEDIAN AND VOCALIST

The New York Clipper was the theatrical and sporting paper of the 1890's, the forerunner of *Variety*.

101

music publishers to cross the ocean in an effort to struggle with the new copyright situation. No sooner had he landed than he discovered that he had picked a difficult task. The Londoners went about their affairs at a leisurely pace. They were accustomed to doing business with elderly, staid gentlemen, not with mere boys. He could see by the faces of the men with whom he was trying to deal that they were amazed at his lack of years. He might have said, in the words of Edmund Burke, "The atrocious crime of being a young man, which the honorable gentleman has with such spirit and decency charged upon me, I shall neither attempt to palliate nor deny." What Isidore did was something far different, however, for during one interview he exploded, "See here! In my country, the type of man you have been expecting to meet in me is retired long ago or relegated to the position of bookkeeper!"

That broke the ice, and the foreign ambassador of M. Witmark & Sons began to make friends. Indeed, he returned with handsome contracts.

The arrangements with Charles Sheard & Company and with Reynolds & Company were of especial importance at this time. Through Sheard, the Witmarks imported a number of hits and introduced not a few of their own into England. Sheard's, together with Francis, Day & Hunter, shared the leadership of the British market, the latter firm already provided with representation in the United States. Through Reynolds, who made a specialty of Albert Chevalier's coster songs, a number of the new Chevalier ditties came to Witmark's. Many of the well-known ones, of course, had been issued previous to the copyright agreement of 1891, and were therefore free to anyone who chose to print them in the United States.

In London, Isidore met Charles Warren, an American who, with his wife Marguerite Fish, was a headliner in vaudeville. He was a graduate of the University of Wisconsin, and an all-round business man despite the fact that he was an actor. He was a descendant of the renowned old American player, William

EXPANSION

Warren, who gave distinction to the early theater in Philadelphia more than a hundred years ago. The Warrens, like the Booths and the Jeffersons, passed on the best traditions of strolling players from father to son until their fame has become legend.

Before Isidore left London, he appointed Warren the personal representative of M. Witmark & Sons, which position, in its varying phases, he held for almost twenty-five years until he died on March 13, 1932. Warren made a host of foreign friends for the firm and became more like one of the family than an employee.

4. Tally-Ho!

During his sojourn in England, Isidore decided that he would go to see his first Derby race. He was staying at Morley's on Trafalgar Square with his friend Morrie Golland. The Derby was to be run off the following week, and they obtained their tickets at the hotel.

This was in 1892, before there were motor cars. The hotel had its own tally-ho, which carried large hampers crammed with plenty to eat and drink. It took about three hours to get to Epsom Downs, and all along the line were small boys doing acrobatic stunts and running after the tally-ho crying, "Throw out your musty coppers!" a call that did not go unheeded.

At Epsom Downs, as far as the eye could reach, there were people of every kind and nationality. Gypsies on stilts; others telling fortunes. Bookmakers. Pierrots giving entertainments. Minstrel shows. Singers of all kinds. It was like one vast fair, and all the choice locations were taken. However, after some manoeuvering their driver found them a spot on a hill. Out came the hampers, and lunch was served while the preliminary races were being run a short distance away.

Isidore became interested in the people. In fact, he was interested in everything *except* the races. Everybody who was anybody was there, and there were many theatrical people he knew by

103

sight. Every few minutes he heard a shout, which meant another race was on, but he paid no attention to it. The clamor was intense. Suddenly he remembered what he had come for and shouted, "When are they going to run the big race?"

"Why," was the reply, "they ran it ten minutes ago!"

From horseflesh to horse meat is a more radical change than language suggests. In any event, during this trip abroad the head of the Witmarks found himself with a couple of days between appointments in London. He had an engagement to run over some songs with Miss Vesta Tilley at Birmingham, and her indisposition gave him an excellent opportunity for a glimpse of Paris.

Isidore spoke no French. Fortunately there was a tourist agency, Low's Exchange, which in those days took care of all the routine arrangements for such a journey. In charge of its London office was John E. Wilkie, who was afterwards for many years Chief of the Secret Service Bureau of the United States Treasury Department. Isidore went to Paris with an Englishman named Rider, who was associated with the Low Exchange. Both Rider and Witmark, having finished their respective affairs, decided to hire a guide and see the city and its environs. At Versailles they were hungry, and might have remained so had there not been the guide to order for them.

They were served what they thought was a steak, and, as they ate it, agreed that it tasted sweeter than the beef to which they were accustomed. "They must have fed this beef on clover," suggested Isidore, and he asked the guide when he came over to pay the bill for them, "What do you feed your beef on over here? The meat is so sweet."

"That is not beef, sir. That is 'orse meat."

"My God!" exclaimed Rider. "Horse meat!" Finally, toward the center of the city, they passed a butcher shop bearing a large sign: *Cheval*. They knew enough French for that. Then and there Rider gave up the ghost, and it was with difficulty that he was brought to.

EXPANSION

5. Final Days at 841 Broadway

On September 1, 1892, Julie was signed up by John H. Russell as a member of the Russell's Comedians, an aggregation of stars. He played with them for some three months in the laughing success, "The City Directory." On December 5th of the same year the Russell's Comedians opened at the Bijou Theater, New York, in a new comedy, "Society Fad," in which Julie played the rôle of Hamilton Jefferson. In 1893, he went over to Hoyt and Thomas, in their production, "A Trip to Chinatown," which featured Harry Conor as Welland Strong, the hypochondriac. So great was Julie's success that he was re-engaged for one season after another, through 1896, including a phenomenal run of 700 nights in New York.

While Julie was on the road with "A Trip to Chinatown" he was engaged for the Australian tour of the company. Joyously he sent word to his family. Here was an opportunity to see a new corner of the world, and to make a reputation upon another continent. As usual, however, he desired the approval of his brothers.

Jay and Isidore, upon receiving his announcement, sent him a large envelope inscribed with the legend, "Sealed Verdict." Before opening it Julie sensed disapproval and made up his mind. He told the manager, "I'm not going along." When he opened the letter his fears were confirmed. Mother was not in good health and Australia was a long way off. The coveted opportunity was passed up. "A Trip to Chinatown" proved a brilliant success in Australia, but never a word of regret was heard from Julie.

Harry Conor played through the American run of Hoyt's piece, and then went with it to Australia. Throughout the American engagement he had been an inseparable companion of Julie's. Conor was not only one of the foremost comedians of his day, but also the composer of such songs as *The Smoke Went Up The Chimney Just The Same*, and *Miss Helen Hunt*. It was he who

105

introduced *The Bowery* and made popular that rural classic, *Reuben, Reuben, I've Been Thinking.* He was a Bostonian and on his visits to New York he often made the Witmark home his own.

In his appearances with "A Trip To Chinatown" Julie popularized *You Gave Me Your Love, I Long To See The Girl I Left Behind, Back Among The Old Folks* (1893); *Her Eyes Don't Shine Like Diamonds, We Were Simply Friends, That Old First Love Of Mine* (1894); *Sunshine Of Paradise Alley; Only One Girl In This World For Me* (1895); and *I Love You In The Same Old Way* (*Sue Dear*) (1896).

6. Fitzsimmons—Corbett—Benrimo

It was not only among actors that Julie counted his numerous friends. There was Bob Fitzsimmons, the pugilist, who was passionately fond of music. In his eagerness to hear the latest songs, he used to haunt the little Broadway office as if he were a vaudeville performer seeking new material.

Shortly after his victory over Peter Maher on March 2, 1892, Fitzsimmons sauntered into the Witmark establishment. Julie happening to be out, he sat down to wait for him.

Bob had a queer way of sitting in a chair. He would slump into it so self-collapsingly that he gave the illusion of being very short. At this moment in bounced a well-known club singer and vaudevillian of the day. He was your typical actor of the late Eighties and early Nineties: Prince Albert coat, high silk hat, carnation in his buttonhole, cane, spats and gloves. His success had gone to his head, and he was irritatingly egotistic and patronizing. Noticing the figure slumped in the chair, he turned to Isidore and asked, in a stage whisper, "Who's the truckman?"

Fitzsimmons caught the query.

Isidore answered, "Don't you know? Let me introduce him."

With the introduction, Bob got up, looking like an elevator rising to the seventh story. On his feet, he towered over Harry,

106

who, at once changing conversational tactics, questioned the champion about the Maher fight. This suggested another question to Isidore. "Bob," said the publisher, "give Harry an idea of how you knocked out Maher."

To Bob the suggestion seemed heaven-sent. He had taken a dislike to the dandy from the moment he had overheard the truckman speech. In his three-second demonstration of the knockout scene Fitzsimmons forgot himself, becoming so realistic that Harry's Prince Albert, top hat, and cane and gloves had to be reassembled into an actor.

Success and prominence did not spoil Fitzsimmons. He had a refreshing simplicity and a tenderness hardly to be suspected in a prize-fighter.

Years later there was another visit of Fitzsimmons to the office of his friend, Julius P. Witmark. It was on the occasion of Julie's return to his desk after a long illness and convalescence. An accident had nearly cost him his life and it had been nine long months before he was able to attend to business again. Bob knew that Julie had been dangerously ill, but was unacquainted with the details. He had hastened to congratulate his friend.

Against the wall, behind the desk where Julie sat, stood a pair of crutches. Bob, wishing to add a light touch to their reunion, jokingly inquired, "Whose funny sticks are those?"

Julie swung around in his swivel chair. One of his legs was missing. For the first time, Bob realized what it had all been about. He fainted, and Julie had to call for assistance to bring him to!

Another pugilist friend of Julie's was Gentleman Jim Corbett. They had been companions since before the days when Corbett was training for his great encounter with John L. Sullivan, on September 7, 1892. Julie was a frequent visitor to Corbett's training quarters at Loch Arbor, New Jersey, and used to soothe the fighter's nerves with songs during the hours of preparation.

Corbett had always wished to be an actor with all the fervor of stage-struck youth. It was when one of the earlier "City Directory" companies was visiting San Francisco, indeed, that he made his debut on a gay night when he was admitted to the cast as a "gag." It was a performance "for this night only"; Corbett did not go on the stage professionally until he had long been known as the world's champion heavyweight. But that "night only" is still remembered by Corbett's friends of the early Nineties.

One of them, J. H. Benrimo, the stage director, co-author of "The Yellow Jacket" and of "The Willow Tree," a noted actor and stage manager, used to do much "suping" with the scrapper (*i.e.*, acting as supernumerary in productions) long before Corbett had become "Gentleman Jim"! Benrimo recalls the time when Corbett went on as a messenger boy in "The City Directory." He appeared in the first and last acts; but that last act! Corbett arrived in a long white beard—silent but visible commentary upon the alacrity with which messages were supposed to be delivered. His friends, who had paid twenty-five cents for gallery seats, were waiting for the great moment. With a wild uproar that turned his entrance into the sensation of the evening, they threw on to the stage, not bouquets of flowers, but their hats and caps.

Prize-fighting in the Nineties was a more personal matter than it is today. By the time the fighters stepped into the ring, they were in a mood for blood. Bob Fitzsimmons and Jim Corbett were not exceptions, and no one would have been surprised had they clashed whenever they happened to meet, prize-fight ring or no prize-fight ring.

Some five years after Corbett's historic fight with Sullivan, Jim and Fitzsimmons were training for the championship bout that was to take place between them at Carson City, Nevada, on March 17, 1897. Feelings between the two contenders ran high; it had been running high, in fact, ever since the Corbett-Sullivan match. The Corbett-Fitzsimmons fight was clearly to be not only a pugilistic "classic," but a matter of private vengeance.

EXPANSION

At this time, Isidore's office was upstairs and those of Jay and Julie downstairs. One day Bob Fitzsimmons was sitting beside the piano in Isidore's front office listening to Ernest R. Ball play and sing his latest song. Bob was enjoying it all so deeply that the tears welled from his eyes and threatened to dampen the piano keys. This went on for some time when suddenly a sharp whistle sounded from one of the old-fashioned speaking tubes. There were no inside telephone systems in those days and the tube was directly above Isidore's desk.

"Who's calling?" asked Isidore.

"It's me—Julie," came the anxious reply.

"What is it?"

"You've got Fitzsimmons up there?"

"Yes. Why?"

"For Pete's sake! Keep him there! I've got Corbett down here!"

7. *An Elephant Wags Its Head*

The Witmarks were fast outgrowing the accommodations at 841. There must have been many a time, these days and nights, when the elephant on Isidore's desk wagged its head.

What was that elephant? It was one of those clay animals whose heads are held in place by a pair of flexible rings. It was a benign elephant whose function was to keep the various egos from expanding beyond the point of comfort.

The Witmarks were addicted to conferences. At the least provocation the brothers would rush to the fray with all the eagerness of a fire horse. Many of the confabs were held in the bathroom at home between poised razors and suspended hair-brushes or shoe-brushes. There was many a tense moment in which one or the other seeking to impose his will, would wax eloquent with the first person singular pronoun. It became annoying to the others who had to listen and keep their own pronouns under control.

109

FROM RAGTIME TO SWINGTIME

It was during one of these orations in Isidore's office that they hit upon a symbolic cure. The moment those I's began to rush past the discourse like so many telegraph poles seen from a train window, one of the brothers would walk over and give the elephant's head a push. The tongue-wagger was thus signalled into modest silence by the wagging head. That elephant became a silent, and silencing, partner in every conference.

Elephants suggest long memories. It was during these final days in 841 Broadway that Isidore, whose sense of justice can become—on occasion—all but unjust, developed an unforgetfulness and an unforgivingness that have remained. Although considered indulgent to the point of sentimentality with those friends who have proved their loyalty, though conducting business on principles that sometimes appear to be self-defeatingly idealistic and ethical in the severest sense of the moral code, he has been implacable with anyone who, he felt, did him harm. He had—and has—a creed: "Death does not excuse those who have done wrong. Only one's good deeds are buried with him. I talk of a man as I find him; nor do I hesitate to express my opinion of him, whether he is living or dead. If he has wronged me, he is dead to me before he dies."

CHAPTER VI

TRANSITION

1. 49-51 West Twenty-eighth Street

RANSITION periods often are convenient fictions of the historian. Change is continuous, even when subtle, and occurs in obedience to laws that do not take into account the needs of commentators. Yet such periods, like legal fictions, have their uses. Thus the five years from 1893 to 1898 may be regarded as a transition period in the history of the United States that was mirrored, in miniature, in the history of the Witmark firm.

The immediate cause of the removal from 841 Broadway was less romantic than had been the expulsion from the chaste precincts of 32 East Fourteenth Street. The structure was about to be demolished to make way for the Roosevelt Building, which was erected on the site. Gradual expansion, in any case, would have brought about the change of offices. Sometime in 1893, with the nation in the throes of a depression attributed to the President for whom Isidore had written a *Wedding March,* the Witmarks removed to 49-51 West Twenty-eighth Street. Here they would remain for the five years that began with the Columbian Exposition in Chicago and ended just before the Spanish-American War.

From the historical standpoint those five years are of primary importance in the development of our popular music, for during

111

them the taste of the nation swung, though with a halting, nervous, indecisive rhythm, away from the servitude to three-quarters time and the polite, moral four-four of the sentimental ballad. Already the negroid rhythms of the minstrel show had been insinuating a new tempo into the national consciousness. The more we learn about the early minstrel singers and the minstrel show that grew out of their activities almost a hundred years ago, the more we realize that such shows contained both the fast and the slow rhythms that were to come forth one day in the guise, respectively, of "ragtime" and "blues." The minstrel show is one of the spiritual and material sources of Tin Pan Alley.

If the Nineties were really gay—and this is one of many adjectives that have been applied to the decade—one of the essential reasons is the growing insistence of the new, lively negroid rhythms that were pushing their way up from the South. Only a couple of years separated the slow, lachrymose, anecdotic measures of *After The Ball* from such early symptoms of ragtime as *The Bully Song, All Coons Look Alike To Me,* or *A Hot Time In The Old Town Tonight.* It would be years before the waltz, as a vehicle for popular song, would be definitely conquered by the jagged two-four rhythms of the rag; indeed, the waltz has never been conquered entirely. It is one of the essential tempos of the dance, and of song, never so sure of its charm as when sophisticated youth, tired for the moment of fox-trots, bunny-hugs, turkey-trots, Charlestons, and what-not-elses, revives a rhythm that never died and never will die, and professes to look upon it as a quaint resurrection.

How many social habits can show, in so striking a fashion as the dance, the rapid changes in the popular mind and spirit? Consider the difference in style between the dances of today and those that were the rage between 1885 and the turn of the century. The earliest Witmark publications of any given season were considered incomplete without a medley of the current musical comedy numbers in the form of lancers, quadrille, waltz, polka,

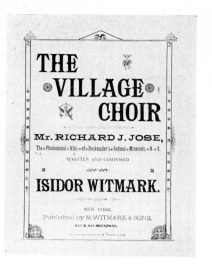
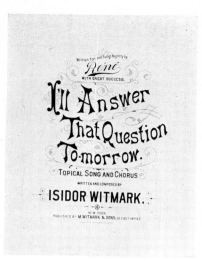

Two of the first songs published by the Witmarks. Title page of
The Village Choir was set up in type by Isidore in 1885.

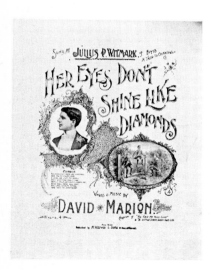
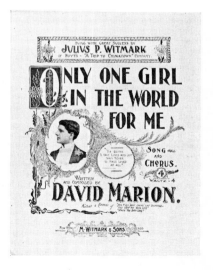

Two famous David Marion song hits.

Original covers of the big Ragtime hits, *Mister Johnson, Turn Me Loose* and *Ben Harney's Rag-Time Instructor.*

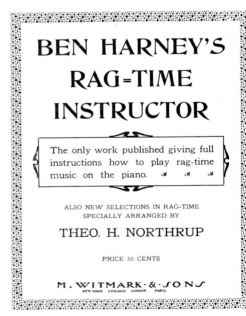

mazurka, gavotte, schottische, and two-step. Beginning with the first operetta to bear the imprint of M. Witmark & Sons—William W. Furst's "The Isle of Champagne" starring Thomas Q. Seabrooke—every operetta had its full complement of arrangements in the dance fashions mentioned. Lancers and quadrilles based upon popular songs were also a seasonal feature of the firm, and numerous hits were arranged as schottische—a very popular dance which one saw everywhere, both on the stage as in the famous *Tell Me, Pretty Maiden* sextette number from "Florodora," as well as in the ballroom—one-step and two-step. This was no mere publishing venture; it was a practical response to an unmistakable demand.

There were other folios that formed a staple of the firm's publications: collections of piano music, vocal music, duets, music for banjo, mandolin, saxophone, cornet, 'cello, violin, guitar, trombone, and so on—all based upon the hits of the day or of the former season. The successes of the previous season could be included in these fifty-cent folios because of an arrangement between the writers and the Witmarks that such reprints would not be subject to royalties. The business of folios grew to the proportions of a special department; thousands were sold.

Then something happened. Was it the decline of piano playing in the home? Was it the coming of the movies, radio, and the talkies? In any case, the folio business suffered a marked decline, and went the way of the old dances—it disappeared.

Who, today, would know the lanciers or quadrille even if he saw them danced? Of all the once-popular dances, the waltz remains, and perhaps the two-step. The waltz has lasted into our own day, despite the evolution of ragtime into jazz, of jazz into sweet and hot, and thence into "swing" and "jam."

It was in the five years between 1893 and 1898 that the ballad and the waltz types gradually yielded, often to the accompaniment of stern moral denunciation, to the allurements of ragtime. Ragtime derived from the familiar minstrel South that, in a different mood, had given us the Negro "spirituals," "the mellows," the work songs. Fast rhythms, however, have always been associated with frivolity, with indecorous ideas; so it is not astonishing that ragtime, considering its origin in the less religious moments of a deeply religious people, should have met with suspicion and scorn. "Hot" jazz still encounters the same hostility.

This is hardly the place to make a musical and psychological analysis of the new appearance. It may be suggested, however, that the syncopated rhythms that proved so exciting to the youth of the Nineties, were not exclusively Afro-American. Even twenty or thirty years later, there was much speculation on the subject, and we found ourselves trying to determine the parentage of jazz. There were those who maliciously intimated that it was a "music without a father." The gypsy rhythms of Hungary, the folk-music of Spain, even the syncopations of the classical masters, were all adduced as ancestral influences. It was a degenerate child of, so to speak, a collaborative ancestry.

The period is important to this story for another and a basic reason: it marks the indubitable beginnings of Tin Pan Alley as a national industry. The Eighties had been a decade of pioneer ventures, but at a hazard. The Nineties witnessed the establishment of a host of music publishing firms by youngsters who had caught on and had a fair notion of the direction in which they were headed. What they knew least about was music and words; what they cared least about might be answered by the same phrase. They had discovered that there was money in popular song.

Symbolic of the whole throng, its background, its innocence of art, its hit-or-miss policies, its back-alley troubadourism, its occasional inspiration on a humble plane, was the flamboyantly successful Charles K. Harris. It was as much the incredible history of *After The Ball* as any one other factor that was responsible for the establishment of mushroom publishing houses financed on a shoestring. Although he remained in the music publishing business until the early 1930's, the seventeen-year-old banjoist was, and remained, a child of the early Nineties. Try as he might, he could never write a song in the new rhythms that were already beginning to be heard in the land when everybody was sighing *After The Ball*. Soon they would be singing Barney Fagan's *My Gal's A High-Born Lady*, and for at least ten years the battle would be on before the victory fell to ragtime.

The Witmarks had already published Harris's first song, which was not very different from the last that Harris was to publish almost forty years later. It was entitled *When The Sun Has Set*. That sun never even rose. The boy composer, not too highly elated over a first royalty fee of eighty-five cents, ironically framed the check. His publishers retaliated by framing the song as a prize failure. It was this episode that turned Harris to becoming his own publisher. The fortune that was made by *After The Ball* was thus lost to the Witmarks, who in the normal course of events might have been the publishers for Charles K. Harris.

Composers and lyricists—Tin Pan Alley knows nothing of poets or versifiers or rhymesters or doggerel bards; words to songs are lyrics, and writers of words to songs are lyricists— frequently take such revenge upon their heartless publishers. For example: George M. Cohan. Cohan's first published song— to jump ahead a moment for a few years—was entitled *Why Did Nellie Leave Her Home?* It was a Witmark number, and the Witmarks offended Cohan at the first crack of the bat by calling in Walter Ford, of the famous Ford and Bratton team, to revise the lyrics. Despite this doctoring, the firm could not put the song across, and Cohan waited twenty-five years to even the score. The Witmarks had sold him and his partner, Sam H. Harris, a musical comedy, whereupon he proceeded to distort the piece almost beyond recognition. And—here was a boomerang!— Gotham took the Cohanized version of "The Royal Vagabond" to its generous heart for a run of fifty-three consecutive weeks.

115

2. Song Slides

One cannot always tell when an old fashion will return in a new form. Who, a few years ago, would have dreamed that the highways would be thronged today with bicycles? Who would have imagined that in 1937, with the talkies at their height and color triumphantly taking its place as a staple of cinematic entertainment, the moving picture houses would be going back to the colored slides of the last century?

For a time at least, the radio brought back singing to the home. Audiences became reacquainted with their own voices and with the fun of making music with one's own throat, however inexpert that music might be. Song-slide manufacture experienced a rebirth.

The man who invented the song slide was, in his clumsy way, a forerunner of the moving picture story. For the song slides presented a story in pictures that moved individually, from incident to incident. The pioneer of the industry was George H. Thomas, who had the inspiration sometime in 1892, when he was chief electrician at the Amphion Theater, Brooklyn, where Denman Thompson was appearing in "The Old Homestead," of happy memory. In that production was sung the song, *Where Is My Wandering Boy Tonight?* illustrated by a solitary slide that showed a saloon with a young man at the bar. Why, thought Thomas, could not an entire song be thus shown, and not from crude drawings? How about actual photographs? Thomas interviewed the publishers of *The Little Lost Child,* and, receiving permission to illustrate that saga of the policeman's daughter, proceeded with realistic zeal to enlist the services of the boys in blue who inhabited the station at Clymer Street and Lee Avenue, Brooklyn.

Then and there, in a police station, the business of the song slide was born. It became a craze. It became, indeed, a recog-

116

nized department of the song industry. Special songs were written for slide accompaniments—chiefly of the "sob" variety. The slides would be on order from the publishers at an average cost of five dollars the set; among song-slide singers they would be distributed free. They were, virtually, "stills" that had been specially posed for. The ordinary popular song would require some fifty sets of slides. As the popularity of the song increased, so naturally did the number of slide sets.

Among the outstanding slide-song singers were a pair known as Maxwell and Simpson. Joe Maxwell did the singing and Simpson manipulated the projector. They became a headline variety act and had quite a vogue. Their big song ballad was written by Ford and Bratton and was entitled *Only Me*. It is difficult for audiences of today to appreciate with what human sympathy the audiences of the Gay Nineties listened to such refrains as

> " 'Only me, only me,'
>   Sobbed in a weary tone,
>   Wrung from an innocent baby's heart
>   That felt so much alone.
>   One got the kisses and kindly words,
>   That was her pet, Marie;
>   One told her troubles to bees and birds,
>   That one was 'Only Me.' "

There were a number of song-slide manufacturers: De Witt C. Wheeler produced many sets for the Witmarks, and Herman A. Rosenberg, who started in 1911 as The Greater New York Slide Company, is still going strong as The Cosmopolitan Studios. During the war period of 1917-18, with all the new patriotic songs, slides came back, but, instead of actors being used to pose, drawings illustrated the action of the verse and chorus. In 1925 came song continuities for special organ presentation, which consisted of a novel idea covering from thirty to forty slides and included a firm's entire song plug, boosting all their outstanding numbers at the same time. The organ department was installed in many of the publishers' advertising sections and became an important consideration, as more than eighteen hundred organists and orchestra leaders were using slides.

With the advent of talkies and radios, song slides were sidetracked for a while. Today, however, it looks as though organists are coming back strongly, and many live-wire publishers realize the value of having their songs plugged through this medium, for when a theater, co-operating with the local music stores, puts on an organ solo, one may be sure that the music sales of the songs are increased. There is a unique slide service today called the Noon Club under the management of Harry Blair, who has his headquarters at Shapiro-Bernstein's.

Unlike the slides of former days, these new slides are not illustrated, but bear the words in white printing on black background, and with these shown on the screen the audiences are enabled to enjoy themselves in joining in with the singing organist.

Mr. Blair explains that this service is maintained, not by the publishers, but by the organists themselves, who find it a remunerative investment inasmuch as it popularizes the organist and assures the permanency of his engagement.

3. Branching Out—Sol Bloom

During 1892 and 1893, Julie was on the road, and when he was on the road the firm of Witmark was on the road, too. With Chicago ablaze—it was the period of the Columbian Exposition, which has come down to us as the Chicago World's Fair—it was natural for Julie, having reached that rising metropolis, to think of Witmark exhibitions. Here he encountered an old San Francisco friend from the days with Billy Emerson's San Francisco minstrels. The friend, Sol Bloom, had come to the Fair in charge of some exhibits.

The relationship was renewed joyfully. On Julie's advice a Chicago branch of the Witmarks was opened and his rediscovered friend was placed in charge. Bloom was a mercurial fellow, but exceedingly capable, as his later career in politics has shown. Under his management the office thrived. He was joined there by brother Frank from New York, who acted as assistant manager and represented the family interests. Bloom had been with the Witmarks for a number of years—when he saw an opportunity to take on another business, that of acquiring the music sections of large department stores. His employers not being prepared to go into this venture, he went in on his own and later embarked on music publishing, in which he remained for some years. When he abandoned this, the Witmarks acquired his catalog, including Arthur Penn's *Carrissima*, the famous *Sammy* song by Edward Hutchison, which Lotta Faust made popular in "The Wizard of Oz," and other big successes.

Sol Bloom next went into the phonograph business and was the first to open up attractive stores, with new ideas in fixtures, in which he was succeeded by Landay Brothers. He proceeded into real estate and built, among other important edifices, the Candler Theater at 226 West Forty-second Street which became the present Harris Theater; and last he went into politics. He is now a Representative in Congress, has served on important committees, and has been returned to Washington eight times in sixteen years.

One incident that stands out vividly in the firm's relations with Bloom concerns an infringement case in which he played a leading rôle. For weeks there had appeared in the streets of Chicago young men selling song sheets containing the lyrics of dozens of popular songs, printed in violation of copyright. Those sheets carried many of the Witmark songs, the unauthorized printing and sale of which, under the copyright act of the time, entitled the authentic publisher to damages of one dollar for every copy found in the possession of the infringer. No notice appeared on the sheets as to who the publishers or printers were, and it was necessary to know so that a case could be made and followed through. The deft detective work it required was right up Sol

Bloom's alley. He put in days and nights on the trail, and after discouraging setbacks was rewarded. He discovered the printer.

How should he approach this important personage? Obviously he could not do it in his true identity. Pretending to be a racketeer, guessing that the printer had the plates already on hand—itself a violation—Bloom whispered to the fellow that he had a gang of men on his payroll and thought he could do some business with the song sheets. The printer, at first suspicious, capitulated; for Sol ordered five thousand each of five different sheets, which were to be ready at a certain date. Meanwhile Sol got in touch with the sheriff's office and laid the case before him. The sheriff assigned several deputies to go with Sol and seize the copies after he identified them.

The day arrived, and Sol and his deputies made for the printer's. The deputies remained outside the door. At the cue, spoken loudly by Sol—"Are there 25,000 copies here?"—they were to enter and make the seizure. The program was carried out. Sol and the deputies, to the amazed chagrin of the printer, carted off the 25,000 copies.

Sol reported this to the home office and was instructed to secure the best legal service possible. The Witmarks were a little apprehensive and wanted to take no chances on a counter-suit.

Months passed; at last the case was called. Sol had engaged a lawyer named Binswanger, who was counsel for such important clients as Nelson Morris, the packers; and also a man named Reed, who specialized in copyright law. For his one appearance Reed was to receive $200, a big fee in those days. The case was brought before Judge Kohlsaat, and if Isidore remembers rightly, the opposing lawyer was named Arndt.

Kohlsaat was one of the most distinguished of American Federal judges. He had not, however, presided over many copyright cases, if his attitude in this case was any criterion.

Isidore came from New York to attend the trial. One look at the lawyer for the other side and he had cause to worry. There was Arndt, a big, blustering fellow, leaning on a pair of crutches, with his left foot shoeless, bandaged up in white gauze, probably for effect. The selection of the jury encountered unusual delay because of the numerous objections by Arndt. He would accept no book publishers, writers, or, in fact, any professional persons. His inclination was toward farmers and small storekeepers—anyone who was blissfully ignorant of copyright or of anything thereunto appertaining.

The lawyer for the Witmarks did not object to this, thinking that the case could be explained in a simple manner; he did not know Arndt. The case was opened; the publishers' side presented its evidence and claims; its wonderful $200 copyright lawyer did his stuff,—which was not understood by anyone, including the judge. In fact, it prejudiced the judge against the Witmarks, as was soon indicated by his charge.

Arndt hobbled painfully on his crutches up and down before the jury box, immediately gaining the sympathy of the jurors. He made a speech as far distant from copyright as the North Pole is from the South, emphasizing all his points in farm language, talking more about straying cows than copyrights, and managing somehow to put the shoe on the other foot. He ended his long harangue by accusing Sol Bloom of being the culprit! He told these men, in language they understood, that Sol had deliberately ordered the copies in a diabolical scheme to make an innocent man do wrong.

The jury brought in a verdict for the defendant, and the judge even thought that there might be a case of conspiracy against the plaintiff. The Witmarks had all they could do to keep out of a counter-suit. The 25,000 song sheets which were to bring to Sol Bloom's employers $25,000 or more were solemnly burned in the furnace of their office building. The Witmarks, to all intents and purposes, had violated their own copyright!

Isidore was so disgusted with the outcome that he decided not to exercise the right of appeal. In a sense, however, as appeared later, the Witmarks had won their case. For a long time no unauthorized song sheets were sold on the streets of Chicago.

4. "In Old New York"

The New York of this era—the decade from 1883 to 1893, when the Fair in Chicago seemed to proclaim a newer and a gayer day symbolized, as much as by anything else, by the mysterious Oriental "Midway Plaisance"—was still a gawky Gotham, as shy and at the same time bumptious as an adolescent tripping over his first pair of long trousers. And yet it returns to memory in a haze of nostalgia for an unrecoverable past. A kaleidoscope of recollections shifts about at the turn of reminiscence, into glittering patterns . . . The squatter farms from Eighth Avenue to the Hudson River, and from Fifty-ninth Street up to Harlem . . . the Elevated railroad being built on Ninth Avenue, the streets dug up, the heavy caissons buried as supports for the stanchions . . . The ride on the Elevated as far as what was known as Carmansville, which made an excellent picnic ground. Where now is the old lady who carried the basket of scalloped bolivars or spice cakes? . . . New York of the free lunches at drinking places—Dowd's on lower Broadway, the Spingler House at Fourteenth Street and University Place, Mc-Keever Brothers at Sixth Avenue and Fourteenth, where the free lunches might have passed as banquets. . . . The institution of the "growler," that could be "rushed" at seven cents for a full can. . . . The old oyster houses,—Jack's, O'Neill's, Bristol's, Dorlan's. . . .

Corsets when corsets were corsets—which is to say, armor. Bustles that followed them about like a too faithful chaperone and rats in the women's hair. Peek-a-boo shirtwaists that acted as the first air-conditioners, and were more exciting as a name than as a fact. Ready-made Ascot ties. Huge watch chains and fobs big as a steeple-bell. Meerschaum pipes, colored yellow, brown and even black at the bowl, and almost everybody had a burnt wood set.

Music from the McTammany Music Box that was operated by the insertion of a perforated roll of paper. This was the first of its kind, and was the forerunner of the player-piano.

The first Brush carbon electric lights on Eighth Avenue— large gray globes with a sizzling white light produced by the contact of two carbon pencils brought point to point. . . . The Broadway stages, the epidemic of throat disease among the stage-horses, and the big swathes of red flannel that were wrapped around their necks to protect them from the epizootic. . . . The first trolleys on Broadway. Wooden Indians in front of the cigar stores, hardly noticed then, and now much sought after as objects for collectors. The crosstown bob-tailed cars with cash-boxes in the front and straw on the floor. The relay of horses for the street cars. The fleet of ferries—at Grand Street and Houston Street for Williamsburg; Fulton Street and Catharine Street for Brooklyn. The Belt Line—a red car that circled the City up the East Side, across town through Fifty-ninth, and south on Tenth Avenue, past all the ferries. The white cars marked University Place. Goat carriages in Central Park at five cents a ride.

The day the Brooklyn Bridge was opened, May 24, 1883. It was Queen Victoria's birthday and the more absurd among the trouble-stirrer-uppers declared that that date was deliberately chosen as an affront to the Irish. Most of the people living near the waterfront in the city of Brooklyn trekked to rooftops in the evening to enjoy the magnificent fireworks display. All day long vast crowds had swarmed over the Bridge like flies and "a good time was had by all." The Bridge was really a traffic artery that made Siamese twins of New York and Brooklyn. On Decoration Day the masses had an opportunity to visit the structure, but through stupidity the day ended in disaster. Late in the day a woman, going down the steps of the promenade, tripped and fell. Somebody cried out, "The Bridge is giving way!" Instantly the cry was taken up by a thousand throats. Pandemonium! The good-natured, laughing crowds became a fear-crazed mob, and as usual in such emergencies few there were who kept level-headed. The screaming mass of humanity plunged toward the New York side of the Bridge. Many stumbled and fell; others piled up on top of them. In the confusion twelve persons were either crushed or suffocated and thirty-five were seriously injured.

In the Eighties, the home was a place where music was sung and played, not listened to at the turn of a dial casually, in the midst of a half-dozen other occupations. Songs, however simple and inexpert, were part of one's personal activities, not an external factor.

Yet, taking as a whole the fifty years of the Witmarks in the business of music publishing, it is a statistical fact that New York City was the worst center for sales in all America. Perhaps this was because the people of the city, except during such holidays as New Year's, had less home life than the smaller communities and did not make such constant use of their pianos.

In the pathos of distance, old New York acquires a quaint, even crude, charm that suggests precisely the feeling one gets today on examining the cover of a popular song of the Nineties. For that New York, too, is an old tune, sweet to the memory that can recapture it, but a memory only, of something that can never return.

5. Bureau of Entertainment—Marie Dressler

The Witmarks had been an entertainment bureau long before they officially established such an adjunct to their growing business. From the beginning the various departments of the firm had been extensions of their individual talents. They had been giving amateur plays, appearing before clubs, associations, and lodges. It was logical—and, for these dynamic youngsters, virtually necessary—to organize such activities. The nucleus of a booking-office was already there; it remained but to name it. Thus was born the Witmark Entertainment Bureau.

The boys were well placed for their new venture. They were performers themselves; they knew the leading artists in variety, burlesque, and musical comedy; they had a numerous acquaintance among prominent social and political organizations. Moreover, in those modest days top-notchers in the amusement world were not "high-hat." They would eagerly accept an opportunity to make a little spare change. The new Entertainment Bureau got off to a quick start.

Small wonder, when one comes to think of it, with millions of dollars worth of talent floating around the city. To be sure, that talent was not yet national currency, but a day would come when it would be. There was Marie Dressler, for example. Isidore had first heard of her through Julie, who had come home one day ablaze with enthusiasm for a clever young performer who was noted for never passing up a dare. Julie was with "The City Directory" at the time, and so was Dan Daly, the fellow who kept teasing Marie Dressler with his crazy dares.

Isidore had seen Marie, long before Julie's glowing account, as one among the delighted audience who had watched her as Ruth in Gilbert and Sullivan's "The Pirates of Penzance" some years before in Yonkers. How could his admiration fail to rise at Julie's tales of her prowess? Dan Daly was the foremost eccentric dancer of his day, and his dares consisted chiefly in challenging Marie to duplicate his fantastic steps and falls. Some of Dan's legmania work, in which he stood alone—if *stood* is the word!—was difficult enough for a man to do, let alone a woman. What is more, Marie was inclined to the higher notes of the weighing scale, even in her girlhood. Yet, avowed Julie, there wasn't a step or a fall or a standing on the head in which the girl did not follow the amazed and delighted Dan.

FROM RAGTIME TO SWINGTIME

It was in 1893, in the first days of the Witmark Entertainment Bureau, that Isidore actually met the acrobatic Marie. He engaged her to do a turn for a number of the local clubs. Her specialty was a burlesque of Schiller's "Glove." For this act she had music, which Isidore discarded, writing his own and playing it to her parody. She was always a great artist, no matter what she did—and she did almost everything in the theater.

Isidore was going about with the idea of writing the great American musical comedy. So when he met Marie Dressler's brother-in-law, the actor and author, Richard Ganthony, and learned that Ganthony had written the book of an opera especially for Marie, it looked like a natural. Marie, impressed with his young talents, was eager to have her accompanist write the music to Ganthony's book, "Baroness Bounty."

When Isidore told George W. Lederer about Marie and the opera—and Lederer was already a big name in the show business —Lederer seemed not to have heard of her. As a result of Isidore's enthusiasm, he was willing to consider her and an appointment was made.

True to the Lederer form, however, he did not put her into Isidore's opera but stole her away from him and placed her in "Princess Nicotine," a musical play he had had written for Lillian Russell. Instead of a straight part, such as she had always done, Marie played a burlesque rôle and proved a sensation. She never went back into opera. Nor was "Baroness Bounty," Isidore's operatic hope, ever produced.

His collaboration with Dick Ganthony, however, had brought them close together and he learned that Ganthony had written about half a dozen unproduced plays. One in particular Isidore felt had tremendous possibilities. Ganthony placed it in his hands and he worked hard for a whole year to sell it. He offered it to everybody who was anybody at that time—the Frohmans, the Holland Brothers, Richard Mansfield, Charles Dickson, Louis Mann,

126

Dan Frawley, Robert Edeson, Arthur Forrest, and many more. E. H. Sothern wanted to act in it, but Daniel Frohman frowned upon the suggestion. All turned it down.

One day Ganthony came to Isidore and said, "I want to start a chicken farm. I need money! I will give you a half interest in this play, and five others, for $250.00."

The Witmarks had not been in the music publishing business long. Their friend, Morrie Golland, was now a big man in his line and a sort of adviser to them. Isidore put the Ganthony proposition up to him, and he said: "Shoemaker, stick to your last! You're not in the play-buying business—you're in the music publishing business." So Isidore declined the proposition.

Ganthony, becoming disgusted with the way his plays were received here, one day took a boat and went to England. There he disposed of the play he had offered to Isidore for $250—the one in which he had had such great faith—and cleaned up $100,000 the first season. It was produced and played by Charles Hawtrey. The name of the play was "A Messenger From Mars."

6. Louis Mann—David Warfield

Talent was cheap in the Gay Nineties. There was, for instance, the amateur minstrel show for the Columbia Club of Harlem, which Isidore staged in 1895. At the last moment the principal end man was called out of town on important business. The producer was in a quandary. The show could not be postponed. What to do? He thought of Louis Mann, then known wherever entertainment was sought, particularly for his still-remembered monologue, *Cohen on the Telephone.*

"Louie," he pleaded, after reaching him, "you must go on as end man for me, and save the day."

"But," protested Louie, "I was never in a minstrel show in all my life."

"Then begin now. You're going to black up."

127

"All right, but I haven't any minstrel material, no gags, no end-songs. And you know I can't sing."

"Who has said anything about songs or minstrel stuff?" asked Isidore. Louie stared blankly.

"You're going to do your *Cohen on the Telephone*, in Hebrew dialect, blacked up on the end."

"You're crazy!"

"We'll see if I am."

The monologue was the sensation of the evening, and no one was more pleasantly surprised than Louie himself. Even back in 1895 he was an artist, and for his artistry that night he received from the Witmark Entertainment Bureau precisely ten dollars. Consider what Louie Mann, if living today, could command as a broadcasting star!

But consider, too, the pay that was being accepted from the Bureau by the best talent of the time. For a club appearance, Isidore hired none other than David Warfield, likewise famous for a monologue, at the price that he had paid to Mann.

Mann and Warfield once met at Forty-second and Broadway. Dave was by this time a stage star, playing in one of his notable successes. To Louie, however, he was, and always remained, the program boy he had known years before in San Francisco, when Louie was one of the chief actors in support of Lewis Morrison, who was famous for his Faust.

The two started arguing about the manner in which Dave played a certain scene in his current piece. They usually wrangled when they met, despite the fact that Dave had lived with the Manns when he first arrived in New York. Mann had a notion how to improve the interpretation. Warfield, perhaps not unnaturally, was riled.

"See here! Mr. Belasco directed that scene, and his direction is good enough for me!"

The argument was on the point of degenerating into fisticuffs, when suddenly the debaters caught sight of an austere gentleman, dressed in the height of fashion, a monocle in his eye, a cane in his hand, sauntering past them in dignified unconcern.

No sooner did they eye him than their altercation was forgotten. In fact, they began chuckling. Said Louis, in a stage "aside," "He thinks he's an actor, too!"

The erstwhile near-pugilists, now friends again, laughed heartily.

The fellow who had passed—who thought *he* was an actor, too? He was Richard Mansfield.

In 1895 Louis Mann married Clara Lipman who had made her fame four years before as the "laughing girl" in "Incog," a successful comedy in which Mann played one of the "three twins." Louis and Clara lived happily together for thirty-five years. Their marriage changed the course of Louis' career. Clara saw in him a great character actor and insisted upon his dropping the rôles of leading men and taking to dialect parts. He fought against it because he could see himself playing only romantic parts. But Clara won, and she was right! This obstinacy was characteristic throughout his life; he fought against playing his outstanding successes, "Friendly Enemies," "Elevating a Husband," "The Girl From Paris," and "The Man Who Stood Still."

After three years of married life—purses low and at their wits' end to find a joint engagement—Louis accidentally ran into Edgar B. Smith, an important author and stage director. Edgar was trying to find a suitable actress for "The Girl From Paris" company which was being organized. Edgar in desperation appealed to Louis, "Your wife speaks French—couldn't she possibly help us out?"

So Clara fell into the greatest success she ever had and dragged Louis in after her—against his will—and he with a false bulbous nose as the manufacturer of a fake spa water and she as the cocotte set New York aflame. The Herald Square Theater became a meeting place, like a club, for many people frequented the theater night after night to see "The Girl From Paris."

To return to the prices current in the Nineties of the Witmark Entertainment Bureau: To the great Helene Mora, England's female baritone, was paid the top price, $30. To the outstanding vaudeville team, Ross and Fenton, $20. The Rogers Brothers likewise split twenty dollars between them.

So, too, Ward and Vokes, who were appearing simultaneously as stars in their own productions! On the same bill with Ward and Vokes, Isidore had engaged Lucy and Margie, sisters of the noted comedian, Dan Daly. It was at this club affair that Lucy and Margie first met Ward and Vokes. Result: Lucy became Mrs. "Hap" Ward and Margie became Mrs. Harry Vokes.

The Abbot sisters used to give their banjo act for twenty dollars apiece. Later, Bessie became a well known prima donna of the Metropolitan. In addition to the variety artists the Bureau had a list of "dependables" who did not leave town; the favorite serio-comic Maude Raymond, who later became Mrs. Gus Rogers; Gus Schlesinger, who became Gus Yorke of Yorke and Adams; Loney Haskell; the versatile Fred Solomon; Press Eldridge, the minstrel comedian; Tom Ballantine, the monologist and Bill Devere.

The Entertainment Bureau flourished for many years until, together with the changes in national mood and progress toward more sophisticated types of theatrical offerings, larger ventures came to absorb the attention of the firm. Chief among these was the association of the Witmarks with Joseph M. Gaites, with whom they entered the field of stage production.

7. Wandering Minstrelsy

Somebody once asked Isidore what was his favorite hobby. He was never a man for cards, nor did he follow any sports.

"My hobby," he answered, "is another man's death."

It sounded far more gruesome than it was. Certainly it was not meant to indicate that the publisher went in for the collection of obituaries, or planning murders on a wholesale scale. All he intended to convey was that he likes his particular hobby so well that he could ride it day and night; it might have exhausted another man. The hobby was a passion born of his childhood delight in theatricals; the staging of amateur entertainments—operettas, revues, musical comedies, and especially minstrel shows.

In the few books devoted to the historical aspects of the subject it is suggested that the minstrel show, which was born before the middle of the nineteenth century, had reached its zenith by the Eighties. In a certain sense this is true. The form had attained definiteness, and its chief possibilities had already been exploited for some thirty or forty years. Rooted in the plantation pastimes of the Negro slaves, it caught both the ecstasies in which subject peoples are so ironically rich: the gleeful abandon and the sober, religious preoccupation with an after-life that shall compensate for the sorrows of the present.

The minstrel show, however, soon acquired a character that is aptly symbolized by the burnt cork. It became, so to speak, pseudo-Negro. Black-face, after all, was not black-skin. Already, then, we have the touch of what is later to become Tin Pan Alley. Even Stephen C. Foster never saw the Swanee River, the occurrence of which in his famous song is simply a geographical accident. Foster no more knew, or cared about, the Swanee River than George Gershwin, years later, when he wrote his song, *Swanee,* and saw it earn a fortune for him. It is quite in the nature of things that *Dixie* was written up North, and that ragtime and jazz, both born of Negro spirits, should have received their intensive commercial development in New York City.

Yet this does not mean that our darkey songs, as written by the whites, are altogether insincere. The Negro has become for us a mask from behind which we speak with less self-consciousness of our own primitive beliefs and emotions. Can one imagine a "white" play made out of "The Green Pastures"? Yet the re-

131

ligious symbolism of the Negro derives from the Hebrew-Christian religion. The Negro, whether in his spirituals or in his ragtime and jazz, has returned the influence of his white masters with rich interest. He has become, in a way that was never suggested by the native Indian, a deep psychological influence upon his fellow Americans. *Swanee* and *Dixie* and the mammies may be, in plain language, pretty much of a fake on the surface, yet they conceal behind their factory-made features a longing for the never-never land of peace and plenty and love. The South, in Tin Pan Alley, has become the symbol of that land of milk and honey. From the folk-poetry of the Negro we have taken over a long list of symbols.

It was natural, then, that in the minstrel show should be found the concentration of these symbols for the first time in a more or less ordered fashion. Whatever else the minstrel show may have been, and it was a number of entertaining and even important things, it was also the first foreshadowing of Tin Pan Alley. It had, as has already been pointed out, its sad songs and its gay, its ballads and its walk-arounds. It contained the germs of what was to break away and become variety and vaudeville. From the minstrel show came the olio—that interlude of specialty acts that was taken over with little change into burlesque, and introduced between the first and second parts of the new entertainment.

To the youthful Witmarks, professional participation in minstrelsy was but another way of being in the show business. And although the minstrel show, even in the early Nineties, was beginning to yield to later developments of burlesque, to the eye-and-ear excitements of comic operetta and extravaganza from England, and to budding musical comedy of our own, it was still a powerful influence in the theater. Powerful enough, in fact, for the Witmarks, under the impulse of Isidore's fondness for the form, Julie's voice, and the vaudevillian capabilities of Frank and Eddie, to build up a highly profitable branch of their business.

A rare program dated April 14, 1894, shows Isidore in the rôle of a Pooh Bah of minstrelsy. Here, too, may well be the beginnings of the much later "spectacular" minstrel show. To be sure, it was but a single performance—"grand" and "spectacular"—given at the Lexington Opera House by the Washington Irving Union, "arranged, coached, and directed by Mr. Isidore Witmark."

The comedy, which made up Part III of the entertainment described as "the laughable Ethiopian absurdity, 'Thirty Minutes For Lunch,' somewhat of a satire on railroad life," was "arranged and written" by the gentleman who had coached and directed the affair. The Assistant Stage Director was Mr. Jay Witmark.

There was something Moscow-Arty (if we may look that far forward) about the request not to encore any numbers in the Novel Medley Opening Chorus. But there were so many numbers that encores would have stretched an already long program into morning. Of the songs listed as the latest Witmark hits, one at least is still well known, with something of a historical value as one of our earliest popular nonsense songs. It is the Dillon brothers' *Do, Do, My Huckleberry Do—Be Careful What You Do Do!*

The success of the venture was not a little responsible for the growing demands of the minstrel amateurs upon Witmark's. Minstrelsy was on Isidore's part an obsession which became an integral part of the firm's activities.

In a few years the Witmarks became the amateur minstrel center of the country. The house published not only minstrel songs, but a full line of joke books, Negro acts, minstrel overtures, and finales. It supplied tambos, bones, high collars and ties for end men, costumes, props and—symbol of all this black madness—burnt cork.

133

FROM RAGTIME TO SWINGTIME

The chief factors in this important department were Frank Dumont and Isidore. It was Dumont who wrote the Negro acts —Dumont whom Isidore calls "the Shakespeare of Minstrelsy." Isidore provided many of the overtures and finales. Dumont was a name to conjure with in the Nineties. He wrote acts for the chief professional minstrel organizations of the day, and had a prominent company of his own in Philadelphia which had succeeded the famous Carncross minstrels of that city.

When the Witmarks decided in 1899 to issue *The First Minstrel Encyclopaedia* and *The First Minstrel Catalogue*, it was naturally Dumont who was selected for the task, and just as naturally Isidore who collaborated in these pioneer ventures. There had been books on minstrelsy before, but hardly such as these. Although not large in size, they covered every want of the amateur quite as well as the mastodonic Sears, Roebuck catalogue covers the needs of its vast patronage.

The Witmarks inaugurated an Information Department which offered its services free to amateurs. The department mail became a deluge of queries. Hereupon Isidore was visited by another inspiration. Why not put on minstrel shows by mail? It was a daring idea, but, like much that is daring, it had about it a beautiful logic that might have been applied—but was not—to legitimate production in the heyday of the stock company and the little theater.

Through a series of questionnaires the Witmark minstrelsy department was able to arrange, to the special requirements of any organization, an individually planned entertainment. For this service there was a nominal fee of five dollars. So nominal, indeed, that it would have been a losing proposition but for the supplies sold to the organizations. The instructions were minute; the materials suggested were so pliable to the capabilities of inexperienced participants that any community leader could rehearse and stage the show. The department became a veritable correspondence school in amateur minstrelsy.

TRANSITION

Many people regret the passing of an entertainment that was very popular up to the late Nineties, the one entertainment that may rightly be styled a purely American product. But it is not without the bounds of reason that the minstrel show, in altered form, will return. There is a popular opinion that this is impossible; that the minstrel show is not sufficiently exciting; that it is too clean; that, for our strenuous age, it is too simple. There is something to all these objections, yet, there is little doubt that it can still provide, with slight modernization, one of the most satisfying evenings possible in the playhouse; especially to lovers of good singing, for, as the very name of the entertainment reveals, minstrelsy was first of all an array of songsters.

Consider today the popularity of such high-salaried balladists as Bing Crosby, Kate Smith, Ruth Etting, Lanny Ross, Rudy Vallee, and their compeers. In the final analysis, aren't they minstrel artists, with the scenery changed? Isn't their fundamental appeal that of the voice, especially when, as on the radio, they remain invisible?

Consider, too, the immense popularity of the prolonged minstrel show over the radio. One radio minstrel show, the Sinclair Oil Hour, held sway for over 300 performances, stretching over three years! The show included a complete first part in the old tradition—and the participants became special favorites of the Chicago audiences, who packed the auditorium every night that the broadcast went on.

It is an old story that out of minstrelsy were graduated some of the most prominent artists of the legitimate stage—men such as Olcott, Sweatnam, Carroll Johnson, Luke Schoolcraft, and, to come closer to our own times, Al Jolson.

But the first-born of the Witmark quintet is hardly content with bemoaning the decline of the minstrel show. His belief that it may, to use journalese, stage a comeback, takes the form of action. He himself, especially in his capacity as a Rotarian, has conceived, directed and staged two performances that may yet

135

play a part in the rehabilitation of the form. The Rotarian minstrel performance given under Witmark's personal supervision at the Plaza Hotel, April 24, 1923, was so well received that, ten years later, on April 4, 1933, it was revived in the ballroom of the Commodore Hotel to the delight of his fellow Rotarians.

8. Marshall P. Wilder

Boys together and attending the same school for a while, Marshall Wilder remained a friend of the Witmarks through life. In 1889 he published a book entitled, *The People I've Smiled With: Recollections of a Merry Life*, in which he wrote, "Dame Nature seemed to be out of sorts when she got hold of me. She put a couple of feet under me but she left a couple of feet off my stature." For Marshall Wilder had been a cripple since birth, not a hopeless cripple even though he frequently was forced to endure agonizing pain. Part of his treatment was to lie in bed, locked in iron braces for hours at a time. But his smile was so expansive, his laugh so tall, they reached to everyone's heart. The whole world was his front door yard. Generals, presidents, and kings paid him homage. Famous the world over as "The Prince of Entertainers and the Entertainer of Princes," meeting thousands of people, including the Prince of Wales, Buffalo Bill (Col. W. F. Cody), General Grant, Henry Ward Beecher—all entered into his service. Marshall Wilder devoted his life to spreading sunshine and laughter. Little wonder exists that the echo lingers in the memories of those who knew him.

Few people knew of his varied accomplishments. He was an excellent magician and a wizard with cards, reserving that accomplishment for his intimate circle. Once in Washington, he went into a bowling alley to spend a half hour doing sleight of hand tricks for a group of boys. The story is told delightfully in his book, *The Sunny Side of the Street*, published in 1905:

TRANSITION

"Just as I had gathered them about me and started to amuse them, Mr. McKinley came to the door and looked in, smiled, came over to us and asked what was going on.

"I replied, 'Well, Mr. President, I was just going over some tricks to amuse the boys.'

" 'Then I'm one of the boys,' said the President of the United States. He sat down in the circle and was one of my most attentive auditors."

CAST OF CHARACTERS—THE MIDDLE NINETIES

1. Evans and Hoey

*L*EAVES from a memory-album of the middle Nineties: Evans and Hoey, in "A Parlor Match." Who remembers them in that screaming farce, elaborated by Charles H. Hoyt from a vaudeville sketch, "The Book Agent," written by Frank Dumont of minstrel fame? In its original form the sketch had been played as early as December 22, 1884, at Tony Pastor's. Ten years later Evans and Hoey were still convulsing their audiences with the elaborated version, which was kept up to date by frequent revisions along topical lines. For more than a dozen years "A Parlor Match" was a reigning comedy success.

Charlie Evans, the senior member of this famous team, is an octogenarian, living in Hollywood and appearing occasionally in pictures with George Arliss and other stars. "Old Hoss" Hoey, his partner and brother-in-law—for they married the French twin sisters who played in their company—was one of the first of the stage hoboes, if not the first of that gentry; what is more, he had a sense of realism that prevented him from yielding to false whiskers. His full beard, in season, was the real thing; in the summer he would shave it off. Naturally a comical fellow, on the stage he was irresistible. The show boasted a cabinet scene,

138

and every year Evans and Hoey would import from England a new attraction that made its first appearance from that cabinet. From it Anna Held was introduced to the audiences of this country. So were the three Levey sisters, the Merrilees sisters, and other foreign artists.

2. "The Yankee-Doodle Dandy"

The reputation that the Witmarks had established in the first ten years of their existence is evidenced in George M. Cohan's book, *Twenty Years on Broadway*. It is indirect evidence, yet the more valuable on that account. It is evidence, moreover, that in certain details George—and all the rest of us—must sometimes be taken with a grain of salt.

The George M. Cohan of the middle Nineties was a self-opinionated youngster, with implicit faith in his gifts. His faith was justified by the years, but in those brash days it took forms at once amazing and irritating, as he himself relates. One of the things he thought he could do was to write songs, and when he was not arguing with theater folk he was tramping the streets of New York with unrecognized masterpieces under his arm. He was no more afraid of publishers than he was of managers, yet there was one firm that he could not quite pluck up the courage to tackle: the Witmarks.

"They were the big song publishers in those days," chronicles Cohan in his book. "They still are, as far as I am concerned. I figured it would be useless to try for a hearing with that house, as they seemed to have first call on the output of every leading composer and lyric writer in the country. They'd be far too busy to bother with a new man; besides, I had them tabbed for a lot of swell-headed guys, anyway."

Everybody in those days was swell-headed to Georgie, except the ardent, impatient boy who made the ready diagnosis. He would pass the Witmark offices and call the brothers big stiffs—

to himself. "Just goes to show how smart those babies in there are, publishing all that bum material written by a lot of 'hams,' and here I am, the best song writer in America, walking right by their door with four or five great big sure-fire hits under my arm."

If the Witmarks intimidated Georgie Cohan, they must indeed have been a formidable firm. But Cohan's self-confidence was equally formidable, and he found himself one day in the office, waiting for an appointment with the president, Isidore, all of twenty-five or twenty-six years, which to Georgie must have represented a well-advanced old age.

He was greeted first by Witmark père; it was a good omen, for Daddy Witmark remembered George's father, Jerry, in a play called "The Molly Maguires," at Niblo's Garden. He made the genius feel warmly welcomed, led him through a railing to a door in the rear, and into a private office, where stood the arbiter of his destiny.

Cohan describes Isidore, in Chapter XV of his book, under the caption, "My First Publisher":

"A tall, dark-complexioned, well-groomed young man, wearing the thickest eyeglasses I'd ever seen, stood behind the busiest desk I'd ever looked at as we walked into the room. This young man turned out to be the Mr. Isidore I'd heard everybody talking about in the front office.

" 'This is my son Issy,' said Mr. Witmark senior. 'This is Jerry Cohan's son Georgie.'

" 'Glad to know you, young man,' said Issy.

" 'Glad to know you, too,' and we shook hands."

It was like Witmark senior to ask his son to give every attention to "this boy," without having stopped to inquire whether he was an insurance agent or a fire inspector. He left the office before he learned.

George sat down and played his compositions. To his amazement, Isidore seemed to like but a single one: *Why Did Nellie*

Leave Her Home? In fact, he made the verdict clear: "It's a pretty bad song as it stands, but if you care to leave the manuscript here I'll see what can be done with it. . . ."

"What about a contract?" asked George.

"Nothing about a contract," replied Isidore. "Call later in the week."

For a moment George was about to snatch his manuscript off the piano rack and leave, but on second thought he decided against so drastic a step. Instead, he left the piece, and departed.

The story should be read in George's own words, as found in his published memories, for he has not spared himself and his youthful cock-sureness. Why, for example, had he fitted Isidore Witmark not only with a pair of glasses, but, for good measure, the thickest he had ever seen? For a long time after he had read the Cohan book, it troubled Isidore, for in those days he wore no glasses. One afternoon, however,—the book was not published until 1924-25, some thirty years after the occurrence—he met George.

"See here, Georgie, what in thunder did you mean in your book by saying that I wore the thickest eyeglasses you'd ever seen, when you know darn well I wasn't wearing any glasses at all?"

"Atmosphere, my boy, atmosphere!" Cohan replied nonchalantly.

The Witmarks have been fond of Cohan since the first day he stepped into their office. He is one of the finest characters not alone in the show business but anywhere. People will never know how many worthy fellow-actors he has helped and is still helping. At one time, when he was too busy to take care of the matter himself, he had a special assistant to superintend his numerous charities.

When Cohan and Harris joined hands as producers, Big Tim Sullivan staked them financially. They had acquired him as an angel after the Washington opening of their first play.

FROM RAGTIME TO SWINGTIME

There was an interlude in which Cohan and Harris themselves took a flyer into music publishing. They were, however, born stage producers, and they had wit enough to realize it. Not that they did not do well as publishers; as a matter of fact they did. They had Georgie Evans of the Honey Boy Minstrels, together with an excellent group of singers, introducing songs from Cohan's "The Yankee Prince" and other Cohan shows; but publishing interfered with producing, and they gave it up. Cohan, as a side issue, backed William Jerome in a song publishing venture, and dropped about $40,000. It was this company that published Cohan's war-song, *Over There*, which was eventually sold to Leo Feist's concern for $25,000.

And here's something that is not generally known. Because of the national appeal of the song and the condition of the country, George did not consider it right to keep this $25,000, so he handed it over to his mother to be distributed under her supervision to soldiers' funds and civic charities.

Then George came back to the Witmarks and he and Julie became great pals. It was at Julie's suggestion that Cohan wrote *When You Come Back and You Will Come Back*, the sequel to *Over There*.

One day while George was writing "The Rise of Rosie O'Reilly," the successor to his hit, "Little Nellie Kelly," Isidore dropped into his office.

"You just cost me a lot of money," George told him. He went on to explain that Edward Bitner, general manager of Leo Feist's music publishing house, had been in the office a short while before, and had offered him a signed blank check which he might fill out in any amount he desired, as advance publishing royalties on his next show. He took pleasure in repeating what he had said: "Mr. Bitner, there's more in this world than money. There's friendship,—and pals. And while you make me a tempting offer, the Witmarks are my pals, and they're going to get my next musical work without putting up a dollar." . . . His eye twinkled,

142

and he went on with a line that Isidore has been proud to quote ever since. "Not that alone, kid. You'll be my publisher as long as I live."

3. "Woozy" Leffler—Ford and Bratton

"Woozy" Leffler, who was John to his parents, got his nickname from a chewing gum, and his start on the roof of the New York Casino, at the corner of Thirty-ninth Street and Broadway, in 1895.

Lottie Gilson, appearing on the roof, was introducing the Witmarks' new Ford and Bratton song, *The Sunshine of Paradise Alley*. The Witmarks, who had already been compelled to silence Daddy's cane, were eager to learn how the song would go on its own. So they had not engaged a water boy. The water boy, whose ostensible duty it was to dispense water to the thirsty patrons, was in reality hired to join in the chorus of the songs and serve thus as a link between the performer and the audience. Lottie sang the first verse and the refrain without benefit of water boy. But the Witmarks had not reckoned with gum boys. Johnny Leffler was peddling "Woozy, the Gum That's Round." No sooner had the diminutive Gilson reached the second chorus than, out of the clear sky, a voice joined in the ditty. It was Johnny Leffler, and, though he did not know it, he was singing himself into a job. "Woozy" proved no better than its name, and was not on the market long. But Leffler was engaged by the Witmarks as a general outside utility man, and the name "Woozy" stuck to him ever after, like gum.

Leffler became a favorite and an asset to the firm. He had a good business head and was quick to grasp an opportunity. The Witmarks, taking pride in his progress, followed it with pleasure. Leffler became manager for the French artiste, Yvette Guilbert. He also managed R. F. Outcault, originator of "The Yellow Kid" and "Buster Brown" newspaper comics. It was

143

Leffler and Bratton who converted the Buster Brown series into a successful musical play.

About this time the Witmarks took on another youngster whom they hired to fold orchestrations and do other utility work. He did not last long with them for he soldiered on the job and was caught sketching, drawing, and making all kinds of figures on wrapping paper or any other object he could obtain. He was Mitchell ("Mitchy") Cirker, who is now the senior member of the New York scenic artists, Cirker & Robbins.

Louis Weslyn was one of the most prolific and versatile writers on the Witmark staff. A Welshman, his name being Louis Weslyn Jones, but he discarded the Jones at Julie's suggestion and legalized the rest of the name. Louis, a lovable chap, was loyal to the Witmarks to the last; he died in 1937. His versatility covered play writing, sketches, material for professional performers, lyrics, and music. His first real hit was *The Witch Behind The Moon,* introduced in "The Wizard of Oz" here and in the "Mother Goose" spectacle in London. He wrote many songs both as special material and for publication. His reputation makers were *The Boy Who Stuttered and The Girl Who Lisped,* made famous by Irene Franklin and others; *Baby Rose,* which he wrote with Ernest R. Ball, and *Send Me Away With A Smile,* which sold over a million copies.

Walter Ford and John W. Bratton were among the writing teams that enjoyed a vogue, through a cycle of songs and instrumental numbers, among them *Sunshine of Paradise Alley, I Love You In The Same Old Way* (*Sue Dear*), *Only Me, In A Cozy Corner, Henrietta, Have You Met Her?, Isabelle, Belle of The Season,* and *Teddy Bears' Picnic.* Then, like so many "cyclists," they were unable to repeat their success. There is the *homo unius libri,*—the author who has a single book in his make-up; and there is the man of just one song. Yet, at the date of writing this, Jack Bratton after more than thirty years, has scored another hit. That's the song business for you!

Ford and Bratton

John Stromberg

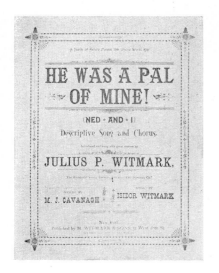

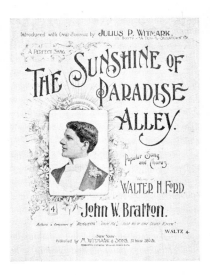

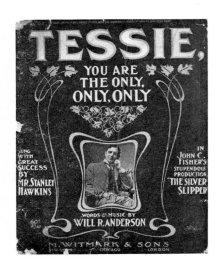

Original title pages of Witmark song hits.

Jack has been trying to place songs during the intervening years. When he teamed up with Leo Edwards he offered to American publishing houses the song *Sweetheart, Let's Grow Old Together*. In the early part of 1936 an English publisher happened to be visiting the United States, and Bratton, as a last hope, played the song for him. It was accepted on the spot and American rights were secured together with the English. With a dozen other songs that he had acquired in this country, the publisher took back the Bratton-Edwards piece, unaware that he had picked what was to become an outstanding hit. Once published, the Edwards-Bratton song sold over 200,000 copies in short order.

Jack is a timid sort of fellow. Recently he went to one of the chief New York publishers to interest him in some new songs. He was turned down just as he had been turned away on the day that he had brought him the song *Sweetheart, Let's Grow Old Together*. Jack is an old-timer; and he took the rebuff in good part.

"Isn't it funny," he said. "Here you turn me down—don't even look at my numbers, and I have a hit in England."

"A hit in England? What's the name of it?" asked the publisher.

Jack named the song.

The publisher shot up from his chair. "You didn't write that, did you? What else have you written?"

"That's what I came up here for, but you wouldn't give me a look-in."

"Who has the American rights of *Sweetheart?*" asked the publisher.

Jack named the English owner.

"I know him," and calling in his secretary, he said, "Take this cable: 'WOULD LIKE TO HAVE THE AMERICAN RIGHTS TO SWEETHEART, LET'S GROW OLD TOGETHER. PROMISE A BIG PLUG. MAKE IT OUR NUMBER ONE SONG. ANSWER COLLECT. . . .'"

The reply came: "ONE THOUSAND DOLLARS ADVANCE."

The New York publisher, who could have had it on a regular royalty basis without an advance, offered five hundred, and lost out. Another publisher paid the $1000 advance for the song that, a few weeks earlier, could not have commanded a cent. The song is having a fine sale on this side now.

4. B. C. Hilliam

Among the staff writers of M. Witmark & Sons was B. C. Hilliam, who wrote the score of "Buddies," book by George V. Hobart, produced by Edgar and Archibald Selwyn at the Selwyn Theater, New York. One number, *Please Learn To Love*, was sung by Peggy Wood; another, *Darling—I*, by Roland Young. Others in "Buddies" were Wallace Eddinger, and Donald Brian, of "The Merry Widow" fame.

A feature in "Buddies" was Hilliam's patter version of Zo Elliott's famous *There's A Long, Long Trail*. The play was so successful that several companies occupied the "road" for several seasons.

Hilliam also wrote *Princess Virtue*, with Gitz Rice, author of *Dear Old Pal of Mine*.

After his War service, Hilliam, as a Canadian lieutenant, toured America in vaudeville under the management of Charles B. Maddock. His versatility as a writer of lyrics and composer of songs was almost equalled by his ability as a cartoonist. He is now playing in England as Jetsam in the stage, screen and radio team of "Flotsam and Jetsam."

At Isidore Witmark's request "B. C.," as he is affectionately known, wrote complete scores for Isidore's musicalized versions of Harold MacGrath's "The Man On The Box" (now known as "Home, James") and the Boyd-Bunner comedy, "Wait Till We're Married" (now known as "Sweet William").

146

CAST OF CHARACTERS—MIDDLE NINETIES

5. Brother Frank

It was in the mid-Nineties that brother Frank, not yet twenty, threw his hat into the ring as aspirant for the honors of the American waltz-kingship. He won the title when he composed the successful *Zenda Waltzes*. The waltzes were dedicated to E. H. Sothern, who was playing in "The Prisoner of Zenda" at the time. The waltzes occurred as incidental music throughout the play and their incorporation was a feature. It was not long before the waltzes were taken up by performers of all kinds, acrobats, jugglers, and dancers, and *Zenda Waltzes* fast became one of the most popular on both sides of the Atlantic.

Zenda Waltzes are heard even today. Frank continued with waltzes named after current theatrical productions. He was, in a word, a theme-song writer, long before the same commercial idea struck the first producers of musical films in Hollywood. In its way the idea was an obvious one. The tie-up between music and drama has always been close, as is witnessed by the term melodrama. In the first days of the talking film the idea of the theme song was so badly overdone that the cinematic wiseacres were sure it was played out forever. But just as the idea long antedated the sounding screen, so was it certain to return after a vacation from the early abuses. The theme song, though regarded today as an ancient Hollywood device and all but discarded as a term, flourishes. So, too, does the "musical" film flourish, despite the facile prediction that it would vanish. Every picture that can possibly interpolate a song with which it will be associated in the popular mind has such a song, no matter how irrelevant the connection may appear. Today, indeed, our popular songs are as likely to come from the musical film as from the musical comedy.

Frank Witmark, sensing the natural tie-up between music and plays of popular appeal, followed up his waltzes to "The Prisoner

147

of Zenda" with a series hitched similarly to stage stars. There were *The American Citizen Waltzes*, dedicated to Nat Goodwin, who was the chief performer in the play of that name. To Richard Mansfield were dedicated the *Cyrano Waltzes*, which were played nightly during the run of "Cyrano de Bergerac." Other waltzes from this waltz prince—we may admit him that high, at least, into the royalty of the Three-Quarter Tempo—were *La Carmela, Mexican Waltzes, The Charmer*, and, as a tribute to his parents, *Health, Wealth and Happiness*.

Frank Witmark's *Lawn Dance* was once in the repertory of nearly every dance team in vaudeville. He was also co-author of the musical comedy, "The Lucky Stone," which had a six months' run at Fisher's Theater in San Francisco. In conjunction with the late Collin Davis, author of *Yama Yama Man* from "Three Twins" he was also composer of the musical comedies, "Miss Society" and "Anchored."

6. Anna Held—and "Ziggy"

Anna Held was one of the toasts of the middle Nineties. It was through her that the Witmarks accidentally stumbled upon another smash hit in their list, became involved with the newspapers, and had a run-in with Flo Ziegfeld, Jr.

One day there came a call from Melville Stoltz, a friend of the firm and one of Ziegfeld's trusted managers. It was about Anna Held and a sensational idea that Stoltz had thought up for her.

"I've come up to you, Izzie," Stoltz confided in the privacy of the sanctum, "for a good song to introduce my novelty. I call it The Animated Sheet."

A huge curtain, painted to represent a song-sheet, with the staff and notes of the song included, was to provide a backdrop to the singer. The notes, however, were to be practical; they were to be cut out so as to allow a human head to thrust through at the moment the note was supposed to be sounded. Moreover, since it was a coon song the heads would be those of colored boys, who would be poised behind the curtain on chairs, ladders, and platforms, according to the required heights.

The important thing was to decide on the song. It must be something virtually made to order for Miss Held's gifts. Dozens of published songs were tried out; manuscripts were brought out of the safe. Nothing could be found. In the desperation of their search the publisher and manager even pounced upon a new batch of "professional" copies just delivered by the printer. A "professional copy"—and the Witmarks were the first to provide them—is a copy without the trade cover. It is otherwise the same as the copy sold to the public, except that it is printed on a cheaper grade of paper. It is furnished free, as advertising, to the members of the acting and singing profession.

Stoltz thumbed the sheets; Witmark paid only half attention, for the sheets were those of Paul West's *I Want Dem Presents Back*, and the manager had already turned down numbers twice as good. Suddenly Stoltz cried, "This is just what we want!" He looked at his watch. "Miss Held will arrive in a few minutes. If she likes the song as well as I do, everything is set."

She came, she saw, she heard, and the Witmarks conquered. So did Paul West, for the song, though clever, had not inspired any too great hopes; in the normal course it would have sold a fair number of copies and been forgotten. Instead, it became a rage.

Music publishers, at that time, were cursed with a condition hard to cope with; they were forced to permit songs to be reproduced in their entirety in the supplements of the Sunday papers. This really meant giving away a fifty-cent piece of music for nothing. Because of the enormous circulation of the papers, and the printing of the music plainly enough so that it could be put on the piano and played, there was a considerable loss of legitimate sales. The publishers of the newspapers stopped at nothing to compel the music publishers to grant these permissions. When they wanted a song from a theatrical or musical production, they would strike the music publisher through the medium of the theatrical producer, by holding out the bait of one-page and two-page spreads of press matter, with pictures advertising the show in which the number was sung. The publisher, pressed by the producer, had to agree, else he might not get the publishing rights for the next production.

Matters got so bad that the song publishers went into conference and refused to release their best numbers to the newspapers. They were backed by the writers, who had felt the shrinkage in their royalties. In those days sheet music sold in large quantities. The theatrical producer was now "on the spot." He realized the injustice done to the song publishers and writers; at the same time, he did not want to lose valuable free advertising. So a compromise was reached whereby the newspapers would get a moderately good song, a comic, or a "business" number, one that normally was not expected to sell as much as the featured hits.

A newspaper publisher now wanted to reproduce *I Want Dem Presents Back,* and the Witmarks turned him down. He was persistent and offered all kinds of inducements. The Witmarks were adamant. Finally the publisher offered five hundred dollars for the use of the song; this, too, was turned down. And now, the *pièce de résistance.* One day Ziegfeld came up personally, carrying a big portfolio under his arm. The Witmarks were standing in his way, he cried, and thereupon opened the portfolio. There lay the most beautiful two-page spread, which could not have been bought at any price.

"See what you're making me lose if you don't give them permission!" he all but wept.

They told him that they had turned down five hundred dollars, and that if they gave the coveted permission they might as well kiss the sale of the song good-bye.

He said, "Maybe I can make it up to you some other way."

The Witmarks went into a huddle; they decided that they might as well be liberal about it, in the hopes that Ziegfeld would keep his promise. They told him that, in spite of having turned down five hundred dollars, they were going to give him the permission for nothing, so that he could get his double-spreads.

Six months later they had to sue Ziegfeld. It was over a bill for some song books that they had made for one of his companies. That was a way Ziggie had.

As a matter of fact, the Witmarks' experiences with Ziegfeld were most unfortunate. Some years after this episode, he produced "Mam'selle Napoleon," by Gustav Luders, composer of "King Dodo" and "The Prince of Pilsen."

The Witmarks represented Gustav Luders. The production of "Mam'selle Napoleon" was beautiful, and one of the most expensive ever made. The book, however, was bad, and in spite of the piece's other qualities it failed. What a dejected lot one saw around that Knickerbocker Theater! In order to show that they felt for Ziegfeld, Luders and Witmark agreed not to demand royalties until the production went on the road and business picked up. They made one stipulation, that a statement be sent them every week, even if it were not accompanied by a check.

The first week's statement was the only one ever received. After that, no response of any kind to letters, admonitions, or threats. Finally Isidore became so angry that he attached the box office in a far Western town. Erlanger, then the czar of the theatrical business, had his secretary call the publisher and request that he lift the ban. Isidore's reply was, "Tell Mr. Erlanger that I'll do so promptly if he will stand good for the claim."

Erlanger must have had his doubts, for word came back that he would not stand good. The Witmarks, however, collected the claim for Luders. All this trouble could have been saved if Ziegfeld had possessed a sense of obligation. But that was a way that Ziggy *didn't* have.

CHAPTER VIII

PIONEERS

1. Ragtime—Ben Harney—Max Hoffman

*S*OMETIME in the middle of the Nineties a performer by the name of Ben Harney came to New York from Louisville. He was to appear at Tony Pastor's with his colored "stooge," Strap Hill. There was another reason for his coming to Gotham. Somewhere in his portfolio was a collection of music sheets that he called his *Ragtime Instructor*. Harney had already written a couple of songs that had taken the public by storm: *You've Been A Good Old Wagon But You Done Broke Down* and, especially, *Mr. Johnson, Turn Me Loose*. That portfolio, however, bespoke a loftier ambition. Harney was not content to exploit the new craze of ragtime; he had the instinct of the codifier. He wanted to trap the theory behind the fact, and to set it down as a method that others could learn.

Harney, one of the first of the ragtime pianists, quickly became a New York fad. His piano act—in addition to Strap Hill, there was a girl—had the touch of the unique, and those who remember the sensation caused by the earliest jazz-pianists will imagine the furore created by Ben Harney's ragging of the scale. He was an early and an important predecessor of Zez Confrey, composer of *Ragging The Scale*.

152

PIONEERS

Ben Harney had the huskiest voice most people had ever heard in a human being, and this quality made his voice just right for ragtime singing. It had queer breaks in it that affected the words as well as the music. Broadly speaking, he might even be called the first of the crooners. He would sustain certain notes, for special effect, to extravagant, breathtaking lengths; others he would break in a way that he alone could manage.

The Witmarks became interested in the songs that he had already brought out through another publisher. The *Ragtime Instructor* was precisely the kind of novelty they were always looking for. At first they were dubious as to how authentic Harney's authorship of the songs and the *Instructor* might be. He had referred them to certain people in his native city of Louisville.

The matter was important, for this was something new under the musical sun. Isidore, therefore, decided to conduct the investigation personally, and took the train for Louisville, proceeding from that city to Evansville, Indiana, to interview various musical folk and dealers. They all knew Ben Harney, and testified that he had written every note he had claimed as his own.

There was, for example, Mr. John Biller, musical director of Macauley's Theater in Louisville. He had transcribed the tune, *You've Been A Good Old Wagon, But You Done Broke Down*. It had been published, but so small was its success that when, two years later, Harney returned to Louisville with *Mr. Johnson, Turn Me Loose*, the publisher turned the composer loose. Harney had carried that song with him for two years. In 1895 he joined a minstrel troupe; part of his act was to sing his new song and to do his "stick dance" specialty. From this time, because of the hit made by the *Johnson* song in the minstrel show, dates the real interest of American publishers in ragtime.

From this time, too, dated the claim of other writers to the authorship of *Mr. Johnson*—a claim that Isidore's trip to Louisville definitely settled in favor of Ben Harney.

Here was an entirely new type of what was then called a

coon song. The Witmarks took over his two hits. May Irwin, whose singing of *The Bully Song* had already established her as one of the first of the coon shouters, incorporated his new pieces on her program.

Later, when Harney went to Chicago, he wrote and they published his *The Cake-Walk In The Sky. There* was a song! It was the first to be provided with a refrain of ragtime words. That is, the words themselves, independent of musical setting, were in the new zigzag rhythms and set a style for interpolated patter. The innovation, by the way, had been worked out by brother Frank, who was at this time in charge of the Chicago office.

The original lyric of *The Cake-Walk In The Sky* was as follows:

> Put a smile on each face, ev'ry coon now take your place,
> And then away they went, all on pleasures bent,
> The harps were a-ringin', in ragtime they were singing,
> And they all bowed down to the king of coons
> Who taught the cake-walk in the sky.

Here is Frank's raggy version of the same words:

Pugut agey smigule ogon egeache fagace evvery cagoon tagake yougora plagace,
Agan wagay theygay wagant ogon plagasure begant
Wigith hargarps reginging gin ragag tigime theygay werger saginging
Agan theygay agaul bogowd dogon togo thege kingying agove cagoons
Whogo tagot thege cagake wagauke gin thege skigi.

The Witmark Monthly—of which more anon—for August, 1899, was to salute Harney as "the originator of ragtime music." The expression was still new at the turn of the century. *The Saturday Evening Post* quoted Secretary of State John Hay as saying, "These negotiations on the Alaska boundary question are being carried on in ragtime. I answer their propositions in twenty-four hours and they answer mine in twenty-four days."

Harney, who was but twenty-seven at this time, consistently claimed to be the originator of the new musical style. In addition to such of his new songs as *If You Got Any Sense You'll Go, I Love My Little Honey, Tell It To Me,* and *The Black Man's Kissing Bug,* his performances included the "ragging" of such popular classics as Mendelssohn's *Spring Song,* Rubinstein's *Melody In F,* and the *Intermezzo* from Mascagni's "Cavalleria Rusticana," which he would first play in their orthodox form. The effect was startling.

The same monthly for August, 1899, used a word that threatens, at the moment, to supplant the noun and adjective, jazz. Describing ragtime, Isidore wrote, "According to the best authorities, with whom Mr. Harney perfectly agrees, ragtime means dance time, and takes its imitation steps from Spanish music, or rather from Mexico . . . being nothing but syncopated consecutive music, either in treble or bass, followed by regular time in one hand. The change of accent in the accompaniment is kept up continually in the same way as the beat of a snare drum. There is a 'swing' about it that holds even the most cultivated ear."

The quotation marks around the word "swing" indicate its novelty as both word and musical method in 1899. Ragtime, jazz and swing, though they differ subtly or obviously in one respect or another, are linked by a liberated conception of rhythm. They are free in the very sense that verse, among the new poets of the 1920's, was free, except that, from the nature of verse, poetry did not have to observe the regularity of a bar-line, as music does. Modernist music, for that matter, eventually abolished the bar-line.

2. Bill Devere—Temptations

The firm was not interested in publishing anything but music, though now and again it was persuaded to take a flier in some other field. One of its earliest ventures proved to be one of its last. In 1897 it brought out a collection of verse entitled *Jim Marshall's New Pianner And Other Western Stories*, by William Devere. Maybe it was the piano in the title that provided the link for a music firm. The boys had been taken by the poems, and they had long been devoted to the author. They believed that business and sentiment, for all that has been said to the contrary, could mix. They never found reason, during the fifty years of their activity, to change this attitude of mind.

The little volume had a satisfactory sale. What particularly gratified the boys, however, was that they had been able to preserve what they considered to be some delightful verse-tales of life in the West.

Bill Devere was a character. He was a typical Westerner, much more than six feet tall, and powerful when once he swung into action. He was a cousin of the redoubtable James boys, and something of the misplaced courage that had turned Jesse and Frank into bandits flowed in his own veins and found a more social outlet. Yet he had several notches in his own gun, carried over from the "hey-rube" days of the circus. Paradoxically, too, he was a soft-hearted fellow, and made the best possible reciter of his own little pathetic poems. To hear him declaim *You're Just Like Your Mother, Mandy, Must Allus Hev Yer Way*, was an experience. In its modest sphere this was a classic. For a time he enjoyed something akin to fame for his *Walk, Damn You, Walk, Beautiful Snow Flies In Your Face Wherever You Go, He Can— Like Kelly Can, No Opening—Write Again* (the tale of a theatrical agent), and *Two Little Busted Shoes*. These were all reprinted in *Jim Marshall's New Pianner*.

Bill Devere had a way of his with everything, even the naming of his three daughters. No family Bible, or name lists, for him! If a girl was born in Denver, Denver was her name; if in New York, Yorke; and he never had to wonder where on his travels daughter Frisco had first seen daylight. Bill even achieved the distinction of dramatization. For it was his character that

PIONEERS

Charlie Hoyt wrote into his comedy, "A Black Sheep," in which Devere was pictured as the editor of the *Tombstone Gazette*. To cap it all, Hoyt had the part of the editor played by Devere. "New York is the Tombstone of the East," was his big line. It is not every actor who can play himself!

Bill wrote himself into the history of Denver and more than one other Western town. He deserves to be better remembered. He had in him the pioneering strain that we associate historically with the heroic builders of the West.

There were temptations a-plenty to leave the chosen field and take a flyer at "easy money." It was not always easy to resist. One week in 1897 the Witmark firm virtually passed up a profit of 2000 per cent, owing to its determination not to be sidetracked.

The Freundschaft Club, one of the first German-American social organizations, was giving its first amateur production in English. A rebellion on the part of the younger members had been responsible for the innovation, and Isidore, through his friend Sol Wolerstein, had been called in to do the coaching. There was too little talent for an elaborate review at that time; besides, Isidore was all for minstrel shows, and a minstrel show this became. Isidore wrote, composed, and directed the next two reviews, equally elaborate, of the Freundschaft Entertainers, which was the name that the group adopted. The productions were entitled "The Borough of Manhattan" and "At Home And Abroad." The organization today is known as the Metropolis Club.

Among the participants in the 1897 minstrel show was a young fellow named Walter Content, younger brother of Harry Content, of the well-known Stock Exchange firm. Walter and Isidore had become friendly; so it was not surprising when one Monday morning he called the publisher on the telephone and said, "Isidore, send me down $500 and I'll turn you in $10,000 by the end of the week. There are big doings down here, and I'm thinking of a few of my pals."

157

Knowing Walter to be no flighty dreamer, and knowing also that his house was one of the best-informed in the Street, Isidore took it for granted that what he said was in good faith. At the same time, he hesitated and asked if it would be O.K. to give his answer in the morning.

"All right, Isidore," answered Content. "There's nothing in it for me, but it's an opportunity."

Isidore immediately went into conference with his brothers. They did not deliberate long. They were doing very well in their business, and it was an unwritten law that nothing was to divert them from it. They were afraid that, with such an unusual start in the market, they might become so deeply absorbed in the adventure that in the end the sideshow would dominate to the detriment of the "big tent." So, in spite of the tempting inducement, they decided to decline.

Next morning Isidore called up Walter Content, thanked him profusely, and asked, "Walter, what hospital do you want me to send that $500 to?"

"What do you mean?"

"We're so devoted to our business, we're afraid that such a wonderful opportunity might start us on the wrong track, and your $10,000 might cost us our business; so we're taking no chances."

"I never heard such a thing in my life," declared Walter. "But I admire your stand. Only—watch the papers at the end of the week."

They did—and found that everything he had predicted came true.

"The Borough of Manhattan" was a full-sized "original operatic comedy" in three acts. It had a dozen principals, a dozen "saleswomen of Reuben Fly's Mammoth Bazaar," a male chorus, a "zobo" band, a brass band, and twenty musical numbers. In the cast, as Favorita Scintilla, "a celebrated actress," was "Sis" Witmark, who shared two of the numbers (*The Borough of Man-*

158

hattan; Just a Gentle Touch) and gave a character interpolation, *Since Cousin Susan's Home From School.* The dress rehearsal was given on February 25, 1898, and was produced on the following evening February 26th. "At Home and Abroad" was produced on March 18, 1899. It was in two acts, but equally ambitious, listing twenty-four numbers.

The year of the Freundschaft Club's minstrel show (1897) had been signalized also by Isidore Witmark's "Miss Columbia," an "original operatic review" in two acts, done for the Columbia Club. In this production "Sis"—she was Frankie Witmark on the program—gave her hilarious version of *Sister Mary Jane's Top Note.* "Miss Columbia" was one of the first entertainments of its kind, amateur or professional, a pretentious affair, having had, for example, twelve sopranos who started a finale on high B flat. It vied, indeed, with the Passing Show revues that were being presented professionally at the New York Casino at that time.

3. Julie in the Movies—Early Disc Recordings

The Witmarks, with their pioneering instinct, were in at the beginning of the phonograph, the movies and in time, the talkies. Julie was part of one of the earliest moving-picture features long before it was discovered that there was money in them thar reels— before the public had developed a taste for cinematic entertainment beyond the most elementary variety. The movies of the early days, just before and after the Spanish-American War, resembled the later developments in one respect, they moved. A fire engine responding to an alarm; a train arriving at a station; a kiss, as imprinted upon the ample cheek of May Irwin; scenes out of the conflict in Cuba, reeled off in a department store as an attraction to customers . . . such was the screen fare in the late Nineties.

In 1896, Julie signed a contract for a special six-week engagement with the Loie Fuller tour. Miss Fuller, an American girl who had made a success abroad, had introduced the famous "Serpentine Dance" with electrical mirror effects. She made the American tour traveling in her own car and with her own company, who, as they were playing two towns a day, lived in the car. It was a flying trip, and was a successful one. Besides Julie, other outstanding members of the company were Willis P. Sweatnam, the minstrel comedian, and Fanny Wentworth, piano monologist, the "female Grossmith." Who of the present generation knows the Grossmith of *Piano and I?* Or the Grossmith who created so many of the comic rôles in the Gilbert and Sullivan operettas?

In August, 1897, Julie was appearing in the musical comedy, "The Good Mr. Best," produced by William Harris at the old Garrick Theater at Thirty-fifth Street, off Sixth Avenue. There was an excellent cast, and it may easily be imagined that the introduction of a movie into the action was regarded as the height of novelty.

This particular movie scene, in its rudimentary way, was almost a forecast of such television scenes as graced the action of the Charlie Chaplin film "Modern Times." At the right of the stage, toward the back, was a small screen. At the left was a series of buttons, which, when pressed, would cause to appear upon the screen an image of what was going on in that room of the house which the particular button controlled. Here, long before talk of television and in the very infancy of the movies, were the movies being used to forecast a development that is still in the pre-commercial stage. It was all very primitive, and when the husband, wishing to know what was going on in the room of his wife, pressed the button, it was a crude image that appeared.

The movies in which Julie figured had been taken in New York on the roof of a downtown building, especially for the comedy. While a number of ludicrous situations had been evolved, and the novelty of the idea was indisputable, the musical piece itself did not prove a great success.

Strangely enough, too, Julie, shortly after the experiment in

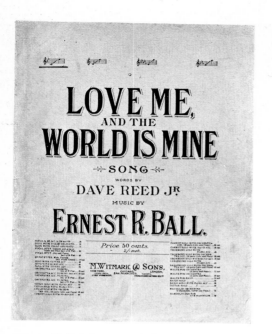

Ernie Balls' first smash hit. It was translated into almost every principal language.

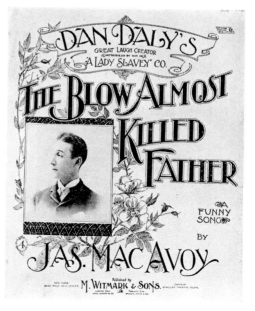

A song that created a catch line.

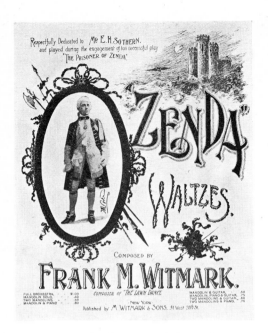

Original title page of the waltz
sensation of its day.

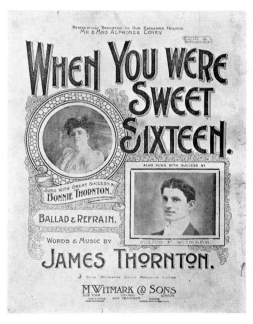

Original title page of James Thornton's
ballad hit, which is still heard
occasionally today.

"The Good Mr. Best," was making phonograph records in disc form, at a time, late in 1898, when the cylinder record was still a novelty. And he was doing it in coöperation with Dr. Emil Berliner whose name looms so large in the perfection of the phonograph. This was before Berliner sold out to the Victor Company. The actual recording was done, under Berliner's supervision, by Calvin G. Child, who was later to direct the recordings of the renowned artists assembled by the Victor Company. The discs do not appear to have been made with commercial exploitation in mind; in fact, judging from some of the scratchings that are still legible upon them, they were made as much in jest as in any other spirit.

Three records remain. Number 1 bears the name of E. Berliner, and the gramophone patent dates, May 8, 1887; May 15, 1887; May 6, 1890; Feb. 19, 1895; Oct. 29, 1895. "Other patents applied for." The legend appears to be rubber-stamped. Scratched in Julie's own hand is the following: *When You Ain't Got No Money, Well, You Needn't Come Around.* Sung by Julius P. Witmark. Accompanied by the boy pianist, Mr. John W. Bratton. Nov. 11, 1898. The second disc, under the same patent dates bears in Julie's handwriting, *"Just One Gal,* Sung by Julius P. Witmark, Nov. 11, '98." There is no date on the third, but it bears, after the patent dates, a typewritten label, *"Mammy's Little Pumpkin Colored Coons,* sung by J. P. W."

The recordings were poor, as the system of voice reproduction was still far from perfect. Owing to a peculiarity of the unperfected acoustical method of recording, the poorer voices registered best, and the best voices registered worst. This proved to be a boon for such lucky fellows as George Gaskin who made a fortune out of his specially adapted voice. There are analogous situations even today in the movie world, where certain beautiful faces somehow fail to screen well, while faces of scant interest off stage are transformed, by the skill of make-up men and photographers, into visions of glamour.

FROM RAGTIME TO SWINGTIME

Gaskin was an ordinary minstrel singer, a tenor with one of the vibrant, nasal voices ideally suited to the limitations of phonograph recording in the late Nineties. Master records, from which any desired number of pressings could be made, were unknown at that stage of the business. If any large quantity of records were required, the singer had to stand before the recorder all day long, singing his song with wearying repetition. Anything like uniformity of product was out of the question. A record made at ten o'clock in the morning was altogether different from one made at three in the afternoon. It was great going for the favorite singer, until new methods of duplication were introduced.

Those who recall the days of the cylindrical records, can still hear in memory the tinny renditions that poured forth from the horns attached to the mechanism; the penny machines, in the arcade shops, with the ear-tubes that were later to return with the first radios in the guise of ear-phones, and transmit renditions that were as primitive, in their electrical way, as the rasping delights of the first phonographs.

The glamour of those arcades! You put a nickel in the slot, and a mechanical piano thumped out the latest tunes. You put a nickel in another slot—later the price sank to a cent—and turned a crank as you watched a movie whirl by under a metal thumb that seemed to flip the pictures into action. This was known as the Mutascope, or Kinetoscope. It is something to have grown up with these various inventions, rather than to walk unawed, hypercritically expectant, into a cinema palace that has risen overnight as if at the rub of Aladdin's lamp.

The same simplicity, even naïveté, that characterized these early ventures into motion-picture photography, into early gramophone recording, and into the mysteries of radio, characterized the songs of the day also. For they were part of the same era, expressive of the same groping after greater achievement. As the convention now has it, the gay Nineties appear rather as the unsophisticated Nineties. They are "dated" as definitely as prints

162

PIONEERS

by Currier and Ives, and their various manifestations are consciously "collected" and hung upon the walls of our remembrance even as those prints of country life and conflagration, seasons and sentiment of a still earlier generation.

163

CHAPTER IX

SOME POPULAR OLD TIMERS

1. *Orchestra Leaders and Arrangers*

THERE were marvelous orchestras in the Nineties that could compare with the brilliant aggregations of today. Not for technical virtuosity, perhaps, for there is many a jazz band, especially among the top-notchers, that boasts members who could take their places in a symphony orchestra. In fact, it might be harder for the symphonic player to change places with his expert jazz brother than for the latter to accommodate himself to the more serious organization.

Among the delights of the variety performer in the Nineties was Tommy Hindley's Orchestra of Miner's Bowery Theater. Hindley and his men were eventually promoted to what was the finest playhouse in town, Miner's Fifth Avenue, at Broadway and Twenty-eighth Street.

He had a rival in Bob Recker, leader of the London Theater Orchestra. This band was so well trained that it could all but do the impossible. For example, at a rehearsal for one of the numerous Sunday night benefits, the Recker orchestra played. During the course of the rehearsal, a singer came down stage and said, "Bob, I've forgotten my music, and it's too far to go and get it and return in time. What shall I do?"

"Hum your song," said Bob, nonchalantly.

The performer hummed the song, and Bob, almost simultaneously, followed on his violin. Then Bob, this time by himself, played the tune through to his men.

"All together now, boys!" he directed. "In E-flat."

And the orchestra then and there went through the piece in full arrangement, as if reading it from notes.

The performer was delighted. "Fine, Bob! But it's just a little too low."

Too low? That was a minor matter for Bob and his men. "Once again, boys. In F." And this time they went through the piece as if they had rehearsed it for a week.

Today arranging is a highly specialized art. There are specialists in "hot" or "sweet" arrangements; there are men who are expert in writing connecting passages—modulations or transitions from one mood or key or style to another. Orchestras maintain their own staff of arrangers. As a result, even the non-musical public has developed a preference for one type of orchestration over another, and a far keener sense of discrimination than was common in the gay—but not too esthetic—Nineties.

Yet it was in the Nineties that this skill in popular arrangement arose, as a natural accompaniment to the new, jagged rhythms.

In the early days most orchestral arrangements of songs were merely accompaniments for singers, with hardly any attempt to introduce a creative element. For such arrangements the Witmarks, when they started, paid Ned Straight or Paul Ritter, whose headquarters were at Harding's, on the Bowery, seventy-five cents, or at most a dollar, for ten parts. Paul Ritter, especially, did a lot of work for the firm in the beginning. A little Italian named Vitozzi made a ten-part arrangement for the same price and also did a lot of copying. The man who at this time did most of the piano arranging for the song publishers was Charles Pratt, one of the outstanding concert accompanists of his day. He charged three dollars for an arrangement, and a piano arrangement by

Pratt was considered standard. He was, in fact, the "big shot" among arrangers until George Rosenberg and Frank W. Meacham came along; they made a "warmer" arrangement, that is, one with more color and special effects—a forerunner of the arrangements that have become "torrid." Their prices were three and five dollars for piano arrangements of an ordinary song. Meacham did not orchestrate; he specialized in piano arrangements, which he wrote only in lead pencil. He was also a composer, and has to his credit a number that his countrymen will never forget: *The American Patrol*. It has become, virtually, a folk-tune. Ironically he had written the *Patrol* for the piano, but it was made famous by bands and orchestras, for which he could not arrange it.

George Rosenberg was more prolific. He was an excellent orchestrator and his arrangements became so popular that he had a numerous patronage of professional singers as well as of publishers. George changed his name to Rosey, and under that name threatened, at one time, to become a rival of the famous John Philip Sousa, as he wrote a number of march hits. His two smashing successes were *The Honeymoon* and *Handicap* marches.

Bob Recker and Tom Hindley may also be regarded as outstanding arrangers of their day. They had a numerous following among the foremost vaudevillians. Their prices averaged three to five dollars for an orchestration, according to length and instrumentation. William Mullaly, noted director of his time, made special arrangements for which he charged ten dollars apiece; to possess a Mullaly arrangement was something to boast about.

An unknown who rose to sudden fame as an orchestrator was Frank Saddler. After being musical director for road shows, he worked in the Witmark Library—a later development—scoring, among other things, orchestrations at fifty cents a page. Before he died he was doing them for the prominent writers of musical comedies and operettas, scoring at five dollars a page and working day and night at that. Then Saddler introduced an entirely new school of orchestration, in fact he was the first modern in this field, and got some very striking effects.

Among the early arrangers for the Witmarks was Herman Hermanson, an orchestra leader who did many of their medleys; Al Pronier, a gifted Frenchman who made many piano parts; Occa, a band arranger who scored the famous battle scenes for Gilmore's Band; Charles Shattuck, noted minstrel basso, who did many of the vocal arrangements for various publishers and was the composer of the standard bass song, *A Hundred Fathoms Deep;* Julius Vogler, orchestra leader at Miner's Eighth Avenue Theater, who had a popular method of teaching harmony and counted many leading orchestra men among his pupils; Herbert Clarke, cornet soloist with Sousa, who was outstanding at arranging band numbers; Harold Sanford, for years Victor Herbert's right hand man in the orchestra of his many productions; Paul Steindorff, a Victor Herbert conductor who also led his own symphony orchestra; David Braham, composer of many Harrigan and Hart song hits; John McGhie, composer and director of several comic operas of twenty years ago; William Schaeffer, lieutenant of Gustav Luders and director of his works; William T. Francis, who directed, among others, musical works for Charles Frohman; John Stromberg, composer of the Weber and Fields' song successes; George May, who presided over the orchestra at Hammerstein's Victoria from its opening to its close; and many others including Arthur Weld, Selli Simonson, Augustus Barrett, Harry Sator, Herman Berl, Anthony Heindl, Paul Schindler, Anthony Reiff, and Victor Baravalle.

William Spielter, son of the musical savant, Herman Spielter, whose *Manual of Harmony* is famous, came to the Witmarks as a youngster and was with them seven years. He joined the Witmark Music Library in 1918 as arranger and assistant librarian, and developed into a prominent composer in the radio and cinema fields.

Exclusively engaged by the Witmarks on a salary was George

Trinkaus, a versatile man, arranging for piano, orchestra, grand orchestra, voices in every combination, and all solo instruments. He was with the house for many years and was one arranger who changed with the times. He became a favorite of Victor Herbert's, under whose supervision he arranged many of Victor's numbers for publication. The endorsement of Herbert was enough to stamp anyone as an excellent musician.

William Christopher O'Hare was another salaried arranger who did excellent work. He specialized in medley arrangements of popular songs for orchestra and band, and in later years devoted himself almost exclusively to vocal and choral arrangements. Being an organist he was especially adapted to this kind of work. A southerner, from Shreveport, Louisiana, he was also a composer of quaint numbers. His outstanding success in this line was a southern interlude known as *Levée Revels*.

Julian Andino was another staff writer. A Puerto Rican by birth, he wrote arrangements with a slightly West-Indian flavor. He made the piano scores for a number of Ernest R. Ball's song hits, particularly *Love Me And The World Is Mine* and *Till The Sands Of The Desert Grow Cold*.

When in August, 1898, Victor Herbert came to the Witmarks he brought with him a fine musician, Otto Langey. He would allow no one else to do the orchestra selections and dance arrangements of his works. Langey received seventy-five dollars for a medley arrangement, which was the highest price the Witmarks had paid an arranger up to that time. The price of his other arrangements was proportionately high. He was a musician in the Herbert class, and a composer of repute; his *Mexican Serenade* was world-famed.

The price of arrangements graduated up to about fifteen dollars. A new arranging star appeared on the horizon, David Kaplan, who asked thirty-five dollars for his dance arrangements, and got it. He was a free lance and was a busy man while his vogue lasted. In later years he was the musical director, arranger, and accompanist for the radio pioneers, Jones and Hare, the Happiness Boys. Carl Williams, an excellent musician, was also associated with the Witmarks and made many arrangements for them.

In the Witmarks' Chicago office they had three orchestrators who made their mark: Hilding Anderson, who became a prominent musical director; Gustav Luders, who made the original piano arrangement of *My Gal's A High-Born Lady* and who became one of our leading composers of musical comedy; and Max Hoffman, the husband of Gertrude Hoffman, the dancer, producer and creator of celebrated dance ensembles.

It was Max Hoffman who became famous as the first white man to make successfully the first rag arrangements. The work was begun in Chicago, which still echoed with the joyousness of the World's Fair of 1893. Additional refrains in the Frank Witmark style provided with rag accompaniments as developed by Max Hoffman, created a nation-wide stir.

Everybody was at his piano, "ragging the keys." The craze developed a special style of playing that today bears all the signs of its age, yet in its time was freighted with thrills. Examined now in the cold light of instrumental technique, it was simple enough in its fundamentals, and not nearly so complicated as jazz, its breaks, its cross-rhythms, and its off-accents would be. Yet jazz, as has been suggested, was a gradual and natural evolution from ragtime, and the pioneer pianists, arrangers, and writers of ragtime are all elder brothers of the present "jazz hounds," "swing cats," and "jam sessioners."

Before being engaged as musical director at the Olympic Theater, Chicago, a post that he occupied for six years, Max Hoffman served in a similar capacity for a number of front-rank travelling companies. As a composer, he began to specialize in ragtime novelties, of which *A Bunch of Rags, Dixie Queen* and *Rag Medley* proved to be outstanding. For these, the Witmarks paid him $25 apiece, and an additional $25 for each of the

169

orchestrations. They published the first rag arrangement he ever made, that of *All Coons Look Alike To Me*. He received $5 for the piano version and as much for the orchestration. The ordinary run of the orchestrations brought him a dollar and a half. This was the average price paid to arrangers in the Chicago office at the time. Hoffman at first arranged exclusively for the Witmark firm; gradually, however, he obtained nearly all the business of the New York publishers who opened up branches in Chicago for the vaudeville artists who appeared at the Olympic Theater under his baton. So great was the demand for his arrangements that he took to hiring for his orchestra only musicians who could make arrangements. In this way was he able to take care of all his orders.

It was about this time that Paul Dresser arrived in Chicago in the interest of Howley, Haviland & Dresser, then at the peak of its career as a music publishing firm. Dresser, who was popular as an actor, was also one of the outstanding song writers of his day. Besides *On the Banks Of The Wabash*, his hits were, *Here Lies An Actor*, *The Letter That Never Came*, *The Pardon Came Too Late*, *The Blue And The Gray*, *My Mother Told Me So*, *Just Tell Them That You Saw Me*, and *My Gal Sal*.

Like so many other popular songsters Paul could not write out his musical inspirations. It was only natural that he should send for Max Hoffman, when he wanted a tune taken down.

It is generally believed that Theodore Dreiser, brother of Paul Dresser, wrote the words to the chorus of *On The Banks Of The Wabash*. Dreiser himself, indeed, has told the story more than once, in magazine articles and in autobiographical writings. Yet, according to Max Hoffman, there is an error in this familiar account, and the words of that famous chorus are as much Paul Dresser's as the rest of the song. This, in Max's own words, is what really took place:

"I went to his room at the Auditorium Hotel, where instead of a piano there was a small folding camp organ, which Paul always carried with him. It was summer; all the windows were open and Paul was mulling over a melody that was practically in finished form. But he did not have the words. So he had me play the full chorus over and over again for at least two or three hours, while he was writing down words, changing a line here and a phrase there until at last the lyric suited him. He had a sort of dummy refrain, which he was studying; but by the time he finished what he was writing down to my playing it was an altogether different lyric.

"When Paul came to the line, 'Through the sycamores the candle lights were gleaming,' I was tremendously impressed. It struck me, at once, as one of the most poetic inspirations I had ever heard.

"I have always felt that Paul got the idea from glancing out of the window now and again as he wrote, and seeing the lights glimmering out on Lake Michigan. We spent many hours together that evening, and when Paul finished he asked me to make a piano part for publication at the earliest moment. I happened to have some music paper with me, and I wrote one right out, on the spot. This I mailed to Pat Howley, one of Dresser's partners, sending it to the New York Office at Thirty-second Street and Broadway. At Paul's request I also enclosed my bill.

"This piano part contained the lyric as Paul (and no one else) wrote it that night in my presence. The song was published precisely as I arranged it. They did not send proofs for me to read; the proofs were read in New York, to save time. During the whole evening we spent together, Paul made no mention of anyone's having helped him with the song.

"This is what I know of the writing of the song, *On The Banks Of The Wabash*."

The Frey brothers, Hugo and Otto, who afterward became important in this specialized field, also did some of the work at the Witmarks' Chicago office. Hugo Frey composed *Shakespearian Love, Havanola, Uncle Tom, Money Blues, Rocking The Boat*, and others.

The dancing craze that was at its height about twenty years ago necessitated an improvement in orchestrations. The many new dances required new styles of musical arranging, more entrancing than before, and this brought forward a new school of arrangers, whose revolutionary innovations had not been recognized until their opportunity had come, among them Joseph Nussbaum, Frank Skinner, and Archie Bleyer. The Witmarks were the first to recognize the new slant; they commissioned many dance arrangements from these men.

To Ferdie Grofé the Witmarks paid $450 for a waltz medley arrangement of the refrains, *Kiss Me Again, I'm Falling In Love With Someone*, and *When You're Away*, from Victor Herbert's "Mlle. Modiste," "Naughty Marietta," and "The Only Girl," respectively. Grofé made the price low for him as a concession because of his love of Herbert's music. In the old days fifty dollars would have been considered a good price. The radical change in orchestration made it necessary for most of the big houses to hire for their service exclusively one of the arrangers of the new school.

Arthur Lange had been signed up by Shapiro, Bernstein & Co., receiving $18,000 a year for his exclusive services, which consisted of two dance arrangements per week. The Witmarks were in the van. They looked around for the best that was available and decided on Louis Katzmann.

Katzmann had been doing excellent work, his arrangements were highly spoken of, and he had a splendid vehicle for the exploitation of his work, his own orchestra, The Anglo-Persians, prominent among the radio orchestras in its day.

The first arrangement made by Katzmann for the Witmarks was of a song entitled *Morning, Noon and Night*; it was in a style entirely new, even for the second decade of the 1900's, and did honor to the firm's publications. For the arrangement, $75 was paid. When Katzmann was engaged by the year, he received a contract at $10,000 per year for part time only. It was one of the highest compensations yet paid to a staff arranger. The Witmarks also engaged his orchestra for the try-out of the arrangements. They were the first publishers to do this and they found that it paid, for, in spite of the remarkable arrangements on which they could depend from this ace musician, there were always little changes to be made. Music on paper is one thing, and in performance it is another.

Katzmann's $10,000 annual salary ran for a three-year term. Out of these days Katzmann recalls other Witmark "firsts." The Witmarks were the first to print arrangements that featured saxophone parts and banjo guide parts; to add a xylophone part, and A and B violin parts; to engage dance orchestras for the try-outs of the commercial dance arrangements, before the orchestrations were committed to print. "You were the first," wrote Katzmann, "to publish symphono-jazz, which trade-mark I registered." The first of these symphono-jazz arrangements was *Fate*, by Byron Gay. The Witmark pioneering in symphonic jazz thus fulfilled the implied prophecy in the early issue of *The Witmark Monthly*, from which will be quoted presently the lines about the ubiquity of ragtime.

The present era—the period of Ferdie Grofé, Russell Bennett, and their compeers—has taken popular arranging definitely into the "symphonic" class.

2. Gus and Gene Salzer

When a musical production is contemplated, next to the stage producer and stars to be engaged, the most important personage is the musical director. That musical director is no ordinary man, for besides being the musical director he is a musical *producer*, doing for the music of the show what the stage director does for the book. He is really a creator and an inventor. There were and are very few such musical producers and Gus Salzer was in that class. He was able to take a completely flat production and after two rehearsals animate it so that life virtually oozed from it and thereby turned hopeless failure into positive success. He was the white hope of many a composer who could safely leave his treasured work in Gus' hands, who, with his little tricks and nuances,

173

often brought such results that the composer did not recognize his own work. Gus produced musically a number of the Victor Herbert pieces and was much appreciated by this Maestro. He was a fine pianist, wrote a number of popular pieces for that instrument, specializing in novelties. The most popular among them being *Lords and Ladies, Snow Queen* and *Laces and Graces.* Gus married Anna Wilks, an ingenue soubrette of her day and left a boy, Edmond, who has inherited much of his father's musical talent. Gus produced—musically—over fifty Broadway successes that are part of America's Theatrical History. His managers were the best—among them, Charles Frohman, Florenz Ziegfeld, George Cohan, Henry Savage, Joseph Gaites, and Cohan & Harris. He died May 22, 1934.

Gus' younger brother, Gene, is also a musical producer (one of the few left) and is in great demand. He goes in for lighter works—the dance musical shows—and has many to his credit, among them "The Gay Divorcee," "On Your Toes," "Babes In Arms," the Murray Anderson and Charlot Revues and at present he is conducting the big New York success "I Married An Angel." Both Salzers were lifelong friends of the Witmarks and produced many of the works they published.

3. William Loraine

William Loraine was one of the earliest writers connected with the House of Witmark. He is famous for having composed the intermezzo *Salome,* and the companion number, *Zomona.* His musical comedies included the "Filibuster," with John T. Wilson, and "Peggy From Paris" with George Ade, produced by Henry W. Savage, both of which were published by Witmarks. Loraine opened and managed a branch Witmark office in San Francisco. He was later director of some of the most prominent musical shows in America.

SOME POPULAR OLD TIMERS

4. *Charles Hambitzer*

Charles was a musical genius, he played every solo instrument in the orchestra, was a composer of great merit, was able to arrange in both the regular and the modernistic styles, and was a teacher of fine attainments. He numbered prominent musicians among his pupils, George Gershwin being one. Hambitzer was the son of a prominent musician and music publisher of Milwaukee. He was an outstanding member of the famous orchestra at the old Waldorf-Astoria under the direction of Joseph Knecht; and was a composer of operettas that were well received, among them "The Love Wager" for Fritzi Scheff, and "The Regular Girl" which he did in conjunction with Wynn Cortelyou, the son of the well-known statesman.

Charles Hambitzer's ending was tragic. In a fit of despondency he committed suicide in Central Park.

5. *Theodore Bendix*

Theodore Bendix came from a family of musicians. He had two brothers: Charles, the New England composer, and Max, one of the foremost American musicians, violin soloist, concertmaster, and director of orchestras including that of Theodore Thomas. Ted was as well known in the lighter sphere of music. He was director of many musical shows, conducted numerous theater orchestras, and had a flair for writing beautiful salon music. His *Hungarian Romance, Longing, In Meadowland,* and *Silly Billy* were representative works. Perhaps his best-known characteristique was *In Beauty's Bower.* Bendix was special orchestral arranger of instrumental novelties for the Witmarks for years.

6. *The Witmark Monthly*

New Year's of 1898—a memorable year for more reasons than one—the firm celebrated with the establishment of *The Wit-*

FROM RAGTIME TO SWINGTIME

mark Monthly, one of the first house organs to be published by a popular-music firm. Its inaugural issue was of four small folio pages, but the contents, under the editorship of the eldest brother, suggested that the company offices were indeed the beehive of industry that served as the symbol on the masthead.

The first picture to appear in the *Monthly* was that of Chauncey Olcott. "When he produced 'Minstrel of Clare,' his *Home Song* and *Love Remains The Same* were in big demand," wrote the editor, "and even today they are selling. His latest and greatest success, 'Sweet Inniscara,' tests the capacity wherever he plays, and the song gems introduced, *Kate O'Donoghue, Sweet Inniscarra,* Olcott's *Fly Song,* and *Old Fashioned Mother* (all his own compositions) are the biggest kind of hits."

Fred Solomon appears, not as an employee of the Witmarks, but as an actor scoring a hit as the disappointed composer in Rice's "new production 'The Ballet Girl' "; though the part was small, Solomon's success was enough to warrant an offer from George Edwardes, who desired him as leading comedian for his famous Gaiety Theater, London.

" 'Rag Time' is now such a craze," comments the editor on page 3, "that one can almost expect to hear it at a grand concert during the rendition of a Beethoven *Sonata.* Already some of Strauss' favorite waltzes have been paraphrased, or shall we say distorted, in this manner, and they have caused no end of amusement. It's 'ragtime' here and 'ragtime' there, and it is getting to be that 'all "ragtime" sounds alike to me.' "

This, in its way, shows the essential likeness, beneath the differences, of ragtime and jazz. Jazz, in its beginnings, was just such a craze as ragtime, only that to jagged rhythms it added piquancies of tone color, instrumentation, special effects. Just as Strauss was paraphrased, so in time were all the classics "jazzified," not always to the edification of the musically fastidious. As for expecting to hear ragtime at a grand concert, side by side with Beethoven, this is precisely what has happened with jazz,

176

which has appeared in the symphony halls of the nation with the revered masters of the tonal art. Indeed, shortly before the appearance of this editorial squib, no less sober a symphonist than Brahms—who certainly knew his syncopated Hungarian rhythms —was writing to a friend that the American ragtime interested him tremendously, and that he was thinking of turning it to personal use. This helps to do away with the argument, frequently heard in the late Nineties, that ragtime was not truly an example of musical Americana, and that it derived from the gypsy music of Spain and Hungary. Certainly if it derived from such sources alone it would hardly have struck the keen ear of Brahms as a new quality deserving of investigation and application!

Among the songs listed as popular at the time are a vocal version of the *Zenda Waltzes*, being sung at Weber and Fields' Music Hall by Gertrude Mansfield; Ben Harney's *I Love My Little Honey*; and Jefferson's *My Coal Black Lady*, as sung by Irene Franklin with the animated song sheet.

Even as early as this—see *Witmark Monthly* for February, 1898—there were pre-Tin-Pan-Alley sobs for the neglected father. "Mother has been praised in all sorts of songs for centuries," said the late lamented J. W. Kelly. "No one seems to think it worth while to bother with sentimental songs about the old man." How recently was it that Father's Day was instituted to soothe a like oversight of the same paternal personality? To be sure, there were a few daddy songs: *Father, Dear Father, Come Home With Me Now*, and *The Old Man's Drunk Again*. "But why," asked Kelly, "don't somebody reach into the soup pot and place Papa on the pinnacle of fame by writing a dacent song about him?"

"Hattie Starr," commented the *Dramatic Mirror*, from which the item was quoted, "must have been moved by the Rolling Mill Man's appeal, for she has recently composed no less than half a dozen ditties in which Dad's goodness and virtues are extolled. One of the song, *You're So Good, Daddy*, has been sung throughout the civilized world." But much good it did to dear old Dad!

177

Years and years later, what was the song that that same civilized world would be singing?

Everybody Works But Father . . .

It is difficult to rehabilitate the old man in Tin Pan Alley!

The same issue contains a rare photograph of Ford and Bratton; they look here as much like two members of a college faculty as two writers of popular ditties. And Jim Marshall's *New Pianner* is endorsed, in a generous letter, by no less a versifier than Eugene Field.

On February 15, 1898, the battleship *Maine* was blown up, and Spanish treachery was suspected. The March issue of the *Monthly* preserved an uncommonly calm attitude, in the face of threatened war. It was for war, if necessary, but was war necessary? Was it not wiser to stretch a point, and to arbitrate the matter? "War in its most successful phases cannot alleviate the gloom of thousands of homes, cannot heal the wounds of mothers' broken hearts."

More in consonance with the purposes of the house organ was the announcement of the "automatic self-playing banjo." Business must have been good, for the *Monthly* was increased to eight pages.

The big news of the month, however, was the announcement that sometime near May 1st the firm of M. Witmark & Sons, after five years in their present quarters, would remove to 8 West Twenty-ninth Street, there occupying a building all its own, the first so to be occupied by a firm specializing in popular music.

7. Hits of the Nineties

The lease at 49-51 West Twenty-eighth Street was about to expire, and, moreover, the Witmarks had begun to feel the need of new quarters. Business had been good, and was getting even better. The Witmark Music Library was demanding quarters of its own. With one exception—and an important exception, for it had been the inspiration for the Witmark venture—this Library was the only business of its kind in the world. Fifteen years before, at almost the moment in which the Witmark children were embarking upon their career, the Tams Music Library had been organized. It became one of the ambitions of the Witmarks to overtake this institution, despite the handicap of a fifteen years' start.

Success seemed to be in the air for the expanding firm. Ford and Bratton's *I Love You In The Same Old Way* was selling extensively; so was Kennett and Udall's hit, *Just As The Sun Went Down*, introduced and sung on tour by the popular counter-tenor, Richard J. José. The same team had written *Stay In Your Own Back Yard, Zizzy Ze Zum Zum*, and that smash hit of two continents, *Just One Girl*. For a while, it seemed almost as if the world were singing Just One Song. In the German-speaking countries it was known as *Du Mein Girl*.

Almost every number the firm had published at 49-51 West Twenty-eighth turned out to be a hit. There were the Dillon Brothers' *Put Me Off At Buffalo*; Francis Bryant's *Be Good, Be Good, My Father Said*; Jim McAvoy's *The Blow Almost Killed Father*, a success with Dan Daly; Jim Thornton's *When You Were Sweet Sixteen*; Ernest Hogan's *All Coons Look Alike To Me*; Dennis Mackin's *We Were Simply Friends*; Ford and Bratton's march songs, *Henrietta, Have You Met Her*, and *Isabelle*; Paul West's *I Want Dem Presents Back*; Billy Cortwright's *Johnny, My Old Friend John*; Horwitz and Bower's *Because, Always*, and *Lucky Jim*; Dunbar and Cook's *Darktown Is Out Tonight*; John T. Kelly's *I Long To See The Girl I Left Behind*; Sloane's *When You Ain't Got No Money, You Needn't Come Around*, and Ben Harney's *Mr. Johnson, Turn Me Loose*, and *You Been a Good Old Wagon But You Done Broke Down*.

Overhead, under the stimulus of these hits, had been increased considerably. Why not an entire building, for the Witmarks? The

179

boys shopped around and found a brownstone residence at 8 West Twenty-ninth Street which had been converted by its owner, Henry C. Eno, a New York realtor, into a business building.

The five years at 49-51 West Twenty-eighth Street had witnessed the publication of a number of other important hits. There had been, from Dave Marion, *Her Eyes Don't Shine Like Diamonds*. It was the subject of numerous parodies, not always reverent to the ocular beauties of womankind.

Ford and Bratton had also signed *Only Me, The Sunshine of Paradise Alley*, and *I Love You In The Same Old Way*. There was a setting, by Gottschalk, of Ella Wheeler Wilcox's,
"Laugh and the world laughs with you,
Weep and you weep alone."

It was in this period, beginning with Olcott's *Home Song*, in 1896, that Witmarks became the publishers of the beloved Irish minstrel whom Julie had known since the days of 1883. And who hasn't heard, even if he hasn't tried to make the perilous descent to that sea-bottom B-flat, Lamb and Petrie's *Asleep in the Deep?* Or Hillman and Perrin's *Mammy's Little Pumpkin-Colored Coon?*

As important as anything on the list was Barney Fagan's ragtime classic, *My Gal Is A High Born Lady*. Fagan, it will be recalled, was a member of the minstrel troupe in which Julie had met Chauncey Olcott; Fagan, the grand old man of minstrelsy and ragtime. *There* was a tune! It was as big a success in its own day and as epochal as *Alexander's Ragtime Band* after Irving Berlin had written and composed it in 1911. In fact, there were more ragtime classics in 1895 than sixteen years later. Fagan was an original spirit, and those who cherished an affection for the man and his times were anticipating the completion of his memoirs, which he was writing in the seclusion of the Percy Williams Home For Actors at Islip, Long Island, when he recently passed away. He wrote and sang a long list of tunes. He had one success, *When The Robins Nest Again*, with which he was never credited, for he had sold the rights, including authorship, for a small sum to Frank Howard, the minstrel tenor. He originated, too, the military extravaganza, "Phantom Guards" which caused a sensation not only in the United States but in England. He was invited to the royal box on the opening night and was complimented by King Edward VII. Fagan was married to Henrietta Byron, his partner in vaudeville, in 1898.

8. Louis and Paul Meyer

Louis and Paul Meyer were born in Paris, nephews of the great French publisher Calman Lévy who brought out the works of Alexandre Dumas, father and son, George Sand, Ludovic Halévy, Ernest Renan, Gyp, Octave Feuillet, Augier, and most of the great French writers. In their early life they lived in an artistic atmosphere. They came to this country in 1890 to join their father. They opened a French bookstore at 1130 Broadway, next to the famous Martin restaurant, after having been with Brentano's for several years where they had organized the foreign book department. Their store became the rendezvous of all French celebrities as well as the musical and stage folks. To it came Sarah Bernhardt, Coquelin, Melba, Calvé, Caruso, the de Reszke brothers, Eleonora Duse, Plançon; the great conductors Anton Seidl and Colonne; the painters, Chartran, de Madrazo, Forain, and so many others that it would take pages to name them all. One of the Meyers' departments was the sale of photographs of the celebrities. Their windows became a center of attraction, displaying the photographs of Lillian Russell, Ada Rehan, John Drew, David Warfield, Mary Mannering, Julia Marlowe, Edna May, Cissie Fitzgerald, Clara Lipman, and other popular artists.

At that time, everybody was collecting photographs of celebrities and this gave the Meyers the idea of publishing a magazine which they called *The Theatre*. It started very modestly and grew up to large proportions. From 1900 to 1931, it was one of the finest and most interesting publications the country ever had. It was modelled after the artistic European publications, printed on heavy coated paper with superb half-tone reproductions of photographs, most of them specially taken. They had obtained the full coöperation of photographers such as Falk, Dupont, Sarony, Byron, Schloss, and brought to the front Ira Hill, Evan Evans, Chidnoff, and many others. Each month the front cover, printed in lithography in eight and nine colors, represented an artist having obtained success. It was the first magazine that gave to America the new offset process in colors.

Unfortunately, with the advent of motion pictures and talkies, and refusing to abandon their ideals, *viz.* representing the stage, dramatic and musical, they were forced to stop publication, much to their regret, in 1931.

Paul Meyer was seen at opening nights accompanied by his charming wife. He became a member of the junior board of the Actors Fund of America, and was for several years president, called the prompter, of the Green Room Club.

Both brothers had been honored by the country of their birth and received the coveted order of Knight of the Legion of Honor.

9. The Klein Family

One of the most successful families in the theatrical business was that of Klein: Herman, the international critic; Alfred, the actor; Charles, the playwright; and Manuel, the musical director and composer. Herman, the music critic, died in London on March 10, 1934. He was the author of the book *Thirty Years of Musical Life in London* (1870-1900), which is dedicated to Señor Manuel Garcia, the illustrious singing teacher of the Nineteenth century, by "his grateful pupil." Herman Klein was one of the important men of music in England and had a tremendous influence in musical matters during the last three decades of the Nineteenth century. He was acquainted with all the great musical stars of his time, beginning with Jennie Lind and going down through all the list of musical names to the present.

Charles, the playwright, wrote some of the greatest successes of his day, including "The Third Degree." And the recent passing of Edmund Breese recalled his great hit "The Lion and the Mouse" in which Breese was featured; "The Music Master" and "The Auctioneer," both written for David Warfield; "El Capitan," which starred De Wolf Hopper.

At the height of Klein's fame in May, 1915, he went abroad with Charles Frohman, sailing on the *Lusitania,* on its fatal crossing. Isidore Witmark, among many, begged him not to go. It seems he had a quarrel with one of the prominent New York theatrical managers and he was determined to go, making a resolution that he would never return. He did not.

Alfred was the actor of the family and played many parts. The best known was in the successful operetta "Wang" in which De Wolf Hopper starred. Alfred Klein became ill during this run and passed on.

Charles Klein had a son named Philip, a fine fellow and talented in his own way. Upon the death of his father, he enlisted in the French army and was later transferred to the American army in France. Phil helped to organize one of New York's first motion picture companies. He was more inclined toward the managerial end and directed a number of stage successes, among them "Buddies," by George V. Hobart and B. C. Hilliam. He went to the Coast and became interested in motion pictures, in which he was a pioneer scenarist. Among his screen dramas, the best known was "Four Sons," which won the award of the Motion Picture Academy some years ago. He also wrote Shirley Temple's first starring vehicle, "Baby, Take a Bow." He was stricken with pneumonia while attending the San Diego Exposition in 1935, and died at the age of forty-six. Just before his death he completed the scenario of "Dante's Inferno."

Manuel Klein, the musical composer and director, was in his

own way a genius. When Isidore Witmark first knew him, he was a young man with a red beard, not knowing much about music. In a short time he acquired knowledge and a repertoire. Upon the opening of the New York Hippodrome, through Gus Edwards he obtained the position of musical director, and wrote the music and lyrics of the productions under the Thompson and Dundy management. On account of its size, the Hippodrome was hardly the place in which to introduce song successes; in spite of this Manny had at least one big hit out of every production.

Toward the end of the War, he was musical director of the Gaiety Theater, London, which the Germans were bombing at the time. One night, as he was leaving the theater, one of the principal comedians had stepped out before him just in time to be killed by a bomb. This and the loss of his brother on the *Lusitania* affected him so terribly that it worked on his mind and he did not survive for long.

CHAPTER X

1898: A PIVOTAL YEAR

1. Counter Irritant

THINGS started off swimmingly at the new offices at 8 West Twenty-ninth Street. The building had a businesslike exterior, more notable for its look of confident efficiency than for any esthetic qualities. Ten stone steps, with substantial guide-rails on either side, led to the first floor, beneath which, at the left of the steps, was a basement. The basement room housed the new Witmark Music Library. The wide doorway of the main entrance, flanked by brass signs on both posts, led to the office, which was almost visible through the wide show-window on the first floor. The middle of that window was emblazoned with a heraldic device: across a large shield, like a ribbon of honor, was painted "M W & Sons," while the family motto, "Success Is Work," decorated the bottom with a plain scroll. Rows of sheet music proclaimed the latest hits. Under the firm name, which formed a sort of projecting shield against the top story windows, floated an American flag. Nor was it at all inappropriate that the building should still look, thus transformed, half like a home.

Everything proceeded to the delight of the brothers until the outbreak of the Spanish-American War. Then came a cut in business so sharp that one could almost have seen the flashing drop of the guillotine. It was virtually a complete standstill, and nobody could understand the reason why. The brothers, out of their continuous conferences, at which the elephant's head must have wagged as desperately as their own, could devise nothing to start the ball rolling again. Jay especially—for he was the financial man of the combination—was becoming depressed.

With Jay growing daily more morose, Julius and Isidore determined that something must be done. After all, they felt, the world had not yet come to an end. They were comparatively well off. This was what the elder brothers must bring home to Jay. So Julie and Isidore began to read the newspapers with an eye single to the major catastrophes of the day, just to show Jay how really well off he was. If a ship were lost at sea, or a mine visited by disaster, or a train mangled by a wreck, they clipped the account and laid it on Jay's desk, without comment. Jay's breakfast became a harrowing register of national calamities. It began to look as if Julie and Isidore were succeeding in this fighting of fire with fire, until there came a day when bills had been arriving, an impromptu calamity not clipped from the morning paper. Together with them the cheerful brothers deposited on the desk of their knight of the doleful countenance a lugubrious account that seemed to have happened with timeliness. It was a goose-fleshy report of a group of unfortunates who had fallen into a vat of molten glass and been blown up by the explosion.

Too much medicine is as bad as too little. This time Jay, who had endured this barrage of misfortune as long as he could, blew up.

"Take the damned thing away!" he growled. "This doesn't pay *our* bills!"

But the end of the war was around the corner, and, close on its heels, the beginnings of a new prosperity. Indeed, the year 1898, which had been threatening to ruin the firm, carried it to new heights, and proved one of the banner years in the history of M. Witmark & Sons.

1898: A PIVOTAL YEAR

It was the year when the Witmark Music Library, already founded, definitely began its career; when *The Witmark Monthly*, first of the Tin Pan Alley House organs, was established; when the Minstrel Department really struck its stride; when Caro Roma, one of the foremost women composers of the country, aligned with the Witmarks and began a career that still is lustrous with folk-melody; when perhaps most significant of all, Victor Herbert —and how appropriate was that first name!—joined the Witmark list. And 1898 was perhaps the greatest single year Victor Herbert himself was to know.

With the end of the war in Cuba, business took a turn for the better that, in its irrational suddenness, paralleled the bad turn of a few months before.

It was in the Twenty-ninth Street headquarters that the Witmarks were to take over the famous numbers of Weber and Fields and carry their early association with George M. Cohan to new heights. So many hits would they send forth from this five-story home of song that five years hence they would again be looking for a larger building. So much for the premature melancholy of brother Jay!

2. *Weber and Fields*

The Witmarks had known Weber and Fields since boyhood, when they had appeared with them on a number of programs, but they did not become intimate until around 1896, when the Weber and Fields Music Hall opened. Julie was closest to the famous partners for he had appeared on many benefits with them and from time to time had met them on the road. Traveling friendships are lasting in the show business, and when Weber and Fields made their famous gala tour around the country Julie was taken along as their guest.

Weber and Fields went into the music publishing business when they started their Music Hall. But they realized that they were not organized for business and were too busy with their shows, so they sold out to the Witmarks for ten thousand dollars. The amount was large in 1898, but the Witmarks made money on the transaction because some good forthcoming numbers proved to be hits. In fact, the Weber and Fields' songs were an institution, like the Harrigan and Hart numbers which preceded them. Particularly was there an advance demand for anything that John Stromberg, Weber and Fields' famous composer-director, turned out, one after the other. Who of his generation will forget *Kiss Me, Honey, Do: (Dinah)*; *How I Love My Lu*; *The Pullman Porters Ball*; *Come Back, My Honey Boy, To Me*; *Ma Blushin' Rosie*; *When Chloe Sings A Song*; *I'm a Respectable Workin' Girl*; and *Come Down, Ma Evenin' Star*? They were all simple melodies with the simplest of harmonies, yet there was a virility in those songs that has kept them alive.

Stromberg had a sad end. He was found dead in July, 1902, just before a new Weber and Fields series, "Twirly Whirly," was opened—and his death was thought to have been suicide. The only thing found in his pockets was the manuscript of *Come Down, Ma Evenin' Star*, which he had just written for Lillian Russell.

When the new show was opened it was a gala occasion. Stromberg's place as director was taken by Billy Francis, a well-known conductor and writer on the Witmark list. Lillian Russell was at her best—until the introduction to *Come Down, Ma Evenin' Star* was played. She began to sing it, hesitated, then broke down, and *Come Down, Ma Evenin' Star* was not finished that night . . .

Stromberg wrote a popular success years before joining Weber and Fields—the song entitled *My Best Girl's A Corker*. Shortly before he died, Stromberg had laid out a realty development near Freeport, Long Island, which he named Stromberg Park and for which he had high hopes. The lay-out was unique as he named the streets and avenues after his associates at Weber and Fields' and other musical and theatrical friends. There were

Weber and Fields Avenue, Ross Fenton Avenue, Lillian Russell Street, and a square called Witmark Place. The project, however, was not a success.

Undoubtedly the greatest coterie of high-priced stars ever gathered together under one roof were associated with Weber and Fields. Here are a few of them: Sam Bernard, David Warfield, Fritz Williams, Marie Dressler, Charles Bigelow, John T. Kelly, Charles Ross, Mabel Fenton, William Collier, Louise Allen, Peter F. Dailey, Julian Mitchell, Henry E. Dixey, Lillian Russell, Fay Templeton, Louis Mann, May Robson, Frankie Bailey, Bessie Clayton, Vesta Tilley, Cecilia Loftus, De Wolf Hopper, Lee Harrison, Bonnie Maginn, Carter DeHaven, and the McCoy Sisters. The lyric writers who worked with Stromberg were also the best of their time, including Edgar Smith, Harry B. Smith, and Robert B. Smith.

3. Peter F. Dailey

With Weber and Fields was the outstanding comedian, Pete Dailey. Pete was rather a complex character, at once sympathetic and easy-going. When one of the girls of the company was burned to death, no one cried more profusely than Pete. Yet, when he suddenly looked up and saw a fellow member crying, he made a remark that almost caused a panic.

The same capriciousness characterized him in learning his parts. Pete never played his part as written. It became funnier through his extemporization. The parts were always rewritten by an alert stenographer who took down Pete's version on the opening night; nevertheless, Peter never played the part twice the same.

Pete was always looking for a good song. He popularized quite a few of the Weber and Fields gems, notably *Dinah, Say You Love Me, Sue, Mah Josephine* and *How I Love My Lu.*

189

He liked to have the first chance at a song. Whenever he met one of the Witmarks, invariably it would be, "Hello—in the safe?" Which always meant, "Any new manuscript?" One day they had a song that they thought fitted him, and sent him a message consisting of three words: "In the safe." Pete turned up next day. The title of the song was *Dinner Time*. Peter heard it, liked it, and, being in need of a new number, took off his coat and started to study it with the aid of a pianist in a demonstration room adjoining Isidore's office. Pete became enthusiastic over the refrain and was singing *Dinner Time* at a high pitch when a card was brought to Isidore announcing the arrival of a concert musician, bringing a letter of introduction from their representative in Australia. He had the rolling doors separating the two rooms closed, as the stranger was ushered in. He was slight, extremely pale, looking somewhat like a young Liszt. The message from the Australian people explained that he was a leading violinist who had been given a contract by an American concert director which they wanted to have checked up. While Pete in the other room was singing his head off about *Dinner Time* and Isidore was looking over the contract, the young violinist fainted. The rolling doors flew open, and Pete rushed in to help bring the young fellow around.

At last he opened his eyes and was able to talk. In a feeble voice he whispered, "I haven't eaten since yesterday morning." It came out that he had been robbed and was too proud to borrow in anticipation of his next remittance.

The whole thing affected Pete differently from what one would expect. He became serious. "What a strange world this is!" he said. "Here I am, a faker, getting big money for a lot of hokum and nonsense, and here's a young man who has been giving his whole self to accomplish something worth while, and he's living from hand to mouth—starving. It's all wrong. It's all wrong."

And for once there was missing the usual comic twist to Pete's speech.

4. The Rogers Brothers

The Rogers Brothers, whose real names were Gus and Max Solomon, were rivals to Weber and Fields. They started in vaudeville about 1893, later starring under Klaw and Erlanger in "A Round of Pleasure." They were then featured in John J. McNally's novel musical productions, "Rogers Brothers in Central Park" (1900); "Rogers Brothers in Harvard" (1900); "Rogers Brothers in Washington" (1901); "Rogers Brothers in Wall Street" (1903); "Rogers Brothers in Panama" (1907). The musical settings were made by Maurice Levi, their conductor, and were published by Rogers Brothers Music Publishing Company, which was later purchased by M. Witmark & Sons.

The Rogers were close friends of the Witmarks, especially Gus, whom Isidore had known since the 80's, when Gus made his first stage appearance at the age of nine. It was at Turn Hall, 66 East 4th Street, where many prominent vaudevillians made their first bow.

Gus was a good looking boy with a pronounced lisp. At his premiere he did a neat little song and dance, and for an encore came out with a slab of marble about eighteen inches square, which he sat on the stage as he announced, "Ladie*th* and Gentlemen, I will now give you an imitation of the *Th*ixty-ninth Regiment going up Broadway." Whereupon he did a clog to the music of a popular march tune and made a big hit that night.

Isidore didn't see Gus again for a number of years until he and his brother opened at Tony Pastor's in 1895. Gus always gave Isidore the credit for putting the starring bee in his bonnet. But it was a selfish motive on Isidore's part. With Ward and Vokes in mind, he had written a scenario of a "flexible" comedy called "College Chums." They were a very popular variety team at that time, but were not yet ready for stardom. So the two principal parts being flexible, he tried to interest Rogers Brothers who

191

were tied up with variety contracts and couldn't get out of them. It gave them the idea, however, and at the first opportunity they took advantage of it.

Here is a remarkable thing about the Rogers Brothers: when they were appearing as a team, Max was considered the big man as he was a fine comedian and had a magnificent voice. He was the comedy man and Gus just acted as a "feeder" or straight man (though he also took care of the business end). Some persons were cruel enough to call Gus excess baggage as far as the stage was concerned (while conceding him his business ability), and argued that Max should unshackle himself and go it alone. Then Gus died and Max had his opportunity. But what happened? There was no bigger failure than Max alone in every production in which he appeared, and he became so disheartened that he left the acting profession to become a theatrical agent. He died soon after. "Feeding" is a thankless art.

Gus married Maude Raymond, a popular singer of her day, and she survives him. She was especially known for her impersonation of Topsy in "Uncle Tom's Cabin." To Maude Raymond must go the credit of making a success of a Witmark song, *Bill Simmons* by George Spink.

5. Raymond Hitchcock

One of the most popular characters of the American stage was Raymond Hitchcock, a man with tremendous personality and a very clever artist. Isidore Witmark became acquainted with him when he was with Savage and a warm friendship sprang up between them. In fact, Ray was inducted into their exclusive circle known as the Saturday Night Club. The Witmarks were the publishers of the music of his outstanding hits, "The Yankee Consul," book by Henry Blossom and music by Alfred G. Robyn, and "The Yankee Tourist," book by Wallace Irwin and music by Robyn.

Ray had a style all his own and was perhaps the originator of

Harry Thacker Burleigh   Paul Laurence Dunbar

J. Rosamond and James Weldon Johnson

Witmark's first complete building — 8 West 29th St. — where they met Victor Herbert, George M. Cohan, Weber and Fields and a host of other celebrities.

the "master of ceremonies" type of comedian who familiarly addresses prominent people in his audience. This custom, however, did not always meet with the applause it deserved, as witness this write up from *The Morning Telegraph* of Providence, Rhode Island, dated May 1, 1902:

"Raymond Hitchcock appeared in 'King Dodo' tonight under protest. Mr. Hitchcock, who is the principal comedian in the musical comedy now being exploited by Col. Savage, is permitted by the authors and managers to go about as far as he likes in the way of introducing local 'gags.'

"Mr. Hitchcock on Monday night introduced a verse in one of his topical songs which had to do with the Beef Trust. There wasn't much to the verse, it was simply a little arraignment of the prime movers in the trust. There was a cutting line here and there. None but a butcher in on the deal or one who had been stung by the promoters of it would have taken offense at the verse. But it seems that there are a lot of butchers in Providence, and many of them took exception to the latest 'King Dodo' interpolations.

"After the performance, Hitchcock was attacked by unknown men, supposed to be butchers, on his way home from the theater. He did not care to play tonight, but there was no one to take his place. When Mr. Hitchcock appeared on the stage he had one discolored eye, which was not called for either by his contract, or by the stage business allotted him. Mr. Hitchcock's experience with Providence is about all he cares for, he declares."

And here is the lyric that caused such amazing results:

"Another King has risen up
To contest the rights of Dodo.
The Beef Trust's now to the front, you'll note,
Much scornful of King Dodo.
But its life will be a brief one,
Our King's not to be by beef done;
The finish will be Swift,
Unless Dodo's lost the gift
Of breaking through such Armour as this beef one."

6. Sam Bernard

One afternoon Sam Bernard had been playing cards at the Friars' Club. That evening he had been invited to Julie's house for dinner, where his wife was to meet him. It was his custom, before beginning his afternoon game, to remove his coat and hang it over the back of his chair. He did so on this occasion. When Sam got into a card game, he came near forgetting everything else; so he forgot his dinner appointment, until Julie's wife telephoned. "Sam, have you forgotten that you're dining with us tonight?"

He apologized and said he was jumping into a taxi. He hurried to the card table, excused himself, grabbed his coat, rushed out of the club, hailed a taxi, and dropped into it exhausted. Passing the Fifties and somewhat relaxed, he put his hand into his coat pocket and drew out—a set of false teeth!

"Ah, the gang's played another trick on me," he said to himself, and threw the teeth out of the cab window.

A little later, he put his hand in the other pocket, and found things he had never seen before.

"What's this?" he thought. Then he took a look at the coat. "My God, another man's coat! And his false teeth!" Hurriedly he told the cabby to turn around and drive back slowly over the route, to see if they could find the lost teeth. Those were anxious moments for Sam. Between the knowledge that he was holding up a dinner and that he had thrown away some friend's "dining-room furniture," he was in a tight place. But he went on looking —and he found those teeth! And, although dozens of cars had passed that spot since he had thrown them out of the window, the teeth were unbroken. They happened to land in a pocket in the cobble pavement and were intact. Sam, delighted with his find, ordered the cabby to drive like blazes back to the Friars! There he met a sight. The man whose coat he had dashed off with was standing in the doorway frantic, jibbering, and crying for his teeth. Sam lost no time in making the exchange of coats and was again on his way to the dinner; his hostess was about to chide him, when he said, "Wait and I'll tell you a story that will exonerate me." And in his German dialect he proceeded to tell the story of the teeth in such an excruciatingly funny manner that he had all the guests in convulsions.

CHAPTER XI

"LIFT EVERY VOICE AND SING"

1. Cook and Dunbar

*I*T WAS in July that a new star, one of the earliest of the gifted American colored composers, rose on Broadway. He rose, too, on the Witmark list, only to make, through no fault of his music, a sudden descent. The story of Will Marion Cook belongs to the short but definite catalogue of men who wronged Isidore Witmark and were never forgiven.

The evening of July 5, 1898, was in its way a historic date, for at the Casino Roof Garden "Clorindy," or "The Origin of the Cake-Walk," an operetta by Paul Laurence Dunbar and Will Marion Cook, was disclosed to New Yorkers as the first Negro operetta in the new syncopated style. The entertainment was one of the offerings of "Rice's Summer Nights," and according to the contemporary newspapers was produced with E. E. Rice's "accustomed prodigality." Forty Negroes were in the cast, which was headed by none other than Ernest Hogan, who deserves a niche all his own in the story of American ragtime as the author of *All Coons Look Alike To Me*, a song that he had written, naturally, in a humorous vein. The title became so popular, however, that his own people took offence; his tune became for him a source of unending misery, and he died regretting that he had written it.

It is not generally known, by the way, that the verse part of

195

the song, as now known, was the work of Isidore Witmark. Hogan's original melody did not fit in well with the refrain; Isidore thereupon wrote a new melody, together with some of the words for the second verse.

The Cook-Dunbar operetta was a mélange of comedy, droll dancing, cake-walking, and ensemble singing that combined to make "Clorindy" a sensation. The music, for its vein, was distinguished. Cook had studied under Dvořák and Joachim. Who, of the youngsters who had ears for music in 1898, cannot yet sing or whistle *Darktown Is Out Tonight?*

About a month before the night of July 5, Isidore had had a call from the composer. The Witmarks were publishing many of the Negro song hits of that time, particularly *All Coons Look Alike To Me.* Isidore was impressed with the Will Marion Cook score and felt it had the right stuff in it for success.

Cook was anxious to get a production for it and made him a proposition. He said, "If you will get me a production of this skit, I will give you the publication rights and all the royalties accruing."

Isidore replied, "I will do my best to get you a production, and publish the score, but I will not accept your royalties. You shall enjoy those yourself."

So royalty contracts were drawn and signed. Cook promised to send up the lyric writer for his contracts. He came—Paul Laurence Dunbar, one of the finest of men, white or black. With splendid eyes and soft of speech, he was fascinating. One could hardly think that he had been a poor little elevator boy in an Ohio hotel, when William Dean Howells discovered and sponsored him. He was the outstanding poet of the Negro race, nor were his gifts limited to poetry; he wrote successful novels and stories. His lyrics for "Clorindy" were excellent.

"Clorindy" was produced through no inconsiderable cooperation on Isidore's part. It played a whole season on the Casino

Roof. Six months went by, the time came for royalty reports, and among those who received their statements was Will Marion Cook.

Imagine the Witmarks' surprise when Cook came in accompanied by a white man whom he introduced as his lawyer. Cook lost no time telling us that he had brought his lawyer to discuss his last royalty statement (which actually was his first) inasmuch as he did not think it was commensurate with the success of the play.

His lawyer was a reasonable man, and the Witmarks convinced him of their integrity, and brought out the fact that this was a new style of music which would require some time to take hold. Therefore too much could not be expected of the first royalty statement. When they added that Cook had offered to give them his royalties if they obtained a production for him, and that they had refused to deprive him of them, the lawyer asked logically, "Why should you want to rob him if you could have gotten them for nothing in the first place?"

They insisted that Cook send an accountant to go through the books, but the lawyer refused, saying, "I'm entirely satisfied." Whereupon Isidore turned on Cook and said, "You are a clever man, you have great possibilities as a writer, and you will make money for a publisher some day. But you can't publish another number with this house as long as you live."

Although later others interceded for him, the Witmarks never accepted another of his songs.

2. J. Rosamond and James Weldon Johnson

In 1901, there came to New York from Jacksonville, Florida, two brothers of the Paul Laurence Dunbar type and ability. J. Rosamond and James Weldon Johnson later became leaders of their race, but at that time their greatness was little realized outside of their own community. The former is a composer of serious music although he collaborated with his brother and Bob Cole

197

on some of the outstanding popular hits of the time, among them, *Under the Bamboo Tree, Congo Love Song,* and *Maiden With The Dreamy Eyes.*

James Weldon Johnson tells in *Along This Way*: "As soon as we had settled in a couple of rooms in West 53rd Street we presented our letter of introduction to M. Witmark and Sons. We got an appointment and played the opera for Isidore Witmark. We were with him a couple of hours, and he appeared to be favorably impressed by the songs and choruses. Just as we finished, Harry B. Smith and Reginald DeKoven, then two of the great American writers of light opera, entered. Mr. Witmark introduced us as two young men who had written an opera. 'Well,' said Mr. Smith, 'let's hear it; we might be able to steal something from it.' Mr. DeKoven and Mr. Witmark laughed. We didn't quite see the joke, . . . gathered up our precious manuscript, and made a quick exit. Later we did laugh about it; and later we did collaborate with both Mr. Smith and Mr. DeKoven, realizing that had it not been for our caution and the extremely high value we placed on our work we might have collaborated with them immediately following that first introduction.

"The opera, 'Toloso,' was never, as such, produced, but it served to introduce us to practically all of the important stars and producers of comic opera and musical plays in New York. The great Oscar Hammerstein climbed to our modest rooms in West 53rd Street to hear it played. . . . We ultimately adapted most of the single numbers, and they were produced in one or another Broadway musical show. I have often looked over the score of our opera and seen that a practiced hand could have whipped it into shape for production. It is possible that the managers were a bit afraid of it; the Spanish-American War had just closed, and they may have thought that audiences would consider a burlesque of American imperialism as unpatriotic. Not long afterwards, however, George Ade, in 'The Sultan of Sulu,' used the same theme successfully."

198

"LIFT EVERY VOICE AND SING"

Although James Weldon Johnson's accomplishments were many and his fame became universal, the song which he always considered his best was one of rich simplicity. It was called *Lift Every Voice and Sing*, written in 1900. His brother Rosamond wrote the music. The Negro school children were the first to sing it at a Lincoln's Birthday celebration in Jacksonville, Florida. Since that far-off day, the whole world has joined in the chorus:

> "Lift every voice and sing
> Till earth and heaven ring,
> Ring with the harmonies of Liberty;
> Let our rejoicing rise
> High as the list'ning skies,
> Let it resound loud as the rolling sea."

3. *Harry Thacker Burleigh*

Another friend of the House of Witmark was Harry Thacker Burleigh, American Negro baritone and composer. He studied under Dvořák at the National Conservatory of Music, and later taught there. In 1894 he became soloist at St. George's Church, New York, and in 1899 at Temple Emanu-El. For many years he has been a well-known concert singer in all the principal cities of the United States.

Harry Burleigh is also famous as a composer of ballads, his outstanding composition being a song entitled *Jean* which is in the repertoire of some of the best-known balladists. He has also collected and arranged a collection of twenty-one *Negro Minstrel Melodies*, published by G. Schirmer in 1909, with a preface by W. J. Henderson. In this book are many of the favorites of Stephen Foster, besides several old melodies which were sung by Dan Rice more than a hundred years ago and of which the author is unknown. But the thing for which he will undoubtedly be longest remembered is his arrangement of spirituals. In 1929, The Century Company, New York, published the *Old Song*

Hymnal, words and melodies collected by Dorothy S. Bolton, music arranged by Harry T. Burleigh. In this collection are the unforgettable *Swing Low, Sweet Chariot* and *Shoes.* In the preface of this book is a sentence that seems to epitomize Harry Burleigh's whole lifework:

"We offer this book with the hope that in these songs the human heart will continue to find expression for its deepest emotions of joy, of sorrow, of inspiration and that exaltation of the soul which gave them the name—spirituals."

How fitting it is that Harry Burleigh should have been the arranger, too, of *Deep River,* which will last as long as the English language is spoken. Spiritual, indeed, is the life of Harry Burleigh.

CHAPTER XII

FLOURISH—ENTER VICTOR

1. *Herbertiana*

A SIMPLE paragraph in *The Witmark Monthly* for August, 1898, announced the addition of Victor Herbert to the Witmark list:

"Mr. Victor Herbert, the celebrated conductor and composer, has entered into an agreement with us whereby our house are to publish his new comic opera, 'The Fortune Teller,' book by Harry B. Smith, which has been written for Alice Nielsen and The Alice Nielsen Opera Company."

The opera received its first metropolitan presentation on September 26th, at Wallack's Theater.

When Victor Herbert came to the Witmarks he was, of course, already established as a composer. He had written a number of songs and piano compositions, as well as *Badinage,* his instrumental success, and the operettas, "Prince Ananias," "The Wizard of the Nile," "The Goldbug," "The Idol's Eye" and "The Serenade."

The general manager of the Witmark Music Library at the time was Otto Weyl, a schoolmate of Mrs. Victor Herbert in Vienna who had become a close friend of her husband. For some years, Weyl was confidential adviser to Victor, and on his advice the rising young composer allied himself with the Witmarks. A

201

few years later, when Herbert was involved in a suit against the *Musical Courier*, which charged him with plagiarism, Weyl took charge of the Herbert cause.

When Isidore Witmark signed the first contract with Victor Herbert for the publication of "The Fortune Teller," they went over to the Gilsey House at Broadway and Twenty-ninth Street and opened a bottle of wine on the agreement.

When Victor made his next visit to the office, he suggested another pilgrimage to the Gilsey. Isidore remembered the experience of a fellow who had been connected with the former publishers of Victor's music: an inseparable companion of Victor's who could not keep pace with the composer.

"Mr. Herbert," he said, "you want us to make money for you, don't you?"

"Yes, yes, my boy, yes, yes."

"We can't do it, and drink champagne during business hours."

Victor was nonplussed for the moment. He had never been crossed, and Isidore had taken a long chance of displeasing him. But he was justified, as was later shown by the letter of appreciation that Herbert sent to the firm upon receiving his first statement. He saw Isidore's point and wine-fests were limited to special occasions. One of those occasions Isidore will never forget.

"You're wanted on the phone, Mr. Isidore—long distance."

"Hello. Who's this?"

"Louie Eckstein, talking from Chicago. I'm coming to New York. I want you to arrange a meeting for me with Victor Herbert, to discuss with him the possibility of putting his orchestra in Ravinia Park next summer, instead of our usual grand opera."

Eckstein, an enterprising entrepreneur, served the nation equally with music and with food; he was the publisher of *The Red Book*, the owner and promoter of important real estate in Chicago, and heavily involved in other business enterprises. At Ravinia Park, known as Eckstein's Folly, every summer he gave grand opera, generally making up a deficit of $150,000 out of

202

his own pocket. He later was one of the Board of Directors of the Metropolitan Opera Company in New York.

"All right," Isidore answered, "I'll get busy at once."

He got in touch with Bob Iverson, Victor's right-hand man at the time, and a luncheon was arranged at the Knickerbocker Hotel, Forty-second Street and Broadway. All who knew Victor Herbert knew what an epicure he was. Food played an important part in his life, and he enjoyed his meals heartily.

As the date for the Eckstein luncheon neared, Isidore got in touch with Victor and was assured that everything was ready. But Victor cautioned him that there should be no business talk during the meal. The composer had an epicurean obsession: to think only of the meal while eating it. He would allow no business to be discussed, if he could help it, until the meal was over. He held that you could enjoy and digest food properly only if you devoted your sole attention to it. He loved to tell and hear stories, and to laugh at his meals; anything serious was taboo. It interfered with proper digestion. This admonition was passed on to Eckstein by Isidore and when they met at the Knickerbocker Hotel, he thoroughly understood his rôle.

Immediately after introductions, cocktails were served with an appetizer. Then came cups of rich mushroom soup while conversation on general topics was going on. Then came *poisson*, a delicious brook trout, with a sauterne of rare vintage. Victor's relish proceeded *accelerando con amore*. Eckstein looked on in growing amazement. "What is this?" he asked Isidore, in an aside. Isidore assured him it was all right. "Just keep on eating." Came another course, an entree of mysterious ingredients, followed by another wine. Victor had only started. Eckstein by now was apprehensive. He managed to whisper again, careful not to offend the host. "I thought I was coming to a luncheon. I hope there isn't any more." Isidore did his best to reassure him, but could promise nothing because there was no written menu.

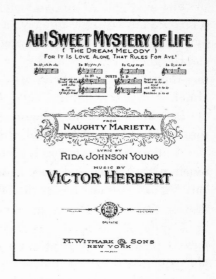

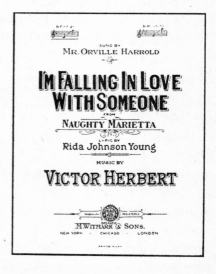

A "foursome" of Victor Herbert's successes. *Gypsy Love Song*, over forty years old and, with the great Herbert endurance, still popular.

The next course was a game bird, floating in its gravies, with a bottle of Pommard. Victor was still at the top of his form, but by this time Eckstein was fairly out. He leaned over to Isidore, and said, "I own two restaurants in Chicago, but never have I served or eaten a *lunch* like this." Eckstein at that time was the owner of Rector's and the North American restaurants in Chicago.

Hereupon the waiter brought an aspic salad (a meal in itself) with another kind of wine. Victor smacked his lips, between ejaculations of satisfaction over the food, the expert cooking, and the excellent chef. This time Eckstein leaned over, not *to* but *on* Isidore, whispering under his breath, "He's killing me." But courageously he stuck.

Finally came the dessert, baked Alaska, a foreign cheese, and a demi-tasse. This out of the way, Victor whispered to the waiter, who soon brought in four large glasses, with cognac in each. Victor raved over the aroma, but Eckstein did not move his hand; he was helpless. For the first time he gave vent to his feelings aloud. "I have never had such an experience in all my life." And turning to Victor, he asked, "Do you eat lunches like these every day?"

Victor nonchalantly answered in his characteristic manner, "That's nothing, my boy, that's nothing. You must lunch with me again."

But between Victor's taboo against talking business at meals, and Eckstein's terror at the prospect of "lunching" with him again, they never got together on the Ravinia Park project. Perhaps Eckstein was afraid to bring Victor out to Chicago for fear that the composer would force him to eat himself to death.

There was to come a comical moment, on July 19, 1905, when Herbert the gourmandizer turned doctor for his publisher. "So glad you are feeling well again," wrote the composer to Isidore who, when dining one night with Paul Dresser, had eaten something that gave him a bad case of ptomaine. "Take good care of yourself now, *strict diet* for *months*, and no more *fish* (or whatever it might have been) . . ."

Physician, heal thyself! If Victor only had partaken as generously of his advice as he did of the food and drink that had prompted it!

Victor, however, was no sluggard. It was not all play and no work with him. Take, for example, the phenomenal season of 1898-1899. Victor Herbert's order book for operas was full up. Nor were these operas written on speculation. Each represented a commission: "The Singing Girl," for Alice Nielsen; "The Ameer," for Frank Daniels; "Cyrano de Bergerac," for Francis Wilson; and "The Viceroy," for the Bostonians.

When one realizes that the writing of one opera is an exhausting task, what prodigious work this four-in-hand must have been! But it did not phase Victor Herbert. On the contrary, that same year as a sort of dessert, he wrote six piano pieces and one of his symphonic poems. He was the original glutton for work. His appetite for toil was equal to his appetite for food.

To give an idea of what it meant to write four operas simultaneously, disregarding the creation of music and considering the scores as a manual job only, he produced more than *a thousand pages of music*. Add to this the actual composing, and the orchestral scoring, which would run to many thousands more!

Take into consideration, too, that the four operas dealt with four distinct periods and sets of characters. "The Singing Girl" was set in a German environment; "Cyrano" was old French; "The Viceroy" was Venetian; "The Ameer" was laid in Afghanistan.

What is here being set down is factual truth, however fantastic is may appear. Victor had in his studio a small washtub filled with ice. On this ice, in true epicurean fashion, he had bottles of beverages to fit each opera. He had his Rhine wine and Moselle for the German; his clarets and burgundies for the

French; his chianti for the Italian; and some specially hard stuff for Afghanistan.

The scores lay face open on three low desks and one tall, bookkeeper's desk, which he used when tired of sitting. He wrote —not one opera at a time until it was finished—but as the Muse moved him, jumping from one score to another and he had them all ready for rehearsal on schedule time! There was an operatic jag for you! Has it ever been equalled by a fellow composer?

Although the story about to be told has been current in musical circles for some years, and has been printed, there may be justification for it here, as Isidore was directly concerned and was the first to relate it. He told it to Harry B. Smith, Herbert's librettist, who used it in his book, *First Nights and First Editions*, from which source Joseph Kaye quoted it in his biography of Victor Herbert.

The Witmarks had just brought out "The Fortune Teller" as though to celebrate their removal to 8 West Twenty-ninth Street. Wherever they had lunch, they had a following of writers, stars, critics. The Gilsey House was in its heyday. Morello's restaurant was next door to them. August Janssen had just opened his Hofbrau around the corner, and often was their host, especially to Daddy Witmark who enjoyed his excellent German dishes and imported beer. They had what is known in German as a *Stammtisch* in the Gilsey restaurant.

One day they were entertaining Raymond Hitchcock, Fred Rankin, Victor Herbert, Ernest R. Ball, and Manuel Klein, when in came Harry Conor, the comedian of "A Trip to Chinatown" and other Hoyt farces. Harry had just returned from Australia, and everybody was glad to welcome him back. In spite of being a successful comedian and an expert with the gloves, he was one of the most modest of men, almost timid. He was carrying a large leather volume under his arm.

While the group were talking around the *Stammtisch*, he called Isidore to the next table and proceeded to reveal what he

207

had in the large volume. On the front cover was a leather label that told the story laconically; *Harry Conor's Mass in F.* He confided that he had written it in Australia, where he had had the assistance of a talented young prelate, who had arranged it for voices and piano accompaniment.

Harry was a good Catholic and a devout church member, despite his authorship of *The Smoke Went Up The Chimney Just The Same* and *Miss Helen Hunt.* He had Isidore look through the score of the *Mass,* and, receiving his approval, shyly asked him to show it to Victor Herbert, who was telling a funny story to the circle.

Assenting, Isidore waited until Herbert had finished his story, and called him aside. "Victor," handing him the *Mass,* "Harry Conor's just written this and brought it from Australia. He wants you to look it over and tell him what you think of it."

"Sure, sure, my boy," said Victor, taking the volume and looking through its pages. Harry stood by on tenterhooks, awaiting Victor's verdict.

Turning to the front of the book again, Herbert read slowly, aloud *"Harry Conor's Mass in F.* Well, well." Then with deliberation he began to thumb the pages, nodding his head now and then, as if reading and digesting the music in approval. The whole party around the table watched, interested. Victor turned more pages, nodding and saying to himself, "F . . . F . . ." in a satisfied manner. Finally he reached the last page.

Looking up, he slammed the book shut. "By God!" he exclaimed, "It *is* in F!"

2. Anecdotage

Victor Herbert had a remarkable memory. Isidore once visited him in his early days at Lake Placid, New York. He had just been made conductor of the new Pittsburgh Orchestra and was preparing his material for his first concerts in the coming fall.

The American maestro, Henry Hadley, had an orchestra in

Willie Howard today in his latest creation Professor Pierre Ginzberg.

Willie Howard as Witmark's Water Boy.

Ernest R. Ball

Chauncey Olcott

164 WEST NINETY-SECOND STREET.

June 21st 99

Dear Witmark

Your semi-annual statement and check received.

Allow me to express to you my gratification at your great promptness and excellent showing in the way of sales.

Thanking you again I remain with best wishes for the continued success of the firm and best regards to the 'boys'

Yours Sincerely

Victor Herbert.

An original Victor Herbert letter.

one of the neighboring Adirondack resorts. He and Victor were devoted friends. Hadley came over for the day to help Victor make up his programs. It was astounding how many classics were at Victor's command, and he knew each work thoroughly, without score or other reference. He was making programs of numbers that were to be not only attractive in themselves but in harmony with each other and the atmosphere of the evening. Before Hadley left and without any other aid than memory, they had more than a dozen programs scheduled for further consideration.

Another proof of his memory was on the occasion of a monster benefit given at the old Madison Square Garden by the musicians of New York for the sufferers of the Galveston flood. With more than four hundred musicians in the orchestra, the feature of the concert was the *Pilgrims' Chorus* from "Tannhäuser," intoned by forty French horns, unaccompanied. It was a gala affair, and some of the most eminent musicians directed, among them Walter Damrosch, Frank Damrosch, Emil Paur, John Philip Sousa, and Victor Herbert who was to direct his *American Fantaisie*. Suddenly there was restrained excitement among the musicians. Being close to Victor that day, I found out the reason. The score of one of the important numbers on the program was missing. The director who was to lead it refused to go on, as he had not memorized it. It could not be omitted, for the program was short as it was. The various leaders were canvassed to find out if any of them would take it through from memory; all refused. All but Victor, who said nonchalantly that he thought he could do it, although he had never conducted it; he had played it as one of the musicians, some years back. He was, of course, an expert 'cellist. He tackled it and came through with flying colors. The members of the orchestra themselves applauded loudest.

To speak of the early Herbert is to recall that genial first-nighter and first-editioner (to borrow from the title of his memoirs), Harry B. Smith. He was a droll fellow. It was long after the good fortune of "The Fortune Teller," and he was writing a play for the firm entitled "The Belle Of The West," in which Florence Bindley was to be starred. Smith delivered the four acts in due course. The acts were read and checked off, in order. Harry had a reputation for falling down in his last act, though Arthur Hopkins, in a fine monograph, asks "How's Your Second Act?" True to form, "The Belle Of The West" slumped in Act Four.

Isidore, something of a play-doctor himself, did everything he could to get Smith to strengthen the weak finale. Smith seemed unresponsive.

Witmark lost patience. "Harry," he cried, "Why don't you put an idea into the act?"

Smith looked at him. "If I had an idea," he replied nonchalantly, "I'd write another play!"

When Victor Herbert was touring the country with his orchestra he had so many friends calling on him in every town that he would have highballs served during intermissions at the concerts. This meant arranging for ice at every stop, and he distributed lavish tips to those who attended to the matter for him.

A story is told of his appearance in St. Louis during a hot spell. Reaching the concert hall, he gave the colored janitor ten dollars and said, "Just get me what ice I need for the highballs during the engagement."

This being the regular amount that he handed out, he knew a liberal tip was included. But he had reckoned without his weather. The excessive heat required the use of far more ice than usual, and the janitor found his tip melting away. It was whispered later that the colored fellow was out forty-five cents on the deal!

That Herbert could play tricks with glasses, as well as with their contents, appears from an anecdote related by the Hon. Greville Le Poer Trench, son of the late Earl of Clancarty, through whose courtesy it is here printed.

Once Victor Herbert stayed at Garbally Court in Ireland with the Earl of Clancarty, who owned a collection of wine glasses. One night at dinner Herbert said that if one put a wine glass down on the table perfectly straight, so that all of the bottom touched at once (an impossibility), the glass would smash to pieces. Lord Clancarty doubted this and asked him to try it, which he did. To the surprise of the host and the guests, the glass snapped at the stem. Five times Lord Clancarty asked Herbert to repeat, until he remembered that the broken glasses were exceedingly valuable. Needless to say, the glasses did not break because they were put down perfectly straight, but because Herbert snapped the stems between his fingers.

3. Songs, Singers, and Names

You can't always tell with a song; the most expert "pickers" make their woeful blunders. When Victor played for Isidore his score of "Cyrano de Bergerac," Isidore picked what he thought was the big song hit of the opera, and Victor agreed. It was a song called *I Wonder*, and was to be sung by Lulu Glaser, one of the foremost comic opera prima donnas of her day, who was appearing with Francis Wilson, for whom the operetta had been written.

On the night of the opening, Victor and Isidore occupied a box with their respective families. They were enjoying the show, but as they had both made up their minds that there was to be one big hit, they primed themselves for it. At last the moment arrived. As if by prearrangement, both Victor and Isidore looked over the audience as Miss Glaser sang, but could feel no unusual emotion sweeping through the theater. The song ended amid silence. Isidore eyed Victor quizzically, and he eyed Isidore. The song had died on the spot. And they never knew why, for Miss Glaser had been superb.

Another song in the show was taken up by the public. Its

success they had foreseen no more clearly than they had foreseen the failure of *I Wonder.*

The question often arises in musical circles as to whether or no the composer's name makes a song or piece? Isidore Witmark has the firm conviction that the public takes to its heart the really good piece, and if a good piece is given half a break, it succeeds regardless of the composer's name.

Once Isidore and Victor entered into an innocent deception to publish *Al Fresco* under an assumed name, the object being to discover whether the number would go over on its own merits, or whether the name of Herbert would be essential to its success.

Originally they issued it under the name of Rowland, and it went very well indeed. But Victor had just completed his musical show "It Happened In Nordland" and needed for the big dance a number like *Al Fresco,* which was just the sort of introduction that would put the number over. So they included it in the "Nordland" score, thus letting the cat out of the bag. Without Herbert's name it would have done well; with it, and in association with the operetta, it fared even better.

Isidore had the honor of naming a number of Victor Herbert's instrumental novelties, including *Al Fresco, Punchinello, Yesterthoughts,* and *Mountain Stream.*

4. *James Huneker's Obsession*

It was at the turn of the century that Isidore, through Victor, met the reigning critic, James Huneker, and asked him who was the greater American composer, MacDowell or Herbert. "Steeplejack" (Huneker) paused for a moment, then tactfully replied, "Victor Herbert is the more versatile."

Herbert and Huneker were great buddies for all their bickering, and it was Huneker who dubbed Herbert "The Irish Wagner." Huneker, like Victor, was fond of his liquid sociability, and equally fond of his pet obsession: that nobody could write good music unless he had a strain of Hebraic blood in his veins, no matter how remote the ancestry. Although he himself was not a Jew—indeed, as his middle name, Gibbons, reminds us, he was nephew to a Cardinal—he lost no opportunity to air his theory.

One day he and Victor had been drinking at Lüchow's, on Fourteenth Street, when suddenly Jim the Penman, self-styled Steeplejack of the Arts, declared that Victor Herbert must possess Jewish blood; how otherwise could he have written all those beautiful strains? Victor was not anti-Semitic, but he had imbibed enough to feel resentful on general principles, so he objected to Huneker's statement.

"I'm Irish," he proclaimed. "Of Irish descent. My mother was Irish. My grandfather, the illustrious Samuel Lover, was Irish!" Huneker's eyes twinkled. "Ha ha! That proves it! Now I do believe, more than ever, that the Irish were one of the lost tribes of Israel!"

5. Grooming A Groom

It was the Herberts who first put the idea of marriage into the head of Isidore Witmark. They chose, so to speak, the idea but not the bride. They thus became matchmakers without the match and they set it to music as well. The story begins, like so many stories that have to do with jolly Victor of the hearty appetite, in a temple—or should this particular place be called a museum?—of gastronomy.

A unique New York eating place, the Arena, had been opened in September, 1889, by William C. Muschenheim, who resigned the superintendency of the New York Athletic Club to manage it. It was at 39-41 West Thirty-first Street, going through to Thirty-second. It was perhaps the most elaborate restaurant in the country and was called "The Epicurean Paradise." Its table d'hôte was famous, its cuisine worthy of so noted a steward as Muschenheim, for whom the Hotel Astor was built. He was an unusual man with unusual ideas, which were exemplified in this establishment.

214

Of a restless, dynamic nature, he was ever for expansion. In 1893 he engaged the best architects and craftsmen to reconstruct the entire place to accommodate the increased patronage of an appreciative public.

Muschenheim had the most complete assortment of wines in America, comprising vintages as far back as 1706. These he sold for outside consumption, as well as serving them. The wine caves of the establishment were of special interest, and were open for inspection.

The Arena was the rendezvous of New York's prominent figures in all walks of life, the groups specially catered to being the athletes, college students, and theater folk. As it was in the neighborhood of some of the leading theaters, Wallack's, the Bijou, Daly's, the Fifth Avenue, and the Manhattan, it attracted a large after-theater patronage. The lunch business was also so extensive that often all its many rooms were filled,—with people waiting for service.

One day Mr. and Mrs. Victor Herbert and Isidore Witmark were having lunch at the Arena.

"Isidore," asked Victor, out of a clear sky, "why don't you get married?"

"I'm too busy," was the reply.

Mrs. Herbert added her voice. "I should marry," she urged. "It is the only life to live."

"But would it be under the circumstances?" asked Isidore.

"What do you mean?"

"This. To marry a girl, I'd have to be very fond of her. And if I were very fond of her, I wouldn't want to neglect her."

"Why would you?"

"Because I shall have to devote every moment of my time to my business until it is built up to the point where I can delegate some of the details to others. Until then I can't consider marriage."

Victor thought a moment, then nodded. "You're right, my

boy. Your reasoning is excellent. But I'll make a compact with you right now. Whenever you *are* ready, I'll write your wedding march."

"That's an inducement, all right," Isidore said. "Don't be surprised to hear from me some day."

6. *Alice Nielsen*

One of the most remarkable careers in musical history of the Golden Nineties was that of Alice Nielsen. She started as a little street singer in Kansas City in her seventh year, and climbed to the top appearing in grand opera in leading cities here and abroad and finally reached the goal of all artists—the Metropolitan Opera House in New York. Previous to this she co-starred with Lillian Nordica in the San Carlo Opera Company throughout this country and played an extended engagement in Boston. She was the first "Madame Butterfly" in Boston and at the request of Mr. Eben D. Jordan, the patron-builder of the then new Boston Opera House, she closed it with that same opera. It might be stated here that Alice Nielsen has the distinction of having been called in by Composer Puccini to go over his "Butterfly" with him when he had it only half finished. They were both summering at an Italian resort at the time.

In London she made her debut in "Don Giovanni" with an all-star cast headed by Caruso at Covent Garden. She traveled all through Europe, particularly Italy, the very font of grand opera, and was triumphant in every continental city in which she appeared. There she met the great Duse and became her special protégée. She also met the poet D'Annunzio. She appeared with all the recognized artists of that day including Melba, Emmy Destinn, Maurel, Constantino, De Luca, Campanari, Muratore, Renaud and Scotti. She knew over fifty grand operas and had a large concert repertoire.

This was her *second operatic career* as a star. Her *first oper-*

atic career was in comic opera in which she reigned as Queen. No other star in comic opera has had a Victor Herbert write three operas especially for her—"Serenade" (Bostonians), "The Fortune Teller," and "The Singing Girl." And few operatic organizations were ever more successful than the Alice Nielsen Opera Company which played extended engagements in all the big cities of America and repeated its triumphs in London. There the American company played the Shaftesbury Theater for an entire season, acclaimed by the critics and public. Isidore Witmark had the pleasure of attending the premières of "The Fortune Teller" in Toronto, "The Singing Girl" in Montreal, and the opening of "The Fortune Teller" in London. The Duchess of Manchester took a special fancy to her and became her sponsor under whose patronage she gave concerts to many distinguished gatherings.

Then came Nielsen's fateful decision—to desert her comic opera career at its very height! In vain, Victor Herbert wrote another operetta for her, to lure her back into that field. When she refused, it became the successful vehicle for launching a grand opera artist into comic opera. The name of the artist was Fritzi Scheff, and the name of the opera "Mlle. Modiste." Thus, while Alice Nielsen went from *comic opera* to *grand*, Fritzi Scheff, reversing matters, went from *grand opera* to *comic*.

Besides Victor Herbert's offer, Alice refused fabulous salaries for those days, among them the offer Isidore brought her from George Tyler—one of the most prominent American managers— of $1,500 a week, stardom, and the production of another Victor Herbert operetta, all of which she turned down with that remark Isidore has never forgotten: "Think of it! I now have two more notes in my voice!"

To explain: after she closed in "The Fortune Teller" in London, instead of coming back home with her company, she remained and took up grand opera seriously under Henry Russell and the noted master, Bevignani. So intent was she on that new career that many times she was actually deprived of the necessities

217

of life and with never a murmur—but it paid for she was acclaimed among the best on the grand opera stage.

To top these achievements Alice Nielsen had a third musical career—the concert platform in which she was tremendously successful, appearing among others with the Boston Symphony under Pierre Monteux and abroad under Hans Richter, Felix Weingartner, Nikisch, Henry Wood, and Landon Ronald. Her notices from such men as H. T. Parker and Philip Hale of Boston, Krehbiel, Huneker, and other outstanding New York critics are evidences of her great artistic success in this particular field. In fact her madcap fascination was so potent that many of her co-artists, among them the world's greatest violinists, Ysaÿe, Kubelik, and Fritz Kreisler, offered to play, and did play, her obbligatos.

Miss Nielsen has been retired for several years, but has recently been working on her memoirs, *She Knew Them All*, to be presented as a book and a series of broadcasts which should be very interesting, as her personal experiences read like fiction. All who remember her with that glorious voice, that individual manner of rendition, and that wonderful madcap personality, will agree that Alice Nielsen was one in a generation.

CHAPTER XIII

WATER-BOYS—AND MEN OF MELODY

1. *Willie Howard*

THE thousands of audiences that have laughed at the antics of Willie Howard in the leading revues will be surprised to learn that he was once a water-boy. What was a water-boy? A water-boy was one who, in the 1900's, served water to audiences in theaters while he joined in the choruses of the artist performing on the stage. He was employed chiefly in the variety houses, and was especially assigned to a singing star. These lads were selected for their voices and for the manner in which they could put over a song; the serving of water was a mere pretext.

This job afforded an opportunity for a bright boy who wanted to work in the theatrical game, and Willie Howard was one of those who took advantage of it. In the year 1901 he came to the Witmarks at their Twenty-ninth Street building; they tried his voice and put him to work immediately. The publisher paid the salary of the water-boy, and Willie Howard was taken on at the munificent figure of $5 a week plus carfare. A good water-boy could get audiences to sing with him after his first refrain; in those days this meant much toward the success of a song. Willie Howard was that kind of a water-boy.

He was an earnest lad and took his job seriously. He had a

219

MEMORANDUM OF AGREEMENT BETWEEN JOHN LEFFLER, PARTY OF THE FIRST PART, AND LEOPOLD LEFKOWITZ, PARTY OF THE SECOND PART.

WITNESSETH: that for and in consideration of the sum of One Dollar ($1.00), to the party of the second part, in hand paid by the party of the first part,

IT IS AGREED that the party of the first part engages the services of Willie Lefkowitz, (professionally known as Master Willie Howard), son of the party of the second part, for the period of one year from date; said Willie Lefkowitz being a minor and legally incapable of signifying his intention.

IT IS ALSO FURTHER AGREED that the said Willie Lefkowitz shall not be under contract with any other person than the party of the first part, nor shall he appear without the consent of the party of the first part, during the continuance of said contract.

IT IS FURTHER AGREED by the party of the first part that the said party of the second part receive, as recompanse, for said services of said Willie Lefkowitz, the sum of Five Dollars ($5.00), per week, and current expenses.

IT IS ALSO AGREED that in the event of the sudden changing, or breaking of the voice of the said Willie Lefkowitz, this contract becomes null and void.

IT IS ALSO FURTHER AGREED that this contract, if mutually satisfactory, can be renewed at the expiration of same.

IN WITNESS WHEREOF the parties hereto have executed this agreement in duplicate at Borough of Manhattan, New York City, State of New York, this day of   1901.

Asher Harris

John Leffler
Leopold Lefkowitz

Sealed and delivered :
in the presence of. :

P.S. Should Master Willie Howard go on tour he is to recieve one half of the net salary derived from by Party of the first Part

The above is a contract "curio" and was seriously followed until Willie Howard's voice broke. This "formidable" document started John Leffler as a theatrical manager and Willie Howard, of Willie and Eugene Howard, as one of the outstanding comedians of the present day. The parties to the contract never bothered to fill in the date line.

220

lovely soprano voice and could read a song to perfection. He used to walk down the aisle at the Casino with a trayful of water glasses in his hand, warbling the refrain of *Pretty Mollie Shannon* with Anna Held, who was playing in "The Little Duchess," and handing out water to the audience as he sang. He did the same thing for Lottie Gilson, singing the refrains of *When You Were Sweet Sixteen* and *Stay In Your Own Backyard;* also for Rooney and Bent, Louise Dresser, and Jack Norworth. Willie had a repertoire of songs, but the principal ones, besides those mentioned, were *Sadie, You Won't Say Nay,* the two ballad successes, *Because* and *Always,* and Lillian Russell's great hit, *Come Down, Ma Evenin' Star.*

Isidore met Willie in June, 1936 in Atlantic City where he was playing with George White's "Scandals" and Isidore was attending the Rotary International Convention. A party of Rotarians saw the show and Howard had them in convulsions with his creation of Professor Pierre Ginzburg.

After the show Willie, his brother Eugene, and some friends sat around and reminisced. Willie proudly told Isidore that his first dress suit as a boy was given to him by Julie, who had worn it himself until he outgrew it. Eugene boasted that he had been the first to sing *Love Me and the World Is Mine* and that it had been taught to him by Ernie Ball, its composer, with whom Eugene was running around at the time.

Willie then related how he was singing with Anna Held and had been taken to Washington to sing in her choruses there. He left New York a boy soprano and when he opened his mouth for the first time in Washington in her chorus of *Mollie Shannon* his voice had changed and he was singing almost bass. He remembered Miss Held's fright the first time he sang with her in Washington and Flo Ziegfeld's asking what was the matter. Not realizing that his voice had suddenly changed, he said, "I don't know." He was unceremoniously fired, and returned to New York, where he wandered the streets trying to figure it out. He kept

221

away from the Witmarks, and Jay, who met him on the back of a street car in New York, was surprised, believing him to be in Washington. The resourceful and ingenious Willie, realizing that his days as a boy singer were over for the time being, started giving imitations of prominent actors, most of whom he had never seen.

Willie Howard's advance is theatrical history. It is hard to reconcile this little sob-singer of 1901 with the super-clown of today.

The contract that bound Willie Howard to the Witmarks is still in existence, though not in force. In its way it is almost as funny as anything that Willie himself ever breathed across the footlights. As he was under age, the contract was signed for him by his father, whose name was Lefkowitz. John Leffler, himself just of age, acted as go-between, thus early becoming an impresario.

2. Gus Edwards

The Witmarks had become acquainted with Gus Edwards during the years 1896-1898. He started his career, not precisely as a water-boy, but singing out front with the artists, much as Willie did. His favorite haunts were Tony Pastor's, Miner's Bowery Theater, Koster & Bial's, and Hyde & Behman's and the Gaiety in Brooklyn. He sang with such artists as Helena Mora, the queen of female baritones; Imogene Comer; Emma Carus and Cora Routt, torch singers of their day; and with Polly Moran who has since become well known in pictures. The songs he plugged for the Witmarks were the hits, *The Sunshine of Paradise Alley, Only Me, Just One Girl*, and *Just As the Sun Went Down*. He too received $5 a week for his services; as he put it, instead of being a water-boy, he "just joined in from the gallery without being asked." He had a soprano voice, not a falsetto, but more *robusto* than Willie's.

Unlike Howard, Edwards leaned toward the managerial end

of the theatrical world and in this department achieved success. First, he graduated into selling sheet music in theater lobbies, particularly at the Circle Theater, Fifty-ninth Street and Columbus Circle, where some weeks he made as much as seven dollars profit. Talk about your Horatio Alger stories! In after years this theater became the Gus Edwards Music Hall.

Again unlike Willie, Gus was a song writer and became an outstanding composer of ballads. He was to have many hits, but the one with which he will always be identified was *School Days*, published by the Gus Edwards Music Publishing Company in 1906. Four of his other song hits were published by the Witmarks. Two that he had already published and that they took over from him were built up into "terrific" sellers: *Tammany* and *Good-Bye, Little Girl, Good-Bye*. Two he placed with Witmarks direct, and they proved almost as successful: *He's Me Pal* and *In My Merry Oldsmobile*. Add to these Anna Held's famous *I Just Can't Make My Eyes Behave*, *I Can't Tell Why I Love You But I Do*, *Two Dirty Little Hands*, *Could You Be True to Eyes of Blue If You Looked Into Eyes of Brown?*, *Way Down Yonder in the Cornfield*, *I'll Be With You When The Roses Bloom Again*, *If A Girl Like You Loved A Boy Like Me*, and some fifty others, and one gains an idea of his writing activities.

In addition to his gifts as a Tin Pan Alley troubadour, Gus Edwards has been noted for sponsoring a formidable list of stars whose names are household words today. He has numbered among his protégés such varied talents as Eddie Cantor, George Jessel, George Price, Walter Winchell, Helen Menken, Ray Bolger, Eleanor Powell, Armida, Groucho Marx, Earl Carroll, Orville Harrold, Lilyan Tashman, Jack Pearl, Herman Timberg, the Duncan Sisters, Charles King, Lila Lee, Mae Murray, Louise Groody, Sally Rand, Eddie Buzzell, Mitzi Mayfair, Bert Wheeler, Ona Munson, Ruby Norton, Bobby Watson, Lew Brice, Johnny Hines, Marion Weeks, Tyler Brookes, Dan Healy, Sammy Lee, Lillian Lorraine, Mervyn Leroy, Ann Dvorak, Larry Adler, Louis Silver, and Yvette Rugel. What a list to conjure with! What a sum their salaries would add up to today!

3. Joe Santley

Yet another water-boy, Joe Santley, now professional manager for a prominent music firm, was a gentlemanly little fellow with an excellent voice and a pleasing personality. He had the natural gift of putting over a song. He made his debut at Proctor's Fifth Avenue Theater as an added attraction, where Dave Fitzgibbons, the pianist, was holding forth; and when Dave played they had no need of an orchestra. Joe served water to the patrons as he joined in the refrains of the current Witmark successes: *Come Down, Ma Evenin' Star, Absence Makes The Heart Grow Fonder, Good Night, Beloved, Good Night, Say You Love Me Sue, Mammy's Little Pumpkin Colored Coon*, and *When You Were Sweet Sixteen*. Joe, in fact, claims to have been the singer who introduced the last-named song.

It may well be, for at this time—1900—Julie Witmark was on tour over the Orpheum Circuit from coast to coast. Coast to Coast! What a difference in the meaning of that phrase today, when a voice is heard over the entire nation simultaneously! What a difference in circuits! In 1900 the Orpheum Circuit comprised exactly five houses: four Orpheums, respectively in San Francisco (the home theater), Los Angeles, Kansas City, and Omaha; plus a Chutes at San Francisco. Julie sent many a song on the road to success during this tour, and it was no small compliment to Joe Santley that he was booked right after Julie in 1901. Nor was it a small achievement to follow up Julie with the success that Joe enjoyed. Santley's tour kept alive the songs that Julie had made popular.

Later, Santley left the theater, went into the music publishing business under the name of "Santley Brothers," and has had gratifying success.

Victor Herbert

Julian Edwards

Madame Schumann-Heink

Alice Nielsen

4. Will R. Anderson

Will Anderson, who was not to make a name as a writer of musical comedy until 1918, with "Take It From Me," to book and lyrics by the popular cartoonist, Will B. Johnstone, had scored a big hit with *Tessie (You Are The Only Only)* two decades earlier. *Tessie*, indeed, became the theme song of the Boston National baseball team. It had been introduced by Stanley Hawkins in the Broadway success, "The Silver Slipper," by Leslie Stuart, composer of "Florodora." *Tessie* was a "natural"; it is still remembered and sung by baseball fans. At the time everybody was singing *Tessie*. Anderson's sister, like so many before and after, came to Isidore with a problem.

"Mr. Witmark," she said, "I have the opportunity of procuring for Will a fine musical education abroad, but it is up to you to tell me whether his talent justifies such an expenditure of time and money. Should he go over, or not?"

He went over, remained abroad for three years, and returned with a musical education that stood him in good stead for years to come. Nor was he a one-hit composer. Among his later hits were *Good Night, Dear,* for Billie Burke; *Here's To The Girls*, interpolated in the English musical comedy "The Girls of Gottenberg"; *Just Someone* for Maud Lambert and *I Love You All The Time.*

"Take It From Me" had a breath of freshness about it that augured well for Anderson's future in musical comedy. He died suddenly while negotiating for the production of his last piece, "The Love Pirate."

5. Julian Edwards

Julian Edwards was another name to conjure with in the early 1900's. He was one of the few contemporaries of Victor Herbert who wrote operas comparable to the Irishman's. He was also a writer of religious works and had many well-known cantatas to his credit. Moreover, he was one of the famous operatic directors of his time, having been associated in his early days with the Duff Opera Company. Afterward he directed his own operettas chiefly, most of them under Fred C. Whitney, one of the prominent managers of the day.

Despite his sweet, boyish nature, his melodies were vigorous, red-blooded, and yet charming, as witness his *My Own United States*. Among composers he was unique; he never complained, no matter how his royalty statement read. On the contrary, he would always ask, "Are you satisfied?"

Among his writings were the sacred cantatas, *Lazarus, The Redeemer, The Mermaid*, and *The Storm*. He wrote incidental music for "In the Palace of the King," and "Quo Vadis?"

His wife was a remarkable woman; being a fine musician she was a helpful companion, copying his scores and at times assisting him in his orchestrations. She was a well-known singer in her day and her brother Ted Siedle was the technician of the Metropolitan Opera House.

After Julian passed on, his wife became interested in musical club work as one of the leaders in the musical life of New York City.

6. Gustav Luders—Frank R. Pixley

Gus Luders had first become known in Chicago, during the Fair epoch, when Frank Witmark represented the firm there. Gus was musical director for a number of local productions, and was also employed as an arranger by Witmarks. His name as such is on the original piano arrangement of *My Gal Is A High Born Lady*. His first success, for which he wrote the score in 1900, was Frank Pixley's "The Burgomeister," which was opened in Chicago and was brought to New York, bringing Luders with it. The success of "The Burgomeister" in New York was so great that the team of Pixley and Luders was soon loaded down with commissions for other works, and they turned them out with considerable rapidity

My Gal Is A High Born Lady.

SONG and CHORUS.

Arr. by GUSTAVE LUDERS.   Words and Music by BARNEY FAGAN.

Moderato.

Professional copy of one of the biggest successes of its day. What is unusual on this copy is the name of the arranger. This was in the early days before Gustave Luders had won renown with such musical comedy successes as *The Prince of Pilsen* and *King Dodo*.

227

11

and success. "The Burgomeister" with its song hit, *Tale of a Kangaroo,* featured William Norris and Henry E. Dixey. It was soon followed by two other notable productions, "King Dodo," starring Raymond Hitchcock, with its popular numbers *Look in the Book and See* and *Tale of the Bumble Bee,* and that perennial hit, "The Prince of Pilsen," with John Ransone, Arthur Donaldson, and a company of stars. Jess Dandy played John Ransone's part in the second company. The song successes of "The Prince of Pilsen" assure frequent revivals of this piece: *Heidelberg, Message of the Violet,* and *The Tale of the Seashell.*

The Witmarks were fond of Gus Luders, and took him to their hearts. Though high-strung and temperamental, he was a most lovable man, easy to get along with, and to know him was a privilege. His music reflected his nature; tuneful, bright, gay. He was a thorough musician, did all his own scoring and orchestrating, and was an excellent conductor. He wrote most of his productions with Frank Pixley, another lovable character, who, besides writing books for musical shows, was a sure-fire lyricist. His series of "tales" (*Tale of the Bumble Bee,* etc.) is proof of this. He and Gus made an ideal team and were very happy in their work together.

Luders had been resting for some time, when Henry W. Savage, for whom he had written most of his productions, and who was fond of him, called him up one day to say he had a commission for him to compose a new musical show with book by Avery Hopwood, the playwright. Gus, who had been chafing under this spell of idleness, was happy to get back into harness, even though it was not with his favorite book-writer. Refreshed by his rest, he turned out a good score, and everything looked auspicious for the opening. It was one of those old-time openings, too, everybody enthusiastic and many predicting another "Prince of Pilsen." Gus and Isidore went to sleep that opening night, assured, from the way the piece had been received, that it would enjoy a long run.

But—that fatal morning after! To their astonishment, the newspapers were cruel. The leading critics "panned" the show. No one could understand it, but it was suspected that the critics had it in for Hopwood. This was the only reasonable explanation they could think of, because truly the show did not deserve such treatment. Whatever the cause, the effect was disastrous. Henry W. Savage, the producer, who under ordinary circumstances would have nursed the attraction, was ill and was so discouraged by the notices that after the third performance he ordered the show closed.

Savage's unexpected action was such a shock to Gus that he never survived it. He was found dead in his bed the next morning of a heart attack. He died, literally, of a broken heart.

7. Dr. Alfred G. Robyn

When "Freddie" Robyn died in October, 1935, the musical world was bereft of a memorable figure. Although he was seventy-five years old he retained his youthful energy and enthusiasm and kept up-to-date. He was born in St. Louis, where he received his musical education from his father, William Robyn, an organist. Fred, too, became an organist of prominence. He was chief organist at the opening of the Rialto Theater, New York, and was at the Capitol Theater during the "Roxy" régime. Fred was best known for having composed the operettas, "The Yankee Consul" and "The Yankee Tourist" for Raymond Hitchcock, and "Princess Beggar" for Paula Edwards. His ballad, *Answer*, will keep the name of Robyn alive for many years.

8. Lyman Frank Baum

Lyman Frank Baum was born in Chitenango, New York, in 1856, started out to be a newspaper man but his efforts in authorship soon eclipsed all his other work. He wrote over fifty volumes

229

most of which were for children. His plays included "Maid Of Arran" in 1881 and "The Queen and the Killarney" in 1885. *The Wizard of Oz,* which he called his most truthful tale, appeared in 1900. Many *Oz* volumes followed. Isidore Witmark has in his cabinet the manuscript of the first and only chapter ever written of a book that he and Frank Baum had planned to write together, entitled, *The Whatnexters.*

The Witmarks published Frank Baum's *Wogglebug* with music by Frederick Chapin and his successful theatrical version of *The Wizard of Oz,* music by Paul Tietjens, which swept Dave Montgomery and Fred Stone to fame and made money for everyone.

One of the most prized volumes in Isidore's library is a little book that bears the following caption on the title-page: *"By the Candelabra's Glare.* Some verse by L. Frank Baum, Chicago, Privately printed By L. Frank Baum, in his own Workshop, 1898. Ninety-nine copies of this Book were Made."

The introduction to this book is a sheer delight:

A friend of mine, who has attained eminence as a critic, once found me glancing through a book of verse.

"What are you looking for?" he demanded.

"His excuse," said I.

"My dear boy," returned the eminent critic, frowning severely, "there can be no excuse for a book of verse."

"Not if it chances to be poetry?" I asked.

"Ah," said my friend, lightly, "that is another matter."

My best friends have never called me a poet, and I have been forced to admire their restraint. Nevertheless, this little book has an excuse. Unaided, I have set the type and turned the press and accomplished the binding. Such as it is, the book is "my very own."

Another peculiar thing about the volume which I believe renders it unique, is the fact that there has not been a penny of expense attending its production. For my good friends, when they found I was going to make a book, insisted upon furnishing pictures and material, and I generously allowed them to do so.

I have done the work evenings, when my business cares were over. It has been my recreation.

9. John Kendrick Bangs

John Kendrick Bangs, author, editor, and playwright, presented the rare combination of a great mind and a great heart. He was in turn editor of *Life, Harper's Weekly, Metropolitan Magazine* and the comic weekly, *Puck.* He wrote many humorous books, the most popular among which were *The Houseboat on the Styx, Coffee and Repartee, The Idiot, The Pursuit of the Houseboat, The Idiot at Home,* and *Mr. Bonaparte of Corsica.* His produced plays were "The Bicyclers," a farce, 1899, "Lady Teazle," a musical version of "The School For Scandal," in which Lillian Russell starred in 1905, for which A. Baldwin Sloane wrote the music, and "The Man From Now" which he wrote in 1905, music by Manuel Klein, produced by Henry W. Savage. There was no warmer friend—no one more loyal or sincere—than John Kendrick Bangs. His character is best summed up in one of his own verses, from *Leaves From a Lecturer's Note Book,* published by the Century Company in 1916:

> "I can't be what Shakespeare was,
> I can't do what great folks does;
> But, by ginger, I can be
> ME!
> And among the folks that love me
> Nothin' more's expected of me."

10. Helf and Hager

Helf and Hager was a young firm of unusual energy and ability when they started in 1904. Fred W. Hager was the leader of the Hager Recording and Park Band when he joined J. Fred Helf in this new enterprise. They were acknowledged hit-writers and hit-makers and between them had some of that period's greatest successes: Helf's *A Picture No Artist Can Paint, A Bit of*

Blarney, How Would You Like To Be The Iceman?, and Hager's *Laughing Water* and *Miss Dixie*. They were also the publishers of the Jean Havez hits, including *Everybody Works But Father*, made popular by the minstrel, Lew Dockstader, the Dillon Brothers' *Every Little Bit Added To What You've Got Makes Just a Little Bit More*, and many others.

11. Harry von Tilzer

Harry von Tilzer, one of the most prolific hit-song writers ever known, was an Indiana boy who loved the circus, the stage, and was always following bands all over town. When he was fifteen he ran away from home with a barnstorming company, and, although his earlier years were spent on the stage, his leisure time was devoted to writing songs which he either sold outright for from $2 to $25; or else simply gave away to singers who would sing them in their acts.

Shortly after arriving in New York he teamed up with Andrew B. Sterling. He wrote many songs before he wrote one that became a hit. This was *My Old New Hampshire Home* originally published by William C. Dunn, and later assigned to another publisher, who assigned it to Shapiro, Bernstein & Company.

Most of the thousands of songs written in those early years went toward gaining him the recognition he was striving for from the publishers. Some of these songs were published, but a great many of them were not. One that never went beyond the professional copy was *Mama Make Goo Goo Eyes At Papa* bought by Sol Bloom as representative of the Chicago branch of M. Witmark & Sons. The Witmarks were afraid the public would think the lyric too suggestive, so the song died a quick death.

Then while on tour through Connecticut with a traveling show, Harry wrote *I'd Leave My Happy Home For You*, one of the first "oo-oo-oo" songs—a tremendous hit. A few months later, while managing an office in Chicago for Shapiro, Bernstein & Co., he wrote *A Bird In A Gilded Cage*, and this was the song that really placed him in the money class. During the next twelve months he wrote many song hits including *Down Where the Cotton Blossoms Grow*. He also became a partner in the firm of Shapiro, Bernstein & Co.

In 1902 he formed his own company, and wrote and published such hits as *On a Sunday Afternoon, In the Sweet Bye and Bye, Strike Up the Band, Down Where the Wurtzberger Flows*, and a rapid succession of "coon songs"—among them *What You Gonna Do When the Rent Comes Round?, Alexander, Moving Day, Jefferson Lee*.

CHAPTER XIV

A LIBRARY AND A HOUSEWARMING

1. Two Basements—Two Millions

BY THE time the Witmark Music Library had been settled in the basement of 8 West Twenty-ninth Street, it was making steady progress. For the musician it was a treasure trove. On its shelves were to be found the complete orchestral scores of virtually every contemporary opera and many of the older ones. A large staff of stenographers and copyists in the working room transcribed words and music for special performances. Frank Saddler, ace among the arrangers of the time, would be seen at his own desk, at work upon an orchestration. There was a main room, an oratorio room, a reception room—the musical world in miniature.

Not least among the treasures were autographed scores from famous composers, many of whom had passed on. There was, for rare example, the original of an Overture, "Composed and dedicated to Charles Kemble, Esq., by M. William Balfe, 1824."

Of all who have listened with sentimental pleasure to the strains of "The Bohemian Girl," how many know that its singer-author entertained symphonic ambitions? He was not to write his famous ballads for twenty years, and he, least of all, dreamed that his Marble Halls would fill the dreams of generations.

The needs and conveniences of the amateur were especially

234

SEPT. 17, 1898.

VAUDEVILLE. VAUDEVILLE. VAUDEVILLE. VAUDEVILLE.

M. WITMARK & SONS

ANNOUNCE

A NEW DEPARTURE. A NEW DEPARTMENT.

The Witmark Music Library,

Witmark Building, 8 West 29th Street, near Fifth Avenue, New York.

TELEPHONE: No. 2403 38th Street.
CABLE: "Wityork," Edlow, New York.

Constantly on hand, for sale and to hire, the *largest* collection of Vocal Concert Numbers and Excerpts in America.

For Musical Directors of Symphony, Oratorio and other high class concerts: Orchestra Scores and Parts of all standard modern Symphonies, Overtures, Operatic Selections and Miscellaneous Compositions (including the Neuendorff and Uhlig collections); also Oratorios, Masses, Cantatas, for Choir and Concert Singers.

For Conductors of Opera and Comic Opera: Orchestra and Vocal Scores, Orchestra Parts (full orchestration and condensed) of all standard Grand Operas, Opera Comiques, Comic Operas, Musical Comedies, Burlesques, &c.; Vocal Solo and Chorus Parts; Prompt Books, Stage Managers' Guides, Scenery and Costumes; in fact, everything appertaining to the production of operatic works.

Music of every description arranged, transposed, copied, hectographed, lithographed, &c. Prompt Books, Librettos, Manuscript Compositions, &c., adapted, translated, localized, printed (for copyright purposes), typewritten and bound.

Repertoire Companies furnished with positively first-class operatic material that is complete in every detail. "We are looking for your business; you will be pleased with the manner in which your interests are cared for."

Are you interested in Amateur affairs? If so, send for our Catalogue of Catalogues, bearing on the subject in every phase. Free on application.

A Novel Departure in connection with our Amateur department is a thorough and most reliable Bureau of Information. This Bureau is in charge of MR. FREDERICK SOLOMON, the well-known comic opera comedian, stage and musical director. He will be glad to assist our out of town correspondents by answering to the best of his ability, any questions of doubt and make plain intricate technicali es regarding stage business or direction of the orchestra, and thereby aid materially toward successful results of a production. Our local and suburban clientele will receive MR. SOLOMON'S advice in person. The services of the Bureau are free of cost to our patrons.

"The Crest" high grade Music Paper (none genuine without watermark), used and indorsed by all prominent composers and musicians. Best material—most practical ruling. Send stamp for sample sheet.

Representatives for Composers having late operatic successes to negotiate.

First advertisement announcing a new departure, September 17, 1898.

235

in the minds of the proprietors. As amateurs, in the ordinary sense, they had themselves begun. As amateurs, in the etymological sense,—that is, lovers of music—they would continue for the rest of their days. A large advertisement, taking a third of a page in *The New York Dramatic Mirror* of September 17, 1898, had officially announced the new department, which was a new departure as well.

The more practical activities of the Library included the preparation of duplicate parts for actual productions. Soon it was operating a day and night shift, making extracts from orchestral scores, copying the principal vocal rôles, and hectographing chorus parts from the leading musical plays of the forthcoming season.

Meantime, what of the prototype of the Witmark Music Library—the Arthur W. Tams Music Library? The rivalry of the two firms was to continue for almost thirty years. Between them, the two Libraries to a degree would divide the world of music. The Tams organization was to acquire primacy in cantatas, oratorios, masses. The Witmarks were to lead in the rental of popular operatic productions. They did not merge until the year 1925, and many a battle was fought until a lasting peace was declared. One legal conflict alone, which involved the German operas in the library of the Conried Opera Company, cost the Tams and the Witmark organizations $50,000 between them. For years, Arthur W. Tams and Isidore Witmark were not on speaking terms.

Tams, too, was of pioneer stuff. He had started his business in a little back room, in 1885. He was a stage manager at the time of the Casino Theater, and spent the bulk of his salary upon the acquisition of scores and orchestrations.

When, at long last, the rivals sank their differences in a merger, the deal involved no less than two million dollars. Not a bad figure for two enterprises each of which started in a basement!

A LIBRARY AND A HOUSEWARMING

2. *A Bierstube—Henry Hart*

On the evening of Thursday, March 15, 1900, the Witmark boys presented to their parents, Daddy and Queen, a beautiful home at 57 West Eighty-eighth Street, then one of the good residential districts of the city. With filial pride, they had furnished it from cellar to dome.

Maybe Queen Witmark, the silent muse who presided over the family fortune, recalled a prophecy made to her on another moving day, when her boys had rented a cubbyhole at 32 East Fourteenth Street and found it all they could do to make their lunch money. They were in their teens then, but they had man-sized ambitions. "Queen," Isidore had said, "we'll be the biggest in our line some day." And the Queen smiled, and answered, in her native German, "Deine Worte in Gottes Ohren." (Your words in God's ears.)

It was a great housewarming on that March evening. There had been a blizzard all day—one that recalled the March of twelve years before—and by night the snow was so high that they had the marquee lead into the basement instead of up the stoop. Beefsteak parties were a novelty in those days, particularly when given in private homes. The boys had secured the services of their friend, Ben Singer, at that time owner of "The Dungeon," a famous beefsteak resort adjoining the Madison Square Theater, in Twenty-fourth Street near Broadway. He sent up his gas stoves, a chef and waiters, and necessary equipment. The stoves, especially made for cooking steaks, were attached to the gas main in the cellar, where the party was given. The cellar had been transformed into a poster room. Collecting theatrical posters in those days was a fad. Some of the French posters, used to conceal the coal bins, were expensive; they were stretched on linen and varnished.

They had an orchestra of five pieces. It had been difficult to

237

get the piano down into the cellar! There were sixty-five guests. Isidore had just produced two minstrel shows at different clubs, and among the guests were enough participants in each to give an impromptu minstrel without rehearsal.

In this new home they found themselves with two dining-rooms, one of which was in the basement. The basement dining-room in such houses was generally turned into a billiard room. None of the boys being interested in billiards, it was thumbs down on this idea. What should it be? An old-time bierstube suggested itself to them, and the suggestion turned into a greater reality than they ever expected. They had special furniture made, special chandeliers and andirons; the steins and other equipment, however, were left to the generosity of friends, who proved open-handed in their contributions. They received *over four hundred steins,* from one inch to six feet in height. Various artist friends vied with each other to paint or sketch originals for the walls. They had many a party in this room, with the imported beer always on tap, and it became a sort of hang-out for the gang. There was one thing, however, that they didn't go in for, and that was cards. No particular reason, except that they had always been too much involved in business.

But one day, Jay rebelled. "Why can't we play cards?" he demanded. "We have the surroundings for a congenial game and we never take advantage of it."

"All right," said Isidore. "Julie, you and Jay invite Henry Hart up tonight for dinner, and while I bring my copyright books up to date at one table, you can have your game at the other." Henry Hart was their first employee. He had come to them in 1885 and was like one of the family.

And so it happened. A new era had dawned for the *bierstube.*

Isidore got busy at his books, and over at the other table the game was on. Such a racket had not been heard in the beer-room since it had been opened for business. They were playing a three-handed game, and were slapping their cards down vehemently, shouting their plays. Isidore looked over casually and saw that they were all absorbed, so he returned to his task.

Gradually the excitement abated. Sensing something, he looked over again, and to his surprise saw that only two were playing; Jay, who had been the one to demand the card game, had fallen fast asleep. Isidore continued his work. He became so engrossed that at first he did not notice another radical change at the other table. The intense stillness finally attracted his attention. Glancing over again, what should he see but brother number two in deep slumber, and Henry Hart playing a game of solitaire. It might be recorded here that this was the first and last card game played in the *bierstube*.

For Henry Hart, who, approaching eighty, still serves M. Witmark & Sons under its ownership by the Warner Brothers, the Witmarks feel a special affection. He was and remains a unique character. For over fifty years, without interruption, he has filled his place of trust faithfully and self-effacingly.

He had come to them as a voluntary assistant on Saturday afternoons, having been introduced by a mutual friend who worked, as did Hart, for the necktie makers, Waterhouse & Co. At once he was christened "Hank the Mail Boy," and many was the glass of beer to which Hank treated his juvenile week-end employers. This inversion of the usual situation took place at the old Spingler House in Fourteenth Street, recently torn down, or McKeever Brothers at Sixth Avenue and Fourteenth Street, where the free lunch spreads assailed the nostrils of the kids from number 32 East Fourteenth with the fragrance of a banquet.

Hart's regular job was tip-printing, which was far more important in the 1880's than it is today. In those days the four-in-hand and the Ascot were manufactured ready to wear. The portion that went around the neck was called the tip and carried, on the inside, the name of the brand: "De Luxe," "Dandy," "Champion," "The Fifth Avenue," and other sobriquets that did not quite attain to the imaginative heights of Pullman-car christening. Printing the trade-name was a craft that called for a heated machine, so that the gold or silver leaf used in the process could be transferred to the tip of the tie. Hart was an expert at the job. About this time, however, the present-day tie was coming into fashion, and soon tip-printing had begun its subsidence into lost arts.

No sooner was Hart available for a full-time position than the Witmark boys offered him a place with them in their cubbyhole. Hart had a pleasant voice, he was a good dancer, and had done considerable work in amateur theatricals. The music business was congenial to him, and he became congenial to the music business. The singing profession, especially, knew him well. He was I.O.U. godfather to many of the actors—and many still owe. He was valuable as a buffer between the boys and Broadway. He was considered first in every instance that called for the establishment of an office of trust.

Despite his advanced age he is as alert as ever. His record is rare in the history of any firm—as rare as his sterling personal qualities.

Gustav Luders and Isidore in Detroit attending the premiere of
"The Fair Co-ed" with Elsie Janis in 1908

Karl Hoschna

Manuel Klein

CHAPTER XV

ADVENTURES

1. "The Chaperons"

THE new century started well so far as concerned Isidore's ambitions to write the great American musical comedy. He had been too busy to do much music-writing since 1894, when he had composed *The Parisian Patrol* (a piano piece) and *The Man Who Plays The Umpah* to words by Webster C. Fulton. The man who played the umpah was an ancestor of *Yuba* who played the tuba down in Cuba. In 1896, too, there had been another piano piece, *Lucinda's Serenade*.

"The Chaperons," however, was a full-fledged musical comedy, with lyrics by Frederick Rankin. It boasted at least ten song numbers, as well as the production music that rarely reaches print: *The Little Girl Who Couldn't Say No; When I Sing My Low C; In My Official Capacity; It Seems Like Yesterday; Somehow It Made Him Think Of Home; Love In A Palace Is Better; Millinery Mary; Noah's Ark;* and the two hits, *Sambo* and *We're All Good Fellows.* A remarkable cast was assembled for the try-out in Middletown, Connecticut. The stars and stars-to-be were Digby Bell, Walter Jones, Joseph C. Miron, Donald Brian (although he did not change from Brine until his success in "The Merry Widow," 1907), Marie Cahill, Louise Gunning, Eva Tan-

241

guay, May Boley, May de Sousa, Nellie Follis, and Sallie Fisher. Sallie was in the chorus, but she wouldn't be there long!

Middletown, Connecticut, in 1901 was a quiet little place and naturally the hotel facilities were limited. The ensemble of "The Chaperons," on the other hand, was a population in itself. One hundred and ten persons left New York for Middletown; and securing accommodations for the company, together with the show people who had come along, was no easy matter.

The musicians, who were of prime importance to the rehearsals, found lodgings in a private home. They also, alas, found time on their hands, not being wanted until the evening for the dress rehearsal. Being for the nonce without "chaperons"— in any sense you please—they thought up a party, and proceeded forthwith to buy up what looked like the entire beer supply of Middletown.

By six o'clock that evening, their inventive genius had devised a plan to stir up somnolent Middletown with a serenade of empty beer bottles, thrown from the top window of their quarters. To the outraged ears and soul of poor Isidore, anxious composer that he was, every bottle that struck the sidewalk exploded like "the shot heard around the world."

Result: That night at dress rehearsal, when the musicians should have been at their desks in the orchestra pit, they were clamped up in the Middletown Jail. After all the expense of transporting an orchestra from New York, the rehearsal had to be given *with a piano*.

In vain did the composer and other sober members of the company try to soften the hearts of the town fathers. These respectable gentlemen had been so deeply outraged that they insisted on keeping the musicians in jail over night, refusing to consider bail until next morning.

Subsequent companies of "The Chaperons" during its five seasons contained such sterling performers as Trixie Friganza,

242

ADVENTURES

Mabel Hite, Harry Conor, and May Boley, who from a minor part in the original cast graduated to the lead two seasons later.

There was the appearance in New Haven, during which Isidore was honored by two hundred Yale students, who learned the show's hit, *We're All Good Fellows*, just made for collegians, and sang it with professional gusto.

Then there was Newark. It was a near-Waterloo, and it made, for Isidore, one of those enemies that he never forgave. Newark, in miles as in name, was too near to New York. If a show played Newark before it had the imprimatur of New York, it was almost sure to have bad business. "The Chaperons" fared no differently from any of the other productions. At the opening, in fact, so meager was the house that the stage contained more people than the seats. Walter Jones, one of the comedians, walked down to the footlights and addressed the customers. "Gosh, folks, you must be lonesome down there. Why don't you all come up here with us?"

Klaw and Erlanger were the theatrical magnates of the time; they controlled the destinies virtually of every new production about which there might be the slightest doubt. They handed down the decision that "The Chaperons" needed plenty of doctoring prior to it venturing before a New York audience. Frank L. Perley, the manager of the company, was among the stage autocrats of the time; he had a remarkable record as manager of the famous Bostonians and of the Alice Nielsen Opera Company. He had not yet been bagged by Klaw and Erlanger, and they were eager to get him under their thumbs.

Perley was not so expert in musical comedy as he had been in operetta. So when Klaw and Erlanger proposed that George W. Lederer be called in, Perley readily agreed. That settled Perley. Klaw and Erlanger now had him where they wanted him.

Lederer was a clever showman, and a henchman of the magnates. He took a professional look at the show in Newark under

243

the worst possible conditions and decreed that, in addition to many minor changes, it must be cut down to two acts. He also decreed that George V. Hobart must be hired to put in new material; with Hobart, Isidore wrote a new song, *Talk, Talk, Talk*. Lederer was to receive $175 per week from that time on. It was a gift, as he did practically nothing. Hobart, too, was collecting a good price.

It was to the interest of Klaw and Erlanger to make out "The Chaperons" as a failure. Naturally, they used the Newark business—or lack of it—as evidence. They reckoned, however, without the never-say-die spirit of the composer.

The next week the piece played Providence, which, much farther than Newark from Broadway, was free of Gothamite influence in the matter of new shows. The opening night was a triumph.

It was still, for stage purposes, the original version of the comedy. Lederer and Witmark sat in a box. People screamed with laughter at the comedy and applauded the songs with the unmistakably spontaneous clapping which no claque can simulate. The show, in fact, was going so well that Lederer, completely forgetting himself—and his $175 per week—turned sharply on Isidore and demanded, "Say, what's the matter with this show? It's great!"

Isidore looked at him blandly. A few minutes later, however, Lederer reverted to type. That spontaneous endorsement had been a mistake; that $175 was slipping through his fingers. So he insisted that the show must be made into a two-acter, despite the reception in Providence. And two acts it was, with Lederer practically in control.

It was tough for Isidore, but there was no other way out. It was hard to agree to the cutting out of five of his numbers in order to rearrange the show. There is a time in the life of a young writer, after he has been hounded to death, when he is rendered indifferent to the artistic end of his production and reconciles himself to what may come out of the box office. That was pretty much how Isidore felt at this juncture.

To get away from it all, he took advantage of a trip to Europe. George W. Lederer promised him faithfully that he would watch over his interests. When he failed to keep this promise, alleging as excuse that he was under orders from Erlanger, Isidore never spoke to him again.

During the next thirty-five years, he did many things to try to regain Isidore's friendship, but Isidore has a sort of creed that has placed him in a similar position with a number of other "dear friends" of the past. He maintains that out-and-out stealing is a business, and that if you're held up by a man he either "gets" you or you "get" him, but that a supposed good friend, abusing a confidence, is the lowest of all low.

Isidore may have lost a number of productions that Lederer could have put his way, but whenever he was approached to make up, his answer was that he could still drive a street-car.

While Isidore was abroad, "The Chaperons" had been brought into New York. By now Perley was leaving almost everything to Lederer. One of the first things Lederer did was to break an important clause of Isidore's contract with Frank Perley. That clause provided against any interpolations, in spite of which, and in violation of his promise to watch over Isidore's interests, Lederer introduced and featured a number called *Bloomin' Lize*, which cost Isidore over three thousand dollars in legal fees to have eliminated. It should never have been in, in the face of the fact that his own numbers were such a success. *Sambo* alone, Eva Tanguay's song, averaged twelve encores a night.

Good old Eva! Eva Tanguay is one of the most peculiar characters that our stage has produced. Isidore had occasion to watch and appreciate her under many circumstances. She made her first success in "The Chaperons," in which she played a female detective. In recognition of her song hit she used to call him her "Sambo man," and in a two-page advertisement, inserted in

Variety, she publicly acknowledged that it was "The Chaperons" and not vaudeville that had made her. She was a sort of stage enigma, which was best explained by the operetta writer and contemporary of Victor Herbert's, Julian Edwards, already mentioned in these pages, who summed it up as follows: "When she was on the stage I wished she were off, and when she was off, I wished she were on."

The dance Eva did in the *Sambo* song tightened up the muscles of her calves so badly that she became muscle-bound every night and had to seek relief by having the property man beat the back of her legs with barrel staves!

Eva was powerful, and few ever gave her an argument—or got away with it if they did. On one occasion she nearly choked Isidore to death, without realizing what she was doing. He was traveling with "The Chaperons" company, making some changes before coming into New York. They were on their way from Buffalo into Canada, and as usual the train was stopped by the customs on Suspension Bridge. The company of the play "The Telephone Girl," another success of the day, coming into the States from Canada, was also held up. It was early in the morning, but the members of both companies had hurried into their clothes in order to get a breath of fresh air on the platform. Always anxious to be on the train when it was moving out, Isidore did not leave his car, but stood on the lowest step watching the procession.

All at once Eva came out, and, standing on the step above him, leaned on him, putting her arms around his neck. She, like him, was reviewing the passersby in hopes of seeing someone she knew. A young woman of the "Telephone Girl" chorus, who must have dressed hurriedly, happened to be striding by, when, without warning, her skirt dropped off, and there she stood in all the glory of her scanty panties.

Eva let out a shriek of laughter, her arms tightened around

Isidore's throat, and there he was, helpless in a grip of steel. She didn't even know he was there.

His shouting was muffled by the way she held him. There was only one thing to do, and he did it: he bit her. Like a tiger she recoiled, and was about to make a spring at him, when he all but collapsed. Then only did she realize what she had been doing. There were explanations all around and they remained just as good friends as ever.

After her success in "The Chaperons," Eva went into vaudeville and became a nationally-known theatrical figure—a headliner wherever she appeared. She had many genuine idiosyncrasies but not a few of them were good business, and she was careful to have them publicized. One instance was when she was invited to a dinner given to the cast of "The Chaperons" by Walter Jones. She refused absolutely to attend because the chorus had not been invited.

2. A Guinea Performance

If, when Isidore had first crossed to London in 1892, the copyright situation in regard to songs had been bad, by the end of the decade, while better, it was still complicated, for it involved a considerable property in musical comedies. When the Witmarks took over the representation of Victor Herbert in 1898, they foresaw that he was to be a figure of international importance in the world of music; the matter of copyright was therefore gone into more carefully than ever before. International copyright was still young—some seven years old, and a number of unpleasant years were ahead for it.

There was a decided difference between the English and the American code of copyright. In this country, everything was—and is—copyrighted under one form. In England there were two distinct copyrights, one for publishing and the other for performing. In those days, the Witmarks saw to it that they were protected under both forms by making simultaneous entries at the Library of Congress in Washington, and at Stationers' Hall in London; in the latter case, copies were deposited on the same day in the British Museum.

In the case of a dramatic composition, so far as England was concerned, the mere deposit of a copy was not enough if the performing rights also were desired; in addition, what was called a "copyright performance" had to be given in public. The detail involved was tedious but inescapable, and here the capabilities of Charles Warren, the English representative of the Witmarks, were doubly appreciated.

In order to protect the Herbert operettas, "The Fortune Teller," "The Red Mill," and their fellows, it was necessary to send to London complete rehearsal material—the book, vocal and piano score, dialogue, solo and chorus parts. The copyright performances, however, differed from those of a regular theatrical performance. Only *one* performance was required; but how entangled it became in the red tape of the process! First, the book had to be read by the Examiner of Plays. The reading fee was £1.1.0. If it met with the approval of that functionary, it was licensed by the Lord Chamberlain for a single performance at a theater or hall designated in the license. Next, the hall or theater had to be rented by the producer, at a rental averaging about the cost of the reading fee. The producer now found himself under the necessity of hiring an entire company of actors for that one performance; if the piece were a musical one, he would have to hire also a chorus and a pianist. (Fortunately, an orchestra was not required by the law!) A musical show demands rehearsals—another expense.

The producer's troubles were not over yet. He had to provide his own audience and to advance to each member of that audience the price of admission, one guinea. The guinea was returned to him, at the box office, after the performance. As a matter of form he had to advertise the show and issue posters.

This formality was gone through regularly with the Herbert and other operettas. Of course, in the end it paid, as it procured to the publisher and producer the rights to regular production. But it was a nuisance!

3. ". . . *In Triumph Shall Wave*"

Isidore had not gone to London in 1901 solely—or even chiefly—for the production of his musical comedy. More important were two other premières: that of "The Fortune Teller" and of a London building for the Witmarks.

The English opening of the Alice Nielsen Opera Company in Victor Herbert's "Fortune Teller" was auspicious. Alice Nielsen made a great personal success and so did Joseph Cawthorn, the comedian, and Eugene Cowles, the basso, especially with the now famous *Gypsy Love Song*. Isidore made an arrangement with the English firm of E. Ascherberg for the publication of the music abroad, and it had a satisfactory sale. Three American companies happened to be playing London at about the same time, and as they were acquainted with each other there was a veritable American colony, with something doing all the time. Many of the players lived in an apartment house on Shaftesbury Avenue known as Regency Mansions; others lived at St. Ermine's Hotel in Westminster. In addition to "The Fortune Teller" company, there were the companies of "Casino Girl" and "The Belle of Bohemia." Some of the people who were featured were Richard Carle, John Hyams, Dave Lewis, Julie Ring, Elfie Fay, Paul Nicholson, Frank Lawton, Trixie Friganza, Viola Gillette, Harry Davenport, Lou Middleton, Lawrence Wheat, Will Armstrong, Vashti Earle, Mildred Devere, and the finest lot of American chorus girls that could be secured, the rage at the turn of the century.

Besides attending the opening of "The Fortune Teller," Isidore's pilgrimage to London was to secure a new home for the publications of M. Witmark & Sons and to superintend the English copyright première of his own "Chaperons." At that time they occupied a floor in one of the Featherstone Buildings at Gray's Court Inn, Holborn.

These buildings were over four hundred years old and wonderfully preserved. Each has some history connected with it. The one next door was the place at which the celebrated Richard Brinsley Sheridan eloped with the beautiful Miss Linley, the belle of Bath. Sheridan, schooling his own scandal, had brought her to the house of an oilman who kept a shop at the corner of Featherstone Buildings. And nearby was the office of W. S. Gilbert of Gilbert and Sullivan. The students there still drink the "health," every evening at sundown, of their favorite Queen Bess.

The offices, however, were away from the theatrical center of London which caused inconvenience. Finding a new place was much easier decided upon than done, for at that time there were few desirable vacancies, and as leases ran into the years, often as many as ninety-nine, it took a good four months' search to discover the most favorable location. This was at 186 Shaftesbury Avenue, at the Oxford end. It was a sort of flatiron building, standing between Shaftesbury Avenue and the street leading into the famous Seven Dials, which at that time could have been compared with our Five Points in New York. However, inasmuch as it was a good situation, and the entrance was on Shaftesbury Avenue, they did not fear the menace of the Dials. It had been their intention to take not a whole building, but a floor or two. The footage in this building, however, was precisely what they required, so Isidore started negotiations for it and learned immediately that bargaining for real estate in London was different from the practices obtaining in the United States.

To begin with, the Witmarks could not negotiate directly. They had to have a lawyer, and the lawyer had to take the matter up with the lawyers of the lessors. The prospective lessees had to make a chart of how they would lay out the rooms and a diagram of what was to appear on the outside of the building.

At last, when these plans had been prepared, they had a conference. Isidore was leaving the next day for America, and, if this negotiation fell through, leaving without a new English home for M. Witmark & Sons.

The conference began, and the plans for the interior were accepted by the lawyers, but dissension arose when it came to the diagram of the outside of the building. They had provided for an American flag and an English flag, in addition to the required signs. Apparently the English owners did not want the American flag displayed at that corner. Charles Warren, who was with Isidore, supported his stand for the United States emblem. The opposing lawyer asked, "What do you want flags for? You don't need flags."

Isidore jumped out of his chair and exclaimed, "Look here, I'm going to put my cards on the table. I've been looking around for four months and this is the only place I've found. Tomorrow I go back to America. But if no American flag goes up on the building, no lease will be signed today."

The opposing lawyer, astonished, asked, "Is it as important as all that?"

Isidore replied that the American flag meant the whole building to him. "This is to be the London headquarters for American professionals," he explained, "and I want them to be welcomed to Witmark's under their own flag—to feel at home under our roof." The opposition went into a hasty huddle. "If it's as important as all that, we will yield."

And while M. Witmark & Sons occupied that building, the American flag and the English flag were displayed side by side.

4. Impromptu Minstrels

It was at about this time that the American "pros" in London were enjoying the hospitality of various clubs, such as the New Lyric Club in Coventry Street, West. The Londoners were so kind that the Americans decided to do something to display their appreciation.

Imagine Isidore's surprise when, coming home one evening after one of his jaunts around town looking for a business site, tired out, ready to go to bed and forget everything, he found his chambers crowded with people.

For the moment he was nonplussed. Then he recognized them as pals, who were noted for plotting practical jokes. He was wary about proceeding. Assuming the rôle of the affable host, but expecting anything, he welcomed them. "Fine. To what am I indebted for this notable assemblage?"

There were Richard Carle, Joseph Coyne, Johnny Hyams, Dave Lewis, Paul Nicholson, Will Armstrong, and a bevy of beautiful American chorus girls.

They were sitting everywhere—on the piano, on the bed—rather more orderly than usual, and in an expectant mood. This made Isidore the more suspicious.

Finally, the spokesman, Dick Carle, began. He said, "Now, Iz, the New Lyric Club has been damned nice to us and we are figuring on getting even by giving them an American show. At first I thought we would give a vaudeville stunt, but as we have all the talent for it we want to give them a swift-moving American minstrel show."

"That's nice," Isidore commented, "but what has this to do with me?"

"It's got all to do with you."

"I don't get you."

"Then get this. We've got to have somebody direct us, and

you're elected. Don't say you can't, because we know you can. We've seen some of your shows."

In spite of which Isidore replied, "I can't, because I'm too tired. I'm going back to America shortly and I haven't yet found suitable quarters for our business. I'm at it every day from nine till four, and I'm worn out."

There was a general uproar of disappointment. Said Carle, "You won't have it so hard with us. We are all professionals, as you know, and all we want you to do is to lay out the show and supervise. We'll do the rest."

Under ordinary circumstances nothing would have pleased Isidore more, for if he ever had a hobby, it was putting on minstrel shows. But he felt he could not do justice to it at this time, and told them so.

When he turned it down definitely, Dick Carle sighed, "All right," and sat down.

A complete silence. No one moved. Isidore was anxious to get to bed, and said, "Well?"

Dick echoed, significantly, "Well?" Then slowly and deliberately, "We may as well tell you that we have pledged ourselves not to leave your rooms until you have consented. And here we are."

It was what we should call, today, a "sit-down strike."

What could Isidore do? Anything to get them out. So he said, "Oh, all right." And with a shout they left, saying they would be back tomorrow at four.

And it was "tomorrow at four" for ten days, when they were all set for their minstrel first part, which took place on Sunday, April 28, 1901.

One outstanding thing was the introduction of the end men. The stage was merely a small platform, but large enough to hold the people when seated. So they couldn't have a grand entry of the end men from behind stage. Necessity, the mother of invention, then played its part. The end men were off the stage when

253

the curtain went up, and at a cue after the opening chorus, to appropriate music, they marched down from the back of the house right through the audience to their seats, playing their bones and tambos, while the girls who were seated on an elevated platform at the back of the stage arose and waved handkerchiefs while everybody sang a chorus of welcome. The effect was electrifying and started off the evening one hundred per cent.

5. "The Cheshire Cheese"

None of Isidore's visits to London was complete without dining at least once at "The Cheshire Cheese." He always took pleasure in bringing a visitor with him. He became acquainted with the waiters, and one in particular was also a sort of guide.

"The Cheshire Cheese," as most people know, was the rendezvous of Doctor Samuel Johnson, James Boswell, Edmund Burke, and others of like prominence. The table where these notables sat in this quaint old hostelry is in the far corner of the big room. To visitors is shown the grease spot on the wall made by the constant leaning of the great Samuel's head, you are assured that this was the original table and these the original chairs.

One day Isidore had a guest with him who was visiting London for the first time. They were entering "The Cheshire Cheese" when they heard a great commotion. There was their waiter-guide with consternation on his face, shouting as if bereft of a child. "My God, somebody has taken Doctor Johnson's chair!"

And surely enough the chair was missing from its regular place. A crowd had gathered around the waiter, shouting questions and offering advice. The result was a Cook's Tour Parade headed by the waiter who was moaning and talking to himself about the impious person who could have committed such a sacrilegious act.

They joined the crowd and walked all over the place. All the time Isidore kept assuring his guest that this was a most unusual occasion and one to be remembered. When the search began to seem almost hopeless, they landed in a dark storeroom where they made out the shape of a man asleep on one chair with his feet on another.

An unearthly scream issued from the waiter-guide as he recognized the lost treasure. With one leap he landed on the desecrator, who happened to be another waiter, and swung the sleeper's legs from the top of the chair with such force that he was flung half way across the room. Throughout this scene the guide was cursing him and threatening to have him fired.

Then, suddenly changing his demeanor, he wrapped his arms around the chair as though it were a long-lost brother; and murmuring words of joy, with pride and dignity led the search party, which by this time had doubled in number, bearing the chair back to the Doctor Johnson table, where it was reinstated with all the pomp and eclat due to a potentate.

6. Harry Harris

Isidore made Harry Harris' acquaintance in London during 1901. He was attracted by his quiet, unassuming demeanor, so unlike that of the average professional boxer. Harris had just beaten the English bantamweight champion, Pedlar Palmer, at the National Sporting Club, thereby winning the world's title of that class, but a casual observer would have been more likely to take him for a young American business man on a tourist trip.

After retiring from the ring he entered the theatrical business and was a familiar figure on the New York Rialto and in the box office of the New Amsterdam Theater. As a sort of side line he also acted as trainer and sparring partner for Abraham Lincoln Erlanger, the then czar of the theatrical world, whom he kept in condition. It was an unwritten law, however, that during their boxing bouts Harry would absorb all the punishment dealt out by Erlanger's gloves, without fighting back. The tutor adhered faithfully to this line of tactics, until it became mechanical.

But one day when sparring in the gym, Harry's mind must have wandered a trifle from the subject in hand. Erlanger was dishing out punches regardless, and several went home with considerable impact. At that moment Abe dropped his guard a bit carelessly. Being somewhat fed up with the sport of being a human target, Harry forgot his caution temporarily, his right shot out to the chin-point and Abe went down in a heap, hardly knowing what had hit him. In a flash the quick-thinking Harris was at the fallen gladiator's side, helping him to his feet. Conscious that his job was at stake, the teacher, with the solemn poker-face that was one of his distinguishing characteristics, remarked sympathetically:

"You must have slipped, Mr. Erlanger. You couldn't have had enough rosin on your shoes."

To which Abe grunted agreement. But there was no more boxing that day!

Later Harris deserted the theatrical field for Wall Street, where Dame Fortune favored him, and he is a successful Curb broker today. In 1929 he paid another visit to London where he was warmly welcomed, feted, and dined by leading sportsmen. The Britons always liked the ex-bantam champion because of the entire absence of arrogance or egotism in his makeup. That kind of athlete never fails to gain appreciation in England.

CHAPTER XVI

"THREE TWINS," BEFORE AND AFTER

1. Karl Hoschna and Otto Harbach

SOON after the establishment of the Witmark Library and the success of "The Fortune Teller," Isidore opened a letter as strange as the hand in which it was written. He was asked to find a place for the writer in his Library; no task, however menial, would be refused. The writer went on to say that he was oboe soloist in Victor Herbert's band, but that he desired to give up oboe-playing as a living. The oboe had been forced upon him. He had studied harmony, composition, and piano at the Vienna Conservatory, and had been obliged, as part of the requirements that went with the winning of a scholarship, to learn a band instrument. He had been assigned to the oboe and had played in the local band for some years. That he had become an expert was attested by his present position as soloist under Herbert. Despite this position he was unhappy, and any other means of livelihood would prove a welcome change.

The chief reason for his eagerness to change was even stranger: he had a notion, indeed, an obsession, that playing the oboe, because of the vibration of the double-reed, would eventually affect his brain. Musicians often are theory-ridden. One pessimist has said—perhaps in a moment of fatigue, following hours

257

of excessive practice—that "eighty per cent of us are wrong in the head." Yet music, in modern times—and not in modern times alone—has been used in the treatment of melancholy and other mental afflictions. At all events, the writer of the letter was ready to surrender a high-salaried position in return for a low wage as copyist in the Witmark Music Library. The letter was so pitiful and so original that it was decided to give the signer a chance. So thorough a musician was hardly expected to remain long at the bottom. It was quickly discovered that he was one of the finest arrangers in the library. And inasmuch as that Library boasted such men as Frank Saddler, this meant a great deal.

The man's name was Karl Hoschna. Perhaps the success of Victor Herbert had inspired him with visions of his own. Isidore took a fancy to him, and for eleven years Hoschna was to be his confidant in the reading of manuscripts and other musical matters. His piano arrangements were especially commendable, and he had a new style in orchestration that made him a favorite in the orchestral department. Gradually he began composing, setting lyrics by the various authors associated with the firm.

Hoschna's melodies had an unusual appeal, and he was much more than one of the one-finger composers then—and now—common in the profession. His chance was not to come until the 1900's, but when it came he was prepared for it.

Charlie Dickson owned the farce "Incog," and came in one day to discuss with Isidore the possibilities of the piece as a musical comedy. "Incog" had been written by the wife of Governor Pacheco of California, and had been a success. Its cast listed an attractive group: Charlie Dickson, Louis Mann, Harry Davenport, Robert Edeson, Lillian Burg, Clara Lipman, and Lillian Burkhardt. Dickson's idea was that Isidore—by this time known for "The Chaperons"—should write the music. Isidore was occupied with others affairs, but agreed to work with Dickson on the book and to supervise the writing of the score.

Here, in Isidore's opinion, was the opportunity for which Hoschna had been waiting. The oboist was elated, and before long he was playing a set of proposed musical numbers that sounded to his employer like a new voice in American song. As Isidore listened, he knew that his faith had been richly justified, and that he had discovered a gift to the national theater. Now, how about the lyricist?

Evidently Hoschna had been thinking of that, too, for one day he brought in some samples of lyrics that a friend of his had written. Isidore looked them over; it was really too good to be true. Here, brought in by one discovery, was another!

"He's waiting outside now," said Karl. "I'd like you to meet him."

Whereupon he introduced to Witmark, and to fame, one of the foremost librettists and lyricists of our theater, Otto Hauerbach. The name was later changed to Harbach. Witmark then and there made a deal to pay Harbach $100 cash for the lyrics. Karl and Otto got to work at once. The result: the score of "Three Twins."

About five weeks later, with the musical comedy still in rehearsal, Isidore had a visit from Harbach, who stood, even as his friend Hoschna had, face to face with an important choice.

"I'm at the parting of the ways, Mr. Isidore," he said, "and I look to you for a decision. My regular business, as you know, is advertising. The Batten people want me to sign another long-term contract. But if you think that I'll make good in the show business, I'll take my chances on that."

Isidore did not hesitate. "The show business, by all means," he answered. "I think there's a big chance for you in that game. I'll stake my reputation on the result."

Harbach's success was phenomenal. "Madame Sherry," "High Jinks," "Rose-Marie," "Mary," "Sunny," "No, No, Nanette," "The Cat And The Fiddle" and "Roberta," in which Harbach has been not only with Hoschna as a composer, but with Rudolf Friml,

Vincent Youmans, Jerome D. Kern, Sigmund Romberg and Victor Herbert.

Despite Hoschna's sudden rise to fame and money, he continued to work at Isidore's side. The demand for his services was so great, however, that he was soon writing new scores for his employers and signing contracts with other producers.

Immediately following "Three Twins" was "Bright Eyes," an adaptation of "Mistakes Will Happen," the rights to which were held by Charlie Dickson. Harbach wrote the lyrics for the new show that starred Cecil Lean and Florence Holbrook. "Bright Eyes," from the box-office standpoint, was moderately successful, but "Madame Sherry" was another smash. Harbach again did the lyrics; the stars were Ralph Herz and Lina Abarbanell. The hit of the show, of course, was *Every Little Movement Has A Meaning All Its Own.* There were also, for Hyams and McIntyre, "Girl Of My Dreams," and, for Ralph Herz, "Doctor De Luxe."

Hoschna was one of the cleverest men in his field and his early death saddened everyone.

2. *"The Song Physician"*

W. T. Jefferson, author of *My Coal Black Lady*—a salient hit of its day—once sent to Isidore Witmark a caricature of the Uncle Sam type, minus the goatee, painted in oil. Across the bottom was an inscription to "I. W.," and the legend, "The Song Physician," as a tribute to Isidore for having doctored his song.

Isidore, a mentor for his younger confrères from the start, had done a deal of doctoring. Besides writing both the words and music to the verse of Ernest Hogan's *All Coons Look Alike To Me,* he rewrote the verse part of the American version of the World War marching hit, *There's A Long, Long Trail.* With regard to how the song came to be written, the composer, Zo Elliott, has said: "In the autumn of 1914, Isidore Witmark accepts the song for publication. He rewrites the verse for American version, changing it from a minor key to a major, and reharmonizes the verse."

There were two published versions of the music of the song, the English with the original verse-melody and the American with Witmark's. The reason for the change on this side was that the original sounded too much like the Chopin funeral march to be acceptable here.

Arthur Penn, a prominent writer and editor of the Witmark staff, was of the opinion that the lyrics of the song were ambiguous. Witmark respected Penn's judgment, but in this case he felt that the very ambiguity was part of the song's charm. To some the long, long trail meant going home; to others, back to the only girl; to others, the Great Beyond.

Isidore put a great deal of work into the comedy "Our Wives," although Frank Mandel received credit for the piece, which later appeared as "The Only Girl" with Victor Herbert's music.

Will B. Johnstone, cartoonist for the New York *World-Telegram*, signed the book of "Take It From Me," albeit Witmark put a tremendous amount of work into it, and even suggested the central theme. This was, as those will agree who saw and heard it, one of the musical comedies that pointed the way to the new sophistication in the field. Johnstone must have been delighted with Isidore's coöperation, for, in an interview, he declared that "Isidore Witmark could dramatize and sell the New York telephone directory."

While Otto Harbach and Wilbur D. Nesbit were credited with the book of "The Girl Of My Dreams," Isidore planned it, and wrote scenes and musical situations while he was in Chicago in 1912, living at the Illinois Athletic Club, where most of the writing sessions took place.

In this, too, Witmark was a hitherto unknown collaborator. Dickson did the actual writing of "Three Twins," and Witmark was constantly in consultation not only for the arrangement of scenes but for the spotting of musical numbers. The continuity of scenes and the "planting" of numbers are two of the essential factors in the success of a musical show. The same song, placed in one position, may register indifferently upon the public, while in another it may "go over big."

Although "Three Twins" became, in time, a sensational success it received a lukewarm reception when first disclosed in Chicago. George W. Lederer charitably suggested that they take the show and dump it into Lake Michigan. Others were less drastic; among them Joseph M. Gaites and Company, of which the Witmarks were the "Company." Gaites had implicit faith in Isidore's judgment, and declared, "If Isidore goes on to Chicago, sees the show, and says that we should bring it to New York, I'll bring it."

Isidore agreed, on one condition: that Gaites engage Clifton Crawford for the New York production. Victor Morley was playing the rôle in Chicago, and Bessie McCoy—as those who saw her cannot readily forget—was the original "Yama Yama Girl."

It was hot, and Izzy wasn't at all eager for travel, but Joe and he left one Friday evening with Clifton Crawford, who might as well not have gone along, for no sooner did they hit Chicago than he was taken down with jaundice and remained *hors de combat.*

Isidore witnessed the two Saturday performances of the show. Instead of an evenly-paced, point-scoring comedy it had been turned into a burlesque. That night he sat up till four in his compartment on the train, making notes in the manuscript of the book. The work completed, he awakened Joe Gaites. "Play the show this way," he prophesied, "and you'll have a knockout."

It sounded egotistical, but Isidore had simply restored the lines and the music that had been eliminated, thus regaining the beautiful atmosphere that the play had originally possessed.

The show was played "this way," and had a triple-company run. The New York company opened at the Herald Square Theater, Thirty-fifth Street and Broadway, and despite a night that seemed to have perched upon the crest of the summer's hottest wave, got off to a sure success. Victor Morley headed the Western company and duplicated the New York event. A number three company with Tom Whiffen in the lead played to $50,000 profit— an unusual figure for a number three troupe.

The Witmarks were laying plans for the next season, and had made up their minds to send out the three companies again. Gaites went to the Erlanger exchange about bookings, and Erlanger called him into his private office. Said Erlanger, "Joe, I don't want you to send out your number three 'Twins' this year."

Joe was taken aback. "What's the matter, Mr. Erlanger? Didn't it give satisfaction?"

"That's the trouble. It's too damned good, and we're not going to let the other fellow have it."

Joe, puzzled, asked Erlanger to explain.

"Well, it looks as if a big battle is on. For years we have booked stars such as Frank Daniels, Anna Held, DeWolf Hopper, in the one-nighters, without any opposition. And we'd take out between eight hundred and twelve hundred a night. Now the Shuberts are cutting in with whatever stars they have, and taking a good slice of that gross away from us. So it looks like we're going to the mat for a real fight, and we're not going to give them any advantage. It seems your number three 'Twins' was booked mostly in their houses last year, because we hadn't many houses on that circuit. Well, I don't want them to have it!"

Joe rushed back and laid Erlanger's ultimatum before the Witmarks. They discussed it at length, finally deciding upon a proposition.

"Joe, go back and tell Mr. Erlanger that we'd be delighted to oblige him and keep the number three company off the road next season. But inasmuch as it cleared $50,000 for us, if he thinks it is worth that much to him, tell him to give you a check for that amount and we won't send it out."

The next two hours were anxious ones for Joseph M. Gaites and company, especially "company."

Finally Joe returned. Did he have that check for $50,000? He certainly did!

And no number three company was sent out that year.

3. *Topsy Turvy*

The music of "Three Twins" was popular, but few know that the two big hits of the show were not written originally for the play. *Cuddle Up A Little Closer* had been done for a vaudeville act, and Karl Hoschna was to receive $100 for it. The money was not forthcoming and Hoschna withdrew the number, adding it to the score of "Three Twins." The other hit, *Yama Yama Man*, was written after the show went into rehearsal in Chicago, and the lyric, which many still think was written by Harbach, was the work of a prolific Chicago writer, the late Colin Davis.

Before coming into New York it was decided to break in the new version, or rather the original version, at New Haven. An unexpected tragedy occurred, now told for the first time. For the opening in New York somebody brought to Gaites a sensational stunt. This "effect" was an upside-down stage setting. Six girls were supposed to be dancing upside down on the floor, which in this case was the ceiling. As a last act finale, the stage was to be shown with everything upside down; the chandelier pointing upwards from the floor; the furniture attached, head down, to the ceiling; the windows and doors were topsy-turvy. Six large columns were evenly distributed on the stage. Each column was hollow, and on the inside, at the top, was a heavy sand-bag counter-weight on a cable. From a slit in each column protruded a gadget that fitted into an iron brace and was clamped there. In each of these braces a girl was placed. When the sand weight at the top was released, the gadget moved up as the sand weight moved down, and at a certain height a cog turned the girl in

264

the brace upside down, so that her feet reached the supposed floor overhead, where she did a repetition of the *Yama Yama* dance.

They should have had two weeks to build the effect, instead of only forty-eight hours, during twenty-four of which the mechanics never slept a wink. The effect was completed about two hours before the show was to go on, with no rehearsals for the dance. Because everyone was so tired out, no one thought of the safety clamp between the gadget and the brace, which kept the girls firmly in position and prevented them from falling out.

When it came to the try-out, volunteers were called for, and a number of the girls shied. It was beginning to look like no effect, when one little girl, the tomboy of the party, spoke up. "I'll go up and show 'em. Who's afraid?"

Whereupon, one of the tired mechanics attached the gadget to the brace, in which the girl was clamped, released the sandbag, and up she went. She had got to the cog and was turning, showing how easily it was done. She began kicking her legs, thus working herself loose—and crash, she fell! Only then did the tired mechanic realize that he had not put the rivet in the gadget to lock the brace.

The girl lay unconscious. She had fallen on her head and shoulder. She was rushed to the hospital where for weeks she hovered between life and death. Eventually she recovered.

Everyone around the place was stunned, helplessly standing around, when Gaites and Isidore arrived from New York. For a moment they could not make out what was wrong, but they learned soon enough. There the company sat, hopelessly helpless, when someone shouted, "Well, are we giving a performance tonight?"

That stirred them out of their stupor.

"Strike!" cried the stage manager, which in theatrical parlance means change of scene. With this the over-fatigued stagehands pulled another terrible bloomer. They unscrewed the columns from the floor, forgetting to release the sandbags, and thus leaving the columns top-heavy. With one thunderous boom the six columns crushed forward, smashing everything in their way, including the leader's violin and missing by inches the pianist's head. This final mishap awoke the stagehands to the realization that they had an evening's performance to prepare.

Although everybody was distressed about the poor little girl who had been hurt, and as a result gave a strained performance, the show went over, and despite Baseball Night in New Haven, when the college boys usually broke up the performance unlucky enough to be playing in the college city. However, the collegians proved quite respectable. In fact, they received the show with acclaim. It foreshadowed the decisive success it attained at the Herald Square Theater in New York, where it ran all that summer and far into the fall.

4. Charles Dickson Sells Witmark to Belasco

"Three Twins," so rich in anecdote, recalls yet another eccentric personality out of those trying, but richly-rewarding days. Charles Dickson was a great favorite with New York theatergoers. He played for the Frohmans in light comedy and wrote many sketches in which he played on the vaudeville stage; among them, "The Salt Cellar" and "Pressing the Suit."

Dickson, having taken up writing and adapting, had come to Isidore with the plan that developed into "Three Twins." That success spurred to new efforts everybody who had been associated in the making of it.

Charles Dickson was a human paradox. He was at once the sweetest, most sentimental, sympathetic fellow imaginable and the most hard-boiled, irascible, and generally cantankerous person one would care not to meet. Like so many of his type, Dickson was a great enthusiast. What is such despair as he used to know but a veritable enthusiasm of moodiness? When he boosted a fellow, he boosted him, not to the sky, but to the stratosphere.

One of the men whom he knew was David Belasco. With "Bright Eyes" ready for production, he thought of Belasco as a backer, although he was hardly partial to musical shows.

It would mean some high-pressure salesmanship, which took the strange form of creating out of Isidore Witmark another Belasco. Dickson, delighted with "Three Twins," brought to the noted producer the name and fame of Isidore Witmark as Exhibit A. Recent musicalizations had failed, among them "Brewster's Millions" and "Baby Mine." The success of "Incog" in its form of "Three Twins" was now laid by Dickson to the credit of Witmark, whom he calmly presented to the Belasco of the legitimate theater as the Belasco of the musical comedy.

Dickson's boosting was so convincing that Belasco became almost eager to meet the musical-comedy wonder and was all but "sold" on "Bright Eyes." A midnight session was arranged between the "two Belascos." Dickson picked up Isidore, and together with their composer and librettist they entered the *sanctum sanctorum*.

It was a large suite over the Belasco Theater. With its paintings, its *objets d'art*, its trophies, antiques, jades, rare volumes, manuscripts, and sculptures, it looked like a museum. They had been seated a few minutes, when in strode Belasco. He was the incarnation of graciousness; but despite his genuine informality they felt instinctively that they were in the presence of greatness.

Dickson lost no time. "Dave, you've met Mr. Hoschna and you've met Mr. Harbach. Now take a look at *it*!" And pointed, with the swing of an introducer's arm at a Madison Square ringside, to Isidore.

"I've met Mr. Witmark before," said Belasco, simply.

"Maybe," countered the irresponsible Dickson, "but not the Isidore Witmark I'm introducing to you tonight!"

To Isidore's abysmal embarrassment he went on: "Dave, he's

all I told you—and more! After he puts on a show in his own inimitable way he has his own fashion of exploiting it. And, big as you are, when it comes to musical shows you can well afford to listen to him!"

"Fine!" came from under the halo.

And from Isidore, nervous and weary of preliminaries, "Let's get down to business."

Charlie started in on a résumé of the whole idea. All listened attentively. It was soon clear that he had swum beyond his depth, and he turned to Isidore for support, asking, "Am I not right, Isidore?" He was not right; he had garbled important points. But Izzy, tactful, replied innocently, "Not exactly, Charlie. I think so-and-so should have been thus-and-thus."

The correction had been made in the spirit of cooperation and in the best of taste. But Dickson was Dickson as Jekyll was Hyde. Suddenly he turned on Witmark—his pal, the Belasco of the musical comedy—with the fury of a mountain-lion.

"What the hell do you know?" he bellowed. Hoschna and Harbach all but fell out of their chairs. Belasco found it hard to believe that he had heard aright. "You think," continued Charlie, in vituperative denunciation, "—you think that you're Isidore Witmark, and that nobody else has an idea in his cranium. Ideas! Why, if anybody did the writing of 'Three Twins' it was *me*, I'll have you understand, and I know what I'm talking about!" He had acquired such momentum that there was no stopping him. His companions sat there, helpless, drowned in the flood of his speech.

Then the paradoxical fellow suddenly realized that he was hearing nothing but his own voice. He stopped short, as if nothing had taken place, and asked, "Well, now, where were we?"

Belasco was obviously amused. Ever the diplomat, he glided over the embarrassment with, "Well, let's talk it over at a little supper."

They went around the corner to one of his favorite restaurants, and ate into the dawn.

A few days later the collaborators heard from Belasco. He had given the matter thought, he reported. If he were going into musical production, he would consider "Bright Eyes," but, for another season at least, he had decided to stick to straight drama.

Had Dickson held his tongue, musical-comedy history in the United States might have read somewhat differently for the early years of the 1900's.

CHAPTER XVII

INNOVATIONS

1. Julie's Marriage

AMONG the chief events important to the Witmarks at the turn of the century was the marriage of Julius to Carrie Rosenberg, of Cambridge, Massachusetts. They had met at Atlantic City and she was in the company of her mother, who seemed to smile upon the match. The pair, however, soon ran into obstacles. The Rosenbergs were summoned home by the illness of a brother. Carrie, a spirited child who had no secrets from her father, told him about her new interest. He received the news with parental happiness—until he discovered that Julius was an actor. At first his feelings about an actor in the family were not antagonistic. Other relatives made the loudest objection, much to the dismay of the girl, for, by sheer force of numbers and reiteration, they began to influence her father. So far nobody but Carrie and her mother had met Julie, whose only crime was that he had given pleasure to thousands with his engaging personality and rare voice.

Carrie herself was determined. The Rosenberg family, for the first time, found itself turbulently in disagreement. Correspondence between Carrie and Julius continued; Julius was eager to go to Cambridge and face the family, but the girl feared a rumpus in earnest. After a persistent campaign, however, she won her father over to a meeting, and it was enough: Julius's presence was the best plea for his cause.

The father, a generous soul, and indulgent toward his daughter, swung over to the side of the sweethearts. The sisters and cousins and aunts, offended at this change in attitude, sulked into a feud, and boycotted the marriage, which was celebrated in Boston on November 5, 1901. This was the only shadow that ever fell across its path. Mr. Rosenberg became proud of his son-in-law, and since he was a splendid business man, his acumen was added to the resources of the publishing firm. He became another daddy to the Witmark boys, and guided them expertly through more than one crisis in the history of the house. He was a tower of strength to lean upon. In his passing the boys lost an irreplaceable support.

On June 6, 1903, was born Julius P. Witmark, Jr., last of the line of the Witmarks. The Witmarks dearly love ceremonies, and the arrival of a son—the only child—called for special observance. A new building had been going up: the Witmark Building in West 37th Street. When, on August 4th of that year, the establishment was inaugurated, Julius P., Jr., was the youngest guest—a couple of days under two months of age.

The Black and White Series, which had been begun a decade before, now started on its path to independent fame. The history of the Series as an institution known the world over wherever "semi-classical" music is appreciated, begins with the birth of Julius P., Jr., and the Witmark Building.

The Witmark Black and White Series, which has been considered the most interesting and valuable catalog of standard ballads in America, took nearly thirty years to establish. It is not alone a catalog of home and concert ballads, but the repository of popular Witmark successes that have become classics, for instance: *Kiss Me Again* and *Gypsy Love Song* by Victor Herbert; *The Long, Long Trail* by Zo Elliott; *My Wild Irish Rose* by Chauncey Olcott; *Mother Machree* and *The Garden of*

My Heart by Ernest R. Ball; *Can't You Hear Me Calling, Caroline?* by Caro Roma.

The series was really begun when Isidore made his first trip to Europe in 1892, becoming interested in some better-class songs by English writers, and securing the American rights to them. It occurred to him that it would be well to use these as a nucleus for a catalog of better-grade songs. The Witmarks tried out these English songs, and retained those that promised to endure. They started then to collect American numbers of equal quality. Julius made the building of this catalog his life-work, and every popular Witmark ballad and operetta success that promised to stand the test of time became part of it. Every jobber and nearly one thousand leading sheet-music dealers in the United States and Canada carried the complete line, giving a special attention to the fifty numbers featured in the pages of the special catalog, *Songland*.

The series contained not only ballads for all voices but sacred songs, arranged for solos, duets, and quartettes, and each song was offered in at least three keys, so that it could come within the range of any voice.

It is with *The Black and White Series* that the Witmark motto, "Success Is Work," became associated and famous although the motto itself goes back to the early Eighties. The New York *Herald* was offering a prize for the best one-act comedy submitted by any of its readers. The piece, as is usually the case in such contests, was to be submitted not under the true signature of the author, but under an identifying proverb or slogan. Isidore, just launched upon his life-work, would hardly be expected to refrain from competing. Together with a friend, Frederick B. Hawkins, he wrote and submitted the comedy, "Uncle George." This is all that has ever been heard of the comedy, but the slogan by which it was identified was destined for a more smiling fate. "Success Is Work" came back to mind when the firm cast about for a trade-mark.

The Bier Stube in the basement of the Witmark home at 57 West 38th Street. Furniture specially made — Over four hundred steins of every description, from six inches to six feet in height. Original paintings and etchings presented by the artists. Imported beer was always on tap.

Gus Edwards

Henry Hart, the first employee
Witmarks ever had. He was with
the firm for fifty years and is
still with M. Witmark and Sons
under Warner Bros. ownership.

INNOVATIONS

2. *The Witmarks Erect Their Own Building*

The Witmarks had used up four years of their five-year lease, and had outgrown the Twenty-ninth Street building. Being well established and in excellent financial condition they were ripe for more pioneering. There were months of looking around, of discussing the type of building they would require; it was not to be had. If, to paraphrase Victor Herbert, they wanted what they wanted when they wanted it, they would have to build it themselves.

Well, they wanted it. The decision was made. The firm announced that they would put up the first building devoted exclusively to the publication of popular music. Much time was devoted to looking for the right site; some were too far uptown; others, not far enough. Forty-fifth Street was far uptown, for when Dad suggested a prospect in that vicinity, the boys said it was impossible—they couldn't get anyone to come way up there! Today the RCA Building, at Fiftieth Street and Sixth Avenue, is the center of music publishing! As a compromise, they decided on Thirty-seventh Street, between Broadway and Seventh Avenue. The move broke up the small, closely-knit locality which was the original Tin Pan Alley. Many firms followed the Witmarks, and before long the music firms were scattered in the midtown district.

On January 24, 1903, the cornerstone was laid. Everything was moving smoothly. They notified their agents that they would not renew at 8 West Twenty-ninth Street, and planned to be in their own building in June. Suddenly a building strike was called. When they approached the agents for an extension of a month in their old location, to their dismay the request was turned down. The agents declared that they must have the building at the expiration of the lease. This was something they hadn't bar-

273

gained for. It spelled almost ruin for them because it meant that they would have to move twice.

Besides, with all the moving, the staff would be demoralized and much business lost. They pleaded with the agents, offered to pay them a bonus, anything within reason; but to no avail. The Witmarks were becoming almost distracted, until someone suggested, "Why not see the landlord himself?" The property was owned by the Eno Estate, which also owned the Fifth Avenue Hotel and many other choice midtown properties. They felt it was a forlorn hope to approach such a large corporation, but in desperation Jay called on Mr. Eno, the president, and was received cordially. Mr. Eno listened attentively and to Jay's delighted stupefaction, announced sympathetically: "Mr. Witmark, stay as long as necessary. It's little enough for us to do, for such good tenants as you've been, to stand by you in this dilemma. You need sign no lease. Just rent from month to month. And good luck in your new place when you get there!"

It was one of the happiest days in their business career. Thus they learned, too, that even hard-boiled corporations sometimes have souls!

The outlook was bright once more, and when the strike was called off in June, they set a new goal—to be in the new building by their mother's birthday, August 4th. It meant work, night and day, not only for the construction gang, which had to be paid extra, but for themselves and their staff. Besides the moving and putting everything in its place, they had to prepare for the opening day, which was a job in itself, as they meant to have the "last word" in inaugurations.

The building had six floors and two basements, an especially designed front with columns, carvings, and a Beehive Clock Tower. At the time it was the tallest building in the neighborhood, and the clock set all the watches for blocks around.

The professional floor was a complete innovation as it was the first studio floor of its kind. The latest improvements and inventions were introduced. There were two elevators, a passenger and a freight elevator in the front, and a private self-running elevator at the back. An innovation for an office building at that time was a fire- and water-proof vault in the sub-basement for the plates, which had to be kept absolutely dry to prevent corrosion.

August 4, 1903! What a day! A double celebration—"the Queen's" birthday, always the big annual event in their family life—and the opening of their own building, the result of the practical use of a toy printing press twenty years before. It was a gala day not only for them but for their friends, including a large group of writers who had participated in their success.

On that opening day everything was early astir. They had all arrived ahead of time; the department heads and their staffs were at their respective desks from the shipping department in the basement to the library on the top floor. Flowers were arranged on the desks, and these, together with the bouquets sent by business, professional, and personal friends made the place resemble a conservatory. From nine o'clock the building was open for inspection, and visitors were greeted by Stewart, the colored, uniformed doorman. It was his first day of service and he remained as long as they occupied the building, some twenty years, making many friends. Eventually he became as well known as the building itself. He was proud of his position and called himself "the Witmark reception committee."

Elaborate exercises had been arranged which started promptly at ten o'clock. The third floor had been set aside as the auditorium for the day, the partitioning of this floor having been postponed until after the inauguration. There was an orchestra of twenty-five pieces. Victor Herbert wrote a march, *Success Is Work*, but couldn't direct it in person as he was on tour with his orchestra at the time.

It was a delightful program, the novelty of which was the directing of most of the numbers by their respective composers.

DeWolf Hopper made the dedication speech on behalf of the theatrical profession and Registrar Ferdinand Levy spoke on behalf of the City of New York. Besides the audience who sat out the concert, there was a constant stream of friends coming and going. The fourth floor was devoted to refreshments that were served all day by Mazzetti, the caterer. A stream of telegrams, cables, and letters of congratulation arrived continually.

Such was the auspicious beginning of twenty years' occupancy of the Witmark Building. In this building they were to publish their leading operatic successes—including Victor Herbert's "Babes in Toyland," "It Happened in Nordland," "Mlle. Modiste," "The Red Mill," "Naughty Marietta," "The Enchantress," "The Only Girl," "Eileen," and "Princess Pat"; Hoschna's "Three Twins," "Doctor De Luxe," and "Madame Sherry"; Gustav Luders' "The Fair Co-ed" and "Woodland"; Robyn's "Yankee Consul"; George M. Cohan's "Little Nellie Kelly," "The Merry Malones," and "The Rise of Rosie O'Reilly"; William Loraine's "Peggy from Paris."

CHAPTER XVIII

COPYRIGHTS—AND WRONGS

1. Julie's Misfortune

*I*T WAS sometime in 1905 that Julie began complaining about pains in his leg, which in spite of treatment did not seem to let up; he suffered a great deal. Very active, he got around in spite of the pain, and when it was not too severe he worked on, paying no attention to it.

One day he was on the way to his doctor in the Seventies off Central Park West. As he was alighting from it, a street car started before he had stepped clear, and twisted him around on his bad leg. He limped to the doctor, and told him what had happened. The physician, thinking there was water on the knee, probed, but found none. Infection set in; the pain became unbearable. Seven specialists were called in, and all agreed that to save his life the leg had to be amputated.

The decision caused almost as much consternation in the family as death. It was not even certain he would come through, so weak was he from his suffering. Julie was considered one of the Beau Brummells of the theatrical profession. With the losing of the leg, his career in the theater would naturally terminate, and there was then no compensation in the way of radio work in which the loss of a leg would have been no hindrance.

However, the decision was finally made. One of Julie's best

chums, Dr. Phil Grausman, and Dr. John Erdman, the surgeon, performed the operation in the year 1906. The operating rooms were overcrowded that day with cases, and this made it necessary for Julie's time to be moved to a later hour, causing a grimly humorous incident. Not knowing the reason for the delay, he became impatient and in his matter-of-fact way inquired, "When are they going to do this thing? What's the delay? If they don't hurry up, I won't let 'em do it at all!"

Jay tried to calm him. "The operating rooms are all still busy." But assuringly, "Don't worry, Julie, it will come off."

Julie retorted, "I know what's coming off, all right!"

With the characteristic stoicism that he had shown through all his suffering, he was talking with his wife over the telephone only an hour after the operation. She was in another part of the hospital as they would not let anyone see him.

He was away from his desk for nine months and when finally he returned, he was received with a personal affection that transcended the amenities of commercial association. Julie was not merely liked. He was loved.

Sometimes that love took a strange, contradictory shape. He and David Warfield, for example, were inseparable pals, and had been members of the Russell's Comedians. One can, therefore, easily imagine how Julie felt when after his tragic accident all of his friends either called or communicated with him—all but Dave Warfield. Julie did not want any sympathy; he usually turned that down with, "I'm all right, I'm better than a hundred dead men."

Some months after the accident, Isidore met Dave in the Pennsylvania Railroad Station in Philadelphia. Said Dave, "Gee, Isidore, I'm so glad to see you. Julie must think I'm a skunk. But I just couldn't. I started writing at least twelve letters and then tore them all up. Some day I hope to meet him by chance, and then it will be easier for me."

When Isidore got home he explained the confession to Julie.

It was not long after this that an organization, either the Dramatists' Club or the Friars, gave Dave a dinner, and Julie was bound to go. The affair was on a Saturday night, and they met in the reception room, just before dinner was called. Dave let out a shout, "Thank God, at last! Julie my boy!"

There was a hug, and Dave said, "Now, I can come to see you. I shall be in your office Monday."

2. The Crest Trading Company

From their own experience with amateur productions, the Witmarks realized that there was a dearth of good amateur material in print. They knew also, to judge by the demand from all over the country, that there was a good market for entertainment novelties as well as for standard styles.

For years they had been accumulating material for amateur entertainment that formed part of their regular catalog. The publishing of amateur material would not have appealed to them if they had not been from the first involved in no end of amateur affairs on both the writing and producing ends.

One day, they had a call from Louis Mann, who required some gag books. He was writing a new monologue specialty for his club work and wanted to use some of their material. Looking over their entertainment publications, he became quite excited. "Why don't you make a special department of this?" he suggested. "There should be a great market for entertainment material." Waxing eloquent, he cried, "Why, do you know, there are four million people in America entertaining in some manner or form *all the time*?"

Louis's words gave Isidore the idea that there was a ready market and one worth catering to, particularly through the mail. They decided to establish a separate department to which they would divert the retail end of the business, and to which they would refer all orders for publications that did not come in through the wholesale channels.

The result was the establishment of the Crest Trading Company which entered the mail order field with the slogan "Everything for entertaining." With Louis Mann's words ringing in their ears—"Four million people entertaining all the time"—they decided to get that *ready market at once*. They issued a catalog of entertainment material of every possible kind, even down to spangles for costumes. They manufactured their own tricks for the magic department, their own make-up material for theatricals; they made the Crest facial cream, endorsed by stars of drama, opera, and vaudeville, and their own burnt cork and liniment for gymnasts, their own Crest Soap for removal of make-up, their own comic collars for end men, and many of their own costumes.

The catalog they issued was as large, in proportion to the field, as the Sears-Roebuck Company's. Large sums were devoted to this new branch, on which they spent approximately a hundred and fifty thousand dollars.

Two innovations in minstrelsy were the product of the Witmarks. The first was the *Witmark Amateur Minstrel Guide and Burnt Cork Encyclopedia*, which was so comprehensive that for $1.50 a community group could put on a minstrel show commensurate with its facilities, from the simplest to the most elaborate.

The other was a conception of Isidore's, entitled *Minstrel Shows by Mail*. This was a plan whereby the applicant received questionnaires that asked the necessary questions to give the firm an idea as to what to recommend; for instance, how many end men were available; how many singers; how many instrumentalists; the size of the stage; the size of the orchestra, if any; the number of specialists and their acts; whether the affair was to be given in a hall, theater, or church. When the questionnaires were returned, they studied the answers and filled in a form which provided not alone the names of the songs designated for each

There were about thirty of these Witmark Minstrel Overtures. The instructions, even to the tapping of the bones and tambos, were such that any amateur could produce them with success.

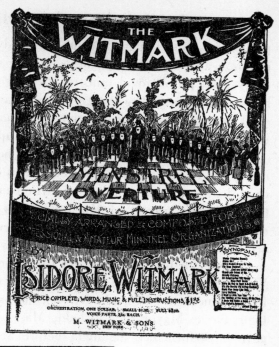

There were about a dozen Crest Minstrel Overtures.

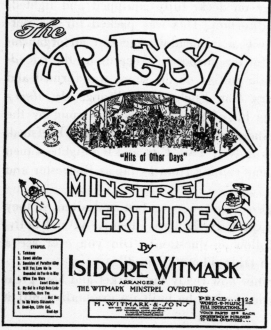

participant, but the gags and other comedy material. Besides the program and the material, there was a page of instructions that every good professional minstrel director used in order to make his show a success. The charge for this mail plan was $5. As each show was individual, the Witmarks actually lost money on the low charge, but anticipated making it up on material ordered.

Since minstrels had always been a hobby with Isidore Witmark, and he had put them on in different countries under various conditions and with all types of participants, it was easy for him to handle this project of Minstrel Shows by Mail. He probably still holds the record for being the only person who ever produced a minstrel show at sea, with passengers as the personnel.

It was on the cruise of the *Princesse Victoria Luise* to the West Indies in January, 1906. Eighteen men from eighteen different American cities, who had not met before, took part, among them the ex-Mayor of Pittsfield, Mass., Daniel England. They gave a performance the night before arriving at Havana. The Captain had built a stage on deck, fully equipped and lighted, and an amphitheater auditorium. This was packed for the performance and the show was a tremendous success; an organization called the P.V.L.'S, for the purpose of keeping up the friendships that were made while putting on the show, was formed and lasted for over five years. Dan England's end-song, *My Merry Oldsmobile,* was the song hit of the show and was sung by the passengers for the remainder of the trip. Thereafter a beefsteak dinner was held annually in New York City and the eighteen men never failed to attend, some coming from as far as Rochester and Cleveland.

The mail-order business didn't move as fast as desired, so they consulted a mail-order expert. He listened attentively, and delivered judgment in the following question: "Did you ever see a three-year-old child eat a table d'hôte dinner?"

He added that no matter how ready the market and how great its possibilities, mail order had to be built up gradually until it reached the point when the cumulative effect would assert itself. In other words, the Witmarks had been misled by the fact that there was a market into thinking that they could immediately acquire it. The market would require educating.

The expert knew what he was talking about, the Witmarks changed their policy, and in time got results.

3. Paris Office

The Witmark office in Paris at 92, Rue St. Lazare, opened July 1, 1906, as a modest, experimental place. Within a year and a half they found it necessary to remove to larger quarters at 58, Rue du Faubourg, Montmartre. Here was the only house on the Continent devoted exclusively to English and American music. It was under the management of Charles Denier Warren, son of the London manager of Witmarks'. The younger Warren was but nineteen; the Witmarks, however, could hardly have been expected to harbor prejudice against youth. Young Warren enjoyed a London reputation as "the child comedian" for his comic performances in pantomime, and had toured the world with his father.

Interviewed on January 28, 1908, in the Paris quarters of the firm, young Warren gave the reporter for the New York *Herald* an excellent idea of what it was like to be an average musical American in the Paris of the twentieth century, first decade:

"We had a little place upstairs in the Rue Saint Lazare at first. But Americans don't understand going upstairs to shop. They want to look for a sign on the door and step in, so we have come here, and now they are finding us. When an American wants a piece of music he wants it in a hurry. He has read about its success in New York, at the Broadway or Hammerstein's. It is the only thing on earth that can make him happy. Heretofore he had to send to New York for it. That meant three or four weeks. He had to guess at the price and perhaps send more than was necessary. By the time the music arrived his hunger for it had passed and the tune did not sound good to him after all. Now he gets it hot off the griddle, for he can rush in here and find any song that is making a success in New York almost as soon as he could get it there.

"It is the same thing in the cafés. It used to be two or three years before the orchestras got the scores of successful musical comedies. Now we barely wait to see that a piece is a success before getting the scores at work. Over here the orchestra leaders fall into the idea quickly enough, for they know their business is to tickle Americans whenever they can. All they wanted was a ready way to obtain popular American music.

"'The Prince of Pilsen' has given American light music a great boom, too, among the French. We have the words in French as well as in English. It is a question which version is more in demand.

"There is one great difference, however, between New Yorkers and Parisians. In New York we are still selling songs that were successes in musical comedies three, four, or even half a dozen years ago. You can still hear *Tessie* and *The Honeysuckle and the Bee*. But the Paris vogue of a song is much shorter. For this reason I dare say *The Message of the Violet*, much admired as it is in Paris, will not long outlast the run of 'The Prince of Pilsen.'

"Here, of course, we have many old songs on sale, but they are new to Parisians.

"There is a change coming over New York's taste in songs. They are built on better lines than they used to be, with ragtime and coon songs. The influences predominant in the new songs are more classical, so to speak. Ernest Ball's *Love Me and the World Is Mine* was the beginning of a new fashion in sentimental music. Every writer is now trying his best to reach that pace and be sentimental without being sloppy. Even the coon song folk have got the fever. One of the latest things of that stamp runs *I Won't Be Your Honey Till You Sing Love Me and the World Is Mine.*"

4. The Macy-Siegel-Cooper Music Feud

The question of copyright and allied considerations, during this decade as during the past, was like an intermittent fever. Hardly had one aspect of it been settled, or at least mitigated, when another arose to trouble the publishers and the dealers. Contests were brewing between the publishers and the sellers of popular music, and the manufacturers of reproductive musical instruments. The publishers had their hands full.

All the more welcome, then, during the visit of "Tay Pay" O'Connor to the United States in 1906 was the assistance of this Irish parliamentarian and newspaper owner in the cause of the American music publishers. O'Connor's London *Era* was the English *Variety*. From the beginning he had sided with the popular song men.

Accordingly, on October 19, 1906, a dinner of welcome and thanks was given at the Hotel Astor to "Tay Pay" and attended by representatives from the grateful firms. Who could keep Victor Herbert away from his brother Irishman? On November 10th *The Era* printed a formal acknowledgment:

"For the brilliant success of the recent banquet, given to Mr. T. P. O'Connor, M.P., by the Music Publishers' Association of the United States, the bulk of the credit must be awarded Isidore Witmark, head of the great house of M. Witmark & Sons. He looked after the details and the beauty and appropriateness of the souvenirs; the elegant table decorations, etc., were his work, and it kept him busy night and day for a week."

Some months afterwards when Isidore went to London he was entertained by "Tay Pay" at the House of Commons. Fortunately, T.P. was in the vein that day and delivered an oration on the floor of the house in glowing tribute to the United States that his American guests remembered for years. Later, at tea with his guests on the terrace of the House of Commons, T.P. reaffirmed his support for the publishers in the double battle that they were waging against violators of copyright and against the "mechanicals." O'Connor remained a staunch champion of both causes.

On this trip, Isidore—who was accompanied by Nathan Burkan, the lawyer for the firm—visited in Berlin the firm of Lincke & Ruelle to sign up representatives for the Witmark publications.

The House of Witmark was publishing so many songs that no single foreign firm, no two or three firms, for that matter, could represent it adequately. The boys conceived a chain plan by which they sent to a half dozen publishers abroad parcels of the latest issues, with a time limit set upon their decisions. The rejected numbers were thereupon moved on to the next publisher in the chain.

During the trip which lasted through July and August, 1907, Isidore renewed the firm's contract with Charles Warren as manager of their London interests. Charles Warren, Junior, was made manager of the Witmark branch in Paris. He quickly exhibited the energy and the push of his father. "I have been away from London for five years," said Isidore in an interview, "and I could stay away five years longer without a thought but that our interests would be served in the best possible manner by our manager."

Witmark not only brought songs to Europe; he brought songs back. There was an important reason why he could not afford to stay in Europe much longer at that time. The fight between the cut-rate department stores and the music business was fast approaching a show-down. A crisis had been reached while Isidore was in Paris, and on August 1, 1907, the cables dispatched to the United States a prediction, attributed to the senior of the Witmark brothers, that sheet music would be sold at 1 cent per copy in the department stores.

The statement was nonsensical. Jay Witmark refused to believe that his brother had made it. "Why," he commented to the reporters, "the royalty on popular music runs from 3 cents to 5 cents on each copy published. We have, with Leo Feist, Howley, Haviland & Dresser, F. A. Mills, and Charles K. Harris, formed the American Music Stores, a company having for its first object the maintenance of prices and the stopping of the present cut rates."

What Isidore really had in mind, and what was misquoted by

the foreign press, may be suggested by the turn taken by affairs as soon as he stepped off the gangplank.

The big department store at Eighteenth Street and Sixth Avenue was a flourishing concern. It was the New York extension of the new idea in department stores that had been inaugurated during the Columbian Exposition in Chicago, Siegel, Cooper & Company, which had been almost as great an attraction as the World's Fair itself. Its slogan, "Meet Me At The Fountain," is still remembered.

The up-to-date sales methods introduced in the Chicago store were followed in the New York house, which offered serious competition to the other established stores in its class. There was intense rivalry between the New York Siegel, Cooper and R. H. Macy & Company, which by this time had moved up to Thirty-fourth Street on Broadway.

Music publishers were feeling the effects of this feud and were distressed over the manner in which these stores were slashing the prices of their publications. The publishers realized that they had no redress, for Macy had just won the famous price-maintaining case brought against it by the book publishers. Sheet music was selling for as low as six cents a copy at Macy's, who declared that no other department store should undersell them.

The stock in the American Music Stores, Inc., was held by five leading music publishers: Leo Feist, Inc., F. A. Mills & Company, Charles K. Harris, Howley, Haviland & Dresser, and M. Witmark & Sons. It had been formed to take over and establish their own music counters in the principal department stores of America, and to cater as jobbers to the department store business in general.

Its chief aim was to combat a large publishing house that had already signed contracts with prominent department stores, hoping to secure publicity advantage for its publications over those of other houses.

With its powerful combination the American Music Stores,

Inc., was successful in making contracts with about fifty department stores in the United States, which proved excellent outlets for the catalogs it represented.

The American Music Stores had another important object: to bring prices for American music back to normal and to uphold those prices. American Music Stores was faced by many problems in this aspect; outstanding was the feud between Macy and Siegel-Cooper.

Isidore hit upon a few ideas that, if properly worked out, might clear the situation. So he called a special meeting of the directors—the heads of the various concerns interested—and addressed them:

"Gentlemen: I am greatly worried over the Macy-Siegel-Cooper situation. It is unhealthy and unethical, and unless we take heroic action I don't know what will become of us. This price-cutting has been going on for weeks. As publishers you and I realize that to beg, request, or demand is a wasted effort, judging from the recent decision won by Macy over the book publishers who were trying to maintain their prices. I feel that something radical must be done by us as the American Music Stores."

The other directors manifested great interest, and Fred Mills said, "It will mean everything in the world to us if we have the right solution."

Leo Feist said, "What's on your mind, Isidore? We're anxious to know."

He proceeded to unfold his plan.

"It is a well-known fact that Macy jealously guards its right to maintain low prices. We've settled the point that they won't pay any attention to us as publishers. As the American Music Stores, we control departments in New York City. Those departments are the only rivals that a store like Macy or Siegel-Cooper recognizes. Why not use those departments to our interest, with a well-organized campaign? We have done enough pleading. Now we must act. My plan calls for a thorough clean-up, if there ever was one.

Actual advertisement from *The New York Evening Journal* October 11, 1907, of the one cent music sale.

FROM RAGTIME TO SWINGTIME

I propose that we make arrangements with our Rothenberg store in Fourteenth Street *for a one-cent sale* of sheet music. All hits of our five firms—no dead numbers. And that we agree to keep this sale going for twenty weeks, if necessary. And then, if Macy should want to sell cheaper than anyone else in New York, they'd have to sell two copies for one cent. But I can assure you, gentlemen, that they'll sit up and take notice. And you'll agree when I reveal further details of my plan."

Charley Harris: "Isidore, you stun us!"

Fred Haviland: "How are you going to do all this?"

Leo Feist: "It sounds good."

Fred Mills exclaimed: "It's drastic!"

"I'm glad to hear Fred Mills say it's drastic," Isidore went on, "because that's what it must be. You've got to fight fire with fire. As American Music Stores we can do many things that we couldn't do as individual publishers; so we must stick together, if we want to see this through. The House of Witmark is publishing the biggest song hit in the country today—*Love Me And The World Is Mine*—and we're getting 23 cents a copy for it wholesale—but that will go in for one cent a copy. American Music will also go into the open market and buy song hits at the regular trade price, and take its loss. Anything to strengthen our fight. You gentlemen will have to volunteer to supply American Music with your best-sellers, and you won't find me wanting. I'm not anxious to get rid of the Witmark music at a cent a copy, nor am I anxious to have sales running through twenty weeks. But in a fight like this we have to provide for everything. To win this battle I've tried to cover every angle. And here's another suggestion: to rehearse fifty or sixty people to go to Macy's and Siegel-Cooper's on the day of our sale and have them tantalize the music clerks and managers by showing them the Rothenberg's penny ad and asking Macy's, who claim always to be cheaper than anybody else, to meet it. I am having some of my friends buy a dozen pieces of music and then put down twelve cents for their pur-

290

chase, as though it were understood that Macy would beat all prices. And when the clerk protests, my people will be trained to raise a row that will not be comfortable for that music department.

"You see, gentlemen, I realize that something more than just a penny ad by a rival concern is necessary to waken them to the issue. As for American Music, we will not sell more than one copy of our music to each customer at our department and we will accept no mail or C.O.D. orders. If you approve of my plan, I should like one of you gentlemen to offer a resolution, and we'll get busy at once."

The plan was accepted with acclaim and a resolution was offered whereby American Music should sell the popular successes at the department in Rothenberg's at one cent a copy and place striking advertisements in the leading dailies. It was further agreed that the individual firms interested in the American Music Stores were to supply free all copies required of them. The resolution was seconded and activities were begun with a will. Arrangements were made with Mr. Price, the owner of Rothenberg's, to hold these sales, and preparations were made in the department to take care of the crowds. The first sale being scheduled for October 12, 1907, announcements appeared in all the dailies the day before.

They were all on their toes for the first act in the big show. But —"the best-laid schemes o' mice an' men gang aft a-gley." They got the result they were after, but all did not turn out as planned. Everything was ready at Rothenberg's. They put on an extra staff to cope with the situation. Their rehearsed crowd started out for Macy's and Siegel-Cooper's, and the battle was on. The music publishers assembled at the offices of the American Music Stores, and reports began to come in.

At first everything seemed as expected, big crowds buying. Early reports from Macy's said that their people were having controversies with the clerks who, becoming more and more irritated, were calling the floor manager for every sale. This did not keep him in any too happy a mood. The sending of customers to Macy's and Siegel-Cooper's was well timed. Meanwhile, the crowd at Rothenberg's had reached menacing proportions. When the end of the sale was announced there was a veritable riot. Fixtures were smashed, stock in other departments was thrown about, and Rothenberg's had to send out an alarm for the police reserves.

In the meantime, the rehearsed customers were going from Macy's to Siegel-Cooper's and repeating their rôles to the consternation of the sales force. By this time, Isidore's friend Max Meyer was staging his little act at Macy's. After buying some tinware in the household department, he went to the music department and ordered a long list of numbers which the salesgirl wrapped up. Then he offered to pay a penny per copy for them. When informed that the music was six cents a copy, he began to protest at the top of his voice, showed the salesgirl the Rothenberg ad, and asked whether they considered him a boob. They couldn't put things like that over on him, he shouted. He started to walk away, keeping up a long harangue, at intervals of which he dropped pieces of tinware that sounded like cannon reports. It took most of the floorwalkers to get him out. But they all knew he was there.

As the eventful day drew to a close, they had reason to feel that the campaign was succeeding. They had a call from a representative of Macy's, who was anxious to know all about it, although he didn't know that they had given their first and last sale at Rothenberg's. They let him understand that they were in the fight to the bitter end, and were prepared for twenty sales, because they were bound to clear up this situation once and for all. He saw that they meant business, and realized that he was dealing with an organized competitor. Their determined stand must have impressed him, for he asked them to let up, promising to adjust matters.

Now, to take inventory at Rothenberg's. The place, when they arrived was a sight. Mr. Price was hardly in a congenial mood. "No more of these sales!" he cried. "Look what one did to me! And you figure on having twenty! The only way you can sell music at a cent a copy in my store is to wrap up ten in a package for ten cents, and I'll provide an empty floor for your sale."

They gave Mr. Price to understand that selling their music at a loss was no advantage—that paying nine cents for *School Days* to sell for one cent was not rational except for such a purpose. They further told him they were taking a big loss, which they were quite willing to do if they could correct the deplorable conditions.

He saw their point, but against holding any more sales in their way he was adamant. They were in an unenviable position. The one saving feature was that the opposition didn't know.

They had to work fast before the next week-end, and kept in touch with the Macy representative, letting him know, piece-meal, their "future intentions," at the same time telling him that they were ready to let up if his firm would show any evidence of meeting them. This they did during the week. And there was no sale the following Saturday.

As a matter of fact, there wasn't to be one in any case.

CHAPTER XIX

THE BATTLE OF "CANNED MUSIC"

1. On To Washington

COPYRIGHT laws have never been satisfactory. No sooner has one point been settled than another crops up. The Witmarks were involved in copyright altercations almost from the moment that their firm had been founded. In 1891 Isidore had been compelled to go to London to adjust differences between American and English firms; in 1901 he was back in the British capital with an operetta of Victor Herbert's and another of his own, again compelled by differences between the American and English law to protect Witmark property by a perfunctory première in England.

In 1906 the vexed matter of copyright had been revived by problems associated with the marketing of music for mechanical instruments, particularly the phonograph. In a happy moment, John Philip Sousa had christened the phonograph record, and other devices for the mechanical reproduction of compositions, "canned music." The phrase caught the fancy of the editorial writers and became linguistic currency. After thirty years it persists, and has been extended to the cinema, as "canned" drama or entertainment.

The question that soon ranged the manufacturers and the music publishers on opposite sides of the battle-line was this:

did the existing copyright law protect the composer and author against the unrewarded appropriation of their creative labors? The manufacturers said No; the publishers yelled Yes. The publishers affirmed that the law gave to the writer exclusive rights to his writings for a term of years. The manufacturers agreed that this was so, but they maintained, by what today appears as a quibble, that their method of dispensing music was not a "writing" because it could not be read. It does not appear that anybody with a little Greek pointed out the etymology of the words "phonograph" and "gramophone," each of which is based upon words meaning "write" and "sound." A phonograph is an instrument for "sound-writing."

The manufacturers were thoroughly organized and ready to fight their opponents to the last ditch. The publishers' organization was inadequate to the task ahead of it. It met once a year and was known as the United Music Publishers of America. It was composed of the foremost music houses in the country including Oliver Ditson & Co., Boston, White, Smith & Co., Boston, John F. Ellis, Washington, D. C., Sherman, Clay & Co., San Francisco, Charles H. Ditson & Co., New York, and almost all the well-known popular publishers. One of its principal members was Lyon & Healy, Chicago—the largest wholesale and retail music house in America. They manufactured their own pianos, harps, and stringed instruments and had one of the rarest collections of old violins extant. They carried the publications of every publisher here and abroad and represented exclusively for the Middle West some of the foremost music and musical instrument houses in the world. James F. Bowers, their general manager, was president of the United Music Publishers of America and was so popular that he was re-elected year after year. He made a fine executive and it looked as if his presidency was a life job. Then something happened.

The mechanical instruments, especially player pianos, were taking a strong hold on the buying public, and it was not long before the Aeolian Company became a power. It was only natural that Lyon & Healy should become its representative in the Middle West and that Bowers should hobnob with these people, who were making money for his house. Bowers disinterestedly engineered a project whereby the Aeolian Company at its own expense was to carry litigation up to and including the Supreme Court of the United States to find out if the then present copyright law protected the publishers in their mechanical rights for which, if the bill were affirmed, many of the prominent publishers, including the Witmarks, were to give the Aeolian Company the exclusive reproducing rights to their publications for a number of years on terms that were to be agreed upon. They thought this fair and of benefit if they got the favorable decision. Litigation is expensive; the publishers did not feel like assuming the liability on a gamble, and the mechanical manufacturers, on the theory that the copyright bill did not protect the publishers, were already helping themselves to their product without the least idea of remunerating them.

Theodore Roosevelt, the "Trust Buster," sat in the White House and "monopoly" had become a word to be abjured. The Witmarks did not consider their contract with the Aeolian a monopoly, any more than the signing up of a writer exclusively so that he could give no other publisher the benefit of his writings; certainly no more than the Victor Phonograph Company's (one of their opponents) signing up of Caruso and other great artists to make records to the exclusion of the other manufacturers. But it was just "pie" for the opposition and they made a "mountain" out of it. The cry of "monopoly" was. raised at once and it reacted on the publishers in Washington. Congressmen, approached by spokesmen for the publishers, shrank from them as if they were lepers.

The Supreme Court of the United States decided against the publishers on the ground that the law as it stood did not apply to the new mechanical industry. The Aeolian people had lost out at a great loss to themselves; their arrangements with the publishers who had promised them exclusive rights naturally became void. The manufacturers continued to cry "monopoly" and managed to discredit the cause of the publishers seemingly beyond salvation.

To make matters worse, Bowers, who appeared to have been convinced by Isidore that because of his Aeolian connection it would not be politic for him to run again at this crucial time for re-election as president of the publishers' association, under heavy pressure from the standard publisher members, who would not be heavily affected by the mechanical invasion, weakened and changed his mind. Isidore had nothing against Bowers; Bowers was, in fact, aside from this strategic objection, the best man that the office could attract. When, however, Bowers was re-elected, Isidore was not the only publisher to realize that there must be a new organization if they wanted to win in Washington. At once he resigned and was followed by Leo Feist and other publishers who meant to win the fight which they considered just.

It was at this point that Isidore's spirit had been roused. Up to now he had left representation of the Witmarks chiefly to Jay. The determined stand of the manufacturers, however, in refusing to pay a single cent of royalty upon music reproduced upon records and other contrivances stirred his ire.

From that day the copyright fight took a new turn. Isidore and his lawyer, Nathan Burkan, took an early train and reached Washington about noon. They wandered toward the Capitol. The place seemed deserted; in the Senate Office Building and the House Office Building they did not encounter a soul. It was as if the city had taken a holiday. They felt, as Isidore expressed it, like Charlie Hoyt's character in "The Texas Steer"—the minister to Dahomey, the half-baked colored politician on the rampage for an appointment. Although they knew no one in Washington, they were looking for information about the new copyright bill that was pending in Congress.

While standing there they were approached by a man whom

297

Isidore thereafter always referred to as "Bill Hodge," for he resembled the actor who was memorable in "The Man From Home." But this Washington "Hodge" was a different kind of actor. He was a lobbyist. He came over and asked if there was anything he could do. They explained that they had come down to learn about the copyright bill. He became loquacious. "You've hit just the right fellow," he assured them, "I know all about it. What is it you'd like to know?"

"The names of the right people who can help us in our fight," Isidore replied.

"Well, you're too late, I just sold the chairman of the two patent committees to the other side and they gave me $2500 for the job."

Burkan and Isidore exchanged glances. They had stumbled upon a wellspring of information that would repay pumping.

The Delphic Oracle asked them whence they had come. They told him.

"Well," he said, cheerily, "you haven't a leg to stand on."

"What do you mean?" they asked.

"The other side has its majority report in. You have no minority report. You say you come from New York. How would that influence Minnesota, for instance? Don't you see, you have no constituency? In order to put through a bill you have to have a constituency all over the United States. The best thing you can do is go home, and think up a compromise."

2. A "Constituency"

He expatiated upon how well the other side was organized, how much money it had to spend on the fight, and how determined it was to win by hook or crook. He was patronizing and said he was sorry they had not seen him first. But now that he had cast his lot with the other side he would have to stick with them.

THE BATTLE OF "CANNED MUSIC"

His parting shot was "When you have a minority report and a constituency, come down and see us again!"

Among the things they had gleaned from their garrulous acquaintance was that nobody could be seen that day, as it was a local holiday.

For two-thirds of the way home, they both sat looking into space. Suddenly Isidore turned to Burkan. "Can you write a minority report?"

Burkan looked at him quizzically. "I suppose I can. But what good will that do?"

"Well, if you'll furnish a minority report, I'll *furnish the constituency!*"

Burkan turned on Isidore sharply and looked at him without speaking. "We're not going home," he said finally, "I'm taking you down to Amityville—for observation!"

Isidore laughed, "What I said holds good, nevertheless, and is likely to change the whole plan of operations."

The next morning, as soon as Isidore reached the office, he called his secretary and questioned her:

Q. Are as many manuscripts submitted through the mail as ever?

A. About the same.

Q. What have we done with the names of those whose manuscripts we have returned?

A. We have carded them.

Q. For what reason?

A. They are the names of people interested in music. We want to cover them with our literature and catalogs.

Q. Do they come from one section of the country or are they widely scattered?

A. They come from all over the United States.

Q. How many names have we?

A. Between five and six thousand.

Q. Thank you. Please fetch the box of names.

His brothers asked if he had been able to accomplish anything in Washington. They agreed that it was tough to have lost the two chairmen of the Patents Committees. There was just one thing to be done—to tie up the rest of the committees and throw the opposition into confusion.

The fight was on in earnest. Isidore's trip had taught him that they had to be represented constantly in Washington by some-one with influence, and that he must be ready to be on the job there in person at a moment's notice. Indeed, he practically lived in a bag for a year and a half, running down to the Capital two or three times a week. A man named Feeney, who was engaged to represent him in Washington, was also the Washington repre-sentative of the Bookbinders' Union and was permanently located there. The outstanding labor representative in Washington was a man named Sullivan who was employed by "Big Six," the power-ful Printers' Union of New York City.

But to return to the box of indexed names: Isidore thumbed them over. Here was the most important list of names in the world! He got busy and formulated a plan that he put into action immediately.

He framed a letter addressed to these disappointed would-be song writers, telling them that if it had not been for one thing, their songs might have been published, namely the mechanical instrument situation, which had so cut into the Witmark business that they had been obliged to limit the number of their publica-tions; if the music publishers received the revenue due to them from the sales of the mechanical reproductions, they would be in a position to publish more music. They were, therefore, writ-ing to urge them to get in touch with their Representatives and explain that it was absolutely necessary for the publishers and writers to draw revenue from the mechanical reproductions of their works. Isidore urged them to write long, strong letters.

The response was gratifying. Whereas, previously, there had been no letters on the matter, the Post Office at Washington within three months was obliged to put on extra hands. These five or six thousand names were working overtime. They not only wrote themselves, but had their friends do so. Ladies and gentlemen—the great constituency!

Some of the "great constituency" took the copyright fight too seriously when asked to write strong letters to the legislators. Witmark and his fellow musketeers received complaints that the legislators had been accused by various constituents of having been responsible for the rejection of the constituents' songs. Now the musketeers had another job on their hands—appeasing the lawmakers!

The Patents Committee of the House, previously insignificant, now assumed primary importance. Formerly it had been the committee to which were relegated the old, decrepit members and the young, untried ones. Now appointments to it were sought by the live wires.

Upon the creation of the "constituency" Isidore became active. He had no organization behind him, nor any large subscriptions. Indeed, he fought this copyright battle mainly with the help of two persons, Burkan and Victor Herbert. The opposition, on the other hand, seemed to have doubled its forces.

If there was no actual organization, certainly there was a brave show of one: the Authors' and Composers' League of America, with an imposing list of chief officers. President, Victor Herbert; Treasurer, John Philip Sousa; Secretary, Reginald De Koven. Affiliated "in this righteous fight for justice," quoting from a clip-sheet sent to the press on January 6, 1908, were The Words and Music Club, The Friars, The Green Room Club, The Treasurers' Club of America, The Actors' Society, The White Rats, The Lambs, The Comedy Club, The American Dramatists' Club, The Playwrights' League.

The organization had been formed to impress the "constituency" aforementioned. They paid $1 as a fee, for which they received a membership card to the League, entitling them to work their heads off for the success of the Cause! It was no trouble to get that dollar; wasn't it worth it, from the member's standpoint, to be in the same organization with Herbert, De Koven, and Sousa? All that there was to this magnetic triumvirate was their names and their moral support. The entire organization was really just one man—and Isidore had his hands full!

In reading the statement on the clip-sheet, one observes how much it resembles arguments that were used in contending against the movies, the talkies, and the radio companies—the manufacturers of a later day.

"When the Copyright bill was framed years ago the sound-producing instruments, such as the phonograph, gramophone, and automatic piano, were unheard or unthought of; naturally, no specific provision for the protection of the composer against them was made into law. . . .

"Thousands of records and perforated rolls are turned out, and before long the country is surfeited with the 'composition canned for the home,' and ere long the talking machines are grinding the melody out by the yard in every gaudy penny theater in the country.

"When the composer's work reaches this stage it is killed, as far as the publishing profits are concerned, for as soon as a musical composition becomes too popular the public ceases to buy it. Hence the composer not only loses his royalties due him from the talking and playing machines, but from the aforesaid short life of music sales as well."

They introduced their Minority Bill, which was looked over and approved by such men as Senator Philander C. Knox of Pennsylvania. Herbert performed herculean labors. He was a veritable minute-man and never failed Isidore when he called on him at short notice to go on to Washington, and they went constantly.

They devised the plan of getting senators and representatives out to meet Victor Herbert personally. Eventually they went through the entire roster with an educational campaign, telling each one, as he met Herbert, what their mission was in Washington: how they were being unjustly treated by the big interests and that the whole future of the song-writing art was at stake. Herbert made an indelible impression on everyone he met and they were gaining recruits in favor of their cause more quickly than Isidore had expected.

Victor Herbert had a close friend in Congress named Barchfeld from Pittsburgh. He was a big, hail-fellow-well-met sort, a doctor by profession, and a real statesman. He worked enthusiastically for the writers any time of the day or night. It seems ironic that such a good, helpful friend should later have come to such an untimely end. He and his little daughter were among the victims of the collapsing roof of a movie theater in Washington a few years later.

Their nemesis in this battle was a representative named Currier from New Hampshire, the chairman of the House Committee on Patents whom "Bill Hodge" had claimed he had sold to the opposition. He was in complete control of the other side.

Isidore had a visit from the secretary to the president of Dartmouth College, a student named Henry Wellman, who was producing a musical show at the college and wanted his help. Isidore liked him and was glad to do anything he could for him. Isidore was invited to Dartmouth to see the performance and pass on it professionally. They gave him a good time and he saw a corking good show, and brought away a new stage director for the theater, Fred Bishop, who entered the professional field by directing "Three Twins," to start with, and thereafter made his living by directing shows.

While at Dartmouth, Isidore was introduced by Wellman to some of the politicians, to whom he complained about the unfair tactics of Currier. Currier was soon complaining in Washington, "That man Witmark came up to Hanover and tried to turn my friends against me." Isidore's answer was that when one had real friends nobody could turn them against him. Isidore never knew whether or not his trip to Dartmouth helped him politically, but Mr. Currier now realized that he was someone to be reckoned

303

with; he sought a meeting with him and they met on a number of things. But it was an uncertain business. No sooner would they get out a copyright bill with some changes in it than along would come Currier with the same changes, plus a joker. Then they would have to get out another bill to take care of that bill, until there was no end of copyright bills floating around.

The fight was now on for fair. While all the publishers were ready to share the benefits of such a battle, it was hard to get them to "kick in." Not wishing to lose any time trying to raise funds, and realizing that if they won, they could then make collections, Isidore didn't wait, but advanced the money as it was needed. By the time the fight was over he had laid out many thousands of dollars.

He realized that an educational campaign was necessary both for his "constituency" and for the men in Washington. So he engaged a bright young man named Bretzfelder and put him in charge of the educational department, from which was sent a cargo of broadsides. It was helpful, if expensive, and told the senators and representatives something about their side of the issue. An empty floor in the new building on Thirty-seventh Street was devoted to their propaganda department. From practically nothing the campaign had grown into a formidable undertaking.

Now, here's a secret Isidore has kept for over thirty-five years that, inasmuch as the principals have passed on, he can now tell. During this copyright fight down in Washington Victor Herbert and he were invited to what was known as the Inner Sanctum. It has always been an unwritten law that no liquor was allowed under the dome of the Capitol. There was one committee room which had not been used for years, the committee having become obsolete, but the room was occupied. To the uninitiated it would have looked like a committee room with its bookcases, tables, and chairs.

It was only a picked few who had entrée there, and one of them was Congressman Barchfeld, who, true to the cause, figured that they might effect some conversions if they had a key to the room. He saw to it that one was supplied to Isidore. It was there that he met Congressman Nicholas Longworth, who had married Alice Roosevelt shortly before. He and Victor were always talking music. Longworth was a violinist of high attainments and played in his local symphony orchestra; he liked to compare notes with Victor Herbert on matters musical. Others who would drop in were Congressmen Lee and McKinley. They would come in for a sandwich and a highball, the latter appearing from an imitation bookcase concealing an icebox. This bar was maintained by the various members of the "club." Victor and Isidore each sent a case to Congressman Barchfeld as their contribution. The room was cared for by a capable colored attendant who knew just what every man ate and drank.

When the bill providing for the soldiers' canteen was brought up and the soldiers lost, warm-hearted Barchfeld felt badly about it, and wrote a card: "Those who voted against the soldiers' canteen are not welcome here." He stuck it on the outside of the door, and some of the habitués of the room were missing for a long while.

In this room Isidore was able to discuss the cause with men whom he might not have reached otherwise. The opposition realized they would have to reconsider their original attitude and agreed among themselves on a compromise in the event that they lost. They were still using the advantage of the word "monopoly," which was dynamite to most of the committee, and made it their chief slogan. They also got busy on some of the song writers, trying to win them over with the prospect of a compromise; this made it hard for Isidore and his group, who were holding out for their exclusive rights with no strings attached.

3. Strategy

He had gone to New York to organize as large a representation as possible of various writing and publishing organizations and had formed what he christened the Allied Copyright Committee, over five hundred strong. This half-regiment he led to Washington. But the opposition won most of them over with the assurance that it was not necessary for them to fight because they were going to get what they wanted!

The copyright group were holding one of their last night sessions; the big room was crowded and things were humming. Isidore was talking with Charley Burnham, the manager of Wallack's Theatre at Broadway and Thirtieth Street, when he looked up and saw a young man standing in the middle of the floor, making one of the finest addresses, in respect to logic and language, that he had heard in a long time. He stopped Charley Burnham and listened intently. While he was so doing, Nathan Burkan came over and asked whether what the young man was saying interested him. "Oh, no, not a bit," he answered, ironically. "If his advice were followed, it would only mean ruin for the entire music business in the United States."

The young man held the rapt attention of the listeners. He was advocating the addition of the word "music" to the manufacturers' clause of the bill. This may not mean much to the layman, but it meant ruin to the music business.

In the copyright bill there is a manufacturers' clause which applies solely to the copyright of books. It means that an international copyright can be secured in this country for foreign books only if the books are printed from type set up in this country. There is an "ad interim copyright" allowed on a book, during the time required for the type to be set up here. In this way, the foreigner's copyright is not lost. This interim copyright applies only to books; music has always been free of this cumbersome and expensive handicap.

The opposition had brought the young fellow from New York to complain that his craft of engraving for sheet music was discriminated against by the publishers and that they sent a lot of their works abroad to be engraved. If what he advocated had been carried out, the prominent foreign publishers, at enormous and unnecessary expense, would have had to engage all the engravers in America to do their work, paying them a bonus in order to save their copyrights, and would virtually have prevented the American publishers from having any engraving done and all but put them out of business. Conditions were really the opposite from what the young fellow asserted; there was a *shortage* of engravers in this country, not a *surplus*.

Isidore soon saw through the whole scheme. The opposition was trying to take the publishers' minds off the main issue by bringing up the labor question; they themselves did not realize the serious consequences to which their strategy might lead. Isidore made up his mind to take instant action. As he sat there with Burnham, listening to the young man's peroration, his man Feeney came into the room. He was recognized by one of the committeemen as one of the prominent representatives of labor. "Mr. Feeney," called out the committeeman, "What do you think of all this?"

Feeney, who had heard hardly a word, but realized that it concerned labor in some way, made a grandstand reply: "I'm for labor always."

Isidore drew him aside and expostulated. "Do you know that you were just talking against my interests? What do you mean?"

"Why, no," said Feeney, "I just heard the fellow say something about labor and I was for it."

"You're not only against what he's talking about, but you are going to fight him tooth and nail. Otherwise the music business is ruined. Feeney, they're trying to have the word 'music' inserted in the manufacturers' clause. Now, it's up to you to win Sullivan over to our side. If 'music' goes into that clause, Mr. Sullivan's printing trade is going to suffer very heavily."

The young fellow had finished talking and was applauded. When he started answering questions Isidore was confirmed in his belief that it was all a frame-up, for the orator had become a different man. His beautiful language and logical thought had been prepared for him; he now revealed himself as just another of the "dese, dem and dose" fellows.

B. F. Wood, a Boston publisher of standard music, asked for the floor and said that he was obliged to send his engraving orders to Leipzig because they didn't have the right tools in this country to carry out his work. He added that he wasn't interested in and did not publish "canned music," and this won him, as a disinterested party, the attention of the committee. He gave a good account of himself. The meeting adjourned until the next morning, as the publishers were sending for the representatives of the foreign publishers to come down from New York to speak for themselves, especially Mr. George Maxwell, then American manager of the Italian house of Ricordi. Isidore did not know it at the time, but the opposition had it in for Maxwell, who had been fighting them single-handed for years; and intended to embarrass him while he was addressing them.

That night after the session, Barchfeld, Herbert, Burkan, and Isidore went to the Willard Hotel, where they sat around, talking and planning. When they went to bed, Isidore said to Burkan who was rooming with him, that he would be up before seven and telephone New York. He was consumed with a passion to defeat the insertion of the word "music," realizing how far-reaching the damage would be. Exasperated, Herbert said, "There's nothing you can do. Keep your mind on the main issue. How are you going to beat labor?"

"With labor," was the startling reply.

Soon after noon the next day the opposition was waiting for Maxwell, in fact, were paging him, when Isidore threw a bomb-shell into their camp by sending word that Mr. Maxwell had nothing to say. He put Maxwell, as a representative of a foreign publisher, together with Sullivan whom he secured through Feeney, and Maxwell soon convinced Sullivan that the word "music" in the manufacturing clause would cause great loss to the printing trade. At the same time, Isidore was searching for the oratorical engraver, who was loitering about. He had fortified himself with authoritative information from Schirmer's, Fischer's, and other important music publishers: there was not a surplus of engravers; any unemployed engravers could get work immediately.

After he had satisfied Sullivan that "music" in the manufacturers' clause would not be so healthy for the printing trade, he put his arm around his shoulder and walked him over toward the young engraver who immediately accosted him.

"How do you do, Mr. Witmark?"

"Do you know me?" he asked.

"Yes," was the reply. "I worked for you once."

"Well, is my word good?"

"Oh, yes, Mr. Witmark, your reputation is of the finest."

By this time a crowd had gathered. Out of a clear sky Isidore shot out at him: "Then you're a damned liar!"

Nonplussed, he stammered, "What do you mean?"

"This, when you said last night that domestic engravers were ignored and orders for engraving were sent abroad, you were lying. I'm ready to give a job to every unemployed engraver you can produce!"

The young man hemmed and hawed, trying to explain his position. Sullivan leaned over and whispered, "You'd better take the next train back to New York."

Sullivan followed this up by going to Chairman Currier of the Patents Committee. "I don't want the word 'music' in the manufacturers' clause," he said.

His wishes were carried out to the letter, and the American and foreign publishers were saved much money and harrying inconvenience.

Prominent among those who helped them in the fight was Representative, later Governor, William Sulzer of New York, who gave most of his time toward the end of that Congressional session to the copyright matter. Also very faithful were Congressmen Jacob Olcott of New York, Focht of Pennsylvania, and Wilson, who afterward became Secretary of Labor; the late Senator Hughes of New Jersey also worked hard. In fact, he was making a speech in Congress, arguing the unfairness of placing a tyro in the same category as a Victor Herbert and arguing against the proposition of the opposition of paying the same amount for each composition mechanically reproduced, no matter who the composer might be, when he was tapped on the shoulder and told that the President had just signed the bill containing the very item he was trying to have deleted.

Harry Rapley, the manager of the National Theater, was kind to Isidore during the fight in Washington. He realized what it would mean to win over as many Congressmen as possible. He also knew the lure of a pair of free seats to a good show. So, one day while they were standing together in the lobby of his theater, he said, "Witmark, you've got a big fight on your hands, and I want to help you. I know you won't abuse my offer." And pointing to the box office, he said, "Whenever you think a couple of tickets will help your cause, don't hesitate to ask for them. They'll be there for you."

Having no real association to sponsor this copyright fight, they handled it themselves, and during the time they were battling the Witmarks advanced around $8,000 of their own money, devoting over a year and a half of personal time and effort. It was a long while before they got any part of that money back.

William A. Boosey of London was here during the excitement, and at a luncheon, slipped Isidore a check for five hundred dollars toward the expense fund in gratitude for saving his company the hardships of the manufacturers' clause.

Isidore's keenest disappointment in the copyright fight was that he had to accept the two-cent royalty compromise. When he realized that they were at the end of a Congressional term, he decided that discretion was the better part of valor, and the wise thing to do was compromise,—especially when Victor Herbert, their mainstay, fearing endless delay, accepted the two-cent compromise, thereby waiving his exclusive right for which their little coterie had been fighting. Once they accepted this compromise, their friends on the Patents Committee got busy, the result was the signing of the copyright bill by President Theodore Roosevelt, his last official act that session, for which it was necessary to turn the clock back five minutes.

The bill, as it then stood, provided for a two-cent royalty for each side of a phonograph disc, a two-cent royalty for each publication reproduced. This they had fought, but when it was realized that in order to carry on the fight it would be necessary to start all over again and educate a new Congress, it was decided to accept the two-cent terms, in the hope of getting, at some future time, their unequivocal rights.

In spite of not getting all they started out for, what they did accomplish brought in millions of dollars in royalties to publishers and writers, instead of nothing at all, which had been the original plan of the opposition.

CHAPTER XX

ROMANCE

1. A Visitor from Omaha

IT IS characteristic of the young Isidore that, during the years of the various copyright complications, he should have been carrying on, in his own equally complicated fashion, a strange courtship. Deeply, beneath the currents of his other preoccupations, ran his attachment to the young woman who one day suddenly gave to his thoughts and emotions a new direction. For five years, romance played a seemingly subdued counterpoint to commerce. It was, in the words of a recent song, "a strange romance"; it led to an equally strange wedding, in which the contradictory aspects of the courtship flared up for the last time in a humorous fashion. Through these five years Isidore kept his mind on both his business and his girl, and conducted both campaigns—for campaigns they were!—to a successful conclusion.

Sometime in 1904 he was rehearsing the Amateur Circle of the Columbia Club of Harlem, in his musical revue, "By The Sea." On this Sunday they rehearsed in the afternoon, as the stage was to be used that night by the German company from the Irving Place Theater. Their troupe was at one table for supper and they were having a jolly time, when one of them who was late, walked in with the most attractive girl Isidore had ever seen. She was a visitor from out of town.

312

ROMANCE

Isidore had always been too busy to think of women seriously. Though he had been active in the Columbia Club affairs for over ten years, the only "girl" he ever took to them was his mother; and though he had always been a subscriber to opera seats, the only girl he had ever taken was his sister. He was not girl-shy. He was well acquainted with many nice girls in the clubs for which he directed amateur shows, and had many agreeable friendships.

He had a goal—to build a big business; and he felt that he should not let himself be hampered by marriage till he reached it. Is it any wonder, then, that when Isidore began to show this visitor from Omaha unusual attentions it was noticeable? A friend of Isidore's, Max Meyer, an Omahan, was a close friend of the girl's family and had known her since she was born. He was delighted to facilitate Isidore's seeing her and showing her attention. Nor was he the only caller. There were many more, and she was royally entertained during her stay in New York.

When they walked down the aisle of the Metropolitan Opera House, all Isidore's friends stared. They were surprised that his regular companion, his sister, was not with him, and were fascinated by the beauty of his new partner.

During this period, he found himself experiencing a new sensation—a desire to be near her. He must have shown it, for there was plenty of tongue-wagging among his friends. It soon ceased, however, as she went on to Baltimore—and he went back to normal. From reports, she was popular in Baltimore, and later proceeded to Chicago as the guest of Mr. and Mrs. Julius Rosenwald. She was only eighteen or nineteen.

While Isidore often thought of her, he did not hear from her until she got back to Omaha. Time passed and then he heard that she had become engaged to a young man from Detroit. She faded slowly from his thoughts. Then his mother passed on, and at about the same time, he learned that her mother, too, had died. One day, Harold Orlob, a popular composer called. Isidore knew him and had, in fact, published some of his productions, but sent out word that he was busy and he had better see his brother. Orlob answered that he wanted especially to see Isidore and would wait. Finally he saw him, and he told Isidore something that gave him rather a shock. He had just received a letter from a friend in Detroit—the man who was supposed to have been engaged to Miss Viola Cahn of Omaha—who reported that the engagement was off and that Isidore was the cause of the break. Isidore was astonished, for it was absolutely untrue; he—at that time—had not seen her for a couple of years. Nevertheless it set him thinking!

The Witmarks had had a practical nurse living with their mother and father who had come to be like a member of the family. Her name was Bard. She was after Isidore at all times, constantly urging him to get married. One particular friend, Charley Hartman, was also determined that he should become a benedict. Close pals, they had made trips together to the Canadian woods as the guests of "King" Charles D. Bingham of Toronto, who had an estate beyond Dorset, Ontario, about one hundred and eighty-five miles from Toronto, on Crozier Lake, and the salmon trout fishing was excellent.

The Canadian woods were the only place in the world where Isidore could dismiss all thoughts of business and do some daydreaming. Romance, which he had never allowed to intrude, cut loose in him up there. The deep pine woods, the silent waters, the clear skies, the lovely glens, an occasional buck or doe, the picturesque corduroy roads, the cottages, all made one forget Broadway.

2. Canadian Woods—and A Poem

This was the picture that again arose before Isidore's eyes when for the second time he arrived at Windsor Castle, the Bingham place. He was tired enough to relish every moment of this vacation. But good old Charley Hartman was with him this time, too, and from the moment they set foot on the train, was repeating his refrain, "Why don't you get married?"

After the second day in camp, in order to stop him, Isidore ventured, "Well, if a certain girl will have me, I'll consider it."

Like a shot out of a gun, Hartman asked: "Where does she live?"

"Omaha," Isidore replied, before he was aware of it.

"Omaha! Let's go!"

"Where?"

"Omaha!"

"You're crazy. We've only been here two days," Isidore said. "I've come up for a rest. Forget it till we get home. These things can't be rushed."

Eventually their vacation was over and they returned home. This time Isidore's thoughts were not entirely on business. As a matter of fact, Charley Hartman would not allow them to be. But as Isidore had sworn him to secrecy, nobody else knew his intentions.

September 19th was Julie's birthday and the Witmarks always celebrated it in the country with a house full of week-end guests. On this occasion, Max Meyer roomed with Isidore. They had been talking about the girl in Omaha. The morning after the birthday, he was out early for golf. When he returned, Max was still in bed.

"Wake up, Max," Isidore said, "I want you to read something I wrote down at the club-house. I had no paper so I wrote it on the back of my golf score."

"It will have to be pretty darned good to interest me this early in the morning," said Max, reaching for his glasses.

He read it, and commented, "That's beautiful. What's it all about?"

"It's about a girl you know. The whole poem came to me at once, like an inspiration. Hartman and Bard are driving me to distraction. A few years ago they would have had no effect on me.

Mother gone, Julie and Sis married, and my business at last up to the point where I can take it easier, I think I'd like to be married —and you know the girl. Now, here's the plan, and it is to be strictly confidential between us. As president of the American Music Stores, I suddenly feel it in my bones that I should make a little inspection tour of the departments!"

Max caught on.

"This tour is to lead *west*, and I'm to sign up some new departments that may be available. I have to be present at the première of Gus Luders' "Fair Co-ed" which opens with Elsie Janis in Detroit, and the Victor Herbert operetta "The Prima Donna" in Chicago, with Fritzi Scheff. We have a department in Hayden Brothers, in Omaha, that may need looking over."

Max nodded significantly.

"You're going to meet me in Burlington, Iowa, and we're going to Omaha together. Previous to this you're going to write to someone in Omaha close to the family and find out the present status of Miss Cahn's sentiments and whether she's receiving attentions from anyone else. If not, we'll be on our way."

Max got in touch with Dr. Oscar Hoffman of Omaha, who had been the family physician since Viola was born, and learned that while Isidore would have plenty of competition her heart was free. So Isidore left for Chicago, where the Witmarks had an office and where the American Music Stores had two departments. Max left New York a week later, and the Witmark brothers, who knew nothing of Isidore's intentions, wrote how sorry they were that he had not waited so that they could have traveled together. Isidore wired home from time to time, as he signed contracts with new departments; he also telegraphed that he was going to Omaha to look over Hayden Brothers' department.

Before leaving New York, he had made a bet of twenty dollars with Nurse Bard that he'd make an announcement within three months. He met Max in Burlington on the midnight train, and they arrived in Omaha on a Friday morning. Max was delighted to see his old home town again.

The first person they called on was Dr. Hoffman, who intimated that on account of Viola's youth, the best he could expect for a while was to be allowed to correspond with her. This dismayed Isidore because he had been dictating for years and to start writing long letters by hand would be an ordeal.

They next called on Mr. Cahn. He was a leading merchant of Omaha, a native son, popular, a "champ" golfer, billiard player, and all-around sportsman. While Isidore was talking to him, he said he expected his daughter at the store at any moment. Isidore's heart beat faster. He wondered what a difference four years might have wrought. When she came in, all his fears were dispelled. She was the same sweet girl, and he could feel that she was glad to see him.

Max and Isidore were invited for Sunday dinner. "Brewster's Millions" was playing on the local stage, and Isidore invited Miss Cahn and her sister Hazel to the Saturday matinee. "Brewster's Millions" was the first entertainment she had attended since she had been in mourning.

While she and her sister were at the matinee, he went to see his department in the Hayden Brothers store and met Joseph Hayden, the head of the company. They chatted until Isidore looked at his watch and said, "I have to meet Miss Cahn now, after the matinee."

Mr. Hayden said, "Miss Cahn? Then you're meeting one of the finest girls in Omaha."

In fact, his enthusiasm was unbounded, and coming from a man of his standing in the community, it was a source of great satisfaction to Isidore.

That evening they all went to Dr. Hoffman's for dinner. Max came in saying he had been able to secure tickets for the Aksarben Ball. The Aksarben (Nebraska spelled backward) was the event of the season, Omaha's Mardi Gras. At a previous

317

Aksarben, Miss Cahn had been a lady-in-waiting. This time she was reluctant to attend, having been so long in mourning, but they persuaded her to go, for they felt that she should get back into the swing of things.

After the ball they had a supper party at Henshaw's. The ice was well broken by this time, and the four years of their separation melting away. By the next day they felt like old friends. They had Sunday dinner at her house, and during the afternoon many friends dropped in, among whom Isidore recognized a few rivals.

Isidore was determined to outstay everybody, and had the presumption to invite himself and Max to supper. As it was Sunday night and the maids were out, the girls said that if they'd take pot luck they would be welcome. After supper, luck was with Isidore. Everybody was going out except Viola. She had got something in her eye earlier in the day; although she had been to the doctor's it still bothered her, and she preferred to stay home until the time came for him to catch the train to Chicago, where Fritzi Scheff was to open in "The Prima Donna" the next evening. Here was Isidore's chance. Now or never! It was seven o'clock—and he had to be on that train by nine.

3. Proposal

While she was out of the room he tried to calm his nerves by playing the piano. On her return she exclaimed, "What a beautiful piece! Play some more."

"No," he answered, getting up, "I want to talk to you." Without any other preliminary he put the big question.

She gave a little gasp. "But how do I know you really care for me?" she asked. "We haven't seen or heard from each other in four years. How do I know that you ever gave me a thought?"

He was nonplussed for the moment. Then he asked, "Do you like poetry?"

318

ROMANCE

"Why, yes," she said.

From his inside pocket he brought out the poem that he had written on the score card at the golf club, *Little Woman of the West,* and gave it to her without comment.

> For you, dear, my heart is yearning,
> Little woman of the West.
> Just for you my soul is burning,
> Little woman of the West.
> Yearning—
> Burning—
> Westward turning
> To the one that I love best,
> That I love best.
>
> To you, dear, my dove is winging,
> Little sweetheart of the West.
> Heart throbs to you, dearest, bringing,
> Little sweetheart of the West.
> Winging—
> Bringing—
> Lines I'm singing
> To the one whom I love best,
> Whom I love best.
>
> ### L'Envoi
> Lonely I wait here in sadness,
> Little mother of the West,
> For your cheering words of gladness,
> Little mother of the West,
> Sadness—
> Gladness—
> Almost madness,
> For the one whom I love best,
> Whom I love best.

She read it, and with emotion whispered, "It's beautiful."

"Well, have I been thinking about you?" he asked.

She smiled and he felt that she had silently consented.

319

He followed up quickly, "Now, let me cure your eye"—which he proceeded to do in his own way!

Suddenly he thought of his train. Just fifteen minutes to catch it!

"I'll call you tomorrow, dear, from Chicago, for my answer!" he cried, as he dashed off.

At the station Max Meyer and Dr. Hoffman were waiting with the baggage. The first thing the doctor asked was, "Well, will she allow you to correspond?"

"Correspond, hell! I'm engaged!"

And the next morning he really was. When he telephoned from Chicago he got his answer, "Yes." And so he has always written his engagement days Oct. 4th *hyphen* 5th.

In Omaha the night he left, as the "engaged" girl was sitting in a daze, everything having happened so suddenly, in walked the most persistent of Isidore's rivals. So distracted was her greeting that he was taken aback. The conversation went on lamely for some minutes. Finally, he gathered the courage to say, "Viola, I'd like to say something to you"—which brought her to. With a "What—again?" expression, she waited—when her sister came in, spoiling what promised to be a second proposal that evening.

The sister was surprised to find Isidore gone and his rival there. Knowing Viola so well she sensed that there was something on her mind, and suggested a game of cards. As Isidore heard later, it was about the queerest game of cards ever played. Not one of the three had the game in mind. And the engaged one made so many mistakes that the game soon died from sheer lack of interest. The sisters kept wishing the young man would leave, and finally he bowed out. One can imagine what the chief topic of the sisters was then, and what happened when the rest of the family came home.

Isidore arrived in Chicago too early to get in touch with anyone, so he went to a hotel, registered, and by the time he had breakfast and got his final "Yes" over the telephone, he was ready to start a busy day. His first visit was to the theater where the Fritzi Scheff show was opening, and as he walked across the stage, who should come in from the other entrance but Victor Herbert. After the usual warm greetings and an agreement to dine together that night, Isidore lost no time: "Victor, remember that lunch we had at the Arena about ten years ago?"

"Yes, yes, my boy."

"Do you remember the compact we made?"

"What compact?"

"That if I got married, you'd write my wedding march?"

"Yes, yes, my boy."

"Well, get busy."

"Get busy?"

"Yes—I'm going to be married!"

"What!"

"I became engaged last night to the most wonderful girl in the world." It sounded like the title of another Victor Herbert success.

Victor congratulated him warmly and wanted to know all about it. He kept his word with one of the most beautiful of his compositions. It was written in two outstanding parts. One theme he called *Isidore* (*energior*) which was martial and broad in its character; the other, *Viola* (*amabile*) which was tender and entrancingly beautiful. He titled it *Wedding Music* and at the end brought the two melodies together in contrapuntal form, in one grand crescendo. The manuscript was dated December 24, 1908.

After his talk with Victor Herbert Isidore went to his Chicago office. Max Meyer had arrived ahead of him, so when Isidore appeared, his manager, Nat Mann, brother of Louis Mann, greeted and congratulated him. The first thing Isidore did was to send a telegram to Brother Julie, as follows: "Signed a life contract with Viola Cahn of Omaha. Very happy. Keep confidential until you hear from me."

This was a new kind of contract! And since it was the first

intimation his family had had of the whole affair, it created a stir. And in spite of his admonition to keep the secret until he released it, they got even with him by telling everybody, and letters and telegrams began pouring into the West.

After telling his family, Isidore realized he had forgotten a most important thing—squaring it with the girl's father. So he put in a call for Omaha.

"Hello. Is that you, Mr. Cahn?"

"Is that you, Isidore? You put one over on me, didn't you? What do you mean—stealing my girl while my back was turned?"

Isidore answered, "I didn't steal your daughter. I brought you a son."

"Well, there's something in that. Are you coming back?"

"No, I'm going home—to correspond."

"What, you're not coming back?"

"Do you want me to come back?"

"Don't you think you ought to come back?"

"Well, I had no idea—"

"But don't you think you ought to come back?"

"Well—not unless you want me to—"

"Well—oh, hell, come back!"

Isidore went back! He never forgot his return to Omaha that Wednesday morning. He met an entirely different girl. When he had left her, she had been under the cloud of grief and mourning for the one who had been dearest to her, but now she was radiant with a new happiness. She greeted him with genuine joy, and he felt more than repaid for having come back.

Her father, too, seemed different. He seemed happy because his girl was once more happy. And being a great kidder, he asked, "What are you going to call me, Dad or Al?"

Isidore said, "If you behave, I'll call you Dad. And if you don't, I'll call you Al."

For twenty-five years they never had a cross word, and Isidore always called him Dad.

On the following Sunday they had a reception and it seemed as though the whole town came. Isidore stayed and met the populace. He was in such a daze at the time that he didn't realize it, but they told him afterward that he followed his betrothed around with a chair wherever she was in the room and planted himself beside her.

After this unexpected week of happiness, he returned to the usual grind in New York. The first thing to greet him on his dresser was an envelope with a weight in it. It was a twenty dollar gold piece, with a laconic note—"You win. Bard." He had difficulty in getting her to take it back. She was happy over the engagement and so was Charley Hartman. They acted as if it were the achievement of their lives!

Bard proved her devotion by standing by him during nights of fevered correspondence. He could not do personal letter writing during the day, and would start in every evening after dinner. He thoroughly enjoyed the new sensation although it was real work for him; feeling bound to have a letter for her every day he denied himself to his friends and wrote into the early morning hours. Bard would bring him a glass of milk or other refreshment and would see to it that the letter went safely on its way, so that the chain would not be broken. Those envelopes looked like official documents, for besides the letters he always put in souvenirs, programs, photographs, anything he thought would be of interest, and they were so thick that Bard had difficulty getting them into the mailbox. It had to be a correspondence courtship, since he could make only a couple of trips to Omaha before his marriage.

4. A Wedding—or A Musical?

The wedding was to be in January. Hundreds of invitations were sent out from Omaha, and arrangements were well under way. Musical friends, among them the outstanding composers of the day, learning that Victor Herbert was writing Isidore's wedding march, also showed their appreciation by writing special music for their chief and his bride. Julian Edwards wrote a beautiful song called *Love's Harmony* with lyric by Mark Zangwill, brother of Israel Zangwill. Manuel Klein, the Hippodrome composer, wrote a serenade for cello and organ. *March Canopy* by Theodore Northrup was another. Gustav Luders, composer of "The Prince of Pilsen" and other successes, wrote *Wedding Bells Waltzes*. Ernest R. Ball, composer of *Mother Machree*, wrote one of his famous twelve-eight numbers, *To The End Of The World With You*, with words by his two famous lyricists, Dave Reed, author of *Love Me and the World Is Mine*, and George Graff, Jr., author of *Till the Sands of the Desert Grow Cold*. Nat Mann wrote a waltz, *The Bride's Dream*. And last, as a surprise, was Isidore's own musical setting to the poem that won the girl: *Little Woman of the West*.

All but one of these numbers are still in manuscript; they were inscribed and presented to Miss Viola Cahn. Each is encased in a leather binding. Wedding presents, they were never published, and never will be; eventually they will be on permanent exhibition in the library of Columbia University to which they have been bequeathed.

The wedding was an event for Omaha. It was the first to be held in a magnificent new temple, which was crowded to the doors. Besides the invited guests, there were many outsiders, because of the popularity of Miss Cahn and the Cahn family and the publicity given to the program of original musical numbers by noted composers. Besides the organ, there were a string quartette and instrumental and vocal soloists.

Arranging for the rendition of all this new music required special and careful rehearsing. This was one wedding utterly devoid of Wagner and Mendelssohn. And what a rehearsal! It took the best part of the day before the wedding to straighten it out, and a big dinner party scheduled for that day was almost spoiled.

Isidore realized that the handling of the rehearsal required a director, and as there was no one else to assume this post, he fell into it. There was much to supervise—the organist, the string quartette in the organ loft, the cello soloist, the singer, the ushers, and bridesmaids. It was more like rehearsing a show than a wedding. The showman in him began to dominate the bridegroom—and here the trouble started. For the moment he forgot that these people were friends, and looked upon them as just so many unmanageable amateurs such as he had rehearsed many times before. In striving for perfection, he rehearsed them over and over again, which, to the uninitiated, made the program seem unusually long. This worried the bride particularly. Isidore was working especially hard on the Herbert music, as that was the most complicated and required the utmost precision because it announced musically the entrance of the various participants and had to be timed exactly. With all this repetition the rehearsal seemed ungodly long.

"You'll have to cut that some," said the bride.

"What? Cut Victor Herbert?" he cried, horrified. "I'd rather cut the wedding itself!" From which it can be seen how far he had lost himself in the "show."

The bride fell on her father's shoulder, weeping, while the bridesmaids looked daggers. The ushers remained unaffected, as most of them came from New York and had performed in many of Isidore's "amateur shows." They proceeded to comfort the rest, saying, "He's all right. He knows what he's about. He has an old slogan—'We'll be all right on the night!' And it always works out. But you've got to let him have his head!"

His bride's tears dismaying Isidore, he apologized, but added, "I've never had a failure in any of my amateur shows, when let alone. If you'll let me do this my way, I'm sure it'll come out all right—and you'll find it won't be too long."

And as predicted, it was not too long. The ceremony was a great success. After everyone had been seated, the jubilant fanfare of Herbert's wedding march pealed forth. At each entrance an appropriate theme was introduced. The minister came on first, followed by Jay as best man, then Isidore. Again he forgot himself, and instead of being the solemn groom, became once more the director. As he was told later, he broke into a smile because everything was going smoothly. The appearance of the bridesmaids and ushers was timed to the second with the music. Even the little flower girls gave an excellent performance! When the beautiful bride entered, to cap the climax, Isidore forgot himself and his audience entirely and beamed and chuckled all over the place.

Thanks to the vigorous rehearsing, the pageant proceeded perfectly, and when the last note of the Herbert music was played, everyone was in proper position. His bride and he were standing before the minister. The Viola theme was being repeated softly. Suddenly he felt a slight tug at his sleeve, and heard his bride's whisper, "You were right, dear. It wasn't too long."

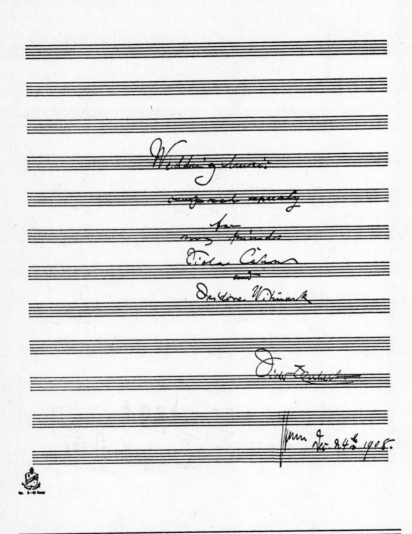

Extracts From Original Victor Herbert Wedding Music.

327

Victor Herbert paid special honor to Isidore and his bride when he wrote music to be played at their wedding. It is reproduced here for the first time, and only in extract form.

CHAPTER XXI

". . . OF BALLADS, SONGS AND SNATCHES . . ."

1. Sweet Adeline

DURING the brief period of courtship that led to the marriage of Viola Cahn and Isidore Witmark, the American ballad era was at its height. As a sort of interlude between ragtime and jazz it sang, often in a thumping, twelve-eight tempo, the eternal longings of the simple soul. The House of Witmark not only published music; it lived, in the persons of its partners, these rhythms, these emotions. It sold songs, yes; also, it *was* song. It was with a ballad, *Little Woman of the West*, that Isidore had won his bride. It was, during this courtship epoch, that the House of Witmark was winning the public all over again—with ballads.

When *Sweet Adeline* was first published, it was included in a thematic catalog of new ballads. At the top of its page was one of the most prophetic blurbs imaginable. It read, "One of the most charming ballads ever written. The story is pathetic, the music of a sentimental nature. The refrain is of the responsive sort, making it valuable for choruses."

What a prediction! "Making it valuable for choruses!" Has there ever been a chorus song like it? Published in 1903, it is still the outstanding popular chorus song, and will remain so, long after its renewed copyright has expired. It is the natural exhaust of pent-up convivial emotion; it probably has made more people sing who had never thought they had voices than any other composition ever written.

The story of *Sweet Adeline* has often been told, in part; the authors of this book are enabled to tell the complete and authentic tale, chiefly because the Witmarks eventually published the song, and because they have received from the composer, Harry Armstrong, an account prepared expressly for this record. No one pretends, least of all Mr. Armstrong or Richard H. Gerard, writer of the words, whose real last name is Husch, that *Sweet Adeline* is a masterpiece of lyrics or music. The history of the piece, however, is yet another in the long catalog of neglected or abandoned writings that have suddenly, through a caprice of the public or an accident of circumstance, been lifted into enduring fame.

For *Sweet Adeline* is now part of American song-lore. It is sacred to the instinctive harmonizing efforts of the street-corner or barber-shop quartette, or whatever name the descendants of these foursomes go by in these sophisticated days. It was the theme song of John F. ("Honey") Fitzgerald's political campaigns, and properly so, since the song was born in the city of Boston, over which Fitzgerald presided as Mayor in 1906-7 and 1910-1914. It achieved the rare popularity of becoming a public nuisance. It possessed such great drawing power that its title was appropriated for one of Jerome Kern's musical comedies. It is, in short, entirely apart from its status as words and music, part of American song history.

In 1896, Harry Armstrong was a youth of eighteen, working in the jewelry store of George Homer on Winter Street, Boston. He belonged to a street-corner quartette that in the good old summer time was attracted to the lampposts as inevitably as moths. They sang by ear, and every once in a while they would hit by happy chance upon a chord that enchanted them with its weird

331

beauty. It was the so-called barber-shop chord, and they would go back to it again and again to impress it upon their memories.

It was this chord and the quartette that gave Armstrong his idea for *Sweet Adeline*. That was not her first name, by the way; in fact, as is usually the case in Tin Pan Alley, the music was born before the words. Part of the chorus—another Tin Pan Alley habit; the chorus is written first—was set down at this time. For Armstrong had begun to have ambitions to write popular tunes.

Even Bostonians under fifty may recall the department store of Pitts, Kimball and Lewis, which was situated near the corner of Washington and Boylston Streets. The music section was run by George Setchel, who now and then ventured into publishing as well. It was here that Armstrong first met Julie Witmark, who was then singing *Her Eyes Don't Shine Like Diamonds*, and, of course, plugging it, too. To show Julie that he knew the song, Armstrong sat down at the piano and played a chorus; Julie, pleased, turned a broad Witmark smile on the youth. Armstrong had no notion that he had played for one of his future employers; nor did Julie dream that there, at the piano, sat the boy who was to produce one of Witmarks' most enduring hits.

Boston proving inhospitable to the work of its suburbanite composer (he came from Somerville), Armstrong made up his mind that New York was the place for a budding genius. Landing in Gotham with $2.65 in his pocket, he began to scan the Help Wanted columns, and found himself at seven o'clock one morning at a Coney Island honky-tonk, applying against several other early birds for the post of pianist. He got the job, and it nearly got him. He played from eleven that morning until two o'clock next, for $2.50. And when he would stop playing, the boss was at his side, with "Don't stop, kid. Go right on!"

There would have to be another job, and this one was at the old Sans Souci Music Hall at Thirteenth Street and Third Avenue. It was this position that turned Armstrong into a New Yorker. A regular visitor to the Sans Souci, who owned a drugstore at Eighty-sixth Street and Third Avenue, used to come around after closing up for the night. His name was Joseph M. Schenck—a rather familiar one to patrons of the movies, and today especially to employees and executives of the Twentieth Century-Fox Film Corporation, of which he is chairman of the Board of Directors. Schenck would hang around until the chairs were stacked up. There was another pal of Armstrong's, Harry Howard. So Schenck suggested one night that the three of them team up and room together. This was as much necessity as companionship; Howard and Armstrong were a week behind in their rent already; if moving were done, 't were well 't were done quickly.

It was about four o'clock one morning when the trio proceeded to the room, removed Howard's trunk—a large, old-fashioned crate—and escorted it down two long flights of stairs. Howard was at one end and Armstrong at the other; Schenck was running ahead on Thirteenth Street, between Second and Third Avenues, watching out for the police to make sure that they would not be taken for burglars.

The poor landlady never received her five dollars back rent. "If I only knew where she was," says Armstrong today, "I'd be happy to send it to her with accumulated interest—and the interest from that time would amount to a tidy little sum."

Schenck later opened a saloon at a small amusement park up Fort George way, and offered Armstrong the job of pianist, but by this time Armstrong had joined the Witmarks, and he declined the offer. Armstrong's direct move from the Sans Souci was to the Old Bohemia, on Twenty-eighth Street. Here he began to enjoy his first success as a composer, placing some of his songs with Witmarks. Selling songs in these days was not a matter of contract and signature; you peddled your wares from publisher to publisher, and in a way that would hardly be understood outside the Alley. The music was written on what are still called lead-sheets, because they provide only the melody, as yet unworded and unaccompanied. This is an economic device, and is meant chiefly for the lyricist, as a guide or "lead" in fitting his words to the contours of the tune. Armstrong peddled his tunes in lead-sheets, to which the lyrics were pinned. He was always careful to pin through the same holes every time, so that the new publisher wouldn't see, from the condition of the manuscript, how many others had considered the composition before him.

It was while submitting a song to Witmarks' that Armstrong was offered a job by Isidore. He was to make himself generally useful around the professional department, at fifteen dollars per week. Here was Harry making twenty-five dollars, and tips extra, at the Old Bohemia. "I don't think I can accept," he answered.

A few weeks later he placed another song with Witmarks', and again Isidore suggested that he join them, this time at eighteen dollars. "If you keep playing around the joints," advised Isidore, "you'll never get anywhere in your life."

The argument sounded too logical to refute. Armstrong, despite the financial drop, accepted. All this time, between the sales of other tunes, there was the chorus for what eventually was to be christened *Adeline*. By now it was completed with the exception of a single bar. It is not only the masterpieces of symphonic structure that are born in long travail. Popular music has its own problems of shrewd adaptation. There were still the words to be supplied, and Armstrong now submitted the lead-sheet to Charles B. Lawlor, who had written the words to the endless *Irish Jubilee*, and who is known to American fame as the author of *The Sidewalks of New York*. Lawlor—observe the artistic leisureliness—kept the music for six months and returned it, saying that he could devise no lyrics for it.

Harry had better luck with Richard H. Gerard. After only a few weeks Dick managed to concoct one line—*You're The Flower Of My Heart, Sweet Rosalie.*

They took the song to Harry's employers, but the Witmarks turned it down. They took it to Howley, Haviland and Dresser, who held it for nine months and then, on the demand either to publish or return, returned it. They took it to the firm of Jerome H. Remick-Whitney-Warner, who held it for a year and then sent it back. In desperation, Harry thought of his old love, Setchel, and forwarded it to Boston. Setchel played with it for another year, and might have had it yet if Armstrong had not met him by accident in New York, and demanded that either he publish or return. He returned.

Back to Gerard went Armstrong. "There's something the matter with the song. Maybe you'd better change the title." Gerard changed the title; he re-christened Rosalie with the name Adeline. With this correction they re-submitted it to the Witmarks. This time the firm said, "Yes."

But how about this name Adeline, that rhymed with pine? "There's no such word as Adeline," objected Julius. "It's pronounced Adel*een*." Gerard nodded. "You're right. I got that name from the name of Adelina Patti. But Adel*een* doesn't rhyme with pine. So it's got to be Adeline." And Adeline it remained. For a year it languished on the shelves of the stockroom. It was too slow, too old-fashioned, they all said. Maybe so. During the adventures of the song the popular taste had changed more than once.

Then happened one of those things that turned a Paul West failure into an Anna Held triumph. A quartette came into the Witmark office—the Quaker City Four—looking for a good number. Fred Rycroft, manager of the professional department, took them into tow and had virtually every song in the catalog played over for them.

"Harry," he called out, at the end of his tether, "you may as well go and fish out *Sweet Adeline*."

And off went Harry to the stockroom, to the top-loftiest shelf, where it had been relegated to its last rest.

Then sat down and played it. Harry Ernest, manager of the quartette, exclaimed at the end, "Why, that is just the song we've been looking for!" Harry Armstrong today is a booking agent and has heard many a tune since that eventful performance; it is doubt-

335

ful, however, that he has ever heard sweeter music than those words from manager Ernest.

The song was put into rehearsal, and was sung for the first time the following week, at Hammerstein's Victoria, 42nd Street and Seventh Avenue. It was an instantaneous hit. John F. Fitzgerald, who was running for the mayoralty in Boston, adopted the song, sang it wherever he went, and won on the *Sweet Adeline*—incidentally the Democratic—ticket. It became, and remained, for him what *The Sidewalks of New York* became and remained for Alfred E. Smith.

This was not to be Armstrong's only association with Mayors. It was shortly after he had begun to peddle the tune of what became *Sweet Adeline* that he met James J. Walker at the Witmarks. He set to music Jimmy Walker's first lyric, *Good-bye, Eyes of Blue.* He remembers Jimmy as a hard worker, who managed to pay his way through college by writing songs and sketches. "The minute his classes were over, he would be down at Witmarks', hard at it."

It was at Witmarks', too, that he first met Ernest R. Ball. Ball he remembers chiefly as a "rollicking, jovial fellow." He was not only a baseball player but an enthusiastic amateur at boxing and wrestling, always looking for a chance to exercise his muscles. Ball's joining of the Witmark forces made history for both the composer and his firm, and is told elsewhere in these pages. His relations with Armstrong—for they became fast friends—appear to have been far more athletic than artistic.

The Witmark staff of writers had private desks out front, in the professional rooms. Ball, coming in for the day's work, thought it a great start to tease the creators at their task. Writing music came so easy to him that he required only the patience to sit down. He would rather keep after Armstrong, for instance, until Harry became so annoyed that he would jump up from his desk and engage in combat.

Nothing could please Ball more. They would roll about on the floor, get up, go at it afresh, and at times crash right through the

Jay Witmark

Witmark Building, 144-46 West 37th St., erected by the boys in 1903.
In left hand corner is a copy of invitation to the opening.

plate-glass window with the sign, "Professional Room." Professional pugilists or catch-as-catch-canners, from the looks of things! Once, after such a crash, both Ernie and Harry ran into the street to escape the Witmark wrath; Julius appeared on the scene just too late. But when, a few months later, the glass crashed again and again the offenders escaped into the street, they were mistaken in thinking that they had "got away with it" once more. That Saturday their pay envelopes were minus $15—the cost of replacing the plate-glass. It was too high a price for office wrestling; they were cured.

2. One-Hit Song Writers

Armstrong wrote some good sellers but *Sweet Adeline* remained his great hit. In fact, few songs of this type have attained the success of this bacchanalian exhaust. It symbolizes, in addition to the fair weather when good fellows get together, another Tin Pan Alley type: the one-hit song writer.

We have all heard of the *homo unius libri*—the one-book man. One of the freaks of the song-writing profession is the writer who turns out one big hit and inexplicably rarely "clicks" again. He produces no end of near-successes, and some songs that promise well but turn out to be comparative failures. One of the ironies of the business, as the Witmarks found, was to sign up a writer on the strength of one hit and then have him hand in almost-successes and flat flops. Another blow was the free-lance writer who would give them his next-best and their competitor his big hit—all entirely by chance. Such had been the case of their friend, Joe Flynn. The Witmarks were his first publishers and brought out his two near-successes, *Paddy Shay* and *Number Four Second Floor*. But his hit, *Down Went McGinty*, went to a firm then new, Spaulding and Gray.

Among the one-hit writers on the Witmark list was the team of

337

FROM RAGTIME TO SWINGTIME

Matthews and Bulger, who were a big success in vaudeville; they wrote their own songs and gags. M. Witmark & Sons were their first publishers. Out of all the material they wrote, one song, *Hey Rube, or A Day at the Circus,* was outstanding. This was another of those long-winded, unending songs like *The Irish Jubilee,* which had a vogue at the time. Oliver and Fay, two Chicago boys, were prolific in the ballad line, but their *Goodnight, Beloved, Goodnight,* was their real success. Herbert Dillea wrote constantly and was a noted musical director, but had one hit, *Absence Makes the Heart Grow Fonder,* which he wrote with Arthur Gillespie. Dillea was the director of the orchestra playing at the ill-fated Iroquois Theater of Chicago on the day of the noted fire. With real heroism, he remained in the orchestra pit until his baton was singed, trying to keep up the public morale by having his orchestra play until it was driven out by the flames. He practically gave his life that day, for he was never the same thereafter.

Will R. Anderson is another example of the one-hit writer. Although he wrote other songs that were good sellers, they were not in the real hit class—as was his *Tessie, You Are The Only Only.* Being his exclusive publishers, Witmarks' were fortunate in getting it, as it sold over a million copies.

Harry L. Freeman of Chicago had one hit, *Honey That I Love So Well,* which was sung by all the leading quartettes in the country. Ernest Hogan's *All Coons Look Alike to Me* was by far the biggest thing he ever wrote.

One of the most versatile and prolific writers known to the song world was Barney Fagan, but he will be remembered by only one song, *My Gal Is a Highborn Lady.*

The one-hit writer is not a purely modern phenomenon. Over fifty years ago Jennie Lindsay wrote many songs, but her one tremendous selling hit, made popular by Julie, remained *Always Take Mother's Advice.* Others who have written many numbers, but have just one outstanding hit, are:

"... OF BALLADS, SONGS AND SNATCHES ..."

Writer	Songs
Lilly May Hall,	*Pretty Pond Lilies*
Ramon Moore,	*Sweet Marie*
Banks Winter,	*White Wings*
George Safford Waters,	*Belle of Avenue A*
James I. Russell,	*Where the River Shannon Flows*
Hattie Marshall,	*Little Willie (He Knew a Thing or Two)*
Zo Elliott,	*There's a Long, Long Trail*
Maude Nugent,	*Sweet Rosie O'Grady*
J. W. Kelly,	*Throw 'Em Down, McCloskey*
Joseph Sullivan,	*Where Did You Get That Hat?*
H. B. Danks,	*Silver Threads Among the Gold*
R. M. Stultz,	*Sweetest Story Ever Told*
Henry J. Sayers,	*Ta-Ra-Ra-Boom-De-Ay*
Jules Jordan,	*The Song That Reached My Heart*
Theodore A. Metz,	*Hot Time in the Old Town Tonight*
Lee Roberts,	*Smiles*
Anita Owen,	*Just a Chain of Daisies*
John T. Hall,	*Wedding of the Winds*
Edward Hutchison,	*Sammy*
Robert Hood Bowers,	*Chinese Lullaby*
Felix Arndt,	*Nola*
James Casey	*Sing Me a Song of the South*
(Norton & Casey),	
Harry Mayo,	*Where the Chicken Got the Axe*
Edward W. Corliss,	*Star of My Life*
Nat D. Mann,	*Honey, Youse My Lady Love*
Francis Bryan,	*Christopher Columbo*
William Courtwright,	*Johnny, My Old Friend John*
Ex-Mayor Jimmy Walker,	*Will You Love Me in December*
	As You Do in May?

3. Ernest R. Ball

"When Ernest R. Ball died, on May 3, 1927, the one writer of his kind passed away. No other has taken just his place." This is the simple tribute of Isidore Witmark for the noblest balladeer of them all.

"I shall never forget a telephone talk with Irving Berlin in which, expressing himself about Ernie, he finished up with, 'I wish I could write a song as good as his.'

"I remember the first time I met Ball. It was in the anteroom of my office, in our building at 8 West Twenty-ninth Street. He had sent in his name, and as I was going to another part of the building I passed him. I stopped and asked what he wanted. He said he would like to join our force of demonstrators. In want of a good man at the time, I asked him a few questions and hired him on the spot.

"We agreed on twenty dollars a week to start with, and as he had had experience I did not have to tell him what his duties were.

"It was not long before his influence was felt, for he was rounding up many new friends for the house."

Ernest R. Ball was born at Cleveland, Ohio, in 1878, and early gave evidence of a remarkable aptitude for music. He laid the foundation of his musical education at the local conservatory, and began giving piano lessons at the age of thirteen, thus earning money to complete the study of his chosen art. When fifteen, he composed his first number, a march that met with pronounced favor. He has been called the American Tosti, his gift being versatile, his ballads appealing to the cultured musician as well as to the boy in the gallery. His melodies were of the kind that reach the heart, having that intangible something which impresses itself indelibly upon the hearer.

One has only to mention the titles of the list of song hits he has written. He was destined to write one song that set the whole world singing and that is still a favorite among the balladists. This was *Love Me and the World Is Mine*, lyrics by Dave Reed, Jr., and it established the composer in the front rank of American writers. From that moment Ernie Ball forged ahead with remarkable rapidity. Song after song came from his pen, nearly all of them numbering among the best sellers. His versatility was matched by his prolific qualities, and the American public soon learned to look

OF BALLADS, SONGS AND SNATCHES

for a Ball song as they looked forward to the coming of springtime. *Love Me and the World Is Mine* was translated into every singable language.

Ernie Ball was blessed with good lyric writers, among them Dave Reed, Jr., George Graff, Jr., Caro Roma, Rida Johnson Young, Arthur Lamb, Louis Weslyn, Bartley Costello, William H. Gardner, J. Kern Brennan, and the famous colored poet, Paul Laurence Dunbar. Aided by this coterie of lyricists, Ball had hardly a season during which he did not turn out a smashing song hit. There was always a demand for his songs and Julie, who took an interest in him from the start, built him up into the Witmarks' number one writer. Ball always declared that he owed everything to Julie, who would go over each of his new numbers; between them they would iron the song out, primarily for the singer and eventually for the public. Julie had tremendous faith in the Ball compositions, and was never "phased" if a new number did not appeal to him on first hearing. He always maintained that Ernie Ball's numbers, like Victor Herbert's, had wearing qualities; Time has borne this out.

As well as a composer, Ernie Ball was a delightful entertainer and singer, with a strong personality. And while variety, or what was later known as vaudeville, was the vogue, he was always a headline attraction wherever he appeared. It was after one of his successful appearances at a vaudeville house in Santa Ana, California, that he suffered a heart attack and died in his dressing-room.

While most song hits may be said to be inspired, Ernie Ball had a sort of formula for writing his heart ballads, which might be best told in his own language. In an interview in *The American Magazine*, printed in the 1920's, he wrote:

"At Witmarks', when I was not busy demonstrating songs, I used to play over airs that came to me; and it was here, in odd moments, that I did my first composing. My first serious effort was a flop. A little later, I wrote *In the Shadow of the Pyramids*. It went over when sung on the stage by May Irwin, but it never became a widely-sold popular favorite. So it was with a number of others I tried.

"One night in New York, in the spring of 1903, I met State Senator James Walker—the same James Walker who was recently elected Mayor of New York City. He handed me some verses for a song. They were crumpled up on a piece of paper. I read them over. Two lines of the original lyric struck my fancy

> Will you love me in December as you do in May?
> Will you love me in the good old-fashioned way?

"I put the bit of paper in my pocket, and for the next two months carried the scribbled lines around with me. At odd moments I tried to picture a golden-haired girl and boy grown gray with the years. Would they love each other when youth and beauty had fled? Bit by bit, I worked out a tune that somehow seemed to fit and, finally, I wrote the music to the words. The result was *December and May*. I awoke one morning to find that I had written a piece that was being sung from one end of the country to the other.

"Now I began to do some puzzling. Why had my earlier songs been flops, and why was *December and May* a hit? I sat myself down to try to figure it all out.

"In my early efforts, I had tried to write hits, and I had failed. With *December and May*, I had simply tried to write a song from my own heart to people's hearts. Then and there, I determined that I would write honestly and sincerely of the things I knew about and that folks generally knew about and were interested in.

"*Down the Trail to Home, Sweet Home* was written when I was in a small city in which I knew no one. I was tired and weary, and down on my luck. I hadn't seen my mother for a long time. So in this frame of mind I sat down and started to compose. I wanted to be hitting that homeward trail myself. The song came from my heart.

342

"... OF BALLADS, SONGS AND SNATCHES ..."

"People seem to like songs that they can take home to themselves. Talk to a man about his home, his wife, his mother, or his children, and you get his attention. That goes for either conversation or songs. Everybody likes a love song. If the sentiment is straight and true—from the heart to the heart—the song has a chance, if the music is attractive and it fits."

The sure-fire feature of Ernie Ball's vaudeville act was a medley that he himself had arranged of the various song hits he had written; to this he would add as song hits were created. This was his *pièce de résistance,* and the vociferous manner in which the first few notes of each of the numbers of that medley were greeted demonstrated the popularity of the singer and the songs.

And what songs! Who is writing a *Mother Machree* today? He wrote *Mother Machree* for Chauncey Olcott; it has been in the repertoire of singers of Irish ballads for decades; it helped vitally in building the reputation of the great John McCormack, who in his beautiful tribute to the composer said, "Ernie Ball is not dead. He will live forever in his songs."

The writer of the lyric of *Mother Machree* was the author of "Maytime," "Naughty Marietta" and "Brown of Harvard"—Rida Johnson Young.

But why stop at *Mother Machree,* when there are so many other songs by the same man? *Till the Sands of the Desert Grow Cold, Dear Little Boy of Mine, I'll Forget You, A Little Bit of Heaven, Let the Rest of the World Go By, My Dear, In the Garden of My Heart, Who Knows? Goodbye, Good Luck, God Bless You, Turn Back the Universe, I Love the Name of Mary, To the End of the World With You, That's How the Shannon Flows,* and *When Irish Eyes are Smiling.* These are just a few of the hundreds of successes by this prolific writer. In addition, Ernie Ball wrote the musical numbers for practically all of the successful stage productions in which Chauncey Olcott starred.

Ernie Ball contributed generously to the Witmark Black and

White catalog of ballads. Some of his outstanding hits in this collection are: *Who Knows?, Mother Machree, My Hour, I Promise You, The Night Wind, In the Garden of My Heart, Mother, Oh, My Mother, Down in the Valley Fair, Goodnight, Goodnight, If You'll Remember Me, When Sinks the Sun So Gently, Wild Rose,* and *Allah, Give Me Mine.*

Ball holds the record for the longest contract with one house in the music publishing business. He had worked out a twenty-year contract with the Witmarks, and when he died he was on his ten-year renewal.

You never can tell about a song. Almost the motto for song publishers to hang above their desks!

Ball had written what was to be one of his last songs. The firm banked upon it as a hit. The sales chart, however, told a different story. There had been a dozen sessions devoted to the song, but each had proved discouraging. Experience had shown the Witmarks that it takes just so long to put a number across; if, at the end of the allotted time, the number does not discover its public (or the public its number!) the song must regrettably be set down as a failure. Moreover, the firm generally worked on one song at a time; it would not be fair to other numbers and their composers to devote an inordinately long campaign to a piece that did not warrant the investment.

The Ball song was doomed. All the brothers favored surrender, except Julie. Hold on a while longer, he counseled; the song had something. The brothers compromised; they would hold on a while longer, but would also begin pushing another song, to see whether they could retrieve the losses on the Ball number.

The losses were retrieved—by Julie's unshaken confidence and by the Ball number itself. It eventually sold 3,500,000 copies. The song was *Let The Rest Of The World Go By.*

It is not generally known, by the way, that the tune, *Mr. Gallagher and Mr. Shean,* was written in one of the offices of M. Witmark & Sons, and that Ball did most of the writing. For this he did not receive credit or remuneration; what he did was done as an act of friendship.

4. Caro Roma

In her day, Caro Roma was one of the foremost women song writers. Born in California, her father having been a Forty-niner, she made her first stage appearance at the age of three. While in her teens she directed a French opera company in a tour through Canada. For a time she even conducted orchestras.

Her musical education was completed at the New England Conservatory of Music, in Boston. At her graduation the citizens of the city awarded her a gold medal, and she entered upon an operatic career. She was the prima donna of the Henry Savage Opera Company, organized in Boston, and returned to San Francisco, playing at the Tivoli Opera House in the principal female rôles from well-known operas, alternating with Alice Nielsen.

When Mascagni came to America, he made a tour of the United States with a company of Italian singers under his own direction. On arriving at San Francisco he conducted a performance of "Cavalleria Rusticana" with Roma as his Santuzza. While the Italian company did not relish having her, and made her days with them unhappy, she was the only artist in the company whom Mascagni brought out with him when he took his bow. This hardly increased her popularity with her fellow-artists. She appeared by command before many of the crowned heads of Europe, and was decorated by several.

Her first composition was written while she was a child and she successfully added a long and varied list. Most of Roma's songs had both music and lyrics by herself. She was an accomplished student of harmony and counterpoint, and did her own arranging for voice and any solo instrument.

She wrote more than two thousand five hundred poems, of which she published two volumes and many of which were set to

345

FROM RAGTIME TO SWINGTIME

music by her. The songs for which she is famous are *Resignation* and *My Jean,* of which she wrote both words and lyrics, and *Can't You Hear Me Calling, Caroline?* for which William H. Gardner wrote the lyric. She made a specialty of writing sea songs and turned out some so virile that they are often mistaken for the work of a man.

She excelled in sacred songs and built up a catalog of this type. Her settings of *Ave Maria, Abide with Me, Nearer, My God, to Thee, Oh, for the Wings of a Dove,* and *Jesus, Lover of My Soul* are still in great demand.

Her song cycle, *The Wandering One,* a group of weird classical ballads with lyrics by the famous English critic and writer, Clement Scott, are in the repertoire of the leading ballad singers on the concert stage.

With the song, *In the Garden of My Heart,* Roma reversed herself, she writing the lyric to Ernest R. Ball's music. Another number by this partnership was *Love Me Today, Tomorrow May Never Come.* She wrote the words and music of *Faded Rose, The Angelus, Thinking of Thee, My One Hour, Forbidden,* and *Separation.* Her setting of James Whitcomb Riley's *There, Little Girl, Don't Cry* is still much sought.

Roma spent the best of her writing years with the House of Witmark. She became more like one of the family than an outsider. She addressed Julie as "My dear old boss" and invariably signed her letters "Roma L. W.," signifying that she was the "left wing" of the establishment, on the Coast, where, in connection with her studio, she had opened a music shop to exploit the Roma songs.

It was to Julie that Roma was indebted for suggestions in rewriting the music of *Can't You Hear Me Calling, Caroline?* As originally composed, the range of the melody had been too wide for the average singer. Roma always appreciated Julie's revision, and maintained that it had been a factor in the success of the song.

Caro Roma led a sort of gypsy life. In her declining years she lived in California where she died in 1937. Upon the

346

occasion of the death of Julius P. Witmark in 1929 she gave a memorial radio concert in Los Angeles; and on September 29, 1932, she gave her Golden Jubilee Concert at Trinity Auditorium, Los Angeles, where she was assisted by a host of artists on a program of nineteen numbers, all her own compositions.

5. Arthur Penn

Few men were more versatile in the music game than Arthur Penn. He is a rare "collection" of editor, critic, columnist, "ad" writer, composer, lyricist, author, and music arranger, and he is proficient in each line. Arthur Penn was exclusively signed up with Witmarks' for many terms of years, and was an important figure in their establishment. His judgment was sought in many matters, and followed. Like many English song writers, he wrote an appealing ballad and gave to the Witmarks a number of successes in this line, among which were *Smilin' Through, Sunrise and You, The Magic of Your Eyes, I Gave a Rose to You, The Salt of the Sea For Me, When I Dream, Sweetheart, of You*, and his Spanish waltz success, *Carissima*. Arthur almost invariably wrote his own lyrics; he also collaborated with other writers.

He has gained attention for the writing of operettas adapted to amateur production, and they are constantly being given in all parts of the country. The successful play *Smilin' Through*, in which Jane Cowl starred, was already half written and still without a title, when Miss Cowl's husband, the late Adolph S. Klauber, who was producing the play, ran across a copy of this Arthur Penn song, just out. He liked the title and the thought conveyed in the song so well that he had the play rewritten to fit it. The result was a tremendous hit, in which the song was used as incidental music. The play was followed by a silent picture starring Norma Talmadge, and later a modern "sound" version starring Norma Shearer.

With his royalties from the song, Arthur Penn bought an old

347

Colonial cottage on Block Island, as a residence for himself and his wife. He named it "Smilin' Through," for the song that had made it possible. He furnished a studio in it where he expected to do most of his writing. Because of the popularity of the song, and the pride of the natives, however, the home became the showplace of the island, and people, especially summer visitors, began to invade the privacy of the Penns. Finally they had to give up the place and move to New London, Conn., where he is now working unmolested.

Popularity has its rewards—and its price.

6. Rida Johnson Young

One of the most beautiful women ever to come from Baltimore —and Baltimore is noted for its beautiful women—was Rida Johnson Young. A mutual friend of Rida and Isidore, Ellis Ephraim, introduced them when she arrived in New York. She became a member of the Witmark staff, assisting Isidore in the press department, at twenty-five dollars a week.

She was the wife of James Young, actor, writer, lecturer, and motion picture director, who was later the husband of Clara Kimball Young.

Mrs. Young did not remain long in the press department, but started writing one-act plays for the publication department, among them "Chatterton" and "The Last of the Cargills." Then she wrote "Lord Byron," in which James Young starred. Her first big play success, "Brown of Harvard," was produced at the Princess Theater in New York, April 2, 1906, with Harry Woodruff in the title rôle, under the management of Henry Miller and had a long run. *When Love Is Young*, words by Rida and music by Melville Ellis, first introduced in this play, was a song success of that day.

There followed "Glorious Betsy," "The Boys of Company B," "Little Old New York," and the libretto and lyrics of Victor Herbert's famous "Naughty Marietta"; also a number of Chauncey Olcott's plays, and the lyric to that never-dying ballad, *Mother Machree.*

She wrote to Isidore in a letter that he prizes: "I always feel somehow that the Witmarks—and you especially—are responsible for my success. You taught me so much while I was with you, and your confidence in my ability made me venture farther than I should otherwise have done. If I ever do anything really worth while in the playwriting line, I shall attribute it to the fact that you gave me a start when no one else would."

7. *Charles Noel Douglas*

In February, 1897, after some years of failing health, Charles Noel Douglas was stricken with an obscure nervous trouble that rendered him almost helpless and put him on a bed of sickness which he never left. It forced him eventually to sacrifice a home and surroundings of refinement for a ward in a hospital. After nine months of hospital life, the doctors could do nothing for him, so he was listed as a chronic case for the public hospital, which is a polite term for the poorhouse. His means were exhausted and, realizing the plight he was in, he begged the hospital authorities to give him a few days' grace. His request was granted. Then an inspiration came to him to write the words for a song. Coon songs were then all the rage, and, as he had sung many during his stage career, he decided he would write a coon song—and, on borrowed paper and with borrowed pen and ink, the words of his first lyrics were dictated to a fellow-patient. He had not held a pen in months and had almost forgotten how to write, but his amanuensis was patient and skillful. His verses went to a celebrated actress. Two days of agonizing suspense passed, and then, to his intense delight, a letter was brought him from the singer, containing a check for twenty dollars. That night he thought out another song "pome," and Weber and Fields, then in the zenith of their fame, sent him twenty dollars for it. He later wrote many poems for magazines which were accepted.

His initial successes were too much for him in his delicate condition, and soon after moving to a new hospital, he collapsed and for three months hardly knew his own name. From this on it was one long, grim, heart-breaking, soul-crashing fight, but he was not discouraged.

He moved to a home for incurables, where he spent three years, in an attic, under a tin roof, roasted in summer, frozen in winter. Here he wrote some two hundred song lyrics and poems, the majority of which he marketed. Sometimes his funds were so low he would have to practically give work away.

His one hope and prayer had been that he might once more have a home of his own. He toiled on, hoped on, prayed on, and finally, in September, 1902, after nearly six years of misery, he turned his back on the hospitals forever, and moved into a home of his own.

"Can you imagine," he wrote, "What that change meant to me? For three years I hadn't seen a vestige of Nature. Spring came; I saw not its verdant splendor; fall rolled on, but the gorgeous tints of autumn were not for me. I could only tell the seasons from the heat or cold.

"You can realize what my delight was to leave all these scenes of suffering, and have my bed in a window that gave me a splendid view of the world, of which I'd seen nothing in six years. I shall never forget my excitement as I watched the first automobile chug-chug past on the street below. But perhaps the most delightful and refreshing sight was a band of lovely children—darling little tots—playing "Ring-a-round, a-rosy" on the lawn of a house opposite me. Ah, me! how little we appreciate the small things of life until we lose them, and then, and not until then, do we realize what we've lost. For a week I could do nothing but gaze out of my window, and laugh and sing, and thank God I was alive. It was glorious."

In March, 1903, his connection with *Comfort Magazine* began.

"... OF BALLADS, SONGS AND SNATCHES ..."

This was an epoch in his life, as it brought him the abiding love of six millions of people. As "Uncle Charlie," in *Comfort*, and "Uncle George," in *Homefolks*, he had become an institution in nearly two millions of homes.

Douglas had written some seven hundred song lyrics and "pomes" during his invalidism. Yet he had never written a line until circumstances forced him to make a supreme effort, knowing that his very life depended upon his success.

The Witmarks' association with Charles Noel Douglas began around 1905 or 1906, when they received a package of lyrics from him. He offered to sell them reasonably. Isidore liked some of the lyrics, mailed him a check, and from that time on received contributions regularly, many of them acceptable. In the main the lyrics were good, although not all had commercial possibilities. Douglas was prolific, able to write on any subject, so occasionally Isidore sent him orders for extra verses of popular songs, especially comic and topical ones, and recommended him to variety artists who needed new material which he was able to supply, for he had once been an actor and singer. His clientele grew until he had a stream of professionals calling on him steadily. For a well man all this would have been a staggering task; for a man as incapacitated as he, it was amazing.

8. A. Baldwin Sloane

A. Baldwin Sloane was another prolific writer of his day, and he had a long day even though he was but fifty-three when he died in 1925. He was born in Baltimore in 1872 and had been a showman from the cradle. He had formed the famous Baltimore Paint and Powder Club, which produced one of his earliest operas. Edward E. Rice, an outstanding producer of the time, recognized his talents and commissioned him to write "Excelsior, Jr.," which was followed by the spectacle, "Jack and The Beanstalk," done for

351

Klaw and Erlanger. He wrote the incidental music for many of the Charlie Hoyt productions.

His musical comedy successes form a long roster: "The Mocking Bird," for Mabel Gilman; "Sergeant Kitty," for Virginia Earl and Helen Byron; "Lady Teazle," for Lillian Russell; "Comin' Through The Rye," "Broadway to Tokio," "The Gingerbread Man," "Tillie's Nightmare," for Marie Dressler; "Li'l Mose," "The Hen Pecks," "The Summer Widowers" (the last two for Lew Fields), and "China Rose," which was playing on Broadway when he died.

Sloane was a convivial spirit. He was president of the Composers' Publishing Company and vice-president of the Authors' and Composers' Publishing Company. He had been a member of The Lambs since 1897, as well as of the American Society of Authors and of the Green Room Club. No matter how much "Baldy" made, he was frequently in need of money. Success followed success. It was he who did the first "Greenwich Village Follies" with its song hit *I Want a Daddy to Rock Me to Sleep*. He will be remembered most of all, perhaps, for such tunes as *My Tiger Lily* and that financial classic, which he must have set to music out of his own constant need of cash, *When You Ain't Got No Money, Well, You Needn't Come Around*. It was sung as only May Irwin could sing it.

He also wrote the score of "Lo," lyrics by Franklin P. Adams (F. P. A.), book by O. Henry.

9. Louis Chevrolet

It was about the year 1910 that the first automobile races were run in the East. These races were promoted by the selfsame Joseph M. Gaites Company (otherwise Joseph M. Gaites, Julie, Jay, and Isidore Witmark). As a matter of fact there was hardly anything novel in the way of entertainment that did not get their attention and, often—their money. So when the matter of 24-hour automo-

Title page of Anna Held's big song hit, showing how the sheet was spread across the stage. The colored boys and men sang through the heads of the notes while standing at different heights in back of the curtain. It was a sensation novelty that was copied by many.

The signing of the copyright renewal for *Sweet Adeline* November 20, 1930. Seated: Henry Hart, Harry Armstrong, Isidore Witmark. Standing: Jay Witmark and Richard Gerard, author.

bile endurance racing came up—it hadn't been done before—they were for it. Joe Gaites was always an opportunist.

The first automobile endurance races took place in Philadelphia, at Point Breeze Track. Joe put in his own lighting system with strong electric floodlights placed at intervals around the entire track—a great innovation for those days. The races started at ten p.m., to finish at the same time the following night.

Gaites and the Witmarks learned with every race they put on. Louis Chevrolet won the race in Philadelphia. He was a famous racer and was known as "Smiling Louie." The Chevrolet car was named after him. The patronage in Philadelphia was not large, as the idea was new and had not yet created much interest. After racing in other eastern cities, with about the same interest manifested, they made a try in Detroit, at the Fair Grounds. The weather was hot and there was a plague of mosquitoes. Two of the spectacles of this race were Cole, the maker of the Cole automobile, riding for twenty-four hours in an open touring car, and Resta with feet on the dashboard of his car, steering it with his right hand and tilting a bottle of beer to his lips with his left.

Then they went to the Sheepshead Bay Race Track near Coney Island for the last race, where they paid $5,000 rental for the race track, for one day. On this track, Ralph De Palma, the champion racer, made a mile in fifty-four seconds, which was considered remarkable at that time.

Among other things they caught speculators selling counterfeit admission tickets, and doormen holding out tickets at the gate and passing them to confederates who re-sold them.

Aside from these little vicissitudes everything went along smoothly. The races were being run off, the small crowd was watching with interest, when suddenly, flash—something terrible happened! One of the cars, rounding a curve, became unmanageable, and, running into the fence, killed the man sitting on the top rail. Excitement ran high; the news got out and reached the city. Attracted by the lure of danger, crowds came. Cars swarmed, jamming the parking places. Taxies arrived. Crowded trains. The grandstand was sold out in a jiffy, and people were still coming when the race was over. The Gaites Company had spent about $16,000 on promoting the race, and would have lost a great deal of money—if that poor fellow had not been sitting on that fence.

The A.A.A., which originally gave Gaites a license to run the races, was pleased with the results. They were friendly to Joe until he asked for a renewal of the license, which they refused. Gaites and the Witmarks did not know what to make of this, because they had done everything possible to run a clean race to the satisfaction of the A.A.A. Joe made a half dozen applications for a renewal of the license, but to no avail. At last, the reason came out. There were to be more automobile races—to be run by the A.A.A. itself. They were run, and the A.A.A. was reported to have made $60,000.

10. Frank Mandel

In the year 1911, a young woman named Helen Kraft brought Isidore a literal translation of the "Jugendfreunde" by Fulda. He liked it, but it needed a lot of reworking to make an American play, and required the best adapter that could be found. First he took it up with Paul Wilstach, who was the literary adviser of Richard Mansfield and author of a number of plays and books of fiction. He was courteous and let Isidore down as easily as possible, saying he could not see anything in it.

Isidore had the same luck with Rida Johnson Young, Otto Harbach, Harold Atteridge, and a number of others. Being the proverbial pest, when he had faith in anything, he haunted these and other writers until, in order to get rid of him, Otto Harbach told him on the telephone, "I know a young red-headed fellow who just came from the west and is doing some work for Belasco. Maybe he'd be interested."

The red-headed fellow came around to see Isidore, heard the story, and at the finish, exclaimed enthusiastically, "That's my life! I like it!" And he did not leave the room until he had signed a

contract. Thus Frank Mandel and Isidore Witmark started col-
laborating on what became the successful comedy "Our Wives."

The play was first performed by Henry Kolker and a good
stock company in Hartford, Conn., and Robert Milton, known as
one of the best directors, staged it. The try-out was promising, but
there was something wrong with the big curtain punch, which had
been expected to thrill the audience.

After the opening, they all sat around, Mandel, Milton, Kolker,
Winchell Smith, who had come to see the show, Gaites, Jay, and
Isidore. A great finale had gone wrong, but no one seemed to know
the reason. It is surprising how little it took to make a success out
of that failure. The reason was at last found, stumbled upon by
Isidore, and the finale was the great success it should have been.
Through a series of damaging conditions over which there was no
control, and because Kolker was not a New York favorite, the play
did not get over in the metropolis, although Alan Dale, one of the
widely read dramatic critics of the time, said in his review that
"Our Wives" "out-Belascoed Belasco." It went to the Cort Theater
in Chicago, where Kolker *was* a favorite, and ran there for three
months.

Now for the sequel. Henry Blossom, the author of "Mlle.
Modiste," "The Red Mill," and a dozen other successes, coming
east from Chicago stopped off in a Pennsylvania town. Between
trains he dropped in at the stock theater where Thurston Hall was
playing in "Our Wives." Blossom became enthusiastic over the
play's potentialities as a musical show.

On reaching New York he called up Victor Herbert and told
him what he had discovered. They looked up the owner of the
rights, the Witmark Music Library, which, besides its own interest
in "Our Wives" represented Mandel, and a contract was signed for
a musical version which became the Herbert-Blossom operetta,
"The Only Girl," produced by Joe Weber, with such song successes as *When You're Away* and *When You're Wearing the Ball
and Chain.*

11. Madam Schumann-Heink

The recent passing of that great artist Ernestine Schumann-Heink has brought up many happy memories of her. As far back as 1899, when she was at the Metropolitan Opera House, her brother artist, Herman Devries, had brought her to visit the Witmarks. He is now living in Chicago where he has been a prominent singing teacher and music critic for years. At the time he was coaching her in French in the rôle of the mother, in "Le Prophète." She, in gratitude, introduced what he called the *Schumann-Heink Valse* song (his composition), which they published.

Their next happy experience with her was when Julian Edwards wrote the comic opera "Love's Lottery," in which she starred under the management of Fred Whitney. It was the first time that she attempted a light work. She played the part of a washerwoman and made a personal success, particularly in her song, *Sweet Thoughts of Home*.

Schumann-Heink was delighted when they were on the train going to Detroit for the opening of "Love's Lottery." Schumann-Heink, in her affable way, came out of her stateroom and sat with the rest of the company, singing and telling stories far into the night. She was particularly pleased with a surprise Isidore had for her—the first copy of the score of "Love's Lottery" published in time for the opening, autographed by the author, composer, and publishers, and presented to her on the train.

The opening at Detroit was auspicious. Schumann-Heink, then in the heyday of her popularity, received an ovation. In later years she was particularly devoted to Julie, whom she would visit at his office, listening by the hour as he tried over new ballads for her. She enjoyed his voice and his reading of songs.

Schumann-Heink was an enthusiastic endorser of the "Let Us Have Peace" movement that Julie conducted during 1911 among the statesmen, clergy, and artists of the day. A feature of this movement was a song written by George Graff, Jr., author of *Till the Sands of the Desert Grow Cold* and other successes. The song was entitled *Let Us Have Peace* and had a musical setting by Ernest R. Ball. It was dedicated to William H. Taft, then President of the United States, and sung for the first time by Ball at the Christian Endeavor Convention at Atlantic City on July 7, 1911, immediately after the address of President Taft.

It is a sad commentary upon human aspirations that in three years the world was to enter upon international slaughter.

CHAPTER XXII

MEMORIES

1. *The Letter*

THE Silver Anniversary of M. Witmark & Sons was a double celebration. The "Gibraltar of the Music World" [1885-'86—1910-'11] was not only a quarter of a century old, but the current year had proved to be the greatest in its career. The Witmark music branches formed a chain across the world: Chicago, San Francisco, London, Paris, Melbourne. "Naughty Marietta" was playing at the New York Theater; "Barry of Ballymore," was on tour, with Chauncey Olcott; "The Red Mill" was on tour; "Madame Sherry" was at the New Amsterdam Theater, and, in addition, two companies of it were on tour. "Mlle. Modiste" was on tour and so were "The Prince of Pilsen"; two companies of "The Three Twins"; "Jumping Jupiter," with Richard Carle; "The Old Town" with Montgomery and Stone; "The Fascinating Widow," with Julian Eltinge.

Yes, 1911 was a gala year, and yet the Witmarks were saddened by the fact that their parents had not lived to celebrate it with them.

"Queen" Witmark had died on December 14, 1906. She had been a quiet, self-effacing mother who had lived in the happiness of her husband and children. Only with her death had come the end of that romance which had begun when young Marcus, leaving

358

for America and adventure, had glimpsed her face as he parted from her and crossed the village bridge—a bridge from the Old World to the New.

In tribute to her, Ronald Burke Hennessy of the *New York Star* wrote:

A good Mother died when Mrs. Marcus Witmark passed away. As the mother of the Witmark boys, she had given decent men to the world; as the wife of her mate, she had been tenderness and loyalty and love; to her sex she gave a sterling example of gracious womanhood. And so she died, mourned by a family and friends, and missed as only a good woman can be missed; but behind she left a memory that shines as gold, and many tender thoughts that assuage the grief even as they bring tears to the eyes. Truly, when a mother dies the stars weep!

On March 29, 1910, her husband followed her, this time across a longer bridge that kept them together forever. . . .

The loss of one's parents, however old one may be at the time of their death, is one of the saddest experiences of life. While they live, one is in part a child. From the loving devotion of this exemplary couple the children had received their design for living. "Queen" and "Dad" had been proud of their brood; the children had been equally proud of their parents. The father and mother, like all beloved friends, found burial in the hearts of those whom they left behind.

Sealed in the envelope with Daddy Witmark's will was a letter to his children which he had written on September 6, 1892, and that letter was a heritage which was more precious to his children than any material possession.

"My dear Children:
"When you all think the matter over you will not wonder why I left all to dear mamma, for you well understand how dearly we all love her. We have been so united, so true to each other, and have worked for each other so earnestly these many, many years, that it will be much better for you, my darling children, and for dear mamma, to let the estate remain intact, until God in his wisdom shall call your dear mamma away.

Then and not till then, let whatever is left be divided equally among you, and may the Gracious God spare you all, to long lives and usefulness, each to receive a like portion, and each to rest content in this distribution.

"I need not say how much I love you all, and how earnestly I wish that you may all prosper during life, and be happy. My heart throbs for you all alike, and not one of you holds a place in my bosom above the other. May God bless you all, is the wish of your affectionate father,

"MARCUS WITMARK."

Life is a circle within the larger circle of death. Less than half a year later a great bandmaster was writing a note of pleasant import.

SOUSA AND HIS BAND

John Philip Sousa, Conductor

Willow Grove, Pa., Sept. 2, 1910.

Mr. Isidore Witmark,
New York City.
My dear Mr. Witmark:—

Allow me to congratulate you on the addition of one more Witmark to the brilliancy of the world.

I am very sure that, with such a father and such a mother, little Carolyn will make a success of life.

I am sending a gift which I beg you to ask my new friend Carolyn Henrietta to accept, with my most earnest felicitation.

Always sincerely yours,

(Signed) JOHN PHILIP SOUSA.

With the letter, Sousa sent a silver cup. For Sousa, fellow composer of Isidore's and fellow fighter in the cause of copyright, was also a lover of children. Today, everybody remembers his marches, and most people have forgotten his novels, especially his curious tale for children, *Pipetown Sandy*.

The big feature of Sousa's concerts was the Sousa March encores which he was so generous in giving. Once at the Metropolitan Opera House where he gave one of his concerts and he played *The Star Spangled Banner*, there was a vociferous demand for an encore. Sousa walked down to the footlights and said: "Ladies and gentlemen, there is no encore to *The Star Spangled Banner*."

MEMORIES

2. Masonic Highlights

Daddy Witmark had been a Mason since March, 1855, when on passing his twenty-first birthday he had been received into Newton Lodge No. 224, at Newton, Dale County, Alabama. In 1857 he was exalted in Lafayette Royal Arch Chapter No. 12, at Fort Gaines, Georgia, and in the same year was affiliated with Darley Lodge No. 17, at Fort Gaines. In New York he became affiliated with Naval Lodge No. 69, on April 15, 1869, and afterwards with Ancient Chapter No. 1.

He was very much a Mason, and therefore nobody could keep him from marching in the parade of October 9, 1880. And nobody even thought to try! It would have been of no avail. A parade day became Witmark Day!

Daddy Witmark loved a parade. Bands leading men in procession fascinated him just as much as he and his piano-accordion fascinated his children, but the parade of October, 1880, was one he never forgot.

The Obelisk in Central Park, incorrectly known as "Cleopatra's Needle" (for Cleopatra had died six years before the removal of the monolith to Alexandria), was a gift of the Khedive of Egypt, Ismail Pasha. He had contemplated the presentation to America as early as September, 1877. The editor of *The World* had visited Egypt a few years previously, and had discussed with its ruler the spread of Egyptology in the United States. On October 7, 1877, *The World* announced that the Obelisk could be procured for New York. William H. Vanderbilt offered to defray the expenses of transportation.

Many problems of engineering were involved in the task. Fortunately, Lieutenant-Commander H. H. Gorringe, in command of the U. S. S. *Gettysburg*, appeared on the scene. He knew the Levant, had studied the Obelisk at Alexandria, and was an accomplished archeologist. He drew up plans for the transportation of

361

the monument, and during the winter of 1879-80 was engaged not only in the solution of the engineering problems but in the frustration of diplomatic intrigues that centered around the presentation of the Obelisk to the United States.

On July 20, 1880, the *Dessoug*, an English steamer that Lieutenant-Commander Gorringe had purchased in Egypt for the express purpose of conveying the precious gift to his country, entered New York harbor.

Renewed public excitement greeted the announcement that the Obelisk could not be landed on Manhattan Island. The *Dessoug* was taken to Staten Island, where began at once the task of transshipping the Obelisk upon caissons prepared according to Gorringe's plans. This required until September 6th; ten days later the monolith was successfully transferred from the caissons to Manhattan Island, at the foot of 96th Street.

Lieutenant-Commander Gorringe had discovered, when the original foundations of the Obelisk had been removed, a number of Masonic emblems engraved upon blocks of syenite: the perfect ashlar, the square, and the rough ashlar. This, confirming the Masonic claims of ancient origin, was considered a historic discovery, and so the laying of the foundation stone was set for October 9, 1880, and the ceremony was entrusted to the Free and Accepted Masons of the State of New York, under the direction of the Grand Master of that Order.

The Witmark household shared the fever that was induced by these ceremonies, for there was to be a parade, and the parade was to be exclusively a Masonic function, in which no other civic body would take part.

About twenty-five years later, the *Masonic Standard* of New York, Saturday, April 1, 1905, ran a special article celebrating Marcus Witmark's fiftieth year in Masonry.

Daddy Witmark's sons, too, were Masons. Too bad that he did not live to enjoy the ceremonies on September 30, 1924, which was a Masonic "Witmark Day" in all official splendor and by special designation!

On May 1, 1894, three brothers—Isidore, Julius, and Jay—were raised in St. Cecile Lodge No. 568. The Master of Ceremonies was Louis Mann. Thirty years later, on September 30, 1924, "Witmark Day," the three brothers received the active honorary membership certificates. Again Louis Mann was Master of Ceremonies.

Some two and a half years earlier—on January 30, 1922—there had been a celebration of a Masonic twenty-fifth Witmark anniversary, in Carnegie Hall. Here the Ancient Arabic Order of the Nobles of the Mystic Shrine, Mecca Temple, of New York, N. Y., had foregathered in annual festivities. But there was, as Louis N. Donnatin, Recorder, reported, a "big show" too, the bestowal of life memberships upon the three Masonic Musketeers, Isidore, Julius, and Jay. Isidore and Jay were called and received their diplomas. When Julius was called, however, his diploma was withheld. He would have to sing for it! He sang for those men who had known him as The Wonderful Boy Soprano, such old-time songs as he had sung when initiated into the order: *Her Eyes Don't Shine Like Diamonds, Just One Girl,* and *Only One Girl in the World For Me.*

It is unusual for three brothers to go through life membership together. In addition, the three Witmarks held life membership in the Consistory of New York; Isidore is a life member of Ancient Chapter, No. 1, Royal Arch Masons, and of Adelphic Council No. 7 of the Royal and Select Masters of the City of New York.

3. "Robin Hood"

It is a point of pride with the House of Witmark that the firm never spent any appreciable amount in advertising its name as distinct from the publications that bore it. Agencies approached them with attractive plans to blazon it forth in special campaigns, and received the same refusal. The firm name went, to be sure, into directories, programs, and the like; this advertising was limited to trade publications. After all, every copy of a Witmark song bore the name of its publishers upon the title page. Of these, there were millions upon millions. What better advertisement could a music-publishing firm desire?

When advertising was desired—for the product, and not for the name—the Witmarks were not inclined to be over-modest. In 1903, the foremost newspaper in New York City was the *New York Herald*, published by James Gordon Bennett. The Witmarks, recently established in their new building and seeking to dramatize the event, hit upon a plan so simple, yet so ambitious for the business, that it has not been repeated by any music publisher in the thirty-five-odd years that have gone by. They took a full-page advertisement in the *New York Herald* of November 22, 1903.

It was an auspicious year. On June 6th, it will be recalled, had been born Julius P. Witmark, Jr., who was chosen at birth to carry on the Black and White Series.

Adolph S. Witmark, better known as Eddie, was making his mark as a concert singer. When his voice broke, it had turned into a baritone as sweet as the soprano had been. Now, at twenty-five, he was at the peak of his singing career.

Earl Carroll worked for the House of Witmark a short while during 1903 in the capacity of professional act getter; he was restless, dynamic, and aggressive. It was through him that the firm took on a professional office next to the Palace Theater on Forty-seventh Street and Broadway, while the main office was still at the Witmark Building on Thirty-seventh Street.

Soon afterwards he left to go to California where he wrote the music for "So-Long, Letty," and "Canary Cottage," his beginning in the production game. Incidentally, he took with him one of the firm's young song demonstrators, all on a half-hour's notice. His companion has become one of the outstanding orchestra directors in the profession, having served many seasons with Al Jolson, at the Winter Garden and elsewhere. He is now one of radio's foremost orchestra leaders, Al Goodman.

The years between that full-page "ad" and the celebration in 1910 of the company's twenty-fifth anniversary, rolled by in musical sequence, rich in activity. There was the mission, sad indeed to Isidore, of closing up the operetta, "Robin Hood," in 1905. It was not only the writing of "Finis" to a grand old piece that troubled him; it was the spectacle of three old-timers at their undistinguished end.

The Witmark Music Library, besides representing authors and composers, owned some valuable properties. From time to time it purchased, from the late Harry B. Smith and other writers, their production rights, for repertoire and stock, of a number of operettas. Among them was the perennial "Robin Hood." The Library, besides owning the authors' share of the work, represented the interests of the composer, Reginald De Koven.

What had once been a magnificent organization, the famous Bostonians, with Barnabee and MacDonald, was on its last legs. It owed thousands of dollars in royalties. As an executive of the Witmark Library, Isidore had been designated to collect the royalties or close the show.

The Bostonians were playing Atlantic City the following week, and it was his job to go there. He found that the operetta was playing on one of the piers instead of in a theater, which must have been humiliating to such a grand old company. For the principals, including a fine old gentleman, Bacon, who had been manager of the company for years, Isidore searched the prominent hotels, only to find the three of them at a little commercial hostelry on the Boardwalk.

As he entered the hotel office, there they sat, those wonderful veterans of comic operas, Barnabee and MacDonald and their faithful manager, Bacon, the most dejected trio he had ever set eyes on. His mind was made up. Instead of making any demand, he had a nice talk with them on general matters and went over to the pier and saw one of the last performances ever given by The Bostonians. Without their knowing what he had come for, he took the next train home. Before going, however, he learned they had decided to close for good.

There was time, on that train-ride home, to think back some fifteen years, when "Robin Hood" and Barnabee and MacDonald were young—the owners of The Bostonians and the stars of that famous organization. Alice Nielsen has told Isidore the story of the song that had "made" the operetta, *Oh, Promise Me*. It was not a part of the original score; the lyric had been written not by Harry B. Smith, but by Clement Scott, the English critic. The song had been published independently.

It had been found that "Robin Hood" needed another song; De Koven for some reason did not relish composing a new tune, so he brought this old one to a rehearsal. He could not interest any of the singers in the song! Finally it was offered to Jessie Bartlett Davis, the contralto, playing the rôle of Alan-a-Dale. Miss Davis, annoyed because she had not been offered the song at first, hummed it over, then disdained it.

Something in the melody, however, remained. She found herself singing it an octave lower. MacDonald happened to pass her dressing-room; all who heard Jessie sing will understand why he stopped. He could not contain himself until the song was finished. "Jessie!" he cried, bursting into her room, "if you ever sing that song as you're singing it now, on the low octave, it will make your reputation."

She sang it, and the prophecy came true. *Oh Promise Me* was always associated with the name of Jessie Bartlett Davis.

4. Chauncey Olcott and Julie

It was in 1907 that Chauncey Olcott, after a sojourn in England, returned to the United States and to his close friendship with Julie, which endured until Julie's death.

Julie supervised the arranging of the songs for most of Chauncey's productions. Ernest R. Ball collaborated with Olcott in several of his songs. Starting with "O'Neill of Derry," his first starring vehicle, Chauncey appeared in ten Irish plays during the time he was associated with Julie. The other nine were "Edmund Burke," "Eileen Asthore," "Garrett O'Magh," "Minstrel of Clare," "Ragged Robin," "Romance of Athlone" (for which Olcott wrote *My Wild Irish Rose*), "Sweet Inniscarra," "Terrence," and "Old Limerick Town."

Chauncey delighted in visiting Julie's home and partaking of Mrs. Witmark's fish dinners, during which they would swap stories over a bottle of Haut Sauterne. Julie prized a beautiful collection of rare Saddler remarque etchings that Chauncey gave him for his dining-room.

Chauncey retired before Julie passed on and spent most of his time at his château on the Riviera, where he adopted a little girl who became a remarkable pianist (one whom Paderewski wanted to adopt—but too late). The Olcotts also had a home in Saratoga, which they called "Inniscarra," after one of the plays. Mrs. Olcott, whom Chauncey had married in 1897, was his constant companion and adviser. She also wrote some of his plays, in conjunction with Rida Johnson Young.

CHAPTER XXIII

A VARIETY OF THINGS

1. *Bert Feldman and Others*

*I*N 1912 the Witmarks had a visit from Bert Feldman, president of B. Feldman & Company, one of the largest popular music publishers of London. Feldman's visit turned out more than social for he proposed that he take over their agency for Great Britain. Their London offices were still going satisfactorily under Warren so they turned the offer down. But Bert was persistent. He made them such flattering inducements that they listened, realizing that he was making a good proposition and that their publications would fare well in his care. They met for a couple of days and argued pro and con and, at last, the terms were practically agreed upon when the Witmarks threw a bomb into the camp—a sort of ultimatum—that wherever the Witmark Catalog went in Great Britain, Charles Warren had to go with it. Bert, realizing how in earnest they were, conceded immediately and it was understood that Warren was to be part of the administration so far as their publications were concerned.

The new business relations with Bert Feldman were pleasant. They made money together, renewed many contracts, and were associated with him until they turned the business over to the Warners.

A VARIETY OF THINGS

In Australia, Witmarks' at first were represented by the music house of Allen & Company. They started in 1903 doing business with their Mr. Charles Tait, of the well-known Australian Tait family, until 1918 when, through a misunderstanding, they severed connections. From 1919 to the time they retired, they were represented by Frank Albert of Sydney and they had about ten years of delightful association with this concern. Frank Albert and his family have made, and still make, frequent trips to the States and even now, after a business separation of over nine years, the devotion to each other is just as strong.

2. "The Aviator"

While temporarily living in Chicago, about 1912, Isidore stepped into a theater for a matinee performance and saw Wallie Eddinger in a Cohan & Harris production, "The Aviator," by James Montgomery. He had been told that the play was dying on its feet. Something prompted him, however, to take a look at it. After the show, he wired his brothers in New York, "Saw 'The Aviator' this afternoon. Failure, but the best show for music since 'Three Twins.' Music situations oozing out of every corner. Should be knock-out." The telegram was signed "One Third." This was the musketeer-like fashion in which the boys signed themselves in personal communications to each other.

Isidore was completely "sold" on "The Aviator" as a musical show. He could see, and almost hear, the possibilities as to numbers, situations, effects. In those days he used to commute between Chicago and New York. In spite of many other important business matters that had to be taken up and disposed of, he dwelt on "The Aviator." His brothers accepted it all as one of his raves, and paid only passing attention to the matter, until one day Harold Atteridge, a writer they had brought from Chicago, and who at this time was doing work for the Shuberts, came in and asked, "What ever became of 'The Aviator'? I understand that it is good for music and might be had."

Only then did his brothers suddenly wake up and become interested in the fate of this play. Isidore gave some evasive answer to Atteridge, but got busy at once. He had met George M. Cohan on the Twentieth Century going back to Chicago, and had told him with vehemence that he had the possibilities of a musical comedy success in "The Aviator." Inasmuch as George owned the rights of the straight play, Isidore went on, he should take advantage of them and secure the music rights also, making a musical comedy version and recouping all the money he had lost on Eddinger.

Strange to say, Cohan couldn't see it Isidore's way and was as vehement in rebuttal as Isidore had been in his proposal. They went at it so strong that George excused himself, saying he had some work to do in his stateroom. He left Isidore until dinner time, when they dined together, and Isidore added to the menu another generous helping of his belief in "The Aviator" as a musical show. Cohan was not to be shaken from his position. It is easily to be imagined that with him feeling as he did, the other "Two Thirds" lost whatever interest Isidore might have stirred in them. However, Isidore never lost faith in the show.

With the Atteridge idea in mind, he investigated, only to learn that besides having proved a failure as a dramatic production, "The Aviator" had also flopped in stock, mainly for the reason that every stock production required the use of a real aeroplane, and aeroplanes were not numerous at that time.

He learned also the important fact that Cohan & Harris had waived all their rights to the play. Through an agency Isidore made an offer of $1000 for the musical rights. It was jumped at. In fact, Jim Montgomery, the author, went up and down Broadway boasting how he had put one over on Isidore Witmark. Isidore got busy, had Otto Harbach make a libretto, and commissioned Lou Hirsch to write the score. Now for the surprise! When it was finished and ready for production, the producers who contracted for it were Cohan & Harris, who had waived their rights to the play! Those who remember, know what a big hit "Going Up" was with Frank Craven, Edith Day and the famous *Tickle-Toe* number. Several companies played it simultaneously, including two in England and two in Australia. All of which goes to prove that the best of us can be mistaken in our judgments.

The Witmarks were associated with Cohan & Harris as producers of "Going Up," and they go on record here to say that it was the finest partnership they have ever experienced. Cohan & Harris ran their business like a bank, assuring the safety of anyone's interest in their enterprises. They were also broad and liberal in their ideas of production, which earned for them the best that was in all who were associated with them.

3. The ASCAP

Music publishers of the early years of the Twentieth Century were beset by complex and increasingly difficult problems. Changes in the amusement habits of the nation brought into being new uses of music. The creators of music, composers, authors, and publishers, were harassed by many injustices. A new factor, the "performing right," began to assume major importance.

To the solution of these problems a little group of far-seeing men devoted themselves. In the heart of the New York theatrical district where men of the stage and music naturally gathered, these men met with increasing frequency to promote their mutual interests. It was natural that the Lambs' Club should become their meeting place, and it was in this historic clubhouse that was discussed the formation of the society for joint action to protect musical copyrights.

A prime mover in this organization was George Maxwell. As the American representative of G. Ricordi & Co., of Milan, world's greatest music publishers, Maxwell held a position of great trust. Associates in the music industry long had relied upon the wise counsel and seasoned judgment of this distinguished executive. Maxwell's intimate familiarity with the methods of foreign publishers in meeting the problems which beset his American associates made him a logical leader. His firm long had been enrolled in the memberships of the Italian, French, and other foreign performing rights societies. He knew how they functioned. The others looked to him for leadership. Similarly active in the early stages of the movement was Nathan Burkan, legal representative of most of the group, a man destined to become through his association with the movement the outstanding authority on copyright law in America. With Burkan to chart the legal course, Maxwell urged the organization of a domestic performing rights society to obtain by collective action protection for copyright owners which would have been beyond the reach of individual initiative.

The last straw, showing the need for such an institution, it is said, had been provided by one of its early members, Victor Herbert, through his experience with a so-called "crooner." Herbert, the reader will remember, had stumbled almost ten years before upon that undying hit, *Kiss Me Again*. It happened in 1905, during the first days of "Mlle. Modiste," in which was an ensemble number called *If I Were On The Stage*. It was a *scena* depicting the emotions of a prima donna, and it was beautifully done by the delightful actress, Fritzi Scheff. In this *scena* one line of melody stood out; it had no name, no major function; it was just a chorus haphazardly called *Kiss Me Again* because such was the last line of the lyric. But it became the base of a triangle, of which Herbert and Fritzi Scheff formed the other two sides.

Julie Witmark conceived the idea of developing that excerpt into a full-sized song, and persuaded Herbert to write a completely new melody for the first part. Further persuasion and persistence were exercised upon Henry Blossom, the author, with

372

the result that an appropriate lyric was written to Victor Herbert's music. The song thus evolved became the success, *Kiss Me Again*, and the sales jumped from about seven thousand copies of the *scena* containing the bit, to more than a million copies of the rewritten version. To millions of persons, the song invariably recalls Miss Scheff, who sings it at every Victor Herbert memorial broadcast. This annual rendition is Miss Scheff's gesture of gratitude to its gifted composer for the song that elevated her to stardom.

Some time during the bellicose year of 1914, Herbert sat in the Shanley Cabaret, then in the Putnam Building at Times Square, since demolished to make way for the structure erected on that site by Paramount Pictures.

When Victor heard a crooner crooning *Kiss Me Again*—crooning it atrociously before the diners, and crooning it illegally as well, he breathed hard, but by no means his last. Nor was it a prayer for his soul, or for the crooner's, that he breathed. This mangling of a man's work, this piracy, must stop! It is such incidents as these that light the fires of revolution. It was thus, in Shanley's, that the explosion took place which resulted finally in the organization of the American Society of Composers, Authors and Publishers, more familiarly known as "ASCAP."

The final step prior to the official organization of the society was taken at an informal meeting of nine enthusiastic men of music in the Lambs' Club, on a blustery wintry afternoon early in 1914. It was the hour of relaxation for men of the theater, between matinee and evening shows. The Lambs' Club was astir. Good cheer, sparkling wit, the camaraderie of the theater, held sway. Scattered in convivial groups about the lounge were Wilton Lackaye, Reginald De Koven, George V. Hobart, Clay Greene, James T. Powers, John Drew, Frank Daniels, Willie Collier, George M. Cohan, Raymond Hitchcock, Sam Bernard, and dozens of others of major and minor importance in the theater.

But apart from these lively groups, seated in a remote corner and engaged in earnest conversation were the nine men of music. There was the beloved Victor Herbert, shaking his massive head to emphasize his arguments. There was George Maxwell, stately and dignified, rapping with his signet ring to concentrate his listeners' attention. There was the urbane and genial Gustav Kerker, acclaimed wherever music was known as composer of the famous musical comedy, "The Belle of New York"; Glen Mac-Donough, who wrote most of Victor Herbert's librettos, such as "Babes in Toyland," "Algeria," "It Happened in Nordland"; the outspoken and aggressive Louis A. Hirsch, composer of dozens of musical comedy song hits including *Hello, Frisco, In a Love Nest,* and the musical comedy, "Going Up"; the gentle and revered Silvio Hein, whose songs the whole nation sang; the well informed, loquacious Raymond Hubbell, who had created *Poor Butterfly* as one of the song hits of the century, and had composed the musical comedy "Fantana"; the conservative, quiet, mild Nathan Burkan, brilliant young lawyer, and the representative of the well known publishing house bearing his family name, Jay Witmark.

Absorbed in their discussion, these men paid little heed to the passing time. Minutes raced into hours, and twilight was giving way to night when Herbert gave a sudden new turn to the parley. He suggested a dinner at Lüchow's, where in the privacy of their own dining-room they could continue the discussion. The response was unanimous. In a few moments the nine were in the horse-drawn hacks of the period, hastening to the historic Fourteenth Street restaurant. And here ASCAP—as the society came to be widely known—was born.

Within a fortnight there was a meeting of more than one hundred charter members at Claridge's Hotel, and there for the first time, American creators of music were banded together for mutual protection of their copyright properties. The organization meeting was a milestone in American musical history. George

Maxwell was unanimously chosen president, and filled the post for seven consecutive years.

The early years of ASCAP were precarious. It had been in existence but a short time when one drastic ruling caused many desertions among the publishers. The house of Leo Feist, through its representative, E. F. Bitner, and the house of M. Witmark & Sons through Jay Witmark, decided to stick under any and all circumstances. Through their efforts most of the deserters were induced to return and the organization was held together.

From 1914 the society fought seven years for bare existence. Opposition to the principle of enforcing performing rights was highly organized. Powerful groups, amply financed, fought the society from court to court, from state to state. Only the loyalty and self-sacrifice of the leaders of the movement sustained it through these trying years. But the darkness of its early struggles at last gave way to the dawn of substantial financial returns. In 1921 the first distribution of royalty checks was possible. The story of the society thenceforth is a record of consistent progress. Receipts for 1937 were a little less than six million dollars.

When first organized, the society met in humble quarters. Today its main offices occupy virtually an entire floor of the great RCA building in the heart of Radio City. There are branches in many states, a legal staff encompassing the whole country, and a headquarters force of more than a hundred employees.

Originally patterned after the performing rights societies of foreign countries, the American unit has become the greatest society of its kind in the world. It embraces more than 1,000 American men and women creators of successful music. Membership does not cease with death. The roster includes the estates of many illustrious men and women whose heirs thus share in the society's collection of royalties for the performances of their copyrighted works.

The American Society of Composers, Authors and Publishers is an absolutely non-profit association. The revenue which it collects for licenses issued to commercial users of music in public performances, after the expenses of operation have been deducted, is entirely divided each three months among the members of the society and the foreign societies with which ASCAP is affiliated. The membership of the entire group exceeds 65,000 of the men and women who write most of the music which the world enjoys. The society is the sole hope and refuge of the indigent, aged, or ailing composer and author in America.

It is dedicated to the principle that "No man or woman in the United States who writes successful music, nor anyone dependent upon him, shall ever want." Membership in the society is available to every citizen of the United States who is a qualified composer, author, or publisher of musical works, regardless of sex, color, or creed.

Jay Witmark was a director of the society for nearly twenty years. He was the assistant treasurer and then treasurer. He was also for a long time chairman of the Relief Committee. He devoted much of his time to the building of the organization, and when the Witmarks in 1929 sold to Warner Brothers, he resigned. In recognition of his faithful services, he was made the first honorary member of ASCAP and for a long time was the only one.

Of the nine founders of ASCAP only two are living: Raymond Hubbell, composer of *Poor Butterfly*, and Jay Witmark.

 Its present officers are Gene Buck, President; Louis Bernstein and Otto A. Harbach, Vice-Presidents; Joseph Young, Secretary; Gustave Schirmer, Treasurer; J. J. Bregman, Assistant Secretary; Irving Caesar, Assistant Treasurer. Its able administrative chairman is E. C. Mills, and its General Manager is John G. Paine.

A VARIETY OF THINGS

4. Towards the "Talkies"

Early in this same eventful year of 1914 the Witmarks had almost participated in yet another revolution of American industry—the "talkies." It will be recalled that as far back as 1907 Julie had figured in one of the first movies made for illusion on the stage, in which the idea of television had been toyed with.

The talkies had been toyed with, likewise by the Witmarks, even earlier—at the turn of the century. The idea had been conceived by Jean Havez, personal representative of Lew Dockstader, and a composer. We have all sung his *Everybody Works But Father*. The Spook Minstrels, as the act was called, owed some of its material to specialties in the Dockstader minstrel shows.

Geoffrey O'Hara, composer of *K-K-Katy, Give a Man a Horse He Can Ride*, etc., and one of the phantom minstrels, tells the story especially for these pages:

"I was the interlocutor. We rehearsed in the private apartment of the then manager of the Woodstock Hotel, then called the Spalding Hotel. Our room overlooked the ground being broken for the Hippodrome by Thompson and Dundy. Herman Berl, the musical director, was our musical man. The Ford Brothers, dance team, were the principal end men. We rehearsed a twenty-five-minute minstrel show, got it ready for the camera. Up to that time no indoor moving pictures had been satisfactory. A stage was set up for us over at the Harley-Merry Studios in Brooklyn. An Edison camera man, Porter, turned the crank for our show. It was a cold November day, with little sun. We waited all morning for it to come out. Finally, after consultation with Havez, Porter decided to use what he called a 'diffused lens,' and take the picture, sun or no sun. He did. We finished at about five o'clock in the afternoon, and a neighbor brought us a large water jug full of coffee, or I think we should have perished.

"We all kept our fingers crossed till the film had been developed. It came out swell. The Finale was a march song, glorifying The Spirit of '76, and this part had to be hand-colored, which was done in Orange,

377

New Jersey, at the factory, under a magnifying glass, with a single hair of a camel's hair brush.

"Five singers, taking the doubling parts of gag men, end men, and so on, now stood behind the moving picture screen, unseen by the audience, and sang and gagged the show. We used a pair of old shoes to tap on the floor, to imitate the Ford Brothers' dance. It was all effective. The orchestra leader, in the vaudeville houses where we appeared, followed the singers behind the screen, making it simple.

"The Keith Circuit head-lined us for a year, then we became an added attraction, and for three years the show was a feature. Seven weeks on Hammerstein's Roof, among other nice spots.

"So far as synchronizing pictures with music, this was the first real show ever done."

A great deal of the rehearsing of the Spook Minstrels took place at the Witmark building, with Fred Rycroft, the Witmarks' professional manager, and Johnny Leffler taking care of the actors. The film had cost all of $2000, a lot of money in the early 1900's! The singers were dressed in Court costume.

At the end of the picture the screen was raised. The concealed singers now stood against another white screen, upon which the final feet of the film were still being shown. Suddenly the house lights went up, revealing more clearly the singers, who walked down to the footlights. It was then that they sang, for the first time on any vaudeville stage, *The Rosary*.

The next association of the Witmarks with more illusive movies was closer. It was in 1914—January 24, to be exact—that Isidore Witmark wrote the following letter to a man who had married a remote cousin of his.

Mr. E. H. Kaufmann,
Hotel Martinique,
New York City.
My dear Mr. Kaufmann:—

Confirming our verbal understanding, I enclose you herewith my check for Two Hundred and Fifty ($250.) Dollars. Said check is to be covered by a three months' note from you, for an equal amount, in the event that the following arrangement between us is not consummated:

A VARIETY OF THINGS

For and in consideration of the sum of One Dollar, each to the other in hand paid, the receipt whereof is hereby reciprocally acknowledged, it is understood and agreed that you will arrange the affairs of the Kaufmann-Kelly Biophone Co. so that I will become half owner of the contract between the said Company and the Messter Projection, of Berlin, Germany, and that I shall receive a half interest in all properties and inventions now owned and controlled by the Kaufmann-Kelly Biophone Co.

I agree to accept a half interest in the above-mentioned contract and properties, provided that the demonstration you are about to make is entirely satisfactory to me and the contract, as revised by Mr. Burkan and sent to the Messter Projection on January 23, 1914, is consummated between the said Messter Projection and the Kaufmann-Kelly Biophone Co. and transferred to a company that I will organize, in which event I agree to attend to the financing, promotion and development of said company.

Your acceptance of this will constitute a contract between us.

Very truly yours,

Isidore Witmark.

A prospectus of the Kaufmann-Kelly Biophone Company reveals that the Witmarks had been considering the talkie enterprise twelve years before it became a reality under the sponsorship of the Warner Brothers. The prospectus reads, in part:

Kaufmann-Kelly Biophone Co.
Exclusive Owners of the Usage
Rights for United States
The Most Wonderful Invention
PERFECT SINGING
AND TALKING
MOVING PICTURES

———

MESSTER'S BIOPHONE EUROPEAN
SUCCESS
Reproducing the Human Voice exactly by
Synchronizing the Motion Pictures with
a Singing and Talking Machine

———

379

FROM RAGTIME TO SWINGTIME

The rest of the title page is devoted to the organization of the Kaufmann-Kelly Biophone Company and the disposition of the shares of stock for sale. On the next page are paragraphs proclaiming the new invention, which would mean little to the layman if the prophecies had not been fulfilled.

Managers of Moving Picture Theatres, as well as the Public, are craving something new and novel in that line.

Singing and Talking Moving Pictures
at Last a Success

Grand opera scenes are pictured with startling fidelity by this new German invention in connection with the wonderful toned phonograph especially built in Paris.

The singing and talking pictures are practically unknown in the United States.

In ninety per cent of all moving picture houses in Europe, they are and for four years have been a standard equipment, and are shown at every performance, changing off with the regular pictures.

They are bound to be equally popular in this country.

The synchronizing attachment of these Singing and Talking Moving Picture Machines enables you to hear the voices of the great opera singers in perfect unison with the movements of the lips in the pictures, without any strain upon the ear or eye.

We have an especially built wonderful-toned Singing and Talking Machine, imported from France; gotten up by Mr. E. H. Kaufmann, vice-president of this company, who has been with Edison for a number of years.

Our machine is patented in all countries, and Kaufmann-Kelly Biophone Co. are the exclusive owners of the usage rights for the United States.

Musical films of Operas, of Popular Songs and of Singers will be a necessity.

These Machines Can Be Installed in
One Hour in Any Theatre

They are adjustable to any Moving Picture Machine now in use, without disturbing present arrangements. They can be operated by any operator running a Moving Picture Machine.

Simplicity—The Machine in itself works without requiring an expert electrician.

A VARIETY OF THINGS

Portability—The Machine can be shipped and handled by any carrier.
Adaptability—To any Machine.
Applicability—To any size of Theatre.

On the third page is the reproduction of a newspaper article that in its description of the device shows a startling parallel to the talkies of the present day:

The San Francisco *Chronicle* of May 19, 1913, contains the following news item:

"The Viennese production of 'The Merry Widow,' and reproductions from the operas, scenes from 'Pagliacci,' 'Mignon,' 'Traviata,' and 'Carmen,' were produced to San Franciscans last evening by a German inventor, Messter by name.

"For the benefit and pleasure of the audience at the Columbia Theatre, the medium through which this wizardry was made possible is the 'Biophone,' a combination of moving picture projector and phonograph. Its mission, according to the inventor, is the production of talking moving pictures, but those who saw it in operation and heard it, believe the term far too modest.

"Science has at last produced a phonograph which does not sound like one. There was an entire absence of the usual rasping metallic obligato common to such an exhibition, and the natural tone of the voice of the actors in the film was easily heard, without straining the ear, in any part of the building, and the field of the camera was sufficient to include a full-sized stage, affording the actors plenty of room to act their parts without crowding each other out of the picture."

While the contract mentioned in the letter of January 24, 1914, was signed by the Messter Projection and the Kaufmann-Kelly Biophone Company, the Messter people eliminated some important paragraphs covering the American patents for the synchronizing device: the omission of these might have necessitated the constant presence of the Witmarks in the law courts, defending their rights. They thought better of the deal and bowed out.

In the meantime, however, they had given successful auditions. One at the Century Theatre, New York, in 1914, was offered through the courtesy of Messrs. Aborn who were playing a season of grand opera there. The finale of "Mignon" was given, and selections from other operas, including "Pagliacci." The results were practically the same as what Warner Brothers achieved when they started, although the mechanism was different. Of course constant experimentation has brought about great improvements today.

The phonograph used was an unusually large one, especially made for extra-size records on which was reproduced an entire selection. While audiences were amazed with the results, it was then found there was not much real interest in the proposition as an investment. The reason was that an organization like Warners was lacking to make feature pictures; what was offered was more like a bill of vaudeville numbers. Also, the public did not seem to be ready for sound as they were to be twelve years later.

A humorous incident occurred at the Century Theatre tryout when they gave the "Pagliacci" number with a German artist playing the chief rôle. The singing in Italian was so beautiful that all were astounded at the voice. Little did they know that the record of the German singer had been lost, and that, to save the day, a Caruso record had been substituted!

5. Emerson Yorke

In 1920 Emerson Yorke, a young live-wire, sold himself to the House of Witmark, organizing a Record and Roll Department—the first recognized mechanical department in the music publishing field, devoted to the coördination of song publications with the phonograph record and piano roll manufacturers. The department became one of the major revenue-producers of the business.

Up to this time every house had someone in some other department taking care of this end. The Witmarks were the first to organize a distinct department for this new line of business. Under Yorke's direction it thrived.

"Yorky," as he was called, was one of those fellows who slept with both eyes open. With the advent of radio he recognized new opportunities for the house. Here was a new field for song exploitation; he became enthusiastic about it. On behalf of Witmark, over station WEAF, he pioneered in the selection of talent and program-preparation and planted the first *solid, sustaining* hour of music, known as the Witmark Black and White Hour, which was built around the series identified by that name. There were few, if any, "commercials" at the time, and the Witmarks in this way were getting free publicity and exploitation that today would cost fabulous sums. There were then few broadcasting artists, but among Yorke's associates on the air were Vincent Lopez, Rudy Wiedoeft, Vaughn De Leath, Joseph White, Billy Jones, Ernie Hare, and Graham MacNamee.

Yorke spent about five pleasant years with the Witmarks, and left to become affiliated with the Brunswick Recording Laboratories. In his own words addressed to Isidore, "a natural move on my part, in view of the contacts I had established over a period of five years in that field—and a compliment to you, your wonderful brother Julius, and your organization, for the invaluable experience during my happy association with M. Witmark & Sons."

CHAPTER XXIV

FACING FAILURE

1. The Great War—The New Jazz

THE war of 1914-1918 began to write, in blood and fire across the mutilated acreage of the battlefields, Finis to a period in the history of the modern world. The ink and the blood still drip over book and battlefield. In Tin Pan Alley, true to their ancient habits, the bards of the commonplace returned to their keyboards and "tickled" journalistic tunes out of the "ivories." When the United States joined the fray, the tunesmiths and wordsmiths experienced a change of heart overnight. They who had not raised their boy to be a soldier discovered that now they were proud to have him shoulder a gun. The piper looks for pay to the man who calls the tune.

The coming of jazz is coincident with the war, and has been attributed by many to the relaxed public morale that followed the cessation of hostilities. Just as the war, however, had its roots far below the contemporary events that led fatally up to it, so did jazz sink roots below the contemporary slaughter. The war, beyond a doubt, accelerated the coming of the jazz age, not alone in music but in painting, in sculpture, in morals, in popular philosophy. The war itself was a cataclysmic jazz grotesque.

Jazz, however, had already been prefigured by the coming of ragtime, which in turn traced one line of its ancestry back to

George M. Cohan

Sigmund Romberg

Julius P. Witmark

Julius P. Witmark, Jr.

Africa. Jazz, in music, was the white man drunk on black potations, just as the Negro spirituals were the black man exalted by white hymnology. The history of American popular music represents a strange mixture of racial qualities: white, black, American, Negro, Jewish, Yankee. Jazz, in history, stands for the latest phase (even in the new terminology, "swing" and "jam") of a trend that is to be discovered even in the old minstrel shows.

[The word jazz, of which the etymology is as uncertain as the date of its earliest use, does not come into the language until some time in 1917.] A glance at the Witmark hits listed during the years of the war shows that it had not begun its true conquest during those eventful days. *Alexander's Ragtime Band*—on Irving Berlin's sheet music—had been blaring since 1911; the *Dixieland Jazz Band* (in the days when jazz was spelled "jass") was blowing and strumming away in obscurity. The country was singing Roma's *Can't You Heah Me Callin' Caroline,* in 1914; Ball's *In The Garden of the Gods, Little Bit of Heaven* (sung by Olcott in "The Heart of Paddy Whack"), and *You Planted A Rose in The Garden of Love* kept it company. Next year Ball was high on the list with *Ireland Is Ireland To Me, If It Takes A Thousand Years, Sprinkle Me With Kisses, That's How The Shannon Flows.* Of course there were always Herbert tunes. In 1916 Ball was still going strong, and everybody was singing *Turn Back The Universe And Give Me Yesterday.* Certainly the jazz invasion was not yet on.

You could hear it in 1917, however, in Louis A. Hirsch's *Going Up,* side by side, so to speak, with McConnell's *Your Country Needs You Now.* And when, in 1918, George M. Cohan wrote *When You Come Back And You Will Come Back*—not to forget *Over There*—its rhythms were definitely in the air. Yet Ernest Ball, for a number of years, would hold his own with the old-time ballads. The ballad is as timeless a song-form as the waltz is a dance-form. Today, in the midst of our "swing" and "jam," the ballad and waltz, after a brief period of eclipse, return to their own even among the self-conscious sophisticates. We satirize the hill-billy song, and adopt it.

Jazz did a number of things to popular music as well as to metropolitan life. It sped up the tempo of things. Whether it was a cause, or the effect of a still more general cause, is here beside the point. Once the new musical spirit had come, it rapidly spread into daily—and nightly!—activities. It was not long before the old type of musical comedy began to appear outmoded. "Pep" was heard in the land. Once we had "ragged" words; now we "jazzed up" everything. Sex and the saxophone—both far older than the "younger generation" appeared to believe—were written long and loud into the national score. Forbidden fruits became sweeter; forbidden drink became harder; dances became wilder. A war had pushed many a youth to the very brink of annihilation; this was the mad joy of youth in the sheer sensation of being alive. Eat, drink, and be merry, for tomorrow there may be another war . . .

But always there must be songs. And soon the radio would add its voice to the general chorus. The radio was but one of a number of important factors that had begun to make inroads upon the music business. For a time, indeed, it threatened to *become* the music business. A shadow was falling over the firm of M. Witmark & Sons, and that shadow, from one angle, resembled a loud speaker.

2. Lean Years

Those famous lines of Dickens, "It was the best of times—it was the worst of times," were never better illustrated than during the occupancy of the Witmark Building in 37th Street. The "best of years" were many, especially in the earlier period. Success followed success. The Witmarks were far uptown at the time and had been trailed by other publishers. This virtually made the neighborhood the new Tin Pan Alley. Then Old Man Progress bestirred himself again and gradually, surreptitiously, sent up new industries, particularly women's wear, to crowd out King Music. Those in the music game who had leased and rented their places did not renew but moved up, up, into the 40's—and those who owned had to remain while the dress shops sprang up around them. Unfortunately, there was just one Music House so situated, as it owned and occupied its own building of six floors and two basements. One other publisher had built in the neighborhood, but he had built for outside occupants as well as for himself and it was easy for him to rent.

"It was the worst of times." Things now went from bad to worse. There was a deadline at 42nd Street and Broadway and it was like pulling teeth to get anyone to come down to 37th Street— the "far uptown" of twenty years before. The Witmarks had to run a car for the artists they wanted to visit them. The World War was raging. The radio was beginning to make itself felt. Mechanical reproductions, phonographs, piano players, etc., a mighty factor for returns in the music business, were falling off. Steadily, too, as the pianos were disappearing, popular song hits were losing the big sales generally accorded them. The Witmarks tried every way to dispose of their building, but up to 1918 there was no sign of a purchaser. Naturally business dropped off and with their extensive overhead the condition was not healthy. Singers would not come down and writers would go where the singers went.

Some time in May, 1918, a man named Samuel Rachman, an international theatrical agent, came to them with the suggestion that the contract of a promising young composer would expire that week and that he would be free to sign up with some representative publisher. When he divulged the name of the composer they were interested, and shortly thereafter they had a conference at his hotel, the Majestic, at 72nd Street and Central Park West, and agreed on terms and conditions.

And everybody was happy; the composer, because the new

contract emancipated him from certain irksome stipulations, and the Witmarks because they felt that they had signed up a good hit-writer who would be congenial to work with.

His name today is a household word throughout musical America, a name synonymous with success in almost any musical work to which it is affixed—Sigmund Romberg.

When he came to Witmarks' he had already written "Maytime" and "Blue Paradise" in which were included, respectively, two of his biggest and most lasting song hits, *Sweetheart* and *Auf Wiedersehen*. "Blossom Time" was another score he rearranged for this country, but one which they did not publish as it had been disposed of by the Shuberts to another house before he came to them. While these operettas had been great successes, his next productions, done for the Witmarks, were not.

They were in post-war times and conditions were not so good. Romberg's advances were climbing up (they had contracted to pay him $150 a week) and as yet there were no selling numbers, no new productions. Money was scarce, but Romberg's check reached him regularly. Finally, he was in debt to them in the amount of $18,000. And the checks were still going out.

Popular publishers were going through hell and Witmarks' had the brunt of it as a result of the lean years winding up at 37th Street. At last they got a nibble for the building, the dear old building of so many memories, and they sold it at a sacrifice, so glad were they to be relieved of it.

3. Sigmund Romberg

With the old building off their hands and a new one chosen, the Witmarks looked forward with confidence to their "next move." This last move was in 1923 to a new building at the corner of 51st Street and Broadway, where they had rented two floors of 7500 square feet each. They had a feeling of surrendering their individuality when moving out of the building that was all their own, yet the new set-up provided more footage and boasted many improvements over the old place. The landlord was the Bethlehem Engineering Corporation, of which Floyd Brown was president. He was one of the most sympathetic men with whom the Witmarks ever did business, as will be evidenced by the following incident.

Upon renting the place, the firm had overlooked a most important detail, yet it could not blame itself for having done so. It thought that this was a loft building, and not one erected for offices only. What particularly deceived the brothers was the fact that the ceilings looked as if they concealed heavy girders. So that they signed the lease with their eyes wide open, thinking that they would have more than the necessary carrying capacity per foot in the floors. This was vital to the business.

Realizing that such a big move required systematic handling, they figured that the whole job should be supervised by one capable person who was to be held responsible. Fortunately there was just such a person in the organization—Tony Kordula, head of the arrangement department. He went at the job like a regular engineer and did an efficient piece of work, saving the firm a lot of money by his shrewdness.

Kordula discovered the serious oversight: he found that what had been taken for heavy girders in the ceilings were only plaster adornment; the carrying weight per square foot was for regular office equipment rather than for deadweight stock as their paper and plates comprised. An architect was employed to check up and found that under the circumstances, and despite the long time lease, it would be perilous to move in, for fear the floors would collapse.

The day this was discovered the Witmarks were stunned. For all they knew, the landlord would hold them to their lease, which he had every right to do, for it had not been his fault that they had overlooked so important a point. What was more, they had no other place to move to. While they were racking their brains as to what to do Kordula walked in and offered a solution. "Why don't you go up and see the landlord, and ask him if these two floors can't be strengthened by reinforcement? *There is only one column to each floor* but it might be accomplished."

At first Mr. Brown was nonplussed over the predicament, but was agreeable to the Kordula suggestion and said he would get in touch with his engineers. He never once declared, as some landlords might have done, that it was no concern of his—that it was the Witmarks' problem. On the contrary, he volunteered to stand his share of the cost, and, as it turned out, he stood more than his share.

One of their greatest problems was how to dispose of their plates, which, in their old building, had been contained in sub-basement vaults. The engineers finally solved it by connecting the one column on the fifth floor with the nearby wall, by means of a seven-foot-deep girder directly underneath the sixth floor; and on the sixth floor they built the vault right over this heavy girder, which was necessary because of the tremendous weight of the plates.

Though nothing was spared in making the two floors the last word in comfort and efficiency, their usual luck did not seem to follow them into this new establishment. They took the usual time to move, had their dedication at the scheduled time, July, 1923, and welcomed back many professional friends whom they had not seen for a long while at the old place. But from the start there seemed to be a jinx on them in the new building. They had spent an unexpectedly large sum on the reconstruction of the new quarters, and the moving bill, of course, had not been small. The last few years in their old building, because their place was out of the proper zone, had not been up to standard, yet the overhead had been as large as ever. They naturally had hoped for a big improvement when they got uptown, but despite their world-famous operatic and standard catalogs, and two big hits,—they had just taken on *I'm Going South*, sung by many artists, including

FACING FAILURE

Al Jolson and Eddie Cantor, and *California, Here I Come,* which was another big Jolson success—their sales upon which they depended were disappointing. With their moving, they had gone in for unusual expansion, organizing for big business. By this time they had accumulated twenty-four branch offices, which took a small fortune to maintain. They had increased their professional staff and put on some high-priced men. They were out for a killing —but were almost killed themselves!

While they had the coöperation of the "real" people in the trade and profession, there were others who gloated over their predicament and did everything to take advantage of it. There was the despicable effort of one of the most prominent houses (for whom they had done many a good turn) to steal Romberg from them, trumping up some charge to the effect that they had broken their agreement with him. This house was willing to finance any lawsuit brought by Witmarks' for breach of contract against Romberg, and were ready to give him $50,000 as a bonus for his shift of allegiance.

To his credit, let it be said at once that nothing like this could influence Romberg. Although strong pressure was brought to bear he flatly refused all offers. He was determined to live up to his contract, which was to run until April, 1930. He declared the treatment he had received at Witmarks' would stamp him as an ingrate if he did anything that was not fair to them. Besides, he considered friendship above money. He continued to give Witmarks' his works, which were destined to become big successes.

It's worth while telling here how they secured the publishing rights of Romberg's biggest success, "The Student Prince." In spite of their contract with Romberg, the score was not his to give; it had already been negotiated and contracted for by J. J. Shubert and young Gus Schirmer with whom he was an inseparable pal, when Gus was one of the big executives of G. Schirmer and Company. At that time Shubert intended to produce this opera and took an advance of $2500 against royalties. Gus Schirmer

391

also had the rights to all the prospective Shubert musical productions, paying an advance on each score he secured. Then something happened at Schirmer's and there was a change of management. Young Gus was out for the time being and the new executives went through the papers and found all the contracts he had made with Shubert. The particular one in question had a time-limit as to the production of this piece; the period had elapsed long before and the new management saw the possibility of getting their advance back, as immediate production did not appear likely.

They made a demand on Shubert for their money, alleging breach of contract, but he paid no attention to them. In the meantime, Romberg, or "Rommy" as they called him, dropped in one day and casually told Isidore that a production of "The Student Prince" was contemplated again, but inasmuch as there had been a number of false starts on this, they weren't to take the report too seriously.

As it happened, Isidore had already learned about the attitude of the new Schirmer management and their determination to get back their advance. So, always being a gambler in business, he took a long chance and called up Mr. Fay, then president of Schirmer's, and discussed the "Student Prince" situation with him. It was then he told Isidore that he intended to sue for his money. Isidore said, "You don't have to sue; I'll take the contract off your hands, and save you the expense of a suit." To which Fay readily agreed and thanked him. And now Witmarks' owned the publishing rights of "The Student Prince." It was a question, with money as scarce as it was, whether Isidore had done the right thing. Conditions seemed to grow worse and worse, and for once they felt themselves quite helpless. Things had never been so desperate in their long business career. They had had panics and close calls before, but never anything like this. Nothing seemed to break right for them. They were desperate, with two supposedly big hits on their hands not selling.

The Witmarks had many a sleepless night, but at last they

called a meeting of their bankers, their lawyers, and other men who had their confidence and laid the whole matter before them. Their lawyer, whom they had practically started in his career and helped make famous, advised that they take the wash: in other words, go into voluntary bankruptcy, and start again from scratch. The others at the meeting did not concur, but had no solution of their own to offer. Needless to tell, the Witmarks felt miserable. The conference adjourned without agreeing on any definite action. They were not for the wash after all these years of building an enviable name! They had been grievously disappointed at their own lawyer's advice and decided to act on their own.

That night Isidore walked the floor, trying to think of an out— and he got it. Next day he called on a number of lawyer friends, each high in his line, and laid the matter before them. They were all sympathetic and were glad to give him their professional opinion. Some of them said that under the circumstances they wouldn't know what to advise, except to carry out his lawyer's instructions. But each sensed, as he said it, that it was like driving a knife through Isidore's heart, knowing how he prized the name and the business that had been built up.

The last of the lawyers he called on was an exceedingly busy man named Harry Zalkin. He had never had any of their patronage and was not obligated to them in any way. But Isidore said he was desperate—and Zalkin was a club friend of his and one of a crowd who used to go away together over Decoration Day. The Witmark type of case was just in his line as he was considered one of the ablest business lawyers in the country. He heard Isidore out, deliberated a while, then exclaimed, "We will *not* take the wash!" A hundred years were taken off Isidore's shoulders.

From that moment, without any understanding as to compensation or arrangement of any kind, that splendid fellow took charge of the case and set out to save the name of Witmark as though *he* had been associated with it from its inception. Being of a sympathetic nature, he devoted a great amount of time to their rehabilitation. In fact, there were days in the early stages when he made their office his office and had his people keep in constant touch with him there.

In his expert manner he eventually straightened out everything through his method of reorganization and retrenchment, and the satisfactory adjustments that he made. More than that, he accomplished what under the circumstances would have seemed impossible but was necessary: their friends being mostly his friends, he went out among them and raised a large sum of money as a loan to tide them over temporarily, he himself being one of the heaviest subscribers.

Because of this and the readjustment, Witmarks' got their second wind and things began to come back. Then came a turn of the tide in business, which began with the stupendous success of "The Student Prince." For strange as it may seem, after so many false starts, this time it did break and the production was assured. There were nine road companies, and they grossed approximately eight million dollars, of which they got their share of Romberg's royalties and the publication sales.

The production of "The Student Prince" was followed by a line-up of other big successes, including "The Desert Song," "My Maryland," "Rosalie," "Nina Rosa," "Princess Flavia," "Louis the Fourteenth" and "The New Moon." Romberg's indebtedness was wiped out, and he carried out his contract to the letter, which enabled the firm to participate in the returns of the above successes, freed of the legal complications that would otherwise have arisen if he had not proved his great loyalty to them.

On May 1st, 1930, Isidore Witmark received a letter from Romberg, a farewell tribute as beautiful as it was rare. Never had he received its equal in fifty years of publishing:

My dear Isidore:

At the beginning of May, 1918, you and your brother Jay signed an exclusive contract with me which in the matter of course lasted twelve years and ended last month. I was a struggling composer, kind of wild, full of ambition and just about to start to produce shows myself. To me your contract, with the necessary guarantee, was about the biggest thing at that time for which my young hopes could aspire. There is no doubt in my mind that you also saw something in me, otherwise of course you wouldn't have signed the contract.

Now, time rolled on and the years passed by, years of hardship, of struggle, of sunshine, and happiness. Our daily troubles and confidential chats brought us closer and closer together. Out of a business arrangement, a friendship grew beyond any clause, rule or regulation which may have been in our contract, our mutual esteem and friendship the bond between us, the other a relic.

During the past years we both had to bear the burden of life. You lost your brother Julius, and I lost my Mother and Father. We jointly shared our misery and found condolence and a ray of sunshine in our daily chats.

So now let the relic of an agreement take its place with other documents of the past and let that friendship continue which never had and never needed a contract. Understand that even if life or circumstances would throw us far apart, you will always remain my big brother, to whom I can give and with whom I can share all my troubles and confidences, who will enjoy and feel happy in the good fortunes which may befall me, and I hope that, as in the past, you will keep up your confidence and let me share your troubles and your happinesses and that there should be only one end to that friendship, that prescribed by God who in his wisdom ends everything.

Also let that friendship go beyond that point and if ever there is anything which I can do in any capacity to stand by your dear ones I will gladly do so.

This letter includes Brother Jay also, and it may sound like a sentimental outburst from an emotional composer, but it is meant rock bottom and had to be told.

> Yours, as ever,
> (Signed) SIGMUND ROMBERG.

Generally, loans from friends are not paid back promptly; often they are written off. But within a year and a half the Witmarks repaid their loans in full plus six per cent interest; and the day this happened, Harry Zalkin was the proudest man in New York. Nevertheless, he *never sent them a bill*. A couple of years later, because of the impetus he had given them, and his watching over them as he did, they were able to make an advantageous sale of the business to the Warner Brothers, which he successfully consummated for them. When everything was settled, the Witmarks had a conference with him wherein he told them of the various obligations they had to take care of. They reminded him that he had mentioned nothing about legal fees. He said, "I will not send you a bill. You boys get together, and anything you decide on will be agreeable to me."

They did, and remembering that he had asked nothing for his previous services, they decided on what they considered an appropriate sum, although at the same time, they felt and will always feel that no matter what the sum, they could never pay Harry Zalkin for his devotion and his determination to keep clear the Witmark name. When they told him the amount agreed upon, he refused absolutely to accept it, although he knew that under the circumstances they were well able to pay it, and insisted upon chopping off a third.

There is a pleasant, characteristic anecdote about Romberg that is known to few. His devotion to his parents was great; in everything he accomplished, his first thought was of them. His father, himself a musician, had been Sigmund's preceptor and throughout the years maintained his status as a critic of all that Rommy did. And Rommy, realizing that his father got a kick out of it, kept up the illusion—and thereby got a kick out of it himself.

When his name had become one of the foremost in the musical world, he went back to Hungary to visit his parents. Having devoured all the press notices about their son and eagerly questioned everyone coming from America about his success, they were excited over his homecoming. After they thought he had rested enough, they began to entreat him to play his new works for them at the piano. His father was especially eager to hear all this music, as he wanted to get in some work as a critic.

But Rommy had something up his sleeve: the more they prodded him, the more he begged off, saying he was tired, not in the mood, and offering other excuses, until one day, when his plans were perfected, he invited them to the prominent concert hall of his native city, whither they went in style. He sent a fiacre for them, and as they were being driven there they wondered what it was all about, because they, keeping track of musical events, knew that nothing was scheduled for that hall for that date.

They were met at the door by the manager of the concert hall, who obsequiously escorted them to their seats—the two best seats in the house. In a semi-daze they beheld an orchestra of about sixty men tuning up on the stage, but not another soul in the house! Just the two of them in that huge auditorium! They looked at each other in bewilderment. But they didn't have long to wait.

The orchestra played a fanfare—and Rommy came on from the wings, with a baton in his hand. He turned toward the auditorium and bowed low, faced the large orchestra, raised his baton, and conducted them through one selection after another of his American operatic successes. The concert, for just those two, lasted the better part of the afternoon. When it was over, Rommy solemnly turned again, bowed low to his audience, and left the stage.

His parents sat dumfounded—and even the old gentleman didn't have a thing to criticize. Rommy then went out front to them, and found them in tears of emotion. And he joined them in a good cry. The concert was followed by a visit to the finest restaurant in town, where Rommy had ordered a banquet for just the three of them, which they enjoyed in regal style.

4. Sargent Aborn Consolidates the Witmark and Tams Music Libraries

The year 1925 opened with an event of some importance to the musical world. A rivalry of thirty years, during which the opponents had waged bitter competition in and out of court, and had for long ceased to be on speaking terms, was at last ended in a reconciliatory merger. The Witmark Music Library and the Arthur W. Tams Music Library, forgetting the rancors of a generation and a half, decided to pool their resources, sink all differences, and thereafter be as one.

The arrangement did not affect the general business of M. Witmark & Sons. The joint properties were entrusted to the Tams forces, under the managing directorship of Sargent Aborn. The Witmarks continued to publish classical and popular music, enlarging these departments; indeed, this had been one of the reasons for approving the consolidation of the Libraries.

"The business of supplying amateurs," said Isidore Witmark, in a statement issued to the press, on January 10, 1925, "has increased a thousand per cent in the past ten years. This is because of the changes brought about through the increased expense of traveling companies. The decreasing number of 'road shows' has caused local theater managers in the smaller cities to fill their time with motion pictures and vaudeville. This has made bookings difficult to managers of traveling companies, decreasing their number still further. But the lovers of light music and spectacular production in those communities must have their favorite diversion occasionally, and they supply this demand in amateur performances, some of which disclose talented individuals who afterward reach Broadway stages. The 'road show' is fast going the way of the horse-drawn vehicle."

It was Sargent Aborn, one of the Aborns now celebrated in the history of popular opera in the United States, who had brought about the merger of the Witmark and Tams Libraries. The Aborns were showmen from 'way back. They started their opera companies in 1901, Milton supervising the artistic end, the selection of the operas and artists, the production and stage management; Sargent took care of financial matters, the bookings of the company, and everything pertaining to the administration. They made

FACING FAILURE

a happy combination, and were most successful, both artistically and financially.

They had opened the first company at the Orpheum Theatre, Brooklyn, N. Y., when Percy G. Williams was alive and connected with that house. The production was a revival of "The Little Duchess," with Elsie Janis featured in the part created by Anna Held. Afterward the Aborns placed Miss Janis under exclusive contract to them, and leased her to George C. Tyler for a starring tour in "The Vanderbilt Cup," which had a long run on Broadway. Among the many artists who started their career with the Aborn Company were Richard Bonelli, now of the Metropolitan, and Clifton Webb, of musical comedy fame, who has drifted from his original parts in opera comique with the Aborns to a versatile career in revues as singer, dancer, and actor.

The Aborns were the first to give good productions of opera at popular prices. For this they won a wide reputation. In 1903 they branched out in a larger way, adding summer repertoire companies to their already established winter tours. At one time they had six to eight companies in different large cities of the United States—New York, Brooklyn, Pittsburgh, Boston, Washington, etc. They had one company every summer for twelve years at Olympic Park, Newark, N. J., and played for two seasons at the Palisade Amusement Park, N. J.

Before the organization of the Witmark Music Library, the Aborns had secured their music material wherever they could, particularly from the House of Tams. But it was not long after the Witmark Library was founded that they concentrated all of their business there because they recognized the Witmark material as correct and easily rehearsed, and the service as most dependable. Besides the standard works, the Witmarks supplied to them all the royalty operas. The Aborns were the first to do in repertory the Victor Herbert and De Koven works, such as "The Serenade," "The Wizard of the Nile," "The Fortune Teller," "Robin Hood," "Rob Roy," and "The Fencing Master."

FROM RAGTIME TO SWINGTIME

In 1914 they gave a ten weeks' season of grand opera at the Century Theatre in New York, since torn down, under the name of Century Opera Company; the late Otto H. Kahn was chairman. "Sarge" relates, in this connection, that Mr. Kahn, who attended the performances almost every night, was concerned regarding the capacity of the house, inasmuch as they were doing such a big business that they were turning people away. Kahn asked Sarge what could be done to increase the seating capacity. "Sarge" took him up the balcony and pointed out where many more seats could be added. "How much would it cost?" asked Kahn. "About one hundred thousand dollars to make the alterations," said Aborn. "I'll let you know tomorrow," said Kahn. Next day he called them up and said, "Go ahead"—as if it would cost about a nickel to do. Aborn had the house altered, and increased the capacity considerably for the following season, but as big as the business was the first season, so much of a failure was it the next. The World War had broken out . . .

The Aborns did not always stick to the conventional mode of producing, but did what one might call a little plunging once in a while. For instance, they staged a spectacular production of "Haensel and Gretel" and of "The Bohemian Girl," using, in the latter, horses and other animals and special scenic effects, augmented choruses, and so on, which was a tremendous success everywhere.

In 1920 the brothers separated. "Sarge" made a production of "The Broken Wing," the first airplane drama ever produced. It was written by Paul Dickey and Charles W. Goddard, with a cast including Inez Plummer and George Abbott, who today is a leading playwright and producer. "The Broken Wing" was a money maker for two seasons.

During this time Milton opened a school of opera, which continued for a couple of years and from which were graduated a number of promising artists.

In 1922 "Sarge" took over the general management of A. W.

George Ade

Frank Craven

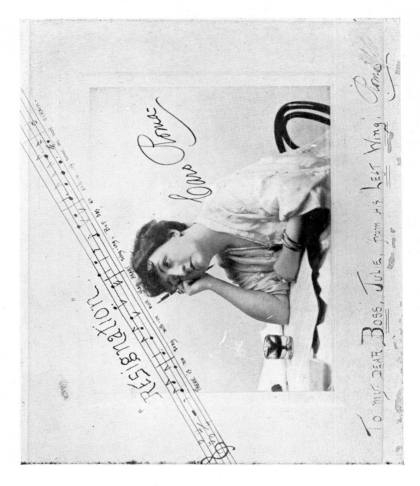

Caro Roma

Tams' Library. Through his efforts, consolidation was made with the Witmark Music Library, a task hitherto impossible because of the enmity between Witmark and Tams. "Sarge," assisted by his clever son Louis, headed the consolidation and made a great success. He has now definitely retired from show business and intends to make the consolidation his life's work. Milton Aborn died November 12, 1933.

5. Tune-Thievery or Coincidence?

For a firm half a century old, the Witmarks encountered comparatively little trouble with that bane of popular-music publishing, plagiarism. There had been, however, a number of cases, more interesting as strange coincidences than as examples of downright stealing. The strangest of these occurred during the middle of the 1920's. It recalls others, however, which make a fitting prelude to the grand climax of the song, *Me Neenyah*.

Writers of popular songs are forever open to charges of plagiarism. They do not always possess the courage to take their accusers into court, as did Victor Herbert in 1902, after a musical magazine had pestered him with the too familiar charges.

The matter of plagiarism is one that is imperfectly understood by the general public. An extensive literature exists on the subject, not alone, of course, concerning music. Coincidences abound, whether in the classics, among composers of indubitable genius, or in the lower ranges of musical composition. Both Gilbert and Sullivan, for example, were plagued in their lifetimes by oft-repeated accusations of plagiarism. This especially irked Gilbert, who was particularly proud of his originality and insisted upon describing his librettos as "new and original." Sullivan, when it was once pointed out to him that *When A Merry Maiden Marries* (from "The Gondoliers") and *Love's Old Sweet Song*, by Molloy, sounded much alike, gave a classic reply: "We had only eight notes between us."

401

In the matter of popular operetta the wonder is not that an occasional resemblance should appear, but that those resemblances should be occasional only. Herbert, like other men of lesser and greater caliber, now and then set down tunes that reminded his hearers of others. The most famous of these instances, perhaps, was the case of *Kiss Me Again,* which bears a striking resemblance—in the early bars only—to Albéniz's *Cordoba,* one of five pieces for the piano. Kaye, one of his biographers, points out that *I Have Been A-Maying,* from "The Wizard of the Nile," recalls the *Legend Of The Bells* from Planquette's "Les Cloches de Corneville" ("The Chimes Of Normandy"). More captious seems the same man's attempt to establish a resemblance between Herbert's *Serenade, Op. 3,* and Schubert's *Heidenröslein.*

Yet Herbert was not entirely unconscious of these similarities, after the fact, and was more or less on guard against them. It is easy to add to the examples. There is a point near the climax of the waltz from "The Serenade" in which a phrase from "Faust," in the song, *Le parlate d'amor* (the famous flower-song) is recalled. One could go through our operettas—from Herbert to Kern and Romberg—and cull a long anthology of such recollections. Perhaps that is just what they are; momentary recollections from a life filled with the hearing and playing of other people's music and the writing of one's own. Sometimes the resemblance is deliberate, but not so often as the public may imagine. Tin Pan Alley, especially, believes in using a known phrase as a good start for a tune. It makes it so much easier to remember and to whistle!

On the other hand, when a man has a distinct style of his own, the recollections may be dismissed as a familiar type of musical accident. Victor Herbert won his case in court. He has won it, too, with posterity.

It was shortly before the Herbert trial that the Witmarks ran into one of the most astounding coincidences that their long record can show. The Whitney Brothers, Howard and Jim, were doing an outstanding musical act in vaudeville. One day the boys came in to Witmarks and asked if they could play a little number that was going well in their program. One unboxed a violin, the other sat down at the piano, and they played an interesting number, of which Jay and Julie thought well. So did Isidore, for that matter, and for a good reason.

When they had finished, he went to the manuscript safe, brought out an *unpublished* number, and asked the boys to play it, too. Inasmuch as they were good musicians, and could read at sight, they tackled it. Half-way through they stopped, and said, "Well, you're naturally going to publish yours."

The numbers were almost identical. The one from the safe had been written by Isidore for an amateur revue. His answer was, "No, we're going to publish yours."

And they did, making fame and money for the Whitneys, as well as great boosters and friends for the house. The name of the piece was *The Mosquito's Parade* and it proved a tremendous success.

The most striking case of all in the records of the Witmarks is that of a song named *Me Neenyah,* an English transliteration of the Spanish, *Mi Niña,* meaning *My Baby,* or *My Little Girl.* It might suggest, to those favoring such solutions, a powerful case of telepathy.

In the year 1925 Herbert Spencer was one of the Witmark song demonstrators, on the floor, and also wrote for them. Herbert composed many song successes, including *Underneath the Stars, Stella,* and *In the Candlelight,* the last of which was published by Witmark.

Consignments of new publications were sent regularly to their London representative, Charles Warren, who made sporadic trips to the Continent to place them with publishers there. In due course the copies and orchestrations of Spencer's *Me Neenyah* went over to England, and Warren took them on his next trip to Germany and other continental countries.

It was not long before an indignant letter arrived from Warren, wanting to know who sent the *Me Neenyah* material direct to the Continent instead of through him. By the time he had reached Berlin and other cities, he complained, he had heard it played frequently, and he couldn't interest anybody in his copies. The Witmarks did not know what to make of this, for they had sent no copies direct to the Continent. One day Isidore was called up by a Mr. Garmaize, attorney for the Columbia Phonograph Company.

"Mr. Witmark, this is Mr. Garmaize."

"How do you do, Mr. Garmaize? What can I do for you?"

"Well, it looks as if we were going to lock horns. My clients, a German publishing firm, assert that you have infringed upon the copyright of a number that they own. You publish a song called *Me Neenyah*, don't you?"

"Yes."

"That's it."

"Have you a copy of the German song?" Isidore asked.

"Yes, right before me."

"Will you send it to me?"

"I'll put it in the mail today."

"Thanks."

The song arrived, and Isidore was astounded. It was not an infringement. It was not a colorable imitation. It was an exact copy, note for note, with the exception of one half-tone in a leading passage, which if left out would have made it exact even to the accompaniment.

"I'll have some fun with this," he thought, and sent for Herbert Spencer, who had the reputation of being a clean writer, so prolific and so charged with melody that he did not need to appropriate anybody else's work.

Isidore turned the German copy inside out, showing the refrain only, and asked Spencer to please play it for him.

At first, he was astonished, then he commenced to chuckle,

then he ejaculated: "Whoopee! They took everything! What are you going to make them pay?"

"Well," said Isidore, "maybe *we'll* have to do the paying!"

"What do you mean?"

Isidore turned to the first inside page, which contained the copyright line. It showed that the German copyright was one year *ahead* of *Me Neenyah*.

Spencer was nonplussed.

"They say," Isidore went on, "that you stole their melody."

Spencer went almost into a frenzy. "How dare they say I stole their stuff? I never stole anything in my life. I don't need to!"

"How do you explain this case?"

"I don't know," admitted Spencer, his anger subsiding. "It's just one of those things."

To which Isidore agreed. It was certainly a remarkable case. After giving it much thought, Isidore called up Mr. Garmaize and said: "I've given the matter a lot of study, and I've come to the conclusion that it was not an infringement but simply a coincidence. For no plagiarist would take a melody note for note. He might take two, four or six bars, and then switch to another melody, particularly if he were an unconscious infringer, when he would naturally weave in some of his own material."

What Isidore stood pat on was that nobody would take a composition lock, stock, and barrel, and popularize it as his own, with the constant menace of having to surrender it after spending time and money to put it over. That in itself would be bad business. Besides, such a writer would have a black eye from that time on and find it difficult to have any publisher take his work.

Mr. Garmaize agreed with him, and the case was dropped.

All of which explains why *Me Neenyah* was a hit in Germany a *year before it was written in this country!*

CHAPTER XXV

CLOSE-UPS

1. *Werner Janssen*

*W*ERNER JANSSEN, born in 1900, was the first native New Yorker to conduct the Philharmonic-Symphony Orchestra. He has also directed the Berlin Philharmonic, the Vienna Symphony, the Helsingfors Municipal Orchestra; orchestras in Rome, Turin, Milan, and Bologna, and conducted in Riga during the city's summer season of orchestral concerts.

Probably the high point of his achievement so far is his conducting an all-Sibelius program at Helsingfors in 1933, at which Sibelius himself was present and was affected deeply. To quote Herbert Peyser, foreign musical correspondent of the *New York Times*, who was present on that memorable occasion:

"Sibelius, at whose side I had the privilege to be seated, turned to me visibly shaken, and stammered: 'You may say that tonight Finland has for the first time discovered my music. This achievement of Janssen's is the deed of a hero. Yes, I know there are other conductors who have done great and memorable things for me, and perhaps I ought not express myself so openly. But the truth is that for the first time I am hearing my work exactly as I conceived it, and my compatriots have never really known me till now.' "

CLOSE-UPS

Werner's father, August Janssen, founder of the famous New York Hofbrau Houses ("Janssen Wants to See You"), is one of the most genial hosts in the city. He is a loyal friend and a fine family man, but he made just one mistake he was big enough to recognize in after years—and that mistake was his boy Werner. This may sound harsh, but the father's intent was good and would have been accepted by any other boy with enthusiasm if that boy had not an entirely different goal in mind. August was at the height of his success as a restaurateur when Werner was going to college (1917-21) and it was such a fine business that he wanted Werner to fall into it.

But Werner had other ideas. August, a strict disciplinarian, was put out by his son's reaction, for while he loved music he wanted his son to have it as an avocation rather than as a vocation. But he could not control Werner. The boy was born for music. August felt that Werner was ungrateful for passing up an opportunity. He took it so to heart that he became bitter, and when Werner started in seriously on his musical career his father practically cast him off, hence Werner had pretty hard sledding.

Werner was obliged to assert his independence, which he did by starting to write popular songs and other "pot-boilers" for a livelihood. He came to the Witmarks, who took his songs perhaps as much to encourage him as to profit by the merit of the numbers.

Werner Janssen wrote songs and a musical show which was produced; during which time Witmarks' made him advances. At the same time he was studying the classics, devoting all his spare energy to serious composition, until his first tone-poem, *New Year's Eve in New York*, was performed by the Cleveland Orchestra in New York on December 3, 1929. This won immediate recognition and was soon being played by prominent symphony orchestras. He went ahead rapidly, and in 1930 went to Europe, where he remained four years. His triumph at Helsingfors, heralded in the New York papers, finally brought his father around and a happy family reunion followed.

407

FROM RAGTIME TO SWINGTIME

His first appearance with the Philharmonic-Symphony Orchestra in New York was scheduled for Thursday evening, November 8, 1934. His reception was one not to be forgotten and he was acclaimed in all the papers the following day.

A few days before that Isidore Witmark had been walking east in 57th Street deep in thought, when in front of Steinway's he was aroused by a loud exclamation: "Mr. Isidore! I am so glad to see you."

Looking up, he saw Werner Janssen. Despite his great success and the position of prominence he held, he was the same boy Isidore had always known.

He said, "Maestro Toscanini just sent me out to take a walk as I had a kind of headache from studying my opening programs." (He was conducting under the general supervision of Toscanini who was in command at the Philharmonic and whom he praised highly for his consideration of his subordinates.) Like Toscanini he conducts without a score—in fact, he rehearses most of his programs without scores.

They began reminiscing, and out of a clear sky, he started laughing, almost boisterously, and cried out, "Do you remember, Mr. Isidore, do you remember when you published my crap?" The reminiscing went on for hours.

Werner Janssen married the famous actress Ann Harding, in January, 1937.

2. Frank Craven

Frank Craven, actor, author, director, is one of the most versatile and best loved characters in the American theater. At times this very versatility has proven somewhat of a problem to him for a day was to come when he discovered that he couldn't sell a play unless he consented to act in it himself; but fortunately no such obstacle stood forth to mar his stage début. He was less than three years old at the time and according to the *New York Dra-*

matic Mirror, even in those days he was an exponent of the natural school of acting and wrote his own lines, which consisted mostly of "Goo-goo." The play was "The Silver King" and his mother appeared with him.

Frank came from a family of troupers. His father, John T. Craven, was one of the original politicians in Hoyt's "A Texas Steer." His mother, Ella Mayer, usually played character parts. His mother was his first teacher and educated him until he was nine. From then on, life was his university and his I.Q. was high.

At sixteen he was playing in repertory in leading cities but quit the stage for the insurance business two years later, bent on insuring his future. The stage, he decided, was not for him. In this his employer did not concur, for after six months he begged him to return to it. At last he capitulated, and returned to the cast of "The Silver King"—but, how he had aged! This time he played the part of an old man.

One of Frank Craven's first ambitions was to be a hack-driver, his second to handle money; whether or not his third was to be a song-writer is not recorded, but in any event in 1905 he was writing lyrics for the Witmarks when the going was a bit rough.

"The Curse of Cain's," his first playlet, was written for one of the "Lambs' Gambols." It was liked by everyone including Frank Craven, who decided to write something else. Thereafter he made a name for himself as an actor in the part of Jimmy Gilley in "Bought and Paid For." He wrote "Too Many Cooks" in 1912. While he was writing it, he told Victor Herbert the subject and story of the comedy. The composer seemed delighted with the idea and suggested that Craven write it as a musical comedy, with lyrics, that Herbert might set it to music. Craven refused, saying that the play could never succeed in that form.

"Why not?" asked Herbert.

"I've told you," explained Craven, "that it is all about building a house; and construction is fatal in a musical comedy."

FROM RAGTIME TO SWINGTIME

One of the best critical estimates of the work of Frank Craven was written by Percy Hammond in 1930:

"When Mr. Craven writes an amusing comedy and appears in it himself, the combination formed thereby is one of the irresistible things of the theater. . . . The most unselfish and therefore the wisest of the stars, he cherishes rather than diminishes the efforts of his fellows with the result that his works are always well acted."

And from the *Boston Herald* of February 13, 1927:

"Frank Craven is a great advocate of the natural school of acting. Mr. Craven, by the way, evidently believes in natural methods off the stage as well as on, for a more quiet, unassuming playwright-actor would be hard to find."

3. *Douglas Fairbanks*

On one of his trips from Chicago in 1908, Isidore met Douglas Fairbanks. He was on the stage then and they had an enjoyable trip swapping stories. He told Isidore that he was joining a show in which he was to get ten per cent of the gross, with a minimum of a thousand dollars per week; he was also lecturing in girls' colleges.

The best story Fairbanks told was about what happened to him and Thomas A. Wise, his running mate in "The Gentleman from Mississippi." Fairbanks was a Cornell favorite but above all he was famous there for walking on his hands. He assured Isidore that it was just as comfortable for him to walk on his hands as for anybody else on his feet. He and Wise finally landed in Ithaca, and on the opening night everybody who knew Doug Fairbanks was there. The curtain rose and the play was moving along smoothly until he made his entrance. There was a riot, and they would not let the show proceed. The more he tried to talk the more they tore up the benches. He bowed, scraped, left the stage, made another entrance, and the audience was getting worse and worse.

CLOSE-UPS

Finally, he and Wise consulted backstage and had about decided to run the curtain down, when Doug was inspired with an idea. All this time the audience was applauding out front.

"Wait!" he shouted. Taking off his coat he walked out on the stage—on his hands. This created another riot. Then, as though it had all been rehearsed, everything became quiet. That's what they had been waiting for, and they were satisfied.

4. Ray Perkins

A promising young song writer, Ray Perkins, began on the staff of the Witmarks in 1921. He left song writing and show business to embark on an advertising career with the *New Yorker Magazine;* but in 1929 Isidore prevailed on him to go back with them as both writer and executive. He sent him to the west coast to take charge of their music activities at the Warner and First National Studios. He had under his direction all their writers, totaling some twenty composers and lyricists, handling the details of song writing and production for all the pictures, as well as the important liaison with the New York office on publication matters. A more delicate and downright difficult assignment would be hard to imagine, for Ray had to be the oil on constantly troubled waters, caused by the problem of adjusting the temperaments of picture folk to those of the newly arrived music makers. Incidentally he wrote several hits during this period himself, but returned to New York after a year. Isidore has always suspected that Perkins felt he put him in a pretty tough spot in Hollywood.

As early as 1924 Ray Perkins, who had attained some fame as an entertainer, particularly in singing his own songs at the piano, was on the air commercially. He was a pioneer commercial broadcaster over WJZ. Now on his return from Hollywood he embarked on a radio career in earnest, and since 1930 has become one of radio's most consistently popular performers nationally.

411

His flair for comedy has resulted in his present high rating as a comedian and master of ceremonies.

5. Richard Carle

Richard Carle, in his time, has played many parts, and all of them well. He was, in his early days, an outstanding comedian who wrote his own musical plays, both the lyrics and the music, and they were staged under his personal management. They included, "The Tenderfoot," "The Maid and the Mummy," "The Mayor of Tokio," "Mary's Lamb," and "Hurdy-Gurdy Girl," all of which the Witmarks published. Richard Carle spent his money lavishly. He had a hobby of helping unknown actors and many an actor owed his first opportunity to him.

When rehearsing "The Tenderfoot," although he was the star of the show, he called his company together and said, "Now, boys and girls, I want you to do everything you can to make your part a success, and if you have any good lines play them up. Don't worry about me—I'll get mine."

It was an exceptional declaration because usually a star demands all the punch-lines of a show for himself.

Today Richard Carle is one of the best loved actors in Hollywood and the esteem in which he is held is a fitting tribute to one who has always dignified the acting profession.

A clipping from the *Chicago Post* of March 30, 1915, reads as follows:

"Since the news of James K. Hackett's action in paying off all his indebtedness in spite of the absolution of the bankruptcy statutes, it has been recalled that once upon a time Richard Carle indulged in a similar outburst of honesty, contributing no less than $30,000 out of a sense of honor. This costly episode in Carle's career was enacted just after the failure of Carle-Marks, Inc., which had undertaken to present Carle in a number of his own plays. The corporation was virtually without assets at the time of its failure, and the indebtedness amounted to approximately

$30,000. Although lawyers, who termed him 'Quixotic,' advised Carle that personally he was not legally responsible for the debts of the corporation, Carle argued that credit had been extended on the strength of his reputation and earning capacity, and notified the creditors that they would be paid in full as soon as he was able to earn the money.

"Gradually the entire amount was wiped out and Carle now treasures among his most valued possessions the receipts and letters of grateful acknowledgment from the men who profited by his sense of integrity."

6. Frank E. Tours

Frank Tours is in the front rank of comic opera and musical comedy orchestra directors and has done conspicuous work in the motion picture field. He has musically produced many of the great successes of the era, including all of the productions made at the Music Box, New York City, and "The Great Waltz" which had a year's run at the Center Theater. He was musical director for the Paramount studios on Long Island and later a director for R. K. O., where he composed the scores for several pictures.

Tours is one of the class arrangers and as a composer of better-grade songs has no peer. His setting of Rudyard Kipling's celebrated poem, *Mother o' Mine*, has made him famous. He comes from generations of musicians who originated in Rotterdam, his father, Berthold Tours, having been an outstanding organist and composer. He received his musical education at the Royal College of Music in London. His piano instructor was Emil Paur and his organ instructor was Sir Walter Barratt. He has been conducting since he was nineteen years old and is equally well known in America and England, where he was musical director for George Edwardes, the leading musical comedy producer at the famous Daly's and Gaiety Theatres. Tours is married and has a family of five children.

After Frank Tours arrived from England with the Gaiety Company, forty-two years ago, he affiliated himself with the Witmarks, Julie helping him in his arrangements with the musical

413

union. Tours is a prolific writer, and his ballads, published by the Witmarks, are among the highly-prized numbers issued by that firm.

7. *George Ade*

In the August, 1933, issue of *Wings,* George Ade wrote: "If I had not turned in at the city desk of *The Chicago Record,* along in the early nineties, little stories which were indefinitely classified as 'human interest stuff' instead of news yarns, I never would have been given a two-column department and a glorious license to go ahead and write about trivial episodes to my heart's content." And he might have added that had he not started writing this "human interest stuff" he might never have started writing musical plays. And if he had never started writing musical plays, he could not have sent Isidore Witmark the complete score of "The Sultan of Sulu" on October 7, 1938, inscribed in his own writing as follows:

"This musical play or light opera or musical satire or what have you, was written at the urgent suggestion of Henry W. Savage, who was ambitious to become a producer. The music was by Alfred Wathall, a young Englishman who had talent and aspirations but no experience with stage work. When the thing was produced in Chicago it was miscast and many of the numbers failed to score. We revised and reconstructed and tried out new numbers and secured Frank Moulan to play Ki Ram and when we finally opened in New York we had an unmistakable hit. All of the good and bad music we ever used while re-writing the play was published by Witmark Brothers. They were kindly and helpful and that is why I am glad, after the lapse of about forty-five years, to inscribe this authentic copy of the musical score for my old friend Isidore Witmark.—George Ade, Hazelden Farms, Brook, Indiana."

The copyright date on the book is 1902, so apparently it only *seemed* like forty-five years to George Ade. Isidore prizes this book highly not because it is bound in full morocco, but because it is bound in friendship that is even more lasting.

CLOSE-UPS

On December 18, 1920, George Ade was guest of honor at a dinner given by the Lotos Club of New York City. His remarks were so delightful, they are reproduced here:

"Mr. Toastmaster, Fellow-Members of the Lotos Club, Guests: Man is never so dismally employed as when he is proclaiming his own unworthiness. The trouble is, he may prove his case. When the heavens open and a great boon descends upon him—and knocks him groggy—the only thing for him to do is to pretend that he expected it sooner.

"If you find a laurel wreath on your brow, 'leave it lay there.' While passing through a pleasant ordeal, as in the present instance, don't ask yourself. 'Why are they doing this to me?' The only question to ask is, 'How can I get through it without being apprehended?'

"Everything was quiet in the Middle West when Secretary Price plucked Cincinnatus from the plow. He called to me and I have come. I have come with a message to the crowded East from the wild and free —more wild than free—open spaces of the corn belt, where nearly every one voted dry and hardly any one refuses a drink. I answered the summons because the Lotos Club is the most wonderful club in the world. For the past twenty-five years it should have been conducting a correspondence school for toastmasters. It has produced the only toastmasters who could acquire the simple art of sitting down. It is the only dining organization that can compel an orator to condense a five-minute speech into eight minutes.

"One day I was an humble agriculturalist and next day I was fairy queen in your Christmas pantomime. After I came to, some one said, 'They must have heard about your golf game.' I said, 'No, I think it is in recognition of my war work. Herbert Hoover and Leonard Wood, and John J. Pershing have received their rewards, before, during, and after the Chicago Convention, and now it is my turn.

"Let me explain. Perhaps you have heard of Will Hays. He is the champion 90-pound Hoosier heavyweight. You may not know that during the war Will Hays and I kept the Germans out of Indiana. In fact, it may not be generally known in New York that Indiana was involved in the war at all.

"I inquired of Mr. Price and he told me not to say too much about my war record, or the Club might withdraw the invitation. He said that war stuff was cold. The man in uniform is now just as popular as Article Ten. He said that the people in New York didn't get up any more except

415

when the orchestra plays *The Wearing of the Green* or *Rule Britannia,* and then they go up about ten feet.

"It occurred to me that possibly the members of the Lotos Club had cultivated their memories by the new magazine methods so that they could remember away back to the time when I was a playwright. A man who works for me out on the farm said he thought they were giving me a dinner because I had never gone into moving pictures. Finally, I came to this philosophical conclusion—the Lotos Club knows what it is doing. The Lotos Club makes very few mistakes. When it gives a dinner there is a reason. . . .

"I am trying tonight to control my emotions and to hold back the platitudes. There are many reasons why I should tell you that I am grateful to you from the bottom of my heart and that this is the proudest moment of my life, but why spoil your evening? Years ago when I found myself footloose and the first easy money in my hands, the logical thing for me to do was to come to New York and grapple with the stock market. Instead of which I took up my voting residence back in Indiana. It is true that I haven't put in a great deal of time there. I built a country house. Not to go to, but merely to refer to. I hung around Indiana long enough to get myself bracketed with General Lew Wallace, James Whitcomb Riley, Booth Tarkington, Meredith Nicholson, David Graham Phillips, Albert J. Beveridge, and George Barr McCutcheon. For years I have been so busy getting myself bracketed with those luminaries that I have forgotten to write anything. My real life work has been the construction of a nine-hole golf course. Often I wonder if I made a mistake in going to Indiana instead of moving on to New York. If I had come here I could now wear spats without being self-conscious but would I have crippled the stock market? Is it better for a man to have a tin box full of standard securities or several cribs full of corn? In either case, he is ready to accept a benefit. Is it better to lead a placid life in the country or remain in contact with the thrilling stimuli of the metropolis? Mr. Emerson was right when he said that each career must pay its way. There are compensations and penalties no matter where we choose to camp. After a man has acquired ten millions, he must accept, with each additional million, at least one gallstone. I have missed a lot of happy nights by being in the country, but I got a lot of sleep that many of the people in your city seem to need, at all times.

"One thing is sure. If I had been hanging around this club every evening for the last fifteen years, I would not now be the central figure

Vaughn De Leath

(*Albert Davis Photo*)

Eva Tanguay

One of the first talking pictures ever made was *April Showers* starring Al Jolson in 1926. Executives of Vitaphone posing with Jolson and his musical director, Al Goodman, on the set at Manhattan Opera House. Left to right, Al Goodman, Herman Heller, Al Jolson, W. J. Rich and the late Sam Warner.

in this tableau. So I am glad I went to the country. I don't know why you called me back, but I am glad you did. God knows why you have pinned a medal on me, but God bless you, just the same."

Will Hays, in a speech immediately following said, "Ade is popular here tonight. Ade is just as popular all the time in Indiana. Ade is easily the most popular man in Indiana. Ade could be and would be nominated and elected Governor of Indiana any time he would say the word, and I speak with some authority and knowledge."

Many years have passed since that night and George Ade has never attempted to become Governor of Indiana. Instead he has been content to remain at Hazelden Farms, preferring to be simply *The Sultan of Sulu*, as President Taft once aptly termed him.

8. *Vaughn De Leath*

The story of Vaughn De Leath is one that should be interesting to millions of radio listeners. Miss De Leath herself tells it:

"In 1919 there was a little quiver of excitement about an activity called wireless telephony. Until then its existence was known mainly only to ship operators (wireless), engineers, or amateurs (nicknamed 'hams'). These 'hams' had small stations of their own and were interested in wireless chiefly as a hobby.

"Dr. Lee de Forest, inventor of the radio vacuum tube and known as the 'Father of Radio,' gave a party in 1919, at which one of the engineers working with Dr. de Forest mentioned that in their experiments they had used a number of my phonograph records and that these had found favor with some of the 'hams' and operators who had written asking for more. Being engrossed in my record work at the time I was naturally delighted.

" 'Why don't you come down some time and record direct?' the gentleman said.

" 'I'd like to,' I answered.

" 'I dare you!' he said.

" 'All right—when?' I countered.

" 'This week?' he queried.

" 'Okay,' I said.

417

FROM RAGTIME TO SWINGTIME

"And so it was that one stormy night that week found me climbing up the steps of the World Tower Building in Fortieth Street near Broadway where de Forest's laboratory was then located. The room was quite small and inasmuch as there had been no previous need there was no piano. I am not an enthusiast of 'a cappella' singing, but in this case it was a necessity. So somewhat dubiously I made my way to the apparatus which consisted of a bell-shaped phonograph horn, with a curtain behind it hiding the 'works.' I was told to go ahead. It seemed so futile and had it not been for the fact that I was accustomed to this same type of recording horn for my disc records, I would have been less at ease. I am not practically gifted with a good memory, but I somehow remember my words on that occasion, due somewhat perhaps to my feeling of inadequacy because of there being no accompaniment. The words were 'Here goes nothing.'

"The response was so reassuring that we decided to do it again—'just for the fun of it.' So I planned that on my next attempt I would take some sort of accompanying instrument along. I persuaded the late Mario Perry, then accordionist with Paul Whiteman's Orchestra to come along. Our third visit was slightly more formal in that we began to assemble the fundamentals of a program form and took several assisting artists with us. Perry, however, still accompanied on the accordion.

"Inasmuch as mine were the first formed programs it still seems that in spite of any questioning I can justly claim the title of 'The Original Radio Girl.' Occasionally there pops up some skeptic who says this one or that one preceded me. To such I quote from Georgette Carneal's *Conqueror of the Air* (Biography of Dr. Lee de Forest), beginning with the eighteenth line on page 273:

"'Shortly after this ban lifted in 1919, de Forest removed the transmitter from Highbridge plant to the World Tower Building, where he worked on an even more elaborate scale than ever before. There, for the first time, regular entertainment was broadcast. Vaughn De Leath, a well known singer, was the first "Radio Girl." She sang and talked over this station in December, 1919, and has a wealth of fan letters recounting the pleasure in receiving her voice.'

"However, I always specify that I was the first American woman to broadcast for I understand that Marconi made an experiment with an Italian opera singer more than twenty years ahead of me. One thing is certain—from then on I devoted much of my time to radio broadcasting and also years to this form of entertainment without any compensation whatsoever. I believe I have given more continuous service to radio from its inception than any other artist. Such lengthy experience in a field

418

which has become so popular sometimes makes people think that I am much older than I am. But it started when I was in my teens and as radio is only eighteen years old, you can put eighteen and seventeen together and find out that I am not much over ninety.

"It is fun, I think, to quote from a letter dated January 5, 1920, as follows (I wonder if the writer knew just how much of a prophet he was when he wrote): 'I am glad to see that you have inaugurated the custom of giving entertainments over the radio. It is certainly a fine idea and will no doubt become very popular in the future.'"

9. Rudy Vallee

Although Rudy Vallee was born in Island Pond, Vermont, most of his childhood was spent in Westbrook, Maine. His real name is Hubert Prior Vallee; the nickname "Rudy" was given him at school because of his admiration for Rudy Wiedoeft, the saxophonist.

His mother, who died in 1931, was of Irish descent; his father's ancestors were French-Canadian. He has one sister, Kathleen, who is married and lives in Westbrook. She teaches piano, plays well, and has been on the air locally in Maine. His brother Bill is younger, and writes for magazines. Rudy went to the University of Maine one year, then to Yale, where he graduated in 1927 after an interruption of one year when he went to London and played an engagement with the Savoy Havana Band. During college years he played with Bolton-Cipriano and was leader of the Yale football band in his senior year. Before college years, he worked in his father's drugstore at Westbrook, then became an usher in the Strand Theatre in Poland, and played sax solos with the house band during intermission. His earliest public appearance as saxophonist was a local appearance at the Elks Club, accompanied by his sister.

He came to New York in the fall of 1927, played club dates under various band leaders, first big engagement (January, 1928) with the Heigh-Ho Club, run by Don Dickerman. Connecticut

Yankees formed for this engagement. Went on air the following month from the club, over WABC, announcing and directing his own program.

And the rest is history. For ten years he has been on the air, and his program has been the first chapter of a success story for many people in radio; among the more outstanding being: Alice Faye, Edgar Bergen, Frances Langford, Tommy Riggs, Bob Burns, Sheila Barrett, Stroud Twins, Frank Fay, Howard and Shelton, Joe Cook, Burns and Allen, Olsen and Johnson. Rudy is constantly on the watch for new talent, and few can equal him as a talent scout.

On July 30, 1936, Rudy Vallee introduced Isidore Witmark's new song, *Thanks a Lot*, over station WEAF with the following words:

"For years the name of Witmark has been synonymous with all that has been fine and great in music. The publication of Victor Herbert's immortal creations, the writings of Ernie Ball, Julian Edwards, Gustav Luders, Karl Hoschna, Sigmund Romberg, and many others—Witmarks' collection has been a veritable treasure chest of valuable music. Isidore Witmark, who is just finishing a history of this famous firm in his memoirs—*The House of Witmark, a Half Century of American Stage and Song*—a founder and former President of the company, celebrates its fiftieth anniversary this year by composing the song *Thanks a Lot* which he feels will express to you through us his debt of thanks and appreciation. The entire proceeds of any presentation or sales of copies of this song go to the Rotarian boys' camp on Fire Island, N. Y., which cares for over three hundred crippled boys each summer."

CHAPTER XXVI

WARNER BROTHERS BUY OUT THE
WITMARK BROTHERS

1. Tin Pan Alley Becomes Hollywood Boulevard

THE definite beginnings of the Hollywood influence over Broadway, which has now resulted in the virtual linking of Broadway and Hollywood across the continental distance that divides them, began in the late twenties with the commercialization of the talkies.

In 1924, the Warner Brothers had bought their first Broadway theatre (the Warner) from the late Lee Ochs. The year 1925 found Herman Heller as managing director, making a good job of putting this theater on the map of the entertainment world, ably assisted by George Morris, director of publicity. The stage was small and the array of artists limited. The theater was always half empty, excepting on the days when an outstanding picture was featured; that was far and in between.

S. L. Rothafel, better known as "Roxy," was deep in plans with Martha Wilchinski, his director of publicity, for the opening of the new theater that now bears his name. Half of his old colleagues were either with him or at the old camping grounds, the Capitol Theater, while the rest drifted elsewhere. Out of the vortex of events, Ottalie Mark, a youngster on Roxy's staff, emerged to a berth with Herman Heller. Experienced in preparing pictures

421

for cueing, because of her association with Roxy and Erno Rapee during the scoring of the silent pictures, she quickly won Mr. Heller's confidence.

Her first suggestion that the Warners install the broadcasting station offered for sale by Frank Mallen, then an editor of the *Evening Graphic,* was taken seriously, with the result that Mr. Heller built an attractive broadcasting studio in the lower lobby of the Warner Theater. It was from this studio that Frank Mallen arranged to have the world hear the first description of the first Vitaphone show ever staged publicly for profit. Minute details were given, and the music played by the Philharmonic Orchestra, which was synchronized to the feature picture, "Don Juan," was broadcast. The exciting cheers that almost drowned the recorded voice of Martinelli came from the first nighters over this new station, then called WBPI (Warner Brothers Pictures, Inc.).

It was during the development of this little theater and radio station that Major Levinson, one of Western Electric's officials, approached the late Sam Warner with a new invention, now "The Vitaphone." This was the interview that was to wipe the radio station out of the theater—make the organ and its organist go the way of all flesh, and empty a pit where heretofore musicians played for a salary of from $80 to $100 per week.

The new invention was shown to Mr. Heller, whose opinion was solicited and accepted. His interest manifested itself in the negotiations carried on between Harry Warner and Eugene Rich, Sr., representative of Western Electric. The new device became the new play toy for the Warner Brothers, who immediately laid plans for its development.

The old Vitagraph Studio in Brooklyn (owned by Warners) was used for ten months, for secret experimenting. Herman Heller was placed in charge of experimentation. The first talking short subject was made in this studio: "The Unexpected," owned by Tom Riley, whose actors and sketch were headlined on the Orpheum Circuit. It was during the recording of this short that the late Sam Warner, assuming that the invention was created for the synchronization of music only, reprimanded Mr. Heller for wasting time on recording the human voice. The amazing result of this "reprehensible" act was enough to show the Warners that they were on the threshold of a new era indeed, one that held endless opportunities.

The first picture synchronized during this experimental stage was "The Sea Beast," a Warner feature starring John Barrymore and Dolores Costello. The score, compiled and conducted by Herman Heller, was played by an orchestra of sixty-five musicians. Among the shorts later made at the same studio during this experimental stage were: Gambarelli and Stanbury; De Vanny and Lang in a sketch from "Maytime"; "The Volga Boatman"; Sydney Jarvis in "The Bride Tamer."

In 1926, the old Manhattan Opera House, 34th Street, West of Eighth Avenue, in New York, was leased. The days of the first experiments were over. Serious work began. The seats were ripped out, sound stages installed, recording equipment brought in and a complete organization formed, consisting of cameramen, engineers, artists, property men, stage hands, etc. The first speech introducing Vitaphone to the world was made by Will H. Hays.

"Don Juan," starring Barrymore and Costello, was the second picture synchronized for release to the public. Herman Heller engaged Major Bowes, Dr. William Axt, and David Mendoza to compile the score. The Philharmonic Orchestra was engaged, and Heller conducted the first synchronization to be released throughout the world. It was in this score that use of copyrighted music owned by Robbins Music Company was made. The result was the first law suit instituted against Vitaphone for infringement.

The phrase "By special permission of the Copyright Owner" took on great significance. Ottalie Mark, well schooled and expert in the use of copyrights from her previous work on silent picture scoring and radio, became a valuable aid in controlling the havoc raised by the international copyright questions that loomed up.

She was immediately brought over to the Manhattan Opera House and placed in charge of the music library and copyright department.

The next picture to be recorded was the comedy, "The Better 'Ole," featuring Sydney Chaplin, brother of Charlie. Original music was composed by Herman Heller, assisted by Fred Hoff, on account of trouble caused by certain publishers and "the Society" —meaning ASCAP. The Philharmonic Orchestra was used and Heller conducted. Another picture to be synchronized was "When a Man Loves," starring Barrymore and Costello, original music by Dr. Henry Hadley. Again the Philharmonic Orchestra of one hundred and nine men was used and Heller conducted. This was the first original score ever written for a drama in the talkies. The recording and beauty of Dr. Hadley's score were instrumental in putting music synchronization on a permanent basis. The score has never been surpassed.

Erno Rapee, present musical director of the Radio City Music Hall, was then engaged to compile a routine picture that was scheduled to be synchronized. Following him came Dr. Hugo Riesenfeld, who scored and conducted one of the many pictures released by the Warners.

About the same time was started the recording of the famous Metropolitan stars, whose music became an international problem. Martinelli, the first opera star to be recorded, sang *Vesti la giubba* from "Pagliacci," and *Celeste Aïda* from "Aïda," with the accompaniment of the entire Philharmonic Orchestra under the direction of Herman Heller. The Warners signed an exclusive agreement between the Metropolitan and themselves for the use of "Met's" artists and names. The following are some of the stars recorded: Martinelli in "Pagliacci," "Aïda," "La Juive," and "Carmen"; Martinelli and D'Angelo in the Duet from "La Juive"; Gigli in "Cavalleria Rusticana" and *Cielo e mar* from "Gioconda"; Gigli, De Luca, Talley and Gordon in the quartette from "Rigoletto"; De Luca in "The Barber of Seville"; John Charles

Thomas in the Prologue from "Pagliacci"; Thomas and Vivienne Segal in "Blossom Time"; Charles Hackett and Mary Lewis in a number of short acts; Schumann-Heink in a group of songs; Rosa Raisa, and Rimini. Anna Case was used in the first elaborate short, and also the Cansinos, famous dancers, the original Marimba Orchestra, and the Metropolitan chorus, accompanied by the Philharmonic Orchestra, all under the direction of Herman Heller.

Among the famous instrumentalists recorded were Mischa Elman, Efrem Zimbalist, Alfred Spalding, Harold Bauer, and the Flonzaley Quartet.

The following are some of the well-known vaudeville artists recorded: Al Jolson, George Jessel, Joe E. Brown, Leo Carillo, Sissle and Blake, Van and Schenck, Blossom Seeley and Benny Fields, The Aristocrats, Whispering Smith, John Barclay, Roger Wolf Kahn and his orchestra, Fred Waring and his orchestra, Vincent Lopez and his orchestra, The Yacht Club Boys, Elsie Janis, The Revelers, with Frank Black at the piano, Mickey McKee (whistler), and others.

A concert orchestra of sixty-five men organized and conducted by Herman Heller was photographed and recorded in some twenty-five popular overtures such as *Mignon, Poet and Peasant, Morning, Noon and Night,* and *Light Cavalry.*

An orchestral number, *Tannhäuser Overture,* was photographed and conducted by Dr. Henry Hadley and played by the Philharmonic Orchestra of New York.

On June 22, 1927, the studio at the Manhattan Opera House was closed and on August 3 the dismantling took place. The equipment was sent to Hollywood, the reason being Union difficulties within the Union itself, lack of space, and better facilities in Hollywood. Mr. Heller went on to California to take charge of the new developments.

For years the moguls of the moving picture industry were getting high blood pressure from fighting and paying for lawsuits by writers and copyright owners forced on them through their performing, often innocently, musical numbers without permission of copyright owners, or, as happened almost as often, paying impostors for such rights.

The Warners, realizing that with the advent of the talkies much more music would be used, and that they would constantly have to be arranging for music rights, made a contract with the ASCAP whereby they were to pay them $125,000 annually, for which they had their choice of the works owned or controlled by all of the members of the society—*except the Witmarks*.

The Witmarks were entering into a separate arrangement with Warners. Everything was agreed upon and contracts were ready for signature when a radical change took place. The Electrical Research Products Inc., generally known as the ERPI, a subsidiary of the Western Electric Company, the principal manufacturers of theater talkie installations, took over the reproduction rights formerly controlled by the Warners so as to be able to distribute them to all moving picture companies that used their installation. It was important that these rights be open to all companies, so that the installation of the Western Electric equipment would be unlimited. Miss Mark, taken from Warner Brothers and made supervisor of music copyrights by ERPI under Donald S. Pratt, manager of the newly organized music rights department, was placed in entire charge of music used by all of the major producers. In 1929 she was sent to Hollywood by ERPI to straighten out and train the various contacts established for her in every major studio there.

In Hollywood, Miss Mark found every major studio plunged into music synchronization of pictures. Routine pictures were scheduled to be released and all were working at a furious pace. The inclusion of one prohibited composition was enough to start a damage suit and retard the release of a picture worth millions. The situation was chaotic.

The late Irving Thalberg welcomed Miss Mark, the ERPI representative, as he would one of his great stars. Harry Cohen, president of Columbia Pictures, and Sam Briskin, manager of the studio, were the first to make use of her services. Little by little, Miss Mark covered each studio. It took her almost a year before she straightened them out. During this time, Donald Pratt at the ERPI Home Office was helping the organization to establish copyright offices throughout the world. Slowly and patiently a filing system for the service of all these offices and studios was installed by Miss Mark, and the copyright history of hundreds of thousands of compositions was recorded on cards. Thus was set up the first and most complete music copyright files for synchronization purposes in the world.

During this time the Witmarks, who were members of the Society, became one of the firms represented by it, for then individual contracts such as the one contemplated with Warners were no longer to be in effect. Meanwhile, in anticipating an individual contract, the Witmarks had given Warners permission to do quite a number of their songs. Inasmuch as that contract was not executed, the Warners were at the mercy of the Witmarks, who could have asked any prices they wanted for those numbers. An amicable settlement was arrived at, contrary to Warners' experience with other publishers, who insisted upon and received high pay for numbers innocently used without permission.

Evidently the Warner Brothers were impressed by the Witmark Brothers, for, not long after this, Isidore received a telephone call from Harry Warner.

"Is this you, Witmark? At last we've gotten around to considering taking over a music publishing firm, and liking the way you do business, we are giving you the first opportunity. Come over and see us."

Isidore was agreeably surprised, thanked him, and said he would drop in on him in a couple of days.

For some time the individual song-publishing firms had realized that the business was gradually becoming what one might call radio-fied, and while the public would be getting as much

427

music as ever, if not more, it would be in a form detrimental to the sale of sheet music. This was also at the height of the boom (1928); mergers were the order of the day. The trend was to buy out or refinance progressive concerns, and this held good for the music field as well as every other. As a matter of fact, when the Witmarks got the offer from Warner Brothers, they were among the nine firms who were already holding conferences, under the guidance of E. C. Mills, then general manager of ASCAP, considering an offer from a group of bankers contemplating a great music merger.

On the day that Harry Warner called up Isidore, one of these conferences was scheduled. Inasmuch as they had the new Warner offer, they did not think it ethical to continue meeting with the other publishers for discussion of the project pending with the bankers. So he sent the following note to Mills:

Dear E. C.:
Will not be with you this afternoon.
Something just came up that makes it necessary for us to defer our attending the meetings. Can't say any more now. Will be down to see you tomorrow or next day and explain everything to your satisfaction.

I. W.

This note was sent to E. C. Mills on November 19, 1928. The message was read at the meeting that afternoon and caused consternation. Those present were puzzled and started guessing what the Witmarks might have up their sleeve; they feared, in case of Witmark withdrawal, that the merger might fall through. And so, indeed, it turned out, for which some of the firms have never forgiven them.

The next day they went to Warners and had a tentative understanding. Harry Warner greeted them with the speech, "I don't know a thing about your business, but I know you are honest and that is what attracted us to you." There was little dickering because they wanted the firm and Witmarks made them a reasonable proposition that was practically accepted. Witmarks agreed to turn over their entire publishing business and the Witmark Music Library with all its valuable properties, for which they were to receive a large sum in cash and were to be retained in their established positions for a number of years.

In accordance with Isidore's promise to Mills, he called on him a couple of days later and told him they were resigning from the merger group and were negotiating independently. Mills expressed his appreciation of their having informed him promptly when they had started dickering with someone else. He was naturally curious to know who the parties were, but Isidore did not tell. Everybody made guesses, nobody hitting the right firm. So well was the secret kept that it proved to be a complete surprise.

In due course the deal with Warners was closed, and M. Witmark & Sons moved into the most elaborate professional offices, at 1657 Broadway, that had ever been devoted to the business of song publishing. M. Witmark & Sons was now the property of the Warners. It had been the only popular-music firm that, through its entire existence of forty-five years, had never changed its original personnel. The self-same "Witmark boys" who had started the business in 1885 were still in charge when they sold out.

It was still a firm of brothers!

The House of Witmark was founded and built by a quintette of boys, all of them under age. The "M" of the legal name was Daddy Witmark, who was needed to give legality to the venture.

Confidentially, Daddy Witmark was never really a member of the firm. In fact, when interviewed, he would tell newspapermen, "I know nothing about the music business—that's how I get along so well with my boys!"

The real firm was composed of the "— & Sons."

2. Julius P. Witmark

Only death could break up the solidarity of the Witmark children. Adolph, last born, had been the first to go. He died on

July 15, 1926. As for Julie, it almost seemed as if his life had coincided with the life of the original M. Witmark & Sons, for, hardly had the ownership of the old firm passed into new hands when he followed his youngest brother. On June 14, 1929, his heart was stilled forever.

Less than a month before, on Saturday, May 25, he had made his first—and what proved to be his last—appearance before a microphone, at Station WJZ, of the National Broadcasting Company, having taken part in the annual memorial program dedicated to Victor Herbert. He sang, in honor of the Witmarks' devoted friend, *Ah, Sweet Mystery of Life*. It was his own memorial he was singing!

It was not only Julie Witmark singing at this memorial to good old Victor; it was the House of Witmark, whom he had helped to make and who had helped to make him. It was the Witmarks' pride that was singing, as well as their commemorative mourning. Nowhere else in the history of American music-publishing, and rarely in the history of music-publishing the world over, had there been such a fruitful, intimate association between composer and publisher. Together, the Witmarks and Herbert had fought for the rights of the composer and the author and the publisher; together they had marched from triumph to triumph on the stage and in the concert-hall.

The musical world was stunned by Julie's sudden death. Telegrams and letters poured in, forming a veritable anthology of sweetest memories. There were so many who had known him from the days when as a child he had opened carriage doors before the fashionable Fifth Avenue Theatre, and who had followed his career since the days, a year later, when he was the singing sensation at the self-same theater with the Thatcher, Primrose & West Minstrels.

For him the Charles Frohmans, the William Harrises, the Alf Haymans, the Charlie Dillinghams, would defer appointments, would lay aside important work, that they might listen to a new song as only Julie could sing it. Frohman, indeed, had been in the habit of sending for the youth just to hear the grateful tones of his voice.

Though Julie's condition, after the accident that had befallen him, kept him often at home, he had not been idle. He sat thinking up ideas that kept the rest of the firm on the jump. And never did his interest in new writers, new singers, new ideas, abate. He had a natural sympathy for the underdog. He never forgot that in his boyhood, after school, unknown to his parents, he had sold newspapers so that he might earn the money for a seat in the gallery of the local showhouses. He had known the thrill of returning home, on the day of the assassination of President Garfield, with pockets bulging with coins made by selling extras. There was nothing "high-hat" about Julie. His employees loved him because they felt all this not in mere words, but in every action of the man. Julie lived his creed.

From Mayor James J. Walker, from Chauncey Olcott, from Raymond Hitchcock, ill in St. Luke's Hospital in Chicago; from the old minstrel team of McIntyre and Heath; from David Warfield; from David Belasco—from far and wide—came expressions of sympathy sincere, simple, and unaffected, to bear witness to the great loss that the theater, the world of music, but above all, human friendship, had suffered.

To the old-timers Julie was still their child. Schumann-Heink called him, to the end, her son. Banks Winter, whom some will remember as the writer of that perennial favorite, *White Wings*, wrote to Isidore:

"As to the tie of friendship between dear Julie and myself, it was more like a father's and son's love for each other, and never will I forget our last meeting in his office, when we sang *White Wings* as a duet, and wound up with our arms around each other's necks, weeping. . . . And may I add, if that boy is not in Heaven, then—let me go where he is, and doubtless I'll meet Ernie Ball with him."

In far-off California, Caro Roma, who had been with the Witmark boys from the very first day, conducted over Station KFWI on July 6, 1929, during the twilight hour from 6 to 7, a memorial program for her old-time friend. Caro Roma too had remained virtually one of the Witmark family.

"I shall always write to you," she had once told Isidore, "and have you answer me—for my life has been bound up with M. Witmark & Sons for half a century. I'm 65 myself and I may not be here much longer. I shall die in your harness, old Dear." Daddy, "Queen," and Adolph had gone on before her. So for that matter had the firm. And now—Julie.

"You boys," she wrote another time, "are very dear to me. I look back now and hear again what Daddy Witmark told me when I was there first. He said, 'Roma, my boys are the dearest things I have in life. Never leave them.' It all comes back so sweetly. You have all done big things and I have appreciated the fact that I have shared some little in your success. Let it go on until the closing of the chapter."

Roma's chapter has just closed. It ended exactly as she had wished.

* * *

As Julie's epitaph, we may choose the words of E. C. Mills, from the notice addressed to the members of the Music Publishers' Protective Association on the day of Julie's death:

"At the moment of writing this I am so shocked as to be unable to do more than make the simple announcement.

"Those who loved Julie, and their name is legion, must remember and find consolation in his own motto in which he had complete belief, and to which he had recourse whenever he was troubled—*Everything happens for the best.*

"It is hard to believe, just now, that Julie was right, yet I think his spirit would echo the sentiment which governed his life."

432

Julie

Miss Christine Roy as a young
teacher in P. S. 28, when she
presented the printing press to
Jay.

Miss Roy today

In Jay's home is a tiny printing press. The ink has long since evap-
orated from its roller. It will print no more. It is the toy that built an
international house and an international reputation.

APPENDIX

APPENDIX

THE VICTOR HERBERT OPERETTAS
Published by M. Witmark and Sons

"The Fortune Teller"—1898

Book by Harry B. Smith. Produced by the Alice Nielsen Opera Company, starring Alice Nielsen.

"The Singing Girl"—1899

Book by Stanislaus Stange. Lyrics by Harry B. Smith. Produced by the Alice Nielsen Opera Company, starring Alice Nielsen.

"Cyrano De Bergerac"—1899

Book and lyrics by H. B. Smith. Produced by the Francis Wilson Opera Company, featuring Francis Wilson and Lulu Glaser.

"The Ameer"—1899

Book and lyrics by Kirke LaShelle and Frederick Rankin. Produced by the Frank Daniels Opera Company, starring Frank Daniels.

"The Viceroy"—1900

Book and lyrics by H. B. Smith. Produced by the Bostonians, featuring Barnabee and MacDonald.

"Babes In Toyland"—1903

Book and lyrics by Glen MacDonough. Produced by Hamlin & Mitchell, featuring Wm. Norris and Mabel Barrison.

"Babette"—1903

Book and lyrics by H. B. Smith. Produced by the Charles Dillingham Opera Company, starring Fritzi Scheff.

"It Happened In Nordland"—1904

Book and lyrics by Glen MacDonough. Produced by Lew Fields Musical Comedy Company, featuring Marie Cahill.

"Mlle. Modiste"—1905

Book and lyrics by Henry Blossom. Produced by the Fritzi Scheff Opera Company, starring Fritzi Scheff.

"Wonderland"—1905

Book and lyrics by Glen MacDonough. Produced by Hamlin, Mitchell & McKee, starring Sam Chip and Eva Davenport.

"Dolly Dollars"—1905

Book and lyrics by H. B. Smith. Produced by Chas. Dillingham, starring Lulu Glaser.

"The Red Mill"—1906

Book and lyrics by Henry Blossom. Produced by Chas. Dillingham, starring David Montgomery and Fred A. Stone.

"The Tattooed Man"—1907

Book by H. B. Smith and A. N. C. Fowler. Lyrics by H. B. Smith. Produced by Charles Dillingham, starring Frank Daniels.

"Prima Donna"—1908

Book and lyrics by Henry Blossom. Produced by Chas. Dillingham, starring Fritzi Scheff.

435

FROM RAGTIME TO SWINGTIME

"Old Dutch"—1909

Book by Edgar Smith. Lyrics by George V. Hobart. Produced by the Lew Fields Musical Comedy Company, starring Lew Fields.

"Sweet Sixteen"—1910

Book and lyrics by Geo. Hobart. Produced by Everole-Wallach Co.

"Naughty Marietta"—1910

Book and lyrics by Rida Johnson Young. Produced by Oscar Hammerstein, starring Emma Trentini.

"The Duchess"—1911

Book and lyrics by Joseph Herbert and H. B. Smith. Produced by Sam S. and Lee Shubert. Previously produced under title of "Mlle. Rosita," starring Fritzi Scheff.

"The Enchantress"—1911

Book and lyrics by Fred de Gresac and H. B. Smith. Produced by Joseph M. Gaites, starring Kitty Gordon.

"Lady Of The Slipper"—1912

Book and lyrics by Anna Caldwell. Produced by Chas. Dillingham, starring Montgomery and Stone.

"The Only Girl"—1914

Book and lyrics by Henry Blossom. Produced by Joe Weber, featuring Wilda Bennett.

"Princess Pat"—1915

Book and lyrics by Henry Blossom. Produced by John Cort, starring Eleanor Painter.

"Eileen"—1917

Book and lyrics by Henry Blossom. Produced by Joe Weber.

"The Velvet Lady"—1919

Book and lyrics by Henry Blossom. Produced by Klaw and Erlanger.

THE JULIAN EDWARDS OPERETTAS

"The Jolly Musketeers"—1898

Book and lyrics by Stanislaus Stange. Produced by Jefferson de Angelis Opera Company, starring Jefferson de Angelis.

"Princess Chic"—1900

Book and lyrics by Kirk LaShelle. Produced by Kirk LaShelle, featuring Marguerite Sylva.

"Gringoire the Street Singer"—1901

Book and lyrics by Willard Holcomb, featuring Homer Lind.

"Dolly Varden"—1901

Book and lyrics by Stanislaus Stange. Produced by Lulu Glaser Opera Company, starring Lulu Glaser.

"When Johnny Comes Marching Home" —1902

Book and lyrics by Stanislaus Stange. Produced by Whitney Opera Company, featuring William G. Stewart.

"Love's Lottery"—1904

Book and lyrics by Stanislaus Stange.

Produced by Whitney Opera Company, starring Mme. Schumann-Heink.

"Belle Of London Town"—1906

Book and lyrics by Stanislaus Stange. Produced by Sam S. and Lee Shubert, starring Lulu Glaser.

"The Girl And The Governor"—1906

Book and lyrics by S. N. Brenner. Produced by Jefferson de Angelis Opera Company, starring Jefferson de Angelis.

"His Honor The Mayor"—1906

Book and lyrics by Campbell and Skinner. Produced by Alfred E. Aarons, featuring Harry Kelly.

"The Patriot"—1907

Book and lyrics by Stanislaus Stange. Tragic opera in one act.

"The Gay Musician"—1908

Book and lyrics by Edward Siedle and Charles J. Campbell. Produced by the Amusement Producing Company, starring Walter Percival.

APPENDIX

"Miss Molly May"—1909

Book and lyrics by Walter Browne. Produced by Alfred E. Aarons, featuring Grace La Rue.

"The Motor Girl"—1910

Book and lyrics by Charles Campbell and Ralph Skinner. Produced by Frank Hennessy, featuring Georgia Caine.

THE GUSTAV LUDERS OPERETTAS

"The Burgomaster"—1900

Book and lyrics by Frank Pixley. Produced by Dearborn Opera Company, featuring Henry E. Dixey.

"King Dodo"—1901

Book and lyrics by Frank Pixley. Produced by John Cort, starring Raymond Hitchcock.

"Prince Of Pilsen"—1902

Book and lyrics by Frank Pixley. Produced by Henry W. Savage, featuring John W. Ransone.

"Mam'selle Napoleon"—1903

Book and lyrics by Joseph Herbert. Produced by Florenz Ziegfeld, starring Anna Held.

"The Sho Gun"—1904

Book and lyrics by George Ade. Produced by Henry W. Savage, featuring Chris Bruno, Edward Martindale, Trixie Friganza.

"Woodland"—1904

Book and lyrics by Frank Pixley. Produced by Henry W. Savage, featuring Doré Davidson, Franklyn Wallace, Ida Brooks Hunt.

"The Grand Mogul"—1906

Book and lyrics by Frank Pixley. Produced by Klaw and Erlanger, featuring Frank Moulan.

"The Fair Co-ed"—1908

Book and lyrics by George Ade. Produced by Charles Dillingham, starring Elsie Janis.

"Marcelle"—1908

Book and lyrics by Frank Pixley. Produced by Sam S. and Lee Shubert, starring Louise Gunning.

"The Old Town"—1909

Book and lyrics by George Ade. Produced by Charles B. Dillingham, starring Montgomery and Stone.

"The Gypsy"—1912

Book and lyrics by Frank Pixley. Produced by John Cort, Featuring John Hazzard, Anna Wilke, Eleanor Kent.

"Somewhere Else"—1912

Book and lyrics by Avery Hopwood. Produced by Henry W. Savage, featuring Taylor Holmes.

THE KARL HOSCHNA OPERETTAS

"Belle Of The West"—1905

Book and lyrics by Harry B. Smith. Produced by the Florence Bindley Company, starring Florence Bindley.

"Girl From Broadway"—1906

Book and lyrics by Chas. Noel Douglas. Produced by Aubrey Mittenthal, starring Grace Edmond.

"Prince Humbug"—1908

Book and lyrics by Mark Swan. Produced by Samuel E. Rork, starring Frank Lalor.

"Three Twins"—1908

Book by Charles Dickson. Lyrics by Otto Hauerbach. Produced by Joseph M. Gaites, featuring Clifton Crawford and Bessie McCoy.

"Bright Eyes"—1909

Book by Charles Dickson. Lyrics by Otto Hauerbach. Produced by Joseph M. Gaites, starring Cecil Lean and Florence Holbrook.

"Fascinating Widow"—1910

Book and lyrics by Otto Hauerbach. Produced by A. H. Woods, starring Julian Eltinge.

437

"Katie Did"—1910

Book and lyrics by W. C. Duncan. Produced by Joseph M. Gaites, featuring Florence May.

"Madame Sherry"—1910

Book and lyrics by Otto Hauerbach. Produced by Woods, Frazee & Lederer, starring Lina Abarbanell and Ralph C. Herz.

"The Girl Of My Dreams"—1910

Book by Wilbur B. Nesbit and Otto Hauerbach. Lyrics by Otto Hauerbach. Produced by Joseph M. Gaites, starring John Hyams and Leila McIntyre.

"Doctor De Luxe"—1911

Book and lyrics by Otto Hauerbach. Produced by Joseph M. Gaites, starring Ralph C. Herz.

"Jumping Jupiter"—1911

Book and lyrics by Richard Carle. Produced by Frazee and Lederer, starring Richard Carle.

"Wall Street Girl"—1911

Book by Margaret Mayo and Edgar Selwyn. Lyrics by Benjamin Hapgood Burt. Produced by Frederic McKay, starring Blanche Ring.

THE MANUEL KLEIN MUSICAL WORKS

"Mr. Pickwick"—1902

Book by Charles Klein. Lyrics by Grant Stewart. Produced by the De Wolf Hopper Opera Company, starring De Wolf Hopper.

"The Man From Now"—1905

Book and lyrics by John Kendrick Bangs. Produced by Henry W. Savage, starring Harry Bulger.

"Top O' The World"—1907

Book by Mark Swan. Lyrics by James O'Dea. Produced by Sam S. and Lee Shubert, starring Anna Laughlin.

"The Pied Piper"—1908

Book and lyrics by R. H. Burnside and Austin Strong. Produced by Shubert Theatrical Company, starring De Wolf Hopper.

"It's Up To You"—1920

Book and lyrics by Augustin McHugh, A. Douglas Leavitt, and Ed Paulton. Produced by William Moore Patch,

featuring Charles King and Betty Pierce.

THE HIPPODROME SERIES

"Society Circus"—1905

Book and lyrics by Manuel Klein. Produced at the New York Hippodrome.

"Neptune's Daughter"—1906

Book and lyrics by Manuel Klein. Produced at the New York Hippodrome.

"The Auto Race"—1907

Book and lyrics by Manuel Klein. Produced at the New York Hippodrome.

"The Battle Of The Skies"—1908

Book and lyrics by Manuel Klein. Produced at the New York Hippodrome.

"Sporting Days And Battle In The Skies" —1908

Book and lyrics by Manuel Klein. Produced at the New York Hippodrome.

MUSICAL WORKS OF A. BALDWIN SLOANE

"Broadway To Tokio"—1900

Book and lyrics by Louis Harrison and George Hobart. Produced by Greater New York Amusement Company, featuring Otis Harlan.

"Aunt Hannah"—1900

Book and lyrics by Clay M. Greene. Produced by Wm. A. Brady and Jos. R. Grismer, featuring May Irwin.

"Miss Printt"—1900

Book and lyrics by Jean C. Havez, Produced at the Victoria Theater, December 25th, featuring Marie Dressler.

"Tillie's Nightmare"—1919

Book by Edgar Smith. Lyrics by Alex Gerber. Produced by Dalton Enterprises Company, Inc., featuring Marie Dressler.

APPENDIX

"Greenwich Village Follies"—1919-20

Book and lyrics by Philip Bartholomae and John Murray Anderson. Produced by Bohemians, Inc., featuring James Watts, Bessie McCoy Davis, Warner Gault.

"China Rose"—1924

Book and lyrics by Harry Cort and George E. Stoddard. Produced by John Cort, featuring Harold Murray and Olga Steck.

THE SIGMUND ROMBERG OPERETTAS

"The Magic Melody"—1919

Book and lyrics by Frederick Arnold Kummer. Produced by Wilner and Romberg, featuring Charles Purcell.

"Poor Little Ritz Girl"—1920

Music by Sigmund Romberg and Richard Rodgers. Book by George Campbell and Lew Fields. Lyrics by Alex Gerber and Lorenz Hart. Produced by Lew Fields, featuring Charles Purcell.

"Love Birds"—1921

Book by Edgar Allan Wolff. Lyrics by Ballard MacDonald. Produced by Wilner and Romberg, featuring Pat Rooney.

"The Rose Of Stamboul"—1922

Book and lyrics by Harold Atteridge. Produced by Messrs. Shubert, featuring Tessa Kosta and Marion Green.

"The Blushing Bride"—1922

Book and lyrics by Cyrus Wood. Produced by the Messrs. Shubert, featuring Cecil Lean and Cleo Mayfield.

"The Lady In Ermine"—1922

Book by Frederick Lonsdale and Cyrus Wood. Lyrics by Harry Graham and Cyrus Wood. Produced by the Messrs. Shubert, featuring Wilda Bennett and Walter Wolf.

"Springtime Of Youth"—1922

From the work of Rudolf Bernauer and Rudolf Schauzer. Lyrics by Matthew C. Woodward and Cyrus Wood. Produced by the Messrs. Shubert, featuring George MacFarlane, Olga Steck and J. Harold Murray.

"Annie Dear"—1924

Book and lyrics by Clare Kummer. Produced by Florenz Ziegfeld, featuring Billie Burke.

"Marjorie"—1924

Book and lyrics by Fred Thompson and Clifford Grey. Produced by Rufus R. Lemaire and Richard W. Krakeur, featuring Skeets Gallagher, Elizabeth Hines, Roy Royston.

"Louie The Fourteenth"—1925

Book and lyrics by Arthur Wimperis. Produced by Florenz Ziegfeld, featuring Leon Errol.

"The Student Prince"—1925

Book and lyrics by Dorothy Donnelly. Produced by the Messrs. Shubert, featuring Howard Marsh.

"Princess Flavia"—1925

Book and lyrics by Harry B. Smith. Produced by Messrs. Shubert, featuring Evelyn Herbert and Harry Welchman.

"The Desert Song"—1926

Book and lyrics by Otto Harbach, Oscar Hammerstein II, and Frank Mandel. Produced by Schwab and Mandel, featuring Robert Halliday and Vivienne Segal.

"Cherry Blossoms"—1927 (also called "Yo San")

Book and lyrics by Harry B. Smith. Produced by Messrs. Shubert, featuring Desiree Ellinger and Howard Marsh.

"My Maryland"—1927

Book and lyrics by Dorothy Donnelly. Produced by Messrs. Shubert, featuring Evelyn Herbert and Nathaniel Wagner.

"Rosalie"—1928

Book by William Anthony McGuire and Guy Bolton. Lyrics by P. G. Wodehouse and Ira Gershwin. Produced by Florenz Ziegfeld, featuring Marilyn Miller and Jack Donahue.

FROM RAGTIME TO SWINGTIME

"New Moon"—1928
Book and lyrics by Frank Mandel. Produced by Schwab and Mandel, featuring Robert Halliday and Evelyn Herbert.

"Nina Rosa"—1930
Play by Otto Harbach. Lyrics by Irving Caesar. Produced by Messrs. Shubert, featuring Guy Robertson and Ethelind Terry.

"Viennese Nights" (moving picture)—1930
Book and lyrics by Oscar Hammerstein, II. Produced by Warner Brothers, featuring Vivienne Segal.

"East Wind"—1931
Book and lyrics by Oscar Hammerstein, II, and Frank Mandel. Produced by Schwab and Mandel, featuring Charlotte Lansing and J. Harold Murray.

THE ALFRED G. ROBYN OPERETTAS

"Yankee Consul"—1903
Book and lyrics by Henry M. Blossom. Produced by Henry W. Savage, featuring Raymond Hitchcock.

"Princess Beggar"—1906
Book and lyrics by Edward Paulton.

Produced by Sam and Lee Shubert, featuring Paula Edwards.

"Yankee Tourist"—1907
Book and lyrics by Wallace Irwin. Produced by Henry W. Savage, featuring Raymond Hitchcock.

THE GEORGE M. COHAN MUSICAL WORKS

"Little Nellie Kelly"—1922
Book and lyrics by George M. Cohan. Produced by Geo. M. Cohan, featuring Elizabeth Hines and Charles King.

"The Rise Of Rosie O'Reilly"—1923
Book and lyrics by George M. Cohan. Produced by Geo. M. Cohan, featuring Jack McGowan and Virginia O'Brien.

"The Merry Malones"—1927
Book and lyrics by George M. Cohan. Produced by Geo. M. Cohan, featuring Polly Walker, Geo. M. Cohan, Alan Edwards.

"Billie"—1928
Book and lyrics by George M. Cohan. Produced by the Geo. M. Cohan's Comedians, featuring Polly Walker.

THE LOUIS A. HIRSCH MUSICAL WORKS

"My Home Town Girl"—1916
Book and lyrics by Frank Stammers. Produced by Perry J. Kelly, Inc., starring John Hyams and Leila McIntyre.

"Going Up"—1917
Book by Otto Harbach and James Montgomery. Lyrics by Otto Harbach, starring Frank Craven.

"The Grass Widow"—1917
Book and lyrics by Channing Pollock and Rennold Wolf. Produced by Madison Corey, featuring George Marion, Robert Emmett Keane, Natalie Alt, Howard Marsh.

"Rainbow Girl"—1918
Book and lyrics by Rennold Wolf. Produced by Klaw and Erlanger, featuring Billy Van and Beth Lydy.

THE CHAUNCEY OLCOTT MUSICAL PRODUCTIONS

"Minstrel Of Clare"
Book by Augustus Pitou, 1896.

"Sweet Inniscarra"
Book by Augustus Pitou, 1897.

"Romance Of Athlone"
Book by Augustus Pitou, 1899.

"Garrett O'Magh"
Book by Augustus Pitou, 1901.

"Old Limerick Town"
Book by Augustus Pitou, 1902.

"Edmund Burke"
Book by Theodore Burt Sayre, 1905.

APPENDIX

"Eileen Asthore"
Book by Theodore Burt Sayre, 1906.

"O'Neill Of Derry"
Book by Theodore Burt Sayre, 1907.

"Ragged Robin"
Book by Augustus Pitou, 1908.

"Barry Of Ballymore"
Book by Rida Johnson Young, 1911.

"Isle Of Dreams"
Book by Rida Johnson Young, 1912.

"Shameen Dhu"
Book by Rida Johnson Young, 1913.

"Terence"
Book by Mrs. Edmund Nash Morgan, 1914.

MUSICAL NUMBERS BY ISIDORE WITMARK

VOCAL

1885—*A Mother's A Mother After All* (Willis Woodward & Co., Publishers).
1885—*Cottage 'Neath the Cliff* (Willis Woodward & Co., Publishers).
1886—*I'll Answer That Question Tomorrow.*
1886—*The Village Choir.*
1886—*The Ship's the Home for Me.*
1886—*Breathe Those Tender Words Again.*
1886—*King of the Swells.*
1886—*Mike Nolan, His Mule and His Cart.*
1886—*Little Mischief, You.*
1887—*Too Whoo (Whistle) You Know* (Words by M. J. Cavanagh).
1887—*Sweet Autumn Flowers.*
1888—*Doncher Know?* (Words by Harry W. Emmett).
1888—*'Tis the Sweetest Song of All* (Words by M. J. Cavanagh).
1888—*Goodnight Baby Darling.*
1888—*Since Reilly Took an Oath He'd Take My Life* (Words by Cavanagh).
1889—*Jack Won't Forget You* (Words by M. J. Cavanagh).
1889—*The Vivandiere* (not published).
1889—*My Sambo* (from "The Chaperons").
1889—*Lullaby* (From "Austerlitz") (Not published).
1890—*He Was A Pal of Mine* (Words by M. J. Cavanagh).
1890—*Just Think of Your Mother* (Words by Fred B. Hawkins).
1890—*My Sweetheart True* (Yodel).
1890—*The Broom Song* (Words by Fred B. Hawkins) (From "The Broom-Maker of Carlsbad").
1890—*I Spy You* (Words by Fred B. Hawkins) (From "The Broom-Maker of Carlsbad").
1891—*Dead Onto Me* (Words by Wm. Jerome).
1891—*Take Your Time, Gentlemen* (Words by Wm. Jerome).
1891—*A Letter To His Dad* (Words by Wm. Collier).
1891—*Everyone Knows O'Reilly Flush But Nobody Knows Him Broke.*
1892—*What Will Tomorrow Bring?* (Words by Wm. D. Hall).
1894—*The Man Who Plays The Umpah* (Words by Webster C. Fulton).
1898—*I Won't Do A Thing To Him.*
1901—*We're All Good Fellows*
1901—*It Seems Like Yesterday*
1901—*The Little Maid Who Couldn't Say No*
1901—*When I Sang My Low C*
1901—*In My Official Capacity* 　　(From "The Chaperons")
1901—*Somehow It Made Him Think of Home* 　(Words by Frederick Rankin).
1901—*Love In A Palace Is Better*
1901—*Millinery Mary*
1901—*Noah's Ark*
1936—*I Said A Little Prayer For You* (not published).

1936—*Thanks A Lot* (Published by Shapiro, Bernstein & Co.).
1936—*Counting The Hours* (not published).
1936—*That's Why I'm Sold on You* (not published).

Love's Lullaby (Words by Frederick Rankin).
In Shanghai (Words by William Cary Duncan).
Just For You (Words by Charles Noel Douglas).
Nobody Know (Words by William Cary Duncan).
I'm in Love With All the World (Words by
  William Cary Duncan).
Here's to Your Health in Tea (Words by Harry
  B. Smith).
Oh You Love (Words by William Cary Duncan).
Chinese Sailor Man (Words by Willard Holcomb).
Game of Love (Words by Harry B. Smith).
You Stick to Me, Dear, and I'll Stick to You
  (Words by William Cary Duncan).
Let's Go! (Duet) (Words by Thomas Grant
  Springer).

} (From "The Pearl of Shanghai"
—1918-1937.)

INSTRUMENTAL

1886—*President Cleveland's Wedding March.*
1886—*Glide Excentrique.*
1888—*Only A Butcher* (Waltz).
1894—*Parisian Patrol*
1896—*Lucinda's Serenade.*

MUSICAL WORKS, BOOKS AND PLAYS WHICH ISIDORE WITMARK HAS WRITTEN OR COLLABORATED IN

PROFESSIONAL AND AMATEUR MUSICAL PRODUCTIONS

"Miss Columbia"
"Madame Pompom"
"By The Sea"
"The Isle Of Palms"
"The Borough Of Manhattan"
"At Home And Abroad"
"The Chaperons"
"The Pearl Of Shanghai"
"Mabel"
"Home, James"
"Take It From Me"
"It's Up To You"
"Three Twins"
"Girl Of My Dreams"
"Sweet William"
"The Flying Honeymoon"
"Love Pirate"
"Llassa"

PLAYS

The Broom-Maker of Carlsbad—with F.
  B. Hawkins.
Getting By—with Thos. Grant Springer.
Our Wives—with Frank Mandel.

PUBLISHED BOOKS

Yama Yama Land, with Grace Duffie
  Boylan.
Minstrel Encyclopedia, with Frank Du-
  mont.

NOVELTY PRODUCTION

"The Evolution Of Minstrelsy"

CATALOGS ABSORBED BY M. WITMARK & SONS

During its career the firm absorbed ten other publishing houses. Almost at the beginning, in 1886, it had acquired the publications of the New York Variety Publishing Company of 117 Park Row; this transaction had given them the title to a

APPENDIX

couple of outstanding hits, *As I Sat Upon My Dear Old Mother's Knee,* by Cavanagh and Skelly, and *Bring Back My Fisher Boy,* by Cavanagh. A few years later, they became the proprietors of the Dobson Banjo Music catalog. In 1892, with the acquisition of the Propheter catalog, the Witmarks became the sponsors for a number of important composers, among them that pioneer Negro writer, Gussie L. Davis. Davis's big ballad hit, at the time of the transfer, was *Baby's Laughing In Her Sleep;* it was being sung by every minstrel show in the business. Other Davis sellers were *When The Cuckoo Goes To Sleep, She Haunts Me In My Dreams, Don't Hide Your Sweet Face From Me, Up Dar In De Sky,* and the two smash hits, *The Lighthouse By The Sea* and *In The Baggage Coach Ahead.*

The Witmarks now took over the publications of Dave Marion. Dave had a flair for melodies in the ballad style; he did not write much, but what he wrote had managed to survive into our own highly sophisticated era. *Her Eyes Don't Shine Like Diamonds* had been written by him in 1894 for Julie, and was introduced with huge success. There was also *You Gave Me Your Love.* But Marion's great achievement—and it was just that, in its own sphere—was the ballad, *Only One Girl In The World For Me.*

The Fred J. Hamill Company catalog with its many western successes came next, followed by the B. D. Nice catalog of popular New York hits. Then came the celebrated Weber & Fields catalog, containing all the song hits of that great house of travesty, including *Dinah, Come Down, My Evening Star, Say You Love Me, Sue,* etc. The eighth catalog to be taken over was the Rogers Brothers', with all the song hits of the Rogers Brothers' productions, composed by Maurice Levi.

Then followed the Gus Edwards publications, including *Goodbye, Little Girl, Goodbye, Tammany, He's My Pal,* and *In My Merry Oldsmobile.* In 1907 the Sol Bloom catalog was bought, which contained, among others, Hutchison's *Sammy* and Arthur Penn's *Carrissima.*

THE ARTHUR A. PENN OPERETTAS, ETC.

(For Amateurs)

"Captain Crossbones"
A comic operetta in two acts.

"The China Shop"
A Chinese operetta in two acts.

"Cindy"
A fantastic modern fairy operetta in two acts.

"The Lass Of Limerick Town"
A romantic operetta in two acts.

"Mam-zelle Taps" or "The Silver Bugler"
A military operetta, prologue and two acts.

"The Swami Of Bagdad"
A musical comedy in two acts.

"Yokohama Maid"
A Japanese comic operetta in two acts.

"Maid Of The Mill"
A rural operetta in one act.

"The Bargain Hunters"
A musical satire in one act.

"The Last Rehearsal"
A musical extravaganza in one act.

"The Middie Maids"
A musical extravaganza in one act.

"The Flowers That Bloom In The Spring"
An operetta for females in one act.

"The Ladies' Aid"
A musical satire for female characters only in one act.

"The Vagabonds"
A romantic comic opera in one act.

"The Dream Boat"
An operetta for grade children in two scenes.

"A Song Of Sixpence"
A semi-humorous operetta in one act.

"Tommy Murphy's Christmas"
An operetta in one act.

"Striking Matches"
A humorous musical sketch.

FROM RAGTIME TO SWINGTIME

OPERATIC AND MUSICAL COMEDY PRODUCTIONS
PUBLISHED BY M. WITMARK & SONS

MISCELLANEOUS LIST

AARONS, ALFRED E.

"Mam'selle 'Awkins"
Book and lyrics by Richard Carle, 1900.

"My Antoinette"
Book and lyrics by Richard Carle, 1901.

"The Knickerbocker Girl"
Book and lyrics by George Totten Smith, 1903.

"A China Doll"
Book and lyrics by H. B. and R. B. Smith, 1904.

ANDERSON, WILL R.

"Take It From Me"
Book and lyrics by Will B. Johnstone, 1918.

AURACHER, HARRY (Harry Archer)

"Pearl Maiden"
Book and lyrics by Earle C. Anthony and Arthur F. Kales, 1911.

BERTON, CHARLES

"Moon Maiden"
Book and lyrics by Geo. E. Stoddard, 1913.

BLAKE, EUBIE

"Shuffle Along"
Words and music by Noble Sissle and Eubie Blake, 1921-2.

"Elsie"
Book by Charles W. Bell. Lyrics by Noble Sissle, Eubie Blake, Monte Carlo, Alma Sanders, 1923.

BOWERS, ROBERT HOOD

"Rubes and Roses"
Book and lyrics by Raymond W. Peck, 1901.

"The Maid And The Mummy"
Book and lyrics by Richard Carle, 1904.

BRADY, WILLIAM S.

"Queen of Laughter"
Lyrics by Ysabel DeWitte Kaplan, 1904.

BRAHAM, GEORGE

"Under Cover"
Words by Edward Harrigan, 1903.

BRATTON, JOHN W.

"Buster Brown"
Founded on the cartoon by R. F. Outcault. Book by George Newman, 1900.

"Hodge, Podge & Company"
Book and lyrics by Walter H. Ford, 1900.

"The Man From China"
Book and lyrics by Paul West, 1904.

"Star and Garter"
Book and lyrics by Walter Ford, 1900.

"The Pearl and the Pumpkin"
Book and lyrics by Paul West, 1905.

"The Newlyweds and Their Baby"
Book and lyrics by Brown and Ayer, 1908.

BRUGUIERE, EMILE

"Baroness Fiddle-Sticks"
Book and lyrics by George De Long, 1904.

CARLE, RICHARD

"Mary's Lamb"
Book and lyrics by Richard Carle, 1908.

CARROLL, EARL

"So Long Letty"
Book by Oliver Morosco and Elmer Harris. Lyrics by Earl Carroll, 1915.

"Canary Cottage"
Book and lyrics by Elmer Harris and Earl Carroll.

CHAPIN, FREDERIC

"The Forbidden Land"
Book and lyrics by Guy F. Steely, 1904.

"The Woggle Bug"
Book and lyrics by L. Frank Baum, 1905.

"The Storks"
Book and lyrics by Guy F. Steely, 1906.

COOK, WILL MARION

"Clorindy," or "The Origin of the Cake Walk"
Lyrics by Paul Laurence Dunbar, 1898.

CRAWFORD, CLIFTON, and AUGUSTUS BARRETT

"My Best Girl"
Book and lyrics by Channing Pollock and Rennold Wolf, 1912.

DE KOVEN, REGINALD

"Yesterday"
Book and lyrics by Glen MacDonough, 1919.

APPENDIX

DELEON, WALKER
"The Campus"
  Book and lyrics by Walter Deleon,
  1912.

DILLEA, HERBERT
"The Merry Clown"
  Book and lyrics by Charles Baswitz.

FALL, LEO
"Girl in the Train"
  Adapted from "Die Geschiedene Frau"
  from the German of Victor Leon. Lyrics
  by Harry B. Smith, 1910.

FRANCIS, W. T.
"Whoop Dee Doo"
  Book and lyrics by Edgar Smith, 1902.
"The Rollicking Girl"
  Book and lyrics by Sidney Rosenfeld,
  1905.
"The Royal Rogue"
  Book and lyrics by Charles Klein and
  Grant Stewart, 1909.

FRANKLIN, MALVIN M.
"Dearie"
  Book by John P. Wilson. Lyrics by
  John P. Wilson and Malvin M. Frank-
  lin, 1920.

FURST, W. W.
"Isle of Champagne"
  Book and lyrics by Charles A. Byrne,
  1892.

GEBEST, CHARLES J.
"Red Widow"
  Book and lyrics by Channing Pollock
  and Rennold Wolf, 1911.

GIRARD, HARRY
"The Alaskan"
  Book and lyrics by Jos. Blethen, 1907.

GOETZ, RAY
"Hitchy Koo"
  Book and lyrics by Ray Goetz, 1917-18.

GOETZL, ANSELM
"Royal Vagabond"
  Book by Stephen Idor Szinnyey and
  Wm. Cary Duncan. Lyrics by Wm.
  Cary Duncan, 1919.
"Rose Girl"
  Book and lyrics by Wm. Cary Duncan,
  1921.

HAMBITZER, CHARLES J.
"The Love Wager"
  Book by Edith Ellis. Lyrics by Wm.
  Cary Duncan, 1912.
"A Regular Girl"
  Book and lyrics by Wm. Cary Duncan,
  1916.

HAMMERSTEIN, OSCAR
"Punch, Judy & Company"
  Book and lyrics by Oscar Hammerstein,
  1903.

HEARTZ, H. L.
"The Tenderfoot"
  Book and lyrics by Richard Carle, 1903.

HEIN, SILVIO
"Furs and Frills"
  Book and lyrics by Edward Clark, 1917.

HILLIAM, B. C.
"Buddies"
  Book by George V. Hobart, 1919.
"Princess Virtue"
  Words and music by B. C. Hilliam and
  Gitz Rice, 1920.

HOFFMAN, MAX
"Me, Him and I"
  Book and lyrics by Vincent Bryan,
  1904.
"The Parisian Model"
  Book and lyrics by H. B. Smith, 1906.

HUBBELL, RAYMOND
"Fantana"
  Book and lyrics by R. B. Smith, 1904.

JOHNSTONE, ALEXANDER
"Fiddlers Three"
  Book and lyrics by Wm. Cary Duncan,
  1918.
"Miss Princess"
  Book and lyrics by Will B. Johnstone,
  1912.

KERKER, GUSTAV
"The Billionaire"
  Book and lyrics by H. B. Smith, 1917.

LEAN, CECIL
"Military Girl"
  Book and lyrics by Cecil Lean, 1912.

LEVI, MAURICE
"Rogers Brothers in Wall Street"
  Book by John McNally. Lyrics by Rich-
  ard Carle, 1899.

"Rogers Brothers in Central Park"
Book by John McNally. Lyrics by D. C. Goodwin, 1900.
"Rogers Brothers in Washington"
Book by John McNally. Lyrics by H. B. Smith, 1901.
"Rogers Brothers in Harvard"
Book by John McNally. Lyrics by Ed Gardenier, 1902.
"Rogers Brothers in Panama"
Book by John McNally. Lyrics by Edward Maddern, 1907.
"The Soul Kiss"
Book and lyrics by H. B. Smith, 1908.

LEWIS, WALTER H.
"The Explorers"
Book and lyrics by Bert Leston Taylor, 1901.

LORAINE, WILLIAM
"A Trip to Buffalo"
Book and lyrics by Harry B. Marshall, 1901.
"Peggy From Paris"
Book and lyrics by George Ade, 1903.
"The Filibuster"
Book and lyrics by John P. Wilson, 1904.
"The Press Agent"
Book and lyrics by John P. Wilson and Mark Swan, 1905.

NEIDLINGER, W. H.
"Sweet Ann Page"
Book and lyrics by Louis Delange, 1901.

NORDEN, ALFRED MULLER
"The English Daisy"
Book and lyrics by Greenbank and Norden, 1903.
"The West Point Cadet"
Book and lyrics by M. Norden, 1904.

PETERS, WILLIAM FREDERICK
"The Mayor of Tokio"
Book and lyrics by Richard Carle, 1905.

ROLT, BERNARD
"Glittering Gloria"
Book and lyrics by Hugh Morton, 1904.

SCHROEDER, WILLIAM
"Lady Luxury"
Book and lyrics by Rida Johnson Young, 1915.

SEARELLE, LUSCOMBE
"Mispah"
Lyrics by Ella Wheeler Wilcox.

SOLOMON, FREDERIC
"King Kaliko"
Book and lyrics by Frank Dupree, 1892.
"Sleeping Beauty and the Beast"
Book and lyrics by J. C. Goodwin, 1901.
"Mr. Blue Beard"
Book and lyrics by J. C. Goodwin, 1903.

STROMBERG, JOHN
(Weber and Fields)
"Girl From Martin's"
Book and lyrics by Edgar Smith, 1899.
"Helter Skelter"
Book and lyrics by H. B. Smith, 1899.
"Hurly Burly"
Book and lyrics by H. B. Smith, 1899.
"Whirl-i-gig"
Book and lyrics by H. B. Smith, 1899.
"Arizona"
Book and lyrics by Edgar Smith, 1900.
"Barbara Fidgety"
Book and lyrics by H. B. Smith, 1900.
"Fiddle Dee Dee and Quo Vass Iss?"
Book and lyrics by Edgar Smith, 1900.
"Sapolio"
Book and lyrics by Edgar Smith, 1900.
"Captain Jinks"
Book and lyrics by Edgar Smith, 1901.
"Twirly Whirly"
Book and lyrics by Edgar and R. B. Smith, 1902.
"Hoity Toity"
Book and lyrics by Edgar Smith, 1905.

TIETJENS, PAUL
"The Wizard of Oz"
Book and lyrics by L. Frank Baum, 1902.

WATHALL, ALFRED G.
"The Sultan of Sulu"
Book and lyrics by George Ade, 1902.

WHITNEY, HOWARD
"Flo Flo"
Book and lyrics by Collin Davis, 1904.

WITMARK, FRANK M.
"The Lucky Stone"
Book and lyrics by Collin Davis, 1904.
"Anchored"
Book and lyrics by Collin Davis, 1907.

APPENDIX

WITMARK, ISIDORE
"The Chaperons"
Book and lyrics by Frederick Rankin, 1901.
"The Pearl of Shanghai" (London production)

Book by Isidore Witmark and Wm. Cary Duncan. Lyrics by W. C. Duncan, Harry B. Smith, Chas. N. Douglas, Thos. Grant Springer, 1918.

CHRONOLOGICAL LIST OF SONG SUCCESSES PUBLISHED BY M. WITMARK & SONS

1886

As I Sat Upon My Dear Old Mother's Knee—M. J. Cavanagh and J. P. Skelly.
Bring Back My Fisher Boy—M. J. Cavanagh.
I'll Answer That Question Tomorrow—I. Witmark.
Is Mother Thinking of Her Boy—George Cooper and J. P. Skelly.
Mike Nolan, His Mule and His Cart—Isidore Witmark.
The Village Choir—I. Witmark.

1887

Too Whoo! You Know—M. J. Cavanagh and I. Witmark.

1888

Doncherknow—Harry W. Emmett and I. Witmark.
Waiting! Waiting!! Waiting!!!—James McAvoy.

1889

Jack Won't Forget You—M. J. Cavanagh and I. Witmark.

1890

He Was A Pal Of Mine—M. J. Cavanagh and I. Witmark.
How to Make a Broom (from "The Broom-Maker of Carlsbad")—I. Witmark.
Irish Jubilee, The—Lawlor and Thornton.
Just Think of Your Mother—F. B. Hawkins and I. Witmark.
My Sweetheart True (yodel)—I. Witmark.

1891

Always Together—W. Andrew Mack.
Hey, Rube—Matthews and Bulger.
Letter to His Dad, A—William Collier and I. Witmark.
Mistakes Are Apt to Happen—James McAvoy.
Picture That Is Turned Toward the Wall, The—Charles Graham.
We Were Sweethearts, Nell and I—John T. Kelly.

You and I—Ramon Moore.
You Better Stay at Home, Lad—Charles Graham.

1892

Ah, Fly Sweet Bird (from "The Isle of Champagne")—W. W. Furst.
Baby's Laughing in Her Sleep—Gussie L. Davis.
He Didn't Split the Wood—William Jerome.
In May—Edward M. Stern.
Irene, Goodnight—Gussie L. Davis.
Peggy Cline—John T. Kelly and Maurice Levi.
Song of All Nations—(from "The Isle of Champagne")—Louis Harrison.
Up Dar in De Sky—Gussie L. Davis.
Wedding of the Lily and the Rose, The—Thomas Le Mack and W. Andrew Mack.
You Gave Me Your Love—Dave Marion and Minnie Bell.

1893

Around the Other Way—James McAvoy.
Back Among the Old Folks—Dave Reed, Jr., and J. W. Wheeler.
Christofo Columbo—Francis J. Bryant
Do, Do, My Huckleberry Do—John and Harry Dillon.
I Ain't A Goin' to Tell—W. C. Parker.
I Long to See the Girl I Left Behind—John T. Kelly.
Little Willie (He Knew a Thing or Two)—Hattie Marshall.
Miss Jones Came Back—Monroe and Mack.
Possum and Sweet Potatoes—Charles Scheffer.
Where the Chicken Got the Axe—Will H. Mayo and William Glenroy.
Your Necktie's Up Behind—E. Wilson Zimmerman.

1894

Airy, Fairy Lillian—Tony Raymond and Maurice Levi.

FROM RAGTIME TO SWINGTIME

Bells of Fate—Ford and Bratton.
Her Eyes Don't Shine Like Diamonds—Dave Marion.
Johnny, My Old Friend John—William Cortright.
Only Me—Ford and Bratton.
Old Stage Door, The—J. W. Bratton.
Our Court Ball—Albert Chevalier.
Poor Little Mary—Maurice Levi.
That Old First Love of Mine—Charles H. Greenfielder and Oscar J. Hockstader.
Tied to Mother's Apron Strings—Charles Graham.
We Were Simply Friends — Dennis Mackin.

1895

Be Good, Be Good, My Father Said—Francis W. Bryant.
Darky Cavaliers—Dave Reed, Jr.
De Leader of Co. B—Dave Reed, Jr.
Henrietta, Have You Met Her—Ford and Bratton.
Night At the Play, A—A. J. Hamill.
Only One Girl in the World For Me—Dave Marion.
Put Me Off at Buffalo—Dillon Bros.
Sunshine of Paradise Alley, The—Ford and Bratton.
What Yer Gwine to Do in De Winter—Harry Earle.
Zenda Waltz (Vocal arrangement) — Frank Witmark.

1896

All Coons Look Alike to Me—Ernest Hogan.
Blow Almost Killed Father, The—James McAvoy.
I Love You in the Same Old Way (Darling Sue)—Ford and Bratton.
I Want Dem Presents Back—Paul West.
Isabelle—Ford and Bratton.
Laugh and The World Laughs With You—Ella Wheeler Wilcox and L. F. Gottschalk.
Lucky Jim—Horwitz and Bowers.
Mr. Johnson, Turn Me Loose—Ben Harney.
My Black Baby Mine—Thomas Le Mack.
My Coal Black Lady—W. T. Jefferson.
My Dad's Old Violin—George Fuller Golden.
My Gal's A Highborn Lady—Barney Fagan.
Olcott's Home Song (from "The Minstrel of Clare")—Chauncey Olcott.
She's Not the Same Sweet Girl I Used to Know—L. W. Jones.

She's the Daughter of Officer Porter—George Schleifarth and M. E. Rourke.
You're So Good, Daddy—Hattie Starr.
You've Been a Good Old Wagon But You've Done Broke Down—Ben Harney.

1897

Asleep in the Deep—Lamb and Petrie.
Bombashay—Max Hoffman.
Honey, You's My Lady Love—Nat Mann.
I Love My Little Honey—Ben Harney.
I'm the Warmest Member in the Land—A. F. Dannic and T. Mayo Gary.
Kate O'Donahue (from "Sweet Inniscarra")—Chauncey Olcott.
Mammy's Little Pumpkin Colored Coon—Eugene Hillman and Sidney Perrin.
Old Fashioned Mother (from "Sweet Inniscarra")—Chauncey Olcott.
Pumpkin Pie That Mother Used to Make, The—James McAvoy.
Sadie, My Lady—Ford and Bratton.
Sweet Inniscarra (from "Sweet Inniscarra")—Chauncey Olcott.
Willie Off the Yacht—John F. Golden.

1898

All Bound 'Round with a Woolen String—Charles Seamon.
Always Do as People Say You Should (from "The Fortune Teller")—Harry B. Smith and Victor Herbert.
Because (Because I Love You)—Charles Horwitz and Frederick Bowers.
Darktown's Out Tonight—Paul Laurence Dunbar and Will Marion Cook.
Don't Ask Me to Forget—Ford and Bratton.
Down Old Tampa Bay—W. T. Francis.
Friends (from "The Jolly Musketeer")—Stanislaus Stange and Julian Edwards.
Gypsy Love Song (from "The Fortune Teller")—H. B. Smith and Victor Herbert.
Honey Dat I Love So Well—L. Harry Freeman.
Hottest Coon in Dixie—Dunbar and Cook.
Jump Back, Honey, Jump Back—Dunbar and Cook.
Just as the Sun Went Down—Karl Kennett and Lyn Udall.
Just One Girl—Kennett and Udall.
Just to Pass the Time Away (from "The Jolly Musketeer")—Stange and Edwards.
Kiss Me, Honey, Do——Dinah (from Weber and Fields)—John Stromberg.
Lazy Bill—A. B. Sloane.

APPENDIX

Lily and the Nightingale, The (from "The Fortune Teller")—H. B. Smith and Herbert.
Miss Helen Hunt—Harry Conor.
When You Ain't Got No Money, Well, You Needn't Come 'Round—A. Baldwin Sloane.
When You Were Sweet Sixteen—James Thornton.
Who Dat Say Chicken in Dis Crowd—Dunbar and Cook.
Zizzy, Ze, Zum, Zum—Kennett and Udall.

1899

Adios Amor (from "Arizona")—Redding and Dane.
Always—Horwitz and Bowers.
Cakewalk in the Sky—Ben Harney.
Cupid Will Guide (from "The Ameer")—Rankin and Herbert.
Deep Down Deep—Charles F. Shattuck.
In Old Ben Franklin Days (from "The Ameer")—Rankin and Herbert.
Little Dutch Garden, A—Harvey W. Loomis.
Love Is Tyrant (from "The Singing Girl")—H. B. Smith and V. Herbert.
If You Were Only Mine (from "The Singing Girl")—H. B. Smith and V. Herbert.
My Little 'Lasses Candy Coon—Nat Mann.
My Sambo (from "The Chaperons")—Isidore Witmark.
My Wild Irish Rose (from "Romance of Athlone")—Chauncey Olcott.
Olcott's Lullaby (from "The Romance of Athlone")—Chauncey Olcott.
Promises of Light—John Carrington.
Say You Love Me, Sue (Weber and Fields) (from "The Whirl-i-gig")—John Stromberg and H. B. Smith.
Sing Me a Song of the South—George A. Norton and James W. Casey.
Stay in Your Own Backyard—K. Kennett and L. Udall.
Turn of the Road, The—Eugene Cowles.
When Chloe Sings a Song (Weber and Fields) (from "The Whirl-i-gig")—John Stromberg.

1900

Absence Makes the Heart Grow Fonder—Herbert Dillea.
Come Back, My Honey Boy, to Me (Weber and Fields)—John Stromberg.
Congregation Will Please Keep Their Seats, The—Ernest Hogan.

Goodnight, Beloved, Goodnight—J. E. Fay and J. B. Oliver.
I Love You, Dear, and Only You (from "The Burgomaster")—Frank Pixley and Gustav Luders.
I'm Looking For An Angel—A. B. Sloane.
Just for Today (from "The Viceroy")—Smith and Herbert.
Ma Blushing Rosie (from "Fiddle-dee-dee")—John Stromberg.
My Home Girl—Edward F. Cogley and William E. Bock.
My Rainbow Coon—A. B. Sloane.
My Tiger Lily (from "Aunt Hannah")—A. B. Sloane.
Tale of the Kangaroo (from "The Burgomaster")—Frank Pixley and Gustav Luders.
Tell Us, Pretty Ladies (from "Fiddle-dee-dee")—John Stromberg.
Talk, Talk, Talk (from "The Chaperons")—G. Hobart and I. Witmark.
When Reuben Comes to Town (from "Rogers Brothers in Central Park")—J. C. Goodwin and Maurice Levi.

1901

Because You Were an Old Sweetheart of Mine—Jacobs and Robinson.
Dolly Varden (from "Dolly Varden")—Stanislaus Stange and Julian Edwards.
For Love I Live Alone (from "King Dodo")—Pixley and Luders.
I'm a Respectable Working Girl (from Weber and Fields)—E. Smith and J. Stromberg.
It Seems Like Yesterday (from "The Chaperons")—Rankin and Witmark.
Look in the Book and See (from "King Dodo")—Pixley and Luders.
Ma Starlight Sue—William Gould.
My Japanese Cherry Blossom (from "Hoity Toity")—Edgar Smith and John Stromberg.
Nobody Ever Brings Presents to Me—Charles Miller.
Pretty Molly Shannon (from "Little Duchess")—Gus H. Ryan and Walter Wolfe.
Pullman Porters Ball, The (from "Hoity Toity")—Edgar Smith and John Stromberg.
Smoke Goes Up the Chimney Just the Same, The—Harry Conor.
Splinter From My Father's Wooden Leg, The—Dillon Brothers.
Tale of the Bumble Bee (from "King Dodo")—Pixley and Luders.

FROM RAGTIME TO SWINGTIME

We Met in Lover's Lane (from "Dolly Varden")—Stange and Edwards.

1902

Artie (from "Prince of Pilsen")—Pixley and Luders.

Boys Will Be Boys (from "Mr. Pickwick")—Grant Stewart and Manuel Klein.

Come Down, Ma Evening Star (Weber and Fields) (from "Twirly Whirly"),—Smith and Stromberg.

Cupid Might Have Been a Little Coon (from "The Explorers")—B. L. Taylor and Walter Lewis.

Dat's De Way to Spell Chicken—Sidney Perrin and Bob Slater.

Dream On, Dream of Me (from "Twirly Whirly")—John Stromberg.

Every Little Dog Must Have His Day (from "Old Limerick Town")—C. Olcott.

Flirty Little Gerty (from "The Stork")—Fred Chapin.

Golden Rules (from "Mr. Pickwick")—Stewart and Klein.

Heidelberg (from "Prince of Pilsen")—Pixley and Luders.

I'll Be Your Honey in the Springtime—L. Harry Freeman.

Katy, My Southern Rose (from "When Johnny Comes Marching Home")—Stange and Edwards.

Manistee (from "The Sultan of Sulu")—Ade and Wathall.

Message of the Violet (from "Prince of Pilsen")—Pixley and Luders.

My Madagascar Maid (from "Mary's Lamb")—Richard Carle.

My Own United States (from "When Johnny Comes Marching Home")—Stange and Edwards.

R-E-M-O-R-S-E (from "Sultan of Sulu")—Ade and Wathall.

Sammy (from "The Wizard of Oz")—E. Hutchison.

Since I First Met You (from "The Sultan of Sulu")—Ade and Wathall.

Tale of the Seashell (from "Prince of Pilsen")—Pixley and Luders.

Tessie, You're the Only Only (from "The Silver Slipper")—William R. Anderson.

Troubles of the Reuben and the Maid (from Rogers Brothers in Harvard")—M. Levi.

Voice of the Violet (from "Old Limerick Town")—C. Olcott.

When You at Last are Mine (from "Prince of Pilsen") — Pixley and Luders.

1903

Ain't It Funny What a Difference Just a Few Hours Make (from "The Yankee Consul")—H. Blossom and A. G. Robyn.

Cupid Has Found My Heart (from "The Yankee Consul")—Blossom and Robyn.

Fascinating Venus (from "The Tenderfoot")—Richard Carle and H. L. Heartz.

Foolishness (from "The Mayor of Tokio")—Richard Carle and Wm. F. Peters.

I Can't Do That Sum (from "Babes in Toyland")—MacDonough and Herbert.

I'm a Jonah Man (from "In Dahomey") (Bert Williams)—Alex Rogers.

I'm On the Water Wagon Now—Ford and Bratton.

In the Days of Old (from "The Yankee Consul")—Blossom and Robyn.

My Alamo Love (from "The Tenderfoot")—Carle and Heartz.

My Little Hongkong Baby (from "A Chinese Honeymoon")—John Bratton.

My San Domingo Maid (from "The Yankee Consul")—Blossom and Robyn.

Star of My Life—E. W. Corliss.

Sweet Adeline (You're The Flower of My Heart, Sweet Adeline)—Girard and Armstrong.

Texas Rangers (from "The Tenderfoot")—Carle and Heartz.

There Once Was an Owl (from "Babette")—H. B. Smith and V. Herbert.

Toyland (from "Babes in Toyland")—Glen MacDonough and V. Herbert.

1904

Absinthe Frappe (from "It Happened in Nordland")—MacDonough and Herbert.

Bandanna Land (from "It Happened in Nordland")—MacDonough and Herbert.

Carissima—Arthur Penn.

Dainty Little Ingenue (from "Woodland")—Pixley and Luders.

Flutter, Little Bird (from "The Shogun")—Ade and Luders.

Goodbye, Little Girl, Goodbye—Will Cobb and Gus Edwards.

I Love You All the Time—Will Anderson.

In Dreamland, In Dreamland (from Weber and Fields)—W. T. Francis.

APPENDIX

In the Shadow of the Pyramids (from "Mrs. Black Is Back")—MacPherson and Ball.

Just My Style (from "Fantana")—H. B. Smith and Hubbell.

Knot of Blue, A (from "It Happened in Nordland")—G. MacDonough and V. Herbert.

Laughing Little Almond Eyes (from "Fantana")—H. B. Smith and Ray Hubbell.

Little Moozoo May (from "The Shogun")—Ade and Luders.

Message of Spring (from "Woodland")—Pixley and Luders.

My Little China Doll (from "A China Doll")—Al Aarons.

Sweet Thoughts of Home (from "Love's Lottery")—Stange and Edwards.

Tale of the Turtle Dove (from "Woodland")—Pixley and Luders.

There Are Fifty-seven Ways to Catch a Man (from "The Man From China")—J. W. Bratton.

Those Songs My Mother Used to Sing—H. Wakefield Smith.

What's the Good O' That, Huh!—Clifton Crawford.

1905

He's My Pal—Gus Edwards.

Good Segar is a Smoke, A (from "Dolly Dollars")—H. B. Smith and V. Herbert.

I Like You (from "The Mayor of Tokio")—Carle and Peters.

I Want What I Want When I Want It (from "Mlle. Modiste")—V. Herbert.

I Was a Stranger and They Took Me In (from "The Man From Now")—J. K. Bangs and M. Klein.

In My Merry Oldsmobile—Gus Edwards.

Jogafree (from "Wonderland") — MacDonough and Herbert.

Mascot of the Troops (from "Mlle. Modiste")—Blossom and Herbert.

Moon Dear (from "A Society Circus")—Manuel Klein.

My Little Lassoo (from "The Belle of the West") — H. B. Smith and Karl Hoschna.

Only One (from "Wonderland") MacDonough and Herbert.

Tammany—Gus Edwards.

Where the River Shannon Flows—James J. Russell.

Will You Love Me in December as You Do in May—James Walker and Ernest R. Ball.

Your Heart Alone Must Tell ("Edmund Burke")—Chauncey Olcott.

1906

Bake Dat Chicken Pie—Frank Dumont.

Because You're You (from "The Red Mill")—Blossom and Herbert.

Bill Simmons (I've Gotta Dance Till the Band Gets Through)—George Spink.

Dinner Time—Addison Burkhardt and Melville Ellis.

Every Day Is Ladies' Day with Me (from "The Red Mill")—Blossom and Herbert.

Good-a-bye, John (from "The Red Mill")—Herbert.

Isle of Our Dreams (from "The Red Mill")—Herbert.

In Old New York (from "The Red Mill")—Herbert.

Kiss, Kiss, Kiss (from "The Parisian Model")—Max Hoffman.

Lemon in the Garden of Love, A (from "The Spring Chicken")—Rourke and Carle.

Love Me and the World Is Mine—Dave Reed, Jr., and E. Ball.

Lucia—M. Klein.

Moonbeams (from "The Red Mill")—Blossom and Herbert.

Nestle by My Side (from "The Grand Mogul")—Pixley and Luders.

On San Francisco Bay (from "The Parisian Model")—Vincent Bryan and Gertrude Hoffman.

Waiting for a Certain Girl (from "The Spring Chicken")—M. Lusk.

When Love Is Young (from "Brown of Harvard")—Rida Johnson Young and Melville Ellis.

1907

Boys Will Be Boys and Girls Will Be Girls (from "The Tattooed Man")—Herbert.

Boy Who Stuttered and the Girl Who Lisped, The—L. Weslyn.

Every Star Falls in Love with Its Mate (from "O'Neill of Derry")—Olcott and Casey.

I Idolize Ida (from "Mary's Lamb")—Richard Carle.

Just Someone—Will Anderson.

My Dear—Ball.

Rock, Rock, Rock (Let Me Rock in My Old Rocking Chair)—G. Spink.

Totem Pole, The (from "The Alaskan")—J. Blethen and Harry Girard.

Wal I Swan—Benj. Hapgood Burt.

Wouldn't You Like to Have Me for a Sweetheart? (from "A Yankee Tourist")—Erwin-Robyn.

1908

As Long as the World Rolls On—E. R. Ball.

Can't You See I Love You, Dear? (from "The Newlyweds and Their Baby")—John Bratton.

Cuddle Up a Little Closer (from "The Three Twins")—O. Hauerbach and K. Hoschna.

Faded Rose—Caro Roma.

Goodnight, Dear (from "Love Watches")—Will Anderson.

Here in the Starlight (from "A Fair Co-ed")—Ade and Luders.

Here's to The Girl (from "The Girls of Guttenberg")—Will Anderson.

I'll Be Married to the Music of the Military Band (from "The Prima Donna")—Blossom and Herbert.

I'll Dream of That Sweet Co-ed (from "The Fair Co-ed")—Ade and Luders.

I'm Looking for a Sweetheart and I Think You'll Do (from "Pied Piper") R. H. Burnside and M. Klein.

In the Garden of My Heart—Roma and Ball.

Little Girl Up There (from "Three Twins")—Hauerbach and Hoschna.

Message of the Red, Red Rose (from "Marcelle")—Pixley and Luders.

Resignation—Caro Roma.

To the End of the World with You—Dave Reed, Jr., George Graff, Jr., and Ball.

When Mary Smiles—Leo J. Curley and E. R. Ball.

When the Summer Days Are Gone—Leo J. Curley and E. R. Ball.

Yama Yama Man (from "Three Twins")—Collin Davis and K. Hoschna.

1909

Bright Eyes (from "Bright Eyes")—K. Hoschna.

Cheer Up, My Honey (from "Bright Eyes")—K. Hoschna.

Meet Me Where the Lanterns Glow—M. Klein.

Take Me Back to Babyland—Pat Rooney.

You Don't Know How Much You Have to Know in Order to Know How Little You Know—L. Weslyn.

1910

Ah, Sweet Mystery of Life (dream melody from "Naughty Marietta")—Young and Herbert.

Birth of Passion (from "Madame Sherry")—Hauerbach and Hoschna.

Doctor Tinkle Tinker (from "The Girl of My Dreams") — Hauerbach and Hoschna.

Every Girlie Loves Me but the Girl I Love (from "The Girl of My Dreams") Hauerbach and Hoschna.

Every Little Movement (from "Madame Sherry")—Hauerbach and Hoschna.

Follow Me (from "The Girl in the Train")—H. B. Smith and Leo Fall.

I Love the Name of Mary (from "Barry of Ballymore")—E. Ball.

I'm Falling in Love with Someone (from "Naughty Marietta")—Herbert.

Italian Street Song (from "Naughty Marietta")—Young and Herbert.

Lane That Leads to Drowsy Land, The—Leo J. Curley and E. R. Ball.

Live For Today (from "Naughty Marietta")—Young and Herbert.

Mother Machree (from "Barry of Ballymore")—Young and Ball.

Plant a Watermelon on My Grave and Let the Juice Soak Through—R. P. Lilly and Frank Dumont.

Save Up Your Kisses for a Rainy Day (from "Katy Did")—K. Hoschna.

Teach Me to Pray—J. M. Jewett.

To the Strains of the Wedding March (from "Jumping Jupiter")—G. Le Roy and G. Kahn.

Your Love Means the World to Me—Leo J. Curley and E. R. Ball.

1911

Art is Calling for Me (from "The Enchantress")—H. B. Smith and Herbert.

Baby Rose—L. Weslyn and G. Christie.

Beyond the Sunset—Frank Tours.

For Every Boy Who's Lonely There's A Girl Who's Lonely Too (from "Doctor De Luxe")—Hauerbach and Hoschna.

Here's Love and Success to You—E. Ball.

I Love Love (from "The Red Widow")—Charles Gebest.

It's a Long Lane That Has No Turning (from "Round The World")—M. Klein.

They All Look Good When They're Far Away (from "The Enchantress")—H. B. Smith and V. Herbert.

Till the Sands of the Desert Grow Cold—George Graff, Jr., and Ball.

APPENDIX

To the Land of My Own Romance (from "The Enchantress")—H. B. Smith and V. Herbert.
We Will Go Go to Gogo (from "The Red Widow")—Pollock, Wolf, Gebest.

1912

Home Is Where the Heart Is (from "Under Many Flags")—M. Klein.
Sweetheart, Let's Go A-Walking (from "Under Many Flags")—M. Klein.
Temple Bells (from "Under Many Flags")—M. Klein.
They Gotta Quit Kickin My Dawg Around—Si Perkins.
When Irish Eyes Are Smiling (from "The Isle of Dreams")—Ball.
When Twilight Falls—Roy King.

1913

I'll Change the Shadows to Sunshine—E. Ball.
In the Candle Light—Brown and Spencer.
Out San Francisco Way—Vincent Bryan and G. Hoffman.
To Have, To Hold, To Love—Ball.
Too-ra-loo-ra-loo-ra (That's An Irish Lullaby from Olcott's (Shameen Dhu")—J. R. Shannon.
Why Is the Ocean So Near the Shore? (from "When Claudia Smiles")—Arthur Weinberg and Clarence Jones.

1914

Can't You Hear Me Calling, Caroline?—Gardner and Roma.
Here We Are Again—Roy King.
Irish Eyes of Love (from Olcott's "The Heart of Paddy Whack")—E. Ball.
Little Bit of Heaven, Sure They Call It Ireland, A (from "The Heart of Paddy Whack")—J. Kern Brennan and E. Ball.
Sweet Kentucky Lady—Louis Hirsch.
When You're Away (from "The Only Girl")—Blossom and Herbert.

1915

Are You from Dixie?—Yellen and Cobb.
Fuzzy Wuzzy—Roy King.
Hello, Frisco (from Ziegfeld Follies, 1915)—L. Hirsch.
Hold Me in Your Loving Arms (from Ziegfeld Follies, 1915)—L. Hirsch.
Kiss Me Again (from "Mlle. Modiste")—Blossom and Herbert.
Neapolitan Love Song (from "Princess Pat")—V. Herbert.

She's the Daughter of Mother Machree—E. Ball.
So Long Letty (from "So Long Letty") Earl Carroll.
There's a Long, Long Trail—King and Elliott.

1916

Goodbye, Good Luck, God Bless You—E. Ball.
I'm Going Back to California—E. Ball.
On the Old Back Seat of the Henry Ford—W. Dillon.
Sorter Miss You—Clay Smith.
Turn Back the Universe and Give Me Yesterday—E. Ball.

1917

All the World Will Be Jealous of Me—E. Ball.
Everybody Ought to Know How to Do the Tickle-Toe (from "Going Up")—L. Hirsch.
Going Up (from "Going Up")—L. Hirsch.
I Did Not Know—Fred W. Vanderpool.
I'd Love to Be a Monkey in the Zoo—F. White.
If You Look in Her Eyes (from "Going Up")—L. Hirsch.
Magic of Your Eyes, The—A. Penn.
'Neath the Autumn Moon—F. W. Vanderpool.
Somewhere in France Is the Lily—P. Johnson and Joseph Howard.
Thine Alone (from "Eileen")—Blossom and Herbert.

1918

Call of the Cozy Little Home, The (from "Take It From Me")—Anderson.
Daughter of Rosie O'Grady, The—W. Donaldson.
Dear Little Boy of Mine—J. K. Brennan and E. Ball.
Have a Smile for Everyone You Meet and They Will Have a Smile for You—B. Rule.
In Flanders Fields—Frank Tours.
Ma Little Sunflower, Goodnight—F. W. Vanderpool.
One More Day—E. Ball.
Smiling Thru—A. Penn.
Sunrise and You—A. Penn.
That Wonderful Mother of Mine—Walter Goodwin.
Values—F. W. Vanderpool.

453

FROM RAGTIME TO SWINGTIME

When You Come Back—and You Will Come Back—George M. Cohan.
Who Knows?—Dunbar and Ball.

1919

Bo-la-bo—G. Fairman.
Darling I (from "Buddies")—B. C. Hilliam.
Golden Crown—H. Gantvort.
Good Bye, Bargravia (from "The Royal Vagabond")—G. M. Cohan.
In a Kingdom of Our Own (from "The Royal Vagabond")—G. M. Cohan.
Lamplit Hour, The—Thomas Burke and Arthur Penn.
Let the Rest of the World Go By—J. K. Brennan and E. Ball.
Little Church Around the Corner (from "The Magic Melody")—S. Romberg.
Once Upon a Time (from "The Magic Melody")—S. Romberg.
Please Learn to Love (from "Buddies")—B. C. Hilliam.
Starlight Love—L. Denni.
When the Cherry Blossoms Fall (from "The Royal Vagabond")—A. Goetzl.

1920

Down the Trail to Home Sweet Home—E. Ball.
I Want a Daddy to Rock Me to Sleep (from "Greenwich Village Follies")—A. B. Sloane.
I Would Weave a Song for You—Geoffrey O'Hara.
My Home Town Was a One Horse Town—A. Gerber.
That Old Irish Mother of Mine—H. Von Tilzer.
Tripoli—Weill.
When a Peach From Georgia Weds a Rose From Alabam—W. Goodwin.
Wyoming—Gene Williams.

1921

Bandanna Days (from "Shuffle Along")—Noble Sissle and Eubie Blake.
Crooning—Wm. Caesar.
Gypsy Blues (from "Shuffle Along")—N. Sissle and E. Blake.
Here Comes Dinah Belle of the Ball—R. Perkins.
I'll Forget You—E. Ball.
I'm Just Wild About Harry (from "Shuffle Along")—Sissle and Blake.
In a Little Town Nearby—Ashmore Clark and Florence Turner Whaley.
June's the Time for Roses—D'Lorah.

Just Been Wondering All Day Long—Irene Ackerly Canning.
Love Will Find A Way (from "Shuffle Along")—Sissle and Blake.
Saloon—E. Llab.
Stand Up and Sing for Your Father—Perkins.
Two Little Love Birds—Ballard McDonald and Sigmund Romberg.

1922

Angel Child—Benny Davis.
I Love You (from "Little Nellie Kelly")—G. M. Cohan.
My Jean—C. Roma.
Rosy Posy (from "The Blushing Bride")—S. Romberg.
Say It While Dancing—Benny Davis.
Till My Luck Comes Rolling Along (from "Little Nellie Kelly")—G. M. Cohan.
You Remind Me of My Mother (from "Little Nellie Kelly").

1923

Bebe—Sam Coslow.
Can It Be Love?—F. W. Vanderpool.
Fate (It Was Fate When I First Met You)—Byron Gay.
Horsy Keep Your Tail Up—Bert Kaplan.
I'm Going South—H. Woods.
I'm Sitting Pretty in a Pretty Little City—Abel Bear and H. Santley.
Me Neenyah—Herbert Spencer.
Out There in the Sunshine With You—E. Ball.
Sing Along—A. Penn.
Ten Thousand Years From Now—E. Ball.
There's Just a Bit of Heaven in Your Smile—Lee David.
Vamping Sal—L. Pollack.
When June Comes Along with a Song (from "The Rise of Rosie O'Reilly")—G. M. Cohan.

1924

California, Here I Come—Buddy De Sylva.
Give Me One Rose to Remember—Gray.
Howdy Do, Miss Springtime—D. Guion.
Mother, Oh, My Mother—E. Ball.
Since Ma Is Playing Mah Jong—Con Conrad.
West of the Great Divide—E. Ball.
When the Sun Goes Down—A. Penn.

1925

Lullaby Lane—Harry DeCosta.
That's Why You're Mary Mine—Roy King.

454

APPENDIX

1926

Dear Heart, What Might Have Been—H. Spencer.

Just an Ivy-Covered Shack—Carl Rupp.

Let the End of the World Come Tomorrow as Long as You Love Me Today—E. Ball.

Mammy's Little Kinky Headed Boy—G. Trinkaus.

1927

I'm Away From the World When I'm Away From You—L. Pollack.

Like the Wandering Minstrel (from "The Merry Malones")—G. M. Cohan.

Molly Malone (from "The Merry Malones")—G. M. Cohan.

Rose of Killarney—E. Ball.

1928

Billie (from "Billie")—G. M. Cohan.

Dance of the Paper Dolls—John Tucker, J. Schuster, J. Shivas.

Memories (Golden Memory Days) — Henry M. Neely and H. Sanford.

Sleep Baby Sleep—J. Schuster.

Where Were You, Where Was I? (from "Billie")—G. M. Cohan.

1929

Am I Blue? (from the picture "On With The Show")—H. Akst.

Let Me Have My Dreams (from the picture "On With The Show")—H. Akst.

My Song of the Nile (from the picture "Drag")—Meyer.

Painting the Clouds With Sunshine (from "The Golddiggers of Broadway")—Burke.

Singing in the Bathtub (from the picture "Show of Shows")—H. Magidson, Ned Washington and M. H. Cleary.

Smiling Irish Eyes (from the picture "Smiling Irish Eyes")—Ray Perkins.

Tip Toe Through the Tulips With Me (from picture "Golddiggers of Broadway")—Joe Burke.

1930

Dancing With Tears in My Eyes—Al Dubin and Joe Burke.

SOME OF THE INSTRUMENTAL HITS
PUBLISHED BY M. WITMARK & SONS

BY GAYLORD BARRETT
The Caress
Love's Voyage

BY THEODORE BENDIX
La Gazelle
In Beauty's Bower
The Busy Bee

BY JOHN W. BRATTON
Belle of the Season (March)
Trilby Waltzes
The Roses' Honeymoon
In a Cozy Corner
Teddy Bear's Picnic
In a Pagoda
Japanese Lantern Dance

BY CHARLES ELANDER
Cotton Land

BY HENRY FINK
Pirouette

BY W. T. FRANCIS
Persiflage
Down Old Tampa Bay

BY LEO FRIEDMAN
Indian Sun Dance

BY LYONS HATCH
Hyacinth

BY VICTOR HERBERT
Al Fresco
Pan Americana
Punchinello
Yesterthoughts
March of the Toys
There Once Was an Owl

BY KARL HOSCHNA
Hypnotic Waltzes

BY EFFIE L. KAMMAN
Dance of the White Rats

BY EDWARD KENDALL
Charme D'Amour (Love's Spell)

BY WILLIAM LORAINE
Zamona
Dance of the Goblins
Martinique

455

FROM RAGTIME TO SWINGTIME

BY MAURICE LEVI
Soul Kiss Waltzes

BY HENRY LODGE
Temptation Rag

BY WM. C. O'HARE
Levee Revels

BY GUSTAV SALZER
Laces and Graces
Lords and Ladies

BY BILLEE TAYLOR
Creepy Creeps (a goblin dance)

BY HOWARD WHITNEY
Mosquitoes Parade
Frog Puddles
Lucky Duck
Donkey Laugh

BY FRANK M. WITMARK
Zenda Waltzes
La Camella Waltzes
American Citizen Waltzes
American Lawn Dance

OUTSTANDING NEGRO SONG WRITERS
AND SOME OF THEIR COMPOSITIONS
(All publishers)

WILL ACCOE
In a Birch Canoe

NATHAN BEVINS
I Ain't Seen No Messenger Boy

J. TIM BRYMN
My Zulu Babe
Josephine, My Joe

HARRY T. BURLEIGH
Jean
Deep River (special arrangement)

HENRY CREAMER and J. TURNER
LAYTON
Sweet Emmeline
My Gal
After You're Gone

GUSSIE L. DAVIS
The Lighthouse By the Sea
In the Baggage Coach Ahead
Baby's Laughing in Her Sleep
Up Dar in De Sky

PAUL LAURENCE DUNBAR and WILL
MARION COOK
Jump Back, Honey—Jump Back
Darktown's Out Tonight
Hottest Coon in Dixie

SHEPARD N. EDMUNDS
I'm Gonna Live Anyhow Till I Die
*You Can't Fool All the People All the
Time*
That Will Bring You Back
Give Me Your Eye

W. C. HANDY
St. Louis Blues
Memphis Blues

J. LEUBRIE HILL
At The Ball

HILLMAN and PERRIN
Mammy's Little Pumpkin Colored Coon

HILLMAN and SLATER
Dat's the Way to Spell Chicken

ERNEST HOGAN
All Coons Look Alike to Me
The Oyster Man's Song
*The Congregation Will Please Keep
Their Seats*

AL JOHNS
Bible Stories
Araby

IRVING JONES
You Missed Your Man
I'm Living Easy

BILLE JOHNSON (originally of Cole and
Johnson)
Porcupine Rag

JAMES WELDON JOHNSON with Cole and
Johnson (Rosamond)
Under the Bamboo Tree
Congo Love Song
Maiden with the Dreamy Eyes

SCOTT JOPLIN
Maple Leaf Rag

APPENDIX

TOM LEMONIER and FRANK WILLIAMS
Just One Word of Consolation

MACEO PINKARD
Mammy O' Mine
Sweet Sue
Here Comes the Show Boat

SHAW and DICKSON
with Alfred Anderson
Fesia
Love Me, Babe, Ma Honey Do

NOBLE SISSLE and EUBIE BLAKE
I'm Just Wild About Harry
Love Will Find a Way
Bandanna Days
All three from "Shuffle Along"

CHRIS SMITH
Monkey Rag
Ballin the Jack
Never Let the Same Bee Sting You Twice

WILL H. TYERS
Maori
Call of the Woods

BERT WILLIAMS and ALEC ROGERS
I'm a Jonah Man
Nobody

Bon Bon Buddy
I May Be Crazy but I Ain't No Fool

WILLIAMS and WALKER
Darkies' Jubilee
You Ain't So Warm

R. C. McPHERSON (Cecil Mack)
In collaboration with Chris Smith
Good Morning Carrie
He's a Cousin of Mine
You're in the Right Church, but the Wrong Pew
with J. Tim Brymn
Please Go Way and Let Me Sleep
with Ford Dabney
That's Why They Call Me Shine
with Ernest R. Ball
In the Shadow of the Pyramids
Prettiest Girl in Borneo
with Albert Von Tilzer
Teasing
with Jimmie Johnson
Charleston, from "Running Wild"
Old Fashioned Love, from "Running Wild"
with J. Tim Brymn
Look Into Your Baby's Face and Say Goo Goo

POPULAR OLD TIME MINSTREL TROUPES

Thatcher, Primrose & West Minstrels
Barlow, Wilson, Primrose & West Minstrels
Primrose & West Minstrels
George Wilson Minstrels
Haverly's Mastodon Minstrels
Al Fields Minstrels
McNish, Johnston & Slavin Minstrels
Sweatnam, Rice & Fagan Minstrels
W. S. Cleveland Minstrels
Lester & Allen Minstrels
Happy Cal Wagner's Minstrels
McIntyre & Heath Minstrels
Neil O'Brien Minstrels
Vogel's Minstrels
Leavitt's Gigantean Minstrels
Cohan & Harris Honey Boy Evans Minstrels
Gorman Brothers Minstrels
Hi Henry's Minstrels
Guy Brothers Minstrels
Gus Sun's Minstrels
Primrose & Dockstader's Minstrels
Simmons & Slocum's Minstrels
Callender's Original Georgia Minstrels (colored)
Billy Kersands Minstrels (colored)

457

FROM RAGTIME TO SWINGTIME

PERMANENTLY LOCATED

New York
  Birch, Wambold & Backus Minstrels
  Billy Birch's San Francisco Minstrels
  Lew Dockstader's Minstrels

Philadelphia
  Carncross' Minstrels
  Frank Dumont's Minstrels
  Emmett C. Welch's Minstrels

Chicago
  Hooley's Minstrels

San Francisco
  Billy Emerson's Minstrels

London
  Moore & Burgess (Pony Moore) Minstrels
  Mohawk Minstrels

LIST OF NEW YORK THEATRES
AND AMUSEMENT PLACES
DEMOLISHED OR NO LONGER USED AS SUCH
FROM 1882 TO 1939

(Changes in theatre names in Italics)

National Theatre, Bowery
Thalia Theatre, 48 Bowery
Atlantic Garden, 50 Bowery
Volk's Garden, Bowery
People's Theatre, Bowery and Houston Street
Windsor Theatre, Bowery
London Theatre, Bowery
Miner's Bowery Theatre
Neighborhood Theatre, 466 Grand St.
Niblo's Garden, Broadway and Houston
Harrigan & Hart, Theatre Comique, 728 Broadway
Old London Street, Broadway and Fourth St.
Poole's Theatre, Eighth St. near Fourth Ave.
  Germania
  Aberle's
  Phillips
Bunnell's Museum, Broadway and Ninth St.
Blank's Music Hall, Twelfth St. and Fourth Ave.
Wallack's Theatre, Broadway and Thirteenth St.
  Star Theatre
Sans Souci Music Hall, Thirteenth St. and Third Ave.
Tony Pastor's, Fourteenth St. near Third Ave.
Tammany Hall, Fourteenth St. near Third Ave.
Academy of Music, Fourteenth St. and Irving Place
Thiess', Fourteenth St. near Third Ave.
Huber's Prospect Garden, Fourteenth St. between Third and Fourth Ave.
  Huber's Museum
Dewey's Theatre, Fourteenth St., between Third and Fourth Ave.
Steinway Hall, Fourteenth St., between Third and Fourth Ave.

458

APPENDIX

Union Square Theatre, Fourteenth St. east of Broadway
  Keith's Theatre
Fourteenth Street Theatre, Fourteenth St. west of Sixth Ave.
  French Theatre
  Lyceum
  Civic Repertory
Chickering Hall, Eighteenth St. and Fifth Ave.
Park Theatre, Broadway and Twenty-second St.
Booth's Theatre, Twenty-third St. and Sixth Ave.
Eden Musée, Twenty-third St. between Fifth and Sixth Aves.
Koster & Bial's, Twenty-third St. west of Sixth Ave.
Lyceum Theatre, Twenty-fourth St. and Fourth Ave.
Madison Square Garden, Fourth Ave. and Twenty-sixth St.
Garden Theatre, Fourth Ave. and Twenty-seventh St.
Madison Square Theatre, Twenty-fourth St. west of Broadway
Miner's Eighth Avenue Theatre, Eighth Ave. between Twenty-fifth and Twenty-sixth
  Sts.
Fifth Avenue Theatre, Broadway and Twenty-eighth St.
San Francisco Minstrels, Broadway between Twenty-eighth and Twenty-ninth Sts.
  Princess Theatre
  Sam T. Jack's
  Herrmann's Theatre
Imperial Music Hall, Broadway and Twenty-ninth St.
  Weber & Fields Music Hall
Wallack's Theatre, Broadway and Thirtieth St.
  Palmer's Theatre
Daly's Theatre, Broadway and Thirtieth St.
Worth's Museum, Thirty-first St. and Sixth Ave.
Bijou Theatre, Broadway and Thirty-first St.
Jacobs's Third Avenue Theatre, Thirty-first St. and Third Ave.
Standard Theatre, Broadway and Thirty-third St.
  Manhattan Theatre
Manhattan Opera House, Thirty-fourth St. between Broadway and Seventh Ave.
  Koster & Bial's (New)
Park Theatre, Broadway corner Thirty-fifth St.
  Herald Sq. Theatre
  Aquarium
Harrigan's Theatre, Thirty-fifth St. east of Sixth Ave.
  Garrick Theatre
Knickerbocker Theatre, Broadway and Thirty-eighth St.
Casino Theatre, Broadway and Thirty-ninth St.
Thirty-ninth Street Theatre, Broadway and Thirty-ninth St.
Mendelssohn Hall, Fortieth St. near Sixth Ave.
Alcazar Theatre, Broadway and Forty-first St.
  Broadway Theatre
American Theatre, Forty-second St. and Eighth Ave.
Hammerstein's Victoria, Forty-second St. and Seventh Ave.
  Rialto Theatre
Lyric Hall, Forty-second St. and Sixth Ave.
  Bryant Hall
George M. Cohan's Theatre, Broadway and Forty-third St.
Berkeley Lyceum, Forty-fourth St. near Sixth Ave.
Hammerstein's Olympia, Broadway between Forty-fourth and Forty-fifth Sts.
  Criterion
  New York Theatre and Roof
Terrace Garden, Fifty-eighth St. and Third Ave.
  Lexington Avenue Opera House
Lenox Lyceum, Sixth Ave. and Fifty-ninth St.

FROM RAGTIME TO SWINGTIME

New Theatre, Sixty-second St. and Central Park West
  Century Theatre
American Institute, Sixty-third St. and Third Ave.
Sonntag's, 110th St. and Lenox Ave.
Mount Morris Theatre, 116th St. and Fifth Ave.
West End, 125th St. west of Eighth Ave.
Hurtig & Seamon's, 125th St. west of Seventh Ave.
Josh Hart's Theatre Comique, 125th St. and Third Ave.
Gotham, 125th St. west of Third Ave.
  Dewey
Olympic Theatre, 129th St. and Third Ave.
Metropolis, 143rd St. and Third Ave.

INDEX

INDEX

462

INDEX

463

INDEX

464

INDEX

INDEX

INDEX

INDEX

INDEX

INDEX

INDEX

477

INDEX

478

INDEX

INDEX

3